Rethinking Mission in the Postcolony

Rethinking Mission in the Postcolony

Salvation, Society, and Subversion

Marion Grau

t&t clark

Published by T&T Clark International
A Continuum Imprint
The Tower Building, 11 York Road, London SE1 7NX
80 Maiden Lane, Suite 704, New York, NY 10038

www.continuumbooks.com

British Library Cataloguing-in-Publication Data
A catalogue record for this book is available from the British Library

ISBN 13: 978-0-567-11619-2 (hardback)
          978-0-567-28088-6 (paperback)

Typeset by Newgen Imaging Systems Pvt Ltd, Chennai, India
Printed and bound in India

Contents

Prologue

Point of (No) Return

Having grown up in the 1960s and 1970s in post-Holocaust Germany, I felt the need not only to interpret history, but also to parse my own soul, personal and social identity. The past possessed an ominous, yet intangible weight. The implications of the Holocaust concerned myself, my identity, heritage, lineage, and place in the world among fellow human beings. My internal landscape became haunted and the territories I knew spoke eloquently of ancient and modern boundaries, walls, and transgressions.

Across time and place, zones of interaction straddling cultural and religious difference tend to be filled with tension, passion, and violence. The negotiation of perceived and real differences, of religiocultural and economic exchanges, are perhaps particularly visible at boundaries, crossroads, and intersections. The archeological remains of the Roman *Limes,* the boundary wall between Roman territories and Barbarian peoples to its north, can still be found throughout southern Germany. Boundaries between cultures often manifest as zones of encounter rather than barriers. Christian faith came to this border region by way of missionary travelers from Ireland and Britain, at the farthest boundaries of Roman imperial reach. I grew up just a few kilometers from the ruin of an ancient Roman farmhouse, a *Villa Rustica,* that is a popular destination for walks and horseback rides.

One summer, some years ago, this ruin was the site of a gruesome murder that can be seen as a striking comment on the layered locations of intercultural encounters along boundaries across time: A young man was killed, dismembered and his body parts deposited in various locations. The murder shocked the entire country as, over time, the gory details of the murder came to light: A girl lured the young man near the ruins where her boyfriend and some of his friends brutally murdered him. They dismembered him, threw some of his body parts into the River Neckar, put his torso into an oil drum and filled it with concrete. Not being able to lift the now heavy container, they left the remains rotting in a friend's basement until a janitor found it, following the stench.[1]

---

[1] For newspaper coverage, see http://www.stern.de/politik/deutschland/610307.html and www.stuttgarter-zeitung.de/stz/page/1793488_0_2147_das-schreckliche-ereignis-ist-stets-gegenwaertig.html

As the details emerged, the police found people from different ethnic backgrounds involved in the murder. The girl, Eritrean-German, had lured a French-German local handball star to the villa, and her paranoid and obsessively jealous Turkish-German boyfriend killed him. The tragic saga serves as a reminder that this place and region in southwest Germany continues to function as a borderland between worlds, cultures, classes, and ethnicities. The *Villa Rustica* was no longer of significance merely as an ancient boundary marker of an empire with a long shadow. Though it is open to speculation in what way ethnic and cultural differences played a part in this murder, the cultural contrasts involved in these events raise many questions about religiocultural identity, community, migration, and violence. After the Second World War, many Turkish workers and their families came to live in Germany. Eritreans fled their wartorn home, some to work and live in Germany. Then, as now, this was a place where cultures and peoples meshed and clashed. Their identities in transition, suspended between nations, cultures, loves and loyalties, became entangled in tragic collision. Stetten is a quaint village in southwest Germany. A French family moved there, the father of the murdered teen working at the *Stettener Anstalt*, a Diakonia Institute for mentally challenged persons. As their identities were complexified by multiple religiocultural identities, personal and social struggles, tragedy ensued.

A migrant worker to a latter day empire, I teach at an Episcopal Seminary in the western United States, not so long ago a frontier of empire itself. Living in a liminal space between cultures, I have been interested in what shapes and forms religious and cultural identities, what Christian mission has meant in the past, and what its postcolonial incarnations might look like. The conflicted religiocultural identity formation that occurs in liminal spaces around empire, Christian mission, and conversion provide my focus. Considering economies of exchange and meaning-making in imperial Roman, Anglo-Saxon, and German locales helps contextualize instances of nineteenth century mission in South Africa, New Zealand, and Alaska.[2] The reader may find in these case studies patterns that resemble contemporary struggles over theological expression, religiocultural alignments, secular and post-Secular Christian identities, and shifts in power.

As a citizen of Germany, a country formerly divided by a wall, I have found the recurring narrative reconstruction of walls as limit, transgression, and access point a poignant echo of multiple openings and confinements. Jericho's walls, the *Limes*, the Great Wall of China, the barbed wires of Auschwitz, the Warzaw Ghetto, and the Berlin Wall continue to be resurrected in ways that mimic that past: walls between Sunnis and Shiites in Baghdad, Palestinians and Israelis,

---

[2] For an account of the shift of understandings of center and periphery in Anglo-Saxon mission, see Nicholas Howe, "Rome: Capital of Anglo-Saxon England," *Journal of Medieval and Early Modern Studies* Vol. 34, No. 1 (Winter 2004): 152 et passim.

North and South Korea, the United States and Mexico. Expensive, ineffective borders, are mustered to keep out the hordes of "Barbarians" storming the gates of struggling empires. Gated communities in the suburbs perform a post-modern, subnational version, while the development of the European Union raises many issues involving religious culture, regionalism, ethnic identities, and economic disparities shaken by the tensions of translocal globalisms. We will attempt here to rethink mission in the face of histories of genocide, repression, colonialism, changing socioreligous and global intercultural relations. There are, as you might expect, no simple answers to come by in such a quest.

For inspiration, help, and support I give thanks to R. S. Sugirtharajah, whose work first introduced me to Bishop Colenso; to biblical scholars Gerald West, Jonathan Draper, Stephen Moore, Roland Boer, Jeffrey Staley, and others, who have highlighted the odd histories of biblical texts within colonial and missionary contexts. I am grateful to the Right Rev. Mark MacDonald, through whom I learned much about indigenous and colonial Alaska and Navajoland, to Andrew Walls, Brian Stanley, and Allan Davidson, who have rendered mission studies exciting for this theologian; to theologians Marcella Althaus-Reid, Kwok Pui-Lan, and Joerg Rieger, for their work in addressing the colonial baggage of theology; to the "Drew Crew" and the "Polodoxy Posse" for pushing new edges in constructive theology, confronting the colonial history of metropolitan theologies, and pointing ways beyond it; to Catherine Keller for continued mentorship, support, counsel, friendship, and wisdom. Thanks go to Mayra Rivera for many hours of discussing ideas and concepts involved in our work; and to Inese Radzins, Annette Weissenrieder, Andrea Bieler, and Dan Joslyn-Siematkoski for their interest and important feedback on early drafts of the manuscript. I am grateful to former and current students at the Graduate Theological Union and the Church Divinity School of the Pacific for keeping me engaged and challenged. Richard Burden helped as my research assistant, and students in my Soteriology class Spring 2010 provided feedback to early drafts of chapters. Jakob Hero, Kate Hug, and Rita Nakashima Brock lent editorial support. Thanks to those other readers who helped shape and influence this book, have given support, editorial help, and feedback: Edward Antonio, Moeawa Callaghan, Monica Coleman, Jean Comaroff, Philip Culbertson, Sigríður Guðmarsdottir, Jeanine Hill Fletcher, Arthur Holder, Melissa McCarthy, Karla Milo-Schaaf, Laurel Schneider, Kathryn Tanner, John Thatamanil, and Hoang-Anh Tran.

I owe a debt to the library personnel and students who helped with access to resources at Kinder Theological Library in Auckland, New Zealand, the University of Kwa-Zulu Natal Theological Library, the Killie Campbell Library, Durban, the Allan Paton Institute at the University of KwaZulu Natal in Pietermaritzburg, the Episcopal Archives in Austin, Texas, and the Diocesan Episcopal Archives at the University of Fairbanks, Alaska. Berkeley and Oakland libraries and coffee house culture provided a space for research, encounter, and conversation.

This work has benefited greatly from a Faculty Fellowship awarded to me by the Association of Theological Schools, from grants given by the Episcopal Church's Conant Fund and the Seminary Consultation On Mission, all of which helped to fund travels, research, and resources. I thank the American Academy of Religion's Summer Seminars on Theologies of Religious Pluralism and Comparative Theology, Cohort 1, for providing another venue for exploring these questions and for offering new collegial relations. For collegial community and engagement, I thank my colleagues at the Church Divinity School of the Pacific and the Graduate Theological Union, the Faculty of Theology at the University of Oslo, the Department of Theology at UKZN Pietermaritzburg, the University of Auckland, St. John the Evangelist's Seminary and Te Rau Kahikatea, Auckland.

Epiphany, 2011.
Berkeley, California.

Works Cited

Howe, Nicholas. "Rome: Capital of Anglo-Saxon England." *Journal of Medieval and Early Modern Studies* Vol. 34, No. 1 (Winter 2004): 147–72.

Chapter 1

Reaching the Limit: Circumambulating the Frontiers of Civilizing Mission

Theory is always written from some "where," and that "where" is less a place than itineraries: different, concrete histories of dwelling, immigration, exile, migration.[1]

Close to my hometown in Germany, hikers and cyclists can still amble along the remains of the *Limes*, the wall erected by Roman imperial forces to prevent incursions of what Caesar called "Germanic" tribes and other Barbarian peoples. The *Limes* reaches from the contemporary Netherlands into Eastern Europe, crossing through Germany.[2] Alongside what began as access roads to Barbarian territory, Roman armies from around the empire built walls, forts, and guard posts. Borders and boundaries generate particular fields of interaction, where alien traditions collude and mingle. In complex processes of interaction they thus bring forth "all manner of strange religio-cultural hybrid."[3] It was also near the Roman *Limes*—marking the "limit" of Roman imperial influence—sometimes river, sometimes wall, that Jews planted their first diasporic communities among Germanic peoples. Jews and Christians planted religious communities along the Roman imperial ledge, in border towns and mercantile centers. The Rhine, the fluid part of the *Limes*, then, like the rivers of Babylon, saw at its banks diasporic presences mourning for lost and precious community and identity, seeking to survive and thrive in lands of exile.

These remnants and rearticulations of gatekeeping efforts are reminiscent also of Jericho's walls. But no promise is made here that edifices will "come

---

[1] James Clifford as quoted in bell hooks, *Belonging: A Culture of Place* (New York: Routledge, 2009), 100. Emphasis mine.

[2] The Latin *Limes*, from where we take the terms limit and liminality, may be more commonly known for its British stretch, Hadrian's wall, and less so for its Scottish stretch, the Antonine Wall. See for example: Erich Schallmayer, *Der Limes: Geschichte einer Grenze*, C. H. Beck Wissen (Munich: Verlag C. H. Beck, 2006) and David J Breeze, *Edge of Empire: Rome's Scottish Frontier, The Antonine Wall* (Edinburgh: Birlinn, 2008).

[3] Catherine Keller, "The Love of Postcolonialism: Theology in the Interstices of Empire," in *Postcolonial Theologies: Divinity and Empire*, Catherine Keller, Michael Nausner, and Mayra Rivera, eds (St. Louis, MI: Chalice, 2004), 222.

crumbling down." After all, archaeological research has shown no sign that Jericho was ever conquered, and certainly not at a time that would fit with the biblical narrative.[4] Hence, the particular narrative formation of the exodus-conquest cycle might be better viewed as telling us something about what stories human communities construct about who and why they are, how different communities adopt and adapt stories to fit changed places and times. Yet, there is a hope that painfully separating walls are often represented as more formidable than they turn out to be, and more permeable than we thought.

When illusions of pure identities and ethnicities give way, when fears of "mixing" of mulatto cultures wane in the recognition that if we dig far enough back in history, not only humans as they exist now emerged from Africa, but many ancient myths and historical narratives give evidence of migration, merging and blending, and emergence of ethnic groups from such interactions—the fiction of control over such encounters and the economies of exchange alongside zones of interaction becomes harder to sustain.

Rather than charging such complex zones of interaction head-on, a battle I would certainly lose, I invite you to walk with me around it as a perplexing *locus theologicus*, in a hermeneutical *circumambulation*—a circling of the barriers, breaches, beachheads, and brambles where messages are encoded and decoded, divine visions and missions translated and transferred, fools and missionaries, soldiers and merchants trade relics, tools, literacy, theology, and money. If you, gentle reader, will remember that this account does not represent an authoritative account, nor an attempt at panoptic surveillance, but rather proceeds as my pondering, meditative circumambulation around a few old stones, *limes*, cairns, and boundary markers, perhaps you can share the path and the itinerary for a time. Theology is always "on the way," it is *via theologica, theologia viatorum*, a perichoretic jagged dance.[5] It travels as a *caminata* undertaken in various states of un/dress, sexual configurations, and economic status, exploring bodies, spaces, lines, transactions, involving "serious doubting as a theological method," interrogating its own hermeneutic principles whenever possible or necessary. As with any travels, there is always the danger of being too preoccupied with one's own thoughts or conversations with others, "without noticing the life of the rebellious poor urban women who do not use underwear," or other important clues, conversations, or encounters we might be missing, and thus missing out on receiving a glimpse of the "richness of the metaphors of God."[6] As postcolonial theologian Marcella Althaus-Reid's

---

[4] James L. Kugel, *How to Read the Bible: A Guide to Scripture, Then and Now* (New York: Free Press, 2007), 373ff.

[5] Jürgen Moltmann, *Theology of Hope: On the Grounds and the Implications of a Christian Eschatology* (Evanston, IL and New York: Harper & Row, 1964), 282.

[6] Marcella Althaus-Reid, Indecent Theology: Theological Perversions in Sex, Gender and Politics (London and New York: Routledge, 2001), 6.

guided tour through her hometown of Buenos Aires reveals the interface between the sexuality and poverty of those we might encounter as we travel with her, this circumambulation, at home and abroad, hopes to participate in the "de-hegemonisation of theology."[7]

Some circumambulate mountains in the directions of the rising and setting of the sun to get a perspective on their lives.[8] Paul Cézanne painted Mont Saint-Victoire numerous times, Denise Levertov described angles and views of Mount Rainier in many of her poems. Mountains can be our orientation, the physical features of the landscapes of our lives. Mountains can be a place to encounter divinity, a sense of insight, epiphany, law, truth, a place of multitudinous perspectives, clarifying heights, and returns to the muddled valleys. Up the mountain Moses follows, while God continues to retreat. Gregory of Nyssa's *Life of Moses* envisions Moses ascending, but perhaps also circling, never exhausting the possible perspectives, far from grasping God, yet seemingly within the titillating reach of touching. Thus, our selves, engagements, and theologies are "touched by that which transcends it and, in the process, transform" themselves and each other.[9]

The practice of circumambulation can be found in a number of contexts and practices around the world. Muslims circle the Kaaba at the end of the pilgrimage to Mecca, Buddhists circle the stupa, in which a Buddhist saint may be buried, some Christian priests circle altars while censing them, the Israelites circumambulate Jericho, sometimes with the sun, sometimes counter the sun. The present theological circumambulation wants to give voice to the ambivalent complexity and hybridity that mark peoples and lands without dissolving resolute senses of positionality and identity. It is important to pay attention to the depth and complexity of the history and the patterns, over generations, of interaction. Certain encounters during my travels and research kept coming back to me as paradigmatic stories that might help illuminate the search for and recognition of patterns that beset and bless our encounters. Some chapters begin with such a paradigmatic encounter. This writing hovers quite consciously somewhere between genres. Theology is a curious discourse, and it fits only unhappily into the categories of English-language genres such as "nonfiction," "fiction," and poetry.

Merchants, missionaries, mercenaries—all travelers across land and sea—employ a variety of coordinates to mark and remember their paths and the lessons learned in passing. They name or narrate the peaks of one or several

---

[7] Ibid., 6–7.

[8] Three California Buddhist poets describe walking around a local mountain, as Gary Snyder writes, "to show respect and clarify the mind." Gary Snyder, "The Circumambulation of Mt. Tamalpais," in *Opening the Mountain: Circumambulating Mount Tamalpais, A Ritual Walk*, Matthew Davis and Michael Farrell Scott (Emeryville, CA: Avalon, 2006), 17.

[9] Mayra Rivera, *The Touch of Transcendence: A Postcolonial Theology of God* (Louisville, KY: WJK, 2007), 128.

mountains. Rock formations herald the markers, boundaries, and forces that bear down upon the landscapes and lives of transient animals and humans. Folk find human and animal forms in landscapes and in objects. People see history, deities, and other forces that shape life on earth, in them. Jesus or Mary detected in pancakes, veneer, stucco, and grease stains enact contemporary urban versions in places with less rugged surfaces. Elsewhere, father sky lies on top of mother earth, pushed apart by tree trunks so humans can breathe and move. Mountains are Grand Tetons, big tits, monkey heads, snake tails, elephant backs, turtlebacks, and so forth. In Navajo territory, rock formations memorialize stories of migration, fights against monsters that threaten the life of the tribe. Giant's blood, virgin spring, bridal veil, Thor's hammer. Moving through the landscapes of their lives, it is as if travelers and inhabitants must find something to recognize, find some connection, interpret the significance of remarkable features, and engage them with the stories of their lives.[10] Earth-shattering events form the basis of narratives that coil with layers of meaning over time. Mapping territories new and old is a common human practice, and when we map, describe, and narrate, we represent, with different religious symbol systems, objectives, and cultural archives.

> Everywhere we look in the encounter of the Old World and the New [. . .] we find an intensive deployment of representations [including] the innumerable crosses erected by Europeans in the harbor mouths and high places of America [. . .] European contact with the New World natives is continually mediated by representations; indeed contact itself, at least where it does not consist entirely of acts of wounding and killing, is very often contact between representatives bearing representations.[11]

Itineraries are rarely traveled without encountering walls, barriers, fences, and boundaries. Real and imagined, physical or spectral, they delineate our worlds. Alongside them manifest many attempts to restrict, channel, and order the itineraries of those who would cross them, trade, and amble near them. As attempts to control the lives, migrations, and movements of people, however, time shows that these attempts to keep out, or root out, the "barbarians," "pagans," "Jews," or "heretics" of the day, are finally unsuccessful. Roman imperial forces moved the walled *Limes* north of my home region several times to adjust to the territorial gains of Germanic tribal peoples. Fences, boundaries, walls eventually are

---

[10] The Barbers trace the possibilities of layered meaning in myth that moves beyond the sometimes reductionist psychologizing of modern interpretations and allows for the potential of multiple layers of meaning coiled within, and shifting over time and place. Elizabeth Wayland Barber and Paul T. Barber, *When They Severed Earth from Sky: How the Human Mind Shapes Myth* (Princeton, NJ: Princeton University Press, 2004).

[11] Stephen Greenblatt, *Marvelous Possessions: The Wonder of the New World* (Oxford/New York: Clarendon Press, 1991), 119.

moved, torn down, are abandoned, and become overgrown. They can vanish, becoming unrecognizable to the untrained eye, fading into the landscape, demarcating a limit no longer recognized or remembered. People find ways around or over boundaries, until they eventually become overrun or insignificant, superseded by successive configurations. Borders and crossroads are places that repel and attract. They generate systems of exchange and withholding, are scaled and embattled. At these limits, where much wonder is found, we will try to "stay with the perilous wonder that resists final resolution, simple identity, and sure teleology."[12] As defense, protection, a means to shape, direct, or survey, if not curb migration and travel,[13] walls and barriers are notoriously unstable. They are built to keep prisoners in and inhabitants safe, while keeping enemies, migrant workers, presumed terrorists, and ethnic others out. They are constantly built, enforced, scaled, scrambled, abandoned, repurposed, and redesigned. And even when they fade away, they, like the *Limes*, continue to be present in the bedrock of ground and history, their ghosts haunting present inhabitants.

Marking geographies as well as human perceptions of self and other, boundaries traverse geographical terrain while marking minds and hearts. Many boundaries have crisscrossed the territories we call home. *Re-member-ing*, reassembling identity in all its facets, religiocultural, socioeconomic, gendered and ethnic, the repetition and differentiation of mimicry and mockery occurs in particularly poignant ways along such boundaries.

Even the frontiers of empires are "zones of interaction,"[14] or "fields of negotiation,"[15] rather than simple barriers:

> A contingent, borderline experience opens up *in-between* colonizer and colonized. This is a space of cultural and interpretive undecidability produced in the "present" of the colonial moment.[16]

The *Limes* was initially an access road, similar to many forest roads today. Such incisions enable quick access to *liminal* territories and trade using wheeled transportation devices, but also serve as boundary markers. Zones of

---

[12] Mary-Jane Rubenstein, *Strange Wonder: The Closure of Metaphysics and the Opening of Awe* (New York: Columbia University Press, 2008), 23.

[13] Thus, the purpose of the *Limes* in Scotland was, most likely, "not military defence, but rather a demarcation line, intended to aid in the task of their control." Breeze, *Edge of Empire: Rome's Scottish Frontier, The Antonine Wall*, 82.

[14] So argues Wells particularly regarding temperate Europe and especially the frontier areas the Romans called *Gallia, Germania Superior* and *Germania Inferior*. Peter S. Wells, *The Barbarians Speak: How the Conquered Peoples Shaped Roman Europe* (Princeton, NJ: Princeton University Press, 1999), 126.

[15] Michael Nausner, "Homeland as Borderland," in *Postcolonial Theologies: Divinity and Empire*, Postcolonial Theologies (St. Louis, MI: Chalice, 2004), 123.

[16] Homi Bhabha, *The Location of Culture* (London/New York: Routledge, 1994), 206.

interaction or not, limits infringe upon and reshape the connection between indigenous peoples and the land. Connection to the land often does not imply sedentariness. Most indigenous peoples knew some degree of seasonal itinerancy. Thus, attempts to posit such limits impacted the sacred and mundane relationships between people and land.

Where "dogma made a prison out of an invitation to freedom, out of poetry,"[17] this circumambulation hopes to stage a prison breakout and suggests that a necessary, ethically, and humanly possible way to engage in such comparison is constituted by "constructive acts of imaginative making" or "imaginative construction."[18] This weaving, this *poesis* can be compared to "poetry and poetics" and participates in a project of "theopoetics that poses a mystery that we do not solve but can only embrace."[19] This theopoetic language, far from being a romantic move, can be moved by the experience "not of beauty but of evil," into a "poetic transmutation of theology." Hence, it may be "better fitted to heal the theopolitical violence of any age," and the deep, old, and ongoing wounds of a Christian option under empire.[20] Given the problematic history of comparison as an instrument for colonial denigration of the ethnic and religious other in particular, there is a great deal of ethical responsibility inherent in such imaginative construction. The work of comparison is fraught with the danger of self-referentiality, of self-interest, the projection of one's denied shadow onto another, and sheer ignorance, the improper linking of texts, patterns, and circumstances across differences of culture, time, and place. One way to remain humble in this undertaking may be to understand it as an *exercise in pattern recognition* rather than an attempt at a universalizing metanarrative, and hence, open to disruption. Thus, such comparisons do not seek "demonstrable proofs, offering secure shelter, but rather tenuous spaces, both for the builder of the comparison and for the audience who temporarily passes under its roof."[21]

As we amble among these ghosts, spirits, bodies, and carnage of past interpretive action, a hermeneutic of places, times, and texts moves into view that not only inquires into the traditional foci of Western thought, but raises questions about the strict opposition rather than the symbiosis of what are sometimes called "East" and "West."

In such intercultural hermeneutic encounters in mission, registering other forms of knowing the divinity, earth, and its inhabitants, can function as an

---

[17] Ivone Gebara, *Longing for Running Water: Ecofeminism and Liberation* (Minneapolis, MN: Fortress, 1999), 178.

[18] Jennifer R. Rapp, "A Poetics of Comparison: Euripides, Zhuangzi, and the Human Poise of Imaginative Construction," *JAAR* Vol. 78, No. 1 (March 2010): 163, 169.

[19] Catherine Keller, *God and Power: Counter-Apocalyptic Journeys* (Minneapolis, MN: Fortress, 2005), 150.

[20] Keller, *God and Power*, 150.

[21] Rapp, "A Poetics of Comparison," 179.

expansion and corrective to the categories and history of "Western" hermeneutics. We will aim here to think towards a coalitional Christian hermeneutics, aiding in overcoming the powers of empire and its blowback, reconsidering how we might think of encountering *God/Divine/Sacred* today, with the best of wisdom from a variety of cultural traditions. One of the guiding questions of this inquiry is how one might continue to stretch and integrate the wisdom and insight of many more interpreters and interpretive communities, without assimilating, conquering, accessorizing, romanticizing, or instrumentalizing these readings. Perhaps this is as impossible now as was proven in ages past. It raises the question whether the sin of omission is greater than the sin of commission; whether to pretend that Western hermeneutics—if there is such a thing—is the only hermeneutics worth discussing, or risk the imperfect representation of interpretive practices from other contexts.

Encounters in mission involve one type of hermeneutical action in imperial zones of interaction. We hear of interpreting bodies: bodies interpreting and bodies interpreted. Of messages getting scrambled, reinterpreted, as different communal bodies manifest: not just the colonially approved churches, but independent churches and "syncretistic" movements like Ratana in Aotearoa/New Zealand or the Shembe Church in Kwa-Zulu Natal.

Any hermeneutics of cultures, and particularly a theological hermeneutics of encounters in mission, cannot help but manifest itself also as an expression of a specific culture, one whose cultural expression includes—for various reasons—an interest in comprehending the Other, whoever and whatever that might be. Hence, it is important indeed to explore the foundations, arguments, and legitimations that underwrite such a practice.[22] Certainly this is good caution when one thinks of hermeneutics as an academic discipline exercised in a particular manner in certain contexts, but the unintended consequence of such caution might be another version of ethnocentrism, including assumptions that certain cultures do not employ hermeneutical practices. The question this *essai* raises—and I use the term intentionally also in this spelling as a reminder that essays always *essayer quelque chose*—attempt something—is rather: The forms of interpretation I am interested in here are embodied. Hermeneutics is done by bodies and interprets bodies. Yet we may not always recognize a hermeneutic when we see it. But if not, why not? How do we know what we know, see what we see, interpret what we interpret? What does it mean for bodies to interpret? What happens when we interpret bodies? Fleshly, earthly, textual, immanent-transcendent? Beyond ethnocentric parochialism and global abstractions this is an attempt for a grounded theology that can encounter difference in ways that transcend narcissistic fascination or abhorrence.

---

[22] Jo Reichertz, "Hermeneutik der Kulturen—Kulturen der Hermeneutik," in *Hermeneutik der Kulturen—Kulturen der Hermeneutik: Zum 65. Geburtstag von Hans-Georg Soeffner*, Jo Reichertz, Anne Honer, and Werner Schneider, eds, (Konstanz: UVK Verlagsgesellschaft, 2004), 13–15.

Rather than separated hermetically by walls, the world I live in manifests every day as a "world without end," where air currents, storms, climate changes, languages and cultures, theologies, philosophies, theories, spiritualities, travel and trade, water, air, fire and earth interact and move with little respect for such boundaries, despite the violent impositions of walls. Within this text we traverse some of the most hermeneutically perplexing and interesting sites I have come across.

Such nonlinear engagement hopes to resist a tight historical trajectory, and hence the temptation to cover and motivate all important features of hermeneutics (as if there were such a thing and it could be done between the covers of one book). This, I hope, will allow for thematic and intuitive connections that may offer a sideways pilgrimage rather than a fly-over hop, skip, and jump.

The quest pursued here includes a critical appropriation of the tradition, taking into account the common conceptual links undergirding genocidal acts in colonialist ventures, ideologies of race undergirding the enslavement of Africans, the genocide of European Jews in the Holocaust, and other genocides of the twentieth century. It must trace the roots of theologically undergirded virulent ethnocentrism[23] and encourage instead appropriate expressions of ethnic identity and intercultural theological identity.[24]

It is precisely that nexus of "strange intermixing and blending" of re-membered anamnesis, of recalibration and transformation of identity in all its intermingled complexity that interests me in these pages. In particular, I am interested in tracing the dynamics of theological reimagination of Jewish, Christian, and indigenous expressions of engagement with God, with the Sacred as understood within such zones of interaction, and how these theologies are embedded in social and economic aspects of culture.

I offer this circumambulation as a contribution to the hermeneutics of soteriology, and as a continuation of the work I have done around the conceptual metaphor of divine economy, this time in its more missiological and global economic implications.[25] As a constructive Christian theologian interested in questions of meaning, salvation, and redemption within Christian traditions and across other religious discourses, I am particularly interested in how the indeterminacy and crossroads functions of communication and interpretation affect the formation of theological language, or, how ways of speaking with and of

[23] I am assuming here that certain forms of ethnocentrism are simply reality and pertain throughout the world. There are more or less virulent and hostile forms of it that can be undergirded by philosophical or religious thought, and we have to be wary here of the particular combination of ethnocentrisms expressed in various European Christianities. I am not assuming that only Western societies or only monotheistic societies have virulent ethnocentric or imperialist tendencies that employ religious and cultural ideologies.

[24] I propose that theological work is always already intercultural, given the diverse history of the Christian tradition. It is important to resist painting the entire vastness of theological traditions as belonging to a particular set or subset of cultures only.

[25] See Marion Grau, *Of Divine Economy: Refinancing Redemption* (London/New York: T&T Clark/Continuum, 2004).

God are subject to these dynamics. I work with an expansive understanding of Christian soteriology, the search for that which saves, redeems, transforms. And especially, where what proclaims to save and redeem disembowels, depropriates, maims, and misappropriates. This includes the field of mission studies as well as theological concerns regarding the logic of atonement, and Christ-focused redemption. Some of the work has the characteristic of a comparative endeavor, and as such ponders the difference and relation between variously contextualized forms of Christianity and various indigenous African, Maori,[26] and Dene/ Athabascan Native American patterns of reasoning and ritual. With the goal of a progressive theology of mission focused around notions of revelation, sacred text, redemption, and transformation, this text seeks to describe patterns of engagement, exchange, and relation. It aims to trace some of the dynamics of cultural loss and lament, cultural adoption, adaptation, assimilation, retraditioning, and reconstruction in relation to theological concepts and perceptions of divinity, deity, and the sacred in the midst of communities in transition.

A circumambulation then, far from a victory march, articulates a lament of the way in which "dangerous memories,"[27] the ghosts of past genocides, of peoples sold for 30 silver coins, haunt us, inform our communities, infect our perceptions of divinity, resurrect fears, whisper warnings, oracles, invoke translucent visions, invite unexpected creative transformations of gospel. You may engage it as a process of spiritual practice, of ceaseless prayer as you move along, *lectio divina*, even as corporate prayer or pilgrimage through text and history. Such spectral sounds and visions may not always be empty of that Spirit that moans for us with sighs beyond words, infusing hope in the ruins of these walls, warning of their temporal and spatial limits and the potently mingled powers that create and undo them. It is my hope that this method of movement offers both structure and allows for creativity.

Haunted by the Specters of Missionary History

The Western metropole must confront its postcolonial history, told by its influx of postwar migrants and refugees, as an indigenous or native narrative internal to its national identity.[28]

There is then some spirit. Spirits. And one must reckon with them.[29]

---

[26] "Maori" is the term indigenous inhabitants of New Zealand generally use to describe themselves, indicating a sense of belonging that goes beyond tribal and familial ties. The term means "ordinary person" in *te reo*, the language of the Maori.

[27] Johann Baptist Metz, "In Memory of the Other's Suffering: Theological Reflections on the Future of Faith and Culture," in *The Critical Spirit: Theology at the Crossroads of Faith and Culture*, Andrew Pierce and Geraldine Smyth (Blackrock: The Columba Press, 2004), 179–80.

[28] Italics in original. Bhabha, *Location of Culture*, 6.

[29] Jacques Derrida, *Specters of Marx: The State of Debt, the Work of Mourning & the New International*, trans. Peggy Kamuf (New York: Routledge, 1994), xx.

Indeed, as Derrida suggests above, there are both spirits and Spirit to reckon with when it comes to missionary history. A few decades into instances of the "Western metropole" beginning to face its postcolonial history, there is still much work to be done on the Christian missionary elements of that history, and the task of rethinking "native narratives" of all shapes and sizes. Confronting missionary history and reckoning with the many Spirit/s involved in post/colonial encounters in liminal zones of interaction means engaging in a kind of archaeology of body and spirit, finding the bodies buried, listening to the unlamented, unresolved voices, and becoming open to possible religiocultural reincarnations.

What interpretive patterns and responsive actions emerged in the circumambulation of the spaces of Spirit/s between cultures in colonial missionary settings? The power struggles and doctrinal controversies we know from the histories of early churches still haunt us today. In certain missionary contexts scenarios strikingly similar to ancient ones arise with forgotten clarity as churches split, emerge, reemerge, and reform themselves in seemingly ever more guises. Mission tends to occur in or create polydox scenarios, where numerous teachings clash, negotiating different worldviews and interpretations of reality.

Studies have continued to describe and emphasize the "porosity" of intercultural encounters, and that such seemingly flat descriptors of nations like "fifteenth-century Portugal" should be seen as "a metaphor" rather than as a literal reference, when it is possible that "more than half of the 'British' navy was not British," and that Native American tribes intermingle to such a degree that "Jesuits complained that it became difficult to preach to the Iroquois in their own language." Elsewhere, Napoleon's "French" army sent to restore slavery in Haiti included Poles and Germans, "trade societies connected cities rather than landmasses," and territorial borders "were routinely ignored," while "smuggling was ordinary business."[30] This kind of porosity, exposes "ungovernable connections" that appear as "many-headed hydras" generated by and simultaneously threatening empire.[31] Such "commerce" involves women, gender, and sexuality as the word "commerce" carries a sexual meaning in multiple languages, and "traffic in women was the prototype of commercial slavery." Indeed, such sexual commerce traversing diverse territories threatened to "dissolve the boundaries of race" and fears of contagion and miscegenation rose.[32] Conversion between religiocultural systems involves a particular economy, engaging many layers of exchange. If, "as humans and Christians, our home is in a sense always at a

---

[30] Susan Buck-Morss, *Hegel, Haiti and Universal History* (Pittsburgh, PA: Pittsburgh University Press, 2009), 112.

[31] See Peter Linebaugh and Marcus Rediker, *The Many-Headed Hydra: Sailors, Slaves, Commoners, and the Hidden History of the Revolutionary Atlantic* (Boston, MA: Beacon Press, 2000).

[32] Buck-Morss, *Hegel, Haiti and Universal History*, 113.

boundary,"[33] it remains important to "resist *both* a simple transgression/transcendence of boundaries and an easy conflation of Christian subjectivity with the bounded turf"[34] where we live.

Rather than seeing this complexity as a problem to be avoided or engaging in missiological relativism, this essay attempts to formulate a constructive vision of mission that can sustain and creatively engage a faithful Christian polydoxy, both internally within forms of Christian life and faith and outwardly manifested as responsibly lived interreligious polydoxy. This investigation circles the limits and traces the intersections of several discourses. Aiming to make a contribution to Christian soteriology and its postcolonial possibilities, it draws deeply from the wells of mission studies, missiology, ethnography, indigenous theories, cultural anthropology, as well as liberation, feminist, and postcolonial theologies. We are concerned here with exploring the possibilities of progressive theological expressions of soteriology in a postcolonial setting and the question of mission and its soteriological implications.

A project seeking to rethink mission must confront colonial history. As Homi Bhabha has urged, it necessitates encounter with what comes weighted with great ambivalence, if not shame: yet, the history of missionary endeavors cannot be forgotten lest "if we repress our colonial and neocolonial histories, they will come back to haunt us all the more."[35] This history continues to haunts us today, marks socioeconomic and political circumstances, frames particular ideological and theological foci in the shape of global political, interreligious, and economic relations. These connections inform, prescribe, and inscribe relationships we did not choose nor have agency to avoid. But we may on occasion have power to "reckon with them" and confront the ancestral ghosts of the past, to exorcise, to recognize, to value, to transform, and transcend. And in this reckoning we encounter what has been so difficult to name without collapsing into incessant claims to destructive power because our relations to the sacred, to life energy, cannot be engaged other than in the fullness of all our relations: the divine, God, Wisdom, Spirit, Christ, the many ways of sacrality we encounter between, beyond, among, and within our psychophysical relations.

So we keep stumbling through the zones of interaction of empire and divinity, liminal places haunted and traversed by a manifold of figures. Some of them are particularly interesting for the scope of this work: there is the ancient impulse to name the processes of transmission by reference to boundary brokers and tricksters. We find Hermes, messenger god and messenger to the gods, haunting the crossroads where merchants, travelers, cultures and

---

[33] Nausner, "Homeland as Borderland," 122.
[34] Ibid., 131.
[35] Joerg Rieger, "Theology and Mission Between Neocolonialism and Postcolonialism," *Mission Studies* 21.2 (2004), 201–27, 202.

religions, empires, missionaries, natives, conquerors and conquered meet, and where a great deal of "hermeneutics" takes place. The "zones of interaction"[36] generated around frontiers are populated by tricksters and coyotes passing through, shuttling goods, meaning, and people to and fro, converting spiritual and economic currencies. Divine messengers enter the fray, slip through the cracks of confinements, provoke, stimulate, announce. Trickster traders shapeshift, deities merge across borders, crossroads blend fabrics, technologies, and traditions, trading spiritual and material energies at the same time.

Jesus' public career can be seen as a kind of circumambulation, traveling under imperial conditions, in occupied land. Hermes, Mercury, Odin, and Christ mingle and merge as their characteristics are recognized, recombined, and blended in the borderlands of Roman imperial presence. Missionaries have been the messengers of such complexly bounded gospel and a boundary-blurring Christ. Traders, artisans, peasants, often drawn from rural lower classes and only slightly educated, at times intellectuals, they struggle to discern what goods can be and should be transmitted. Their motives are often mixed and complex. Their trading partners, too, have multiple motivations, interests, and trade secrets. But while exchanges never are simply equal, forms of reciprocity are manifold. In order to distinguish whatever may constitute "good news" of the gospel from empire, capital, trade, and culture, it is key to examine the way all of these together become embodied and traverse territory.

In this blend of zonal interaction, Christians begin to build their communities, interact with the peoples of the empire and beyond the empire. "Christianity suffers from an imperial condition."[37] That is, Christians have always existed under the conditions of empire, have had to function within it, sometimes hesitatingly, sometimes resisting, sometimes collaborating, sometimes heralding it. These fluid liminal zones where Christian mission and empire interact compound the territory that interests us here. The human-divine Christ, trickster figure that embodies and thereby holds together in powerful the paradoxes of human flesh and divine substance, can be found at many of these crossroads. Often overshadowed, sidelined, and sandwiched between the goods, the muskets, the textiles, the technologies, and monies that titillate exchanges, the manifold readings and interpretations of story and narrative are legion.

This essay attempts to articulate a constructive proposal for rethinking mission in the postcolony. The vision of this project traces versions of giving and taking, imperially sanctioned theft, rape and robbery, but also instances and possibilities of gifting and receiving beyond the positional dualities of perpetrator and victim, colonizer and colonized, oppressor and oppressed. It seeks to find spaces beyond the hardened edges of identity politics towards

[36] Wells, *Barbarians Speak*, 126.
[37] Keller, "Love of Postcolonialism," 221.

coalitional consciousness.[38] Pushing constructive polydoxy towards soteriological significance, it aims for mutual accountability and engagement while laboring towards embodying partnership. This includes an interdisciplinary approach. Though few contemporary anthropologists have acknowledged the role of religion in colonial contexts, anthropological writings of the first generations have participated in shaping knowledge and perception, as well as governance, missionary methodology and other approaches to indigenous peoples and forms of wisdom and knowledge. These discourses and more recent approaches engaging economic and sociological methodologies are part and parcel of this work, despite the difficulties integrating the accounts, as they often are distinct and deal with issues as separate.[39] The hope is that such a polydox approach will map possibilities for mutual transformation, beyond dialogue, and beyond simple pursuits for conversion without considering the impact on the transformation of life and society.[40] For some, especially those in former colonies, this may involve indigenizing Christian faith and practices without falling prey to false rejections or problematically conceived nativisms; for others, in former and current missionary-sending contexts, this will mean considering the various stages of mission, as well as "mission as inreach"[41] beyond self-perpetuating narcissisms, continued fantasies of quasi-omnipotence, or hypertrophic white guilt complexes.

Stuart Hall, scholar of the African diaspora, notes that there is no such thing as a pure identity for diasporic peoples, but rather that all identity is

---

[38] Chela Sandoval, *Methodology of the Oppressed* (Minneapolis, MN: University of Minneapolis Press, 2000), 78–79.

[39] A poignant example of this separation of labor in anthropology can be seen in two books on colonial presences in the same region of Indonesia that were both lacking in their scope of examination. While Webb Keane and Ann Laura Stoler both deal with almost an identical region and populace in Indonesia, Webb never once considers gender relations in his account of the interaction between the representational economies of Dutch Reformed missionaries and local Reformed Christians and indigenous Indonesian culture, nor does Stoler consider religious or missiological issues in her account of intimate gendered relationships among colonized and colonizing communities. See Webb Keane, *Christian Moderns: Freedom & Fetish in the Mission Encounter* (Berkeley, CA: University of California Press, 2007) and Ann Laura Stoler, *Carnal Knowledge and Imperial Power: Race and the Intimate in Colonial Rule* (Berkeley, CA: University of California Press, 2002).

[40] This specification may require some comment. Many of my students from Africa and Asia note that rather than rejecting conversion, they are concerned with the superficiality of conversion in some of their contexts. The nominal adherence and worship at a church is one thing, but the transformation of life towards more just and equitable relationships does not necessarily follow. Thus, some contexts in Northern and Western as well as Southern and Eastern regions of the globe struggle with similar issues once the first flush of evangelical fervor has died down. This is reminiscent of historical controversies regarding what some saw as superficial conversions elicited during periods of revivalism on the eastern seaboard of the United States under Whitefield, Wesley, Tennent, Edwards and others, towards which Anglican priest Charles Chauncy and others remain quite skeptical. Nathan O. Hatch, *The Democratization of American Christianity* (New Haven, CT: Yale University Press, 1989), 181.

[41] I use the term as defined by Joerg Rieger. Rieger, "Theology and Mission," 219.

a production, "which is never complete, always in process, and always constituted within, not outside, representation."[42] People migrate, and with them so
do their languages, religions, cultures, their diseases, economic interests and
ways of cultivating the earth. The directions of migration and power distributions may change. Empires shift and coagulate, grow, die, and are reborn in
the imagination of the previously conquered. How, as people of faith, as scholars implicated but perhaps also resistant to the status quo of power discourse
and distribution, can we read, speak, act within these intensely complex movements? Poring over the sacred texts of multiply dislocated peoples, we attempt
to wrest from them wisdom for today. Having inherited the texts of dislocated
peoples who experience their God first located, then migrating, then trans-
regional, then universal, a "cosmic God of the displaced,"[43] how might such
hard-won and hard fought-over transcontextuality encounter the traditions
of peoples more solidly grounded in traditional place without devaluing and
overriding them?[44]

Local narrations of the powers in life and land—who the people are, and
how they relate to ancestors, neighbors, animals, sacred powers and relations—
feature prominently in creation accounts around the world. Missionaries
engaged these local indigenous narratives and negotiated their contents, their
similarities and differences with the biblical accounts in Genesis. Their theological and pedagogical activity was profoundly infused with hermeneutic
issues engaging the status and potential veracity of indigenous creation narratives, deities, social and moral practices, and how to negotiate a Christian
faith and morality with them. Hence, missionary encounters represent one
fascinating way to explore cross-cultural hermeneutics and "intercultural
mimesis,"[45] the framing and appropriating of cultural practices and knowledge for the purposes of enhancing the interests and aspirations of colonizer
and colonized.

---

[42] Stuart Hall, "Cultural Identity and Diaspora," in *Theorizing Diaspora*, ed. Nandini
Bhattacharya (Malden, MA: Blackwell, 2003), 234.

[43] Laurel C. Schneider, *Beyond Monotheism: A Theology of Multiplicity* (London: Routledge,
2008), 35.

[44] Is then the Christian monotheism that develops, perhaps, in large part, during the Jewish
exile in Babylonia "a remnant of war trauma on the one hand, and a tool of empire on the
other" that informs questions of militant ethnocentrism, questions of nationalism, and so
forth? Cf. Ibid., 10, 28.

[45] Richard King uses this term—elaborating on Charles Halisey—as a manner of mimetic
interaction between cultural interpreters and especially highlights that such mimesis does
not result in the outright silencing of "Buddhist texts or actual Buddhist practices," for
example, but rather that these have been "manipulated, conceptually framed and thereby
transformed by Western interests and aspirations." See Richard King, *Orientalism and
Religion: Postcolonial Theory, India, and 'The Mystic East'* (New York: Routledge, 1999), 148,
149. While this dynamic may be prevalent in colonial discourses, this kind of mimetic
action, is often not unidirectional, but occurs within different settings and at different
levels of visibility and authority, as Bhabha and other postcolonial critics suggest when they
define colonial mimicry.

The Great Commission—Reconsidering Directions

In late October 2010, the chapel of Virginia Theological Seminary in Alexandria, Virginia, burned down. News reports in the media and from eye-witnesses mentioned that during the fire the stained-glass windows popped and melted with sounds that sounded like cries. One of these windows included "a large iconic window underneath the words 'Go ye into all the world and preach the gospel.'"[46] There are not a few who have wondered whether this "Great Commission" did not go up in flames some time ago, and what might be left in the smoldering embers of its claims. Sent from North-Atlantic and Pacific seminaries, missionaries were motivated and enthused by this classic motto of Christian mission, which peaked with great fervor and energy in the nineteenth century.

At the beginning of the twenty-first century, many progressive and mainline Christians, haunted by shame and white guilt regarding the dismal history of colonial missions, seem doubtful about a sense of mission that goes beyond the relief and development agencies they fund and support. As they turn away in shame and disgust from what they associate with mission—colonial exploitation, the export of Western mores and capitalism, conservative proselytizing, divisive hate speech against sexual minorities, and the preaching of prosperity—there seem only few spaces in which to articulate a resolute progressive Christian witness in praxis that gives account of the full complexity of the laments and losses, the hybridities and tensions, as well as the chances and hopes of polydox soteriologies.[47] They also turn away from their many fellow Christians in Africa, Asia, and the Americas, whose very identity as Christians is rendered questionable through the uniform dismissal of the mode of colonial conversion that stood at the beginning of their faith. Engaging Christian faith and practice across cultural difference in the postcolony—in the long aftermath of colonial missions—helps articulate the "creative tenacity of dissent"

---

[46] The loss of this chapel, and in some sense the spirit in which churches were building windows like these, prompts us to ponder what we understand by the term mission, or commission today. ENS Staff, "Virginia: Fire Destroy VTS Chapel," *Episcopal News Service*, 22 October 2010, www.episcopalchurch.org/81803_125350_ENG_HTM.htm.

[47] An initial attempt to define this emerging expression of theology affirms the multiplicity within theological and religious expressions not as "problems to be overcome" but as "starting points," and indispensable resources for ongoing articulations of faith. Such polydoxy can include both the plurality of faith expressions within the Christian tradition that have been with us since its inception, as well as the reality of multiple religious belongings in more than one religious tradition, and, in this book in particular, the multiple possible valid interactions between expressions of gospel culture and its faithful renderings in the context of other ways of perceiving the world. Thereby, "what had always seemed a liability for Christian theology [. . .] has miraculously turned into theology's friend." For a selection of articulation of such polydoxy, see Catherine Keller and Laurel Schneider, eds, *Polydoxy: Theology of Multiplicity and Relation* (London/New York: Routledge, 2010), 1 and passim.

both within and without the liminal zones of a religious tradition and within and beyond the imperial aspirations our quest for the sacred is so often embedded in. Such resonant flexibility is not the *proprium* of theology only but pertains to many aspects of life.

Theology is a curious discipline, with a long, turbulent history. It has been perceived as a cultural practice too successfully assimilated into the purposes of Roman imperial consolidation and thereafter adapted by various intellectual and interpretive traditions in places north and west of Imperial Rome. That is, its inculturations have been troublingly coextensive with colonial cultures, then and now. Meanwhile, many theological methods employed represent a mimesis of long-standing practices of reading and interpreting, carrying forth interpretive and cultural heritages from North African, Roman, Greek, and Middle Eastern cultural circles, as well as adaptations, translations, and transformations with each cultural context Christians have worked with or from. Theology, like other forms of cultural expression of religious consciousness, is always already deeply informed by its ancestry *and* always already adjusting to new circumstances: *Theologia viatorum.* It is through such spaces we are moving here.

Meanwhile, at home, the specter of Augustine's *corpus permixtum* always threatened, that only a small number within the church were truly committed, reiterated by Martin Luther's sense that few people are real Christians in any society, and that therefore the government needed to keep basic laws for the protection of all.[48] Indeed, missiologists have been asking the question of whether Europe was ever truly Christianized or was not rather an effect of *cuius regio, eius religio,* the imposition of religious affiliation from above.[49] This may underestimate the participation of nonelites in events such as the Reformation, and their resistance to clerical abuses, as well as embrace of a new religious option. Of course, one could ask the same question about Africa, or any other place where Christianity now spreads, as claimed by some, with a zeal and commitment that sometimes is harnessed to shame Northern Christians. These struggles about religious and secular identities heighten questions about what constitutes the limits of recognizable Christian faith and practice. Is evangelical fervor and enthusiasm a reliable sign of "real" Christians? Is obedience to "traditional" cultural models of family and gender? Or have contemporary definitions of Christianity and what counts as valid "mission" and "gospel" been dominated by conservative perspectives? Have these approaches then become so hegemonic that they are no longer interrogated as to their validity, not even by progressive and moderate Christians who are tempted to accept the terms of the debate? Missionary encounters are hardly one-way streets: indeed, theological questions raised by potential converts were often already entertained

[48] Martin Luther, *On Temporal Authority,* in *Luther's Works,* Volume 45, ed. Walther Brandt (Minneapolis, MN: Fortress, 1962), 90–91.
[49] Albrecht Beutel, ed., *Luther Handbuch* (Tübingen: Mohr Siebeck, 2005), 82.

in the missionaries' societies, if in radically different ways. Both sides have to negotiate the challenges to resident assumptions and perceptions, generating a force field of mutual interrogation and creative friction.

We suggest here that interactions on the missionary "field," involving conversations of soteriological content—in the widest possible sense of having to do with how to achieve and maintain a good, meaningful personal and communal life in accordance with the sense of the divine as mediated by missionary and/or local culture—help elucidate how religiocultural communication and the representation of the gospel to other cultures occur. How do people communicate experiences of God that structure the world differently for us? How do they relate to others, with variously differing conceptions of the divine, who or what it is, how it relates to them, how one can be in relationship with it, how it manifests in the world? What kinds of methods and technologies of telling and writing are employed? How are bridges to the ineffable claimed, messages received, transported, translated, negotiated, and what kind of reasoning structures, aids, or impedes the communication of religious truths across persons, communities, and cultures?

What concerns us here are the techniques and technologies of mission, the assumptions and dynamics that shape messages and objects. What cultural production will retain its value when exchanged? What translates, what does not? What is the purpose of these transactions? What is the gospel, and how does it appear in a new context? Where do messengers come to the limits of self and blend and bleed into the cultures they encounter? What is conversion and how does it function? What is contagion and syncretism and how do they function? What kind of transformation and encounter are desirable, who decides, and how do we know? What interactions deconstruct the imaginary of the self-certain position of the missionary as well as stark anticolonial and anti-missionary positions and instead highlight the hybrid realities of these exchanges? Those who found themselves confronted with missionaries had their own questions, informed by knowledge regimes of their cultural environments: Why should we trade in what we have for other cultural goods, including the stories that form our identities? What are we asked to give up in the trade? What constitutes "conversion" and how are the economic conversions related to the spiritual ones? Can the many layers of Christian story be a resource for survival when confronted with changing regimes of knowledge under colonialism or capitalist globalization? If so, how?

The Great Omission: Minding the Gaps in Missiological Discourse

[T]he majority of Christians live in the Southern continents, and their coming to Christian faith is ultimately related to the missionary movement. No Western response

to other faiths can hold water that does not take responsibility for the missionary move-
ment; no Western response to other faiths can show Christian integrity if it by implica-
tion cuts itself off from the Christian believers of the non-Western world.[50]

The Great Commission has been the locus classicus for the theological articulation of many missiologies, but the section title angles for more than a cute
wordplay. The many glaring gaps, wounds, and omissions of encounters in
mission call out to be minded, remembered, lamented, and transformed. For
our purposes here, then, the "Great Omission" refers to the gaps in discourses
of mission. Some of these gaps manifest as (1) shame and avoidance of mission discourse among mainline and progressive Christians, (2) the omitted
complexities of disciplinary layers in traditional missiology, (3) an absence
and erasure of the theological and linguistic contributions of local interlocutors in the consideration of mission history, interfaith and intercultural
encounter, (4) the absence in dominant accounts of mission history of the
contribution of women, as missionaries and as local interlocutors and the
implied limitations of what is considered "mission," (5) the rarity of theological as well as functional and historical analyses of the dynamics of encounters
in mission.

Missionary rhetoric, preaching, and teaching involve significant amounts of
hermeneutical activity, and thus trickster technologies. The transformations
and transfers involved in missionary interactions involved also manifold opportunities for trickster activity. What dynamics are involved in persuading, what
techniques are employed to resist or strategically interact with the attempted
recalibration of worldview, loyalty, and interpretation of the world? What is the
message of the gospel and how is it entangled in narratives of history, culture,
sociopolitical, and economic structures? How does this wide scope of intercultural hermeneutical action affect Christian theological thinking, which, in
much of its scope, has been a glorified form of "European clan history?"[51] That
is, how might one go about tending to some of the gaps in church history, and,
beyond that, constructive theological work?

Such efforts are hampered by archival problems familiar to historians:
the patchy canvas of sources. Most widely accessible discourses are written
by imperial agents and are predicated on the focus on the missionary as the
agent of mission whose writings are directed to a panoptikon of eyes located
in the sending cultures. The preference of literacy over orality on the side of
many missionaries comes at the cost of likely obscuring and omitting vital oral

[50] Andrew F. Walls, *The Missionary Movement in Christian History: Studies in the Transmission of
Faith* (Maryknoll, NY: Orbis, 1996), 147.
[51] Andrew F. Walls, "Eusebius Tries Again: The Task of Reconceiving and Re-Visioning the
Study of Christian History," in *Enlarging the Story: Perspectives on Writing World Christian
History*, Wilbert R Shenk, ed. (Maryknoll, NY: Orbis, 2002), 11.

discourses and asides. In many unfortunate cases, variously talented linguists and scholars reduced the culture of the natives to something to be understood, a code to be cracked so it could be more effectively superseded. Discussions of mission and missionary history often omit the realities of cultural and communal loss of aspects of identity shaping narratives in the transitions between or the negotiation among indigenous and Christian religiocultures, alongside the more well-known aspects of the loss of deep connections to land (perhaps often seen as separate from identity!), the invasion of colonial bodies into land and body, and the attending economic and sexual violence.

In some cases, the intent of establishing a relationship to the gospel can be replaced by the relation to the colonizer or missionary. A narcissistic wound in the colonizing missionaries can conflate their own identity with the gospel and their rejection with a rejection of the gospel. This raises the relationship between the messenger and the message. As soon as we claim the gospel as a *kerygma* distinct from the *keryx* (the messenger) we have to think more deeply about what this gospel is and in what relationship it stands with the cultures that produced it, transcribed it, transmitted and interpreted it. At other times, the priests, missionaries, and scholars underwent a process of deep encounter that, at least in part, transformed them, some so substantially that they were dismissed as having "gone native," which was code for what was perceived as disloyalty to the sending culture, church, or society, and having preferred or adapted elements of the host culture.

Another interdisciplinary gap has been the relative lack of thinking economics and mission together in theologies of divine economies. The economic effects of mission have in the last few years received increased attention for the way in which economic dynamics articulated the "civilising mission" through tools, bodily practices, literacy, work, land rights and property, monetary exchange, and gender roles. Another angle on the economics of mission is the way economic situations and organizations were involved in recruiting, training, funding, and supporting missionaries. Still largely overlooked or at least unintegrated with the economic and missiological effects are the ecological effects of missionary and imperial policies on land use, resource extraction, mining, farming, agriculture, water usage, irrigation and dams, air pollution, trash production, deforestation, mineral, oil, and precious metals extraction. All these questions have been pursued especially under the influence of what is now widely called postcolonial theories and discourse analysis, which also form part of the methodological approach of the present inquiry.

This book proceeds from certain points of departure, places of (no) return, and offers a theological account of particular patterns of Christian missionary history and presence from the "North." At the same time, it raises, with Homi Bhabha, suspicions about such imprecise, if convenient labels as West, North, South, and East as synechdoches for presumably solid cultural or moral identities.

Modernity, we would now argue, was not a western invention as such but itself a product of the west's interaction with the rest of the world, including the economic exploitation of colonialism which first provided the surplus gold that was the motor for modern capitalism. [. . .] The debate is not between modernity and its opponents, but rather between different versions of modernity, some of which offer alternatives to what is regarded, not always very accurately, as the western model.[52]

Instead, I suggest that the four directions can serve as an exemplary metaphor for the shared four-foldness that many humans have seen in the organic patterns of world, and the infinity of perspectives a circumambulation can provide as one faces east, south, west, and north.

Along the way, we encounter long-standing symbioses, mutual transformations and adaptabilities of cultures, peoples, and ideas. Though it has been argued that Christianity "has no locality, either sociologically (institutions and people circulate), culturally (ideas and practices circulate), or ontologically (its truth-claims are universal),"[53] a deeper recognition of the incarnate practice of theology finds both striking similarities and sturdy differences. Even if one were to grant a universal essence to Christian faith, or the gospel—it has continued to be translated or transmitted into local cultural space and time. And when translation into a cultural idiom occurs, the "infinite translatability"[54] manifests itself also as the site of *infinite difference*, of *infinite losses in translation*.[55]

Counteracting the tendency to claim universality for some inculturations and re-localizing them adds to the breadth of conceptions of the gospel, since the "failure to consider our colonial heritage may result in failure to understand who we are today."[56] Kwok Pui-Lan suggests that since the "colonial process is doubly inscribed, affecting both the metropolitan centers and the colonies, the postcolonial process must involve both colonizers and the colonized." This, she proposes, means that "not only do the colonized need to disengage from the colonial syndrome, the colonizers have to decolonize their minds and practices as well."[57] Given this need to decolonize, how might one recast "Western" Christianity as comprising a subset of "European" inculturations of

[52] Robert Young, *Postcolonialism: A Very Short Introduction* (Oxford: Oxford University Press, 2003), 98.

[53] Walls seems to follow here some of the less contextual readings of the gospel. Keane, *Christian Moderns*, 45.

[54] Walls, *The Missionary Movement in Christian History*, 25.

[55] While we cannot engage in this issue here, it is also worth discussing, in the context of comparative theology, whether and if so, how Christianity might be more or less translatable than other religious expressions.

[56] Rieger, "Theology and Mission", 202.

[57] Kwok here applies Stuart Hall's insight to the need for a multilateral postcolonial theology. Kwok Pui-Lan, *Postcolonial Imagination & Feminist Theology* (Louisville, KY: WJK, 2005), 127.

the gospel? Thus it shares the fate of all known inculturations of gospel, the ambivalent connection to the cultures that produced and formed it in other locales, as well as the difficulty of linking it to local cultures.

Upon using the local idiom for a seemingly universal and further imported theological articulation of divinity, multiple confusions can occur. Missionary hermeneutics highlight certain biblical narratives and features above others, selecting them for relevance and apparent functionality in the projected encounters. There is no guarantee that disseminated texts are received in ways that missionaries may hope or predict. Rather, they are, rather obviously read within the context of the local culture, and often read as displaying a different logic of divine agency and character than the one intended by the missionaries, who often had particular theological frameworks that were neither shared by the indigenous peoples, nor, in fact with a more plainly heard and interpreted sense of scripture. Despite the gaps in the archives and accounts of mission history, there are traces of biblical and cultural hermeneutics of missionary days that have much to teach about what a globally aware local Christian option in the postindustrial world could look like and what its challenges and changes might be.

How can the "Eurocentric structure of its knowledge forms" be engaged in critical depth and how can multiple contexts engage in a conversation that incorporates "non-Western [cultural] traditions on something like an equal footing"? If mission in the postcolony "begins not with the conversion of the other," but with "the conversion of the missionary self,"[58] what might this conversion entail? Joerg Rieger proposes a "multilogical" approach to mission,[59] beyond monological or even dialogical encounters, something that is "no longer optional but absolutely essential to the future of both mission and theology."[60]

During a class I taught on modern church history, the lone Native American student in the class challenged us by suggesting that the European-descending members of the class (and by extension the churches they represent) fully engage their own ethnic group's colonized past as a precondition for greater solidarity with indigenous peoples today. The challenge was a reminder to consider that something important might be lost if the colonizers' own history and indigenous past are repressed in the quest for something that might approach a post-imperial space. What would it mean to attempt to bring into a deep conversation between some of the conversions of "barbarian" tribes north of Rome and civilizing missions of the nineteenth century, addressing

[58] Rieger, "Theology and Mission," 222.

[59] Ibid., 224.

[60] A nagging question remains: What would keep such an enterprise from being yet another version of gazing at the other, navel-gazing by proxy, because we are seeking answers about our own self-identity? Or is asking this question already hopelessly engaged in such narcissism? Perhaps we must move through such interrogations to come to resolution.

perhaps another gap in knowledge production, the erasure of the loss of indigenous religious practices for most Europeans? Mind you, I do not envision here the possibility of some sort of reconciliation, which, too quickly claimed, cannot but be either an "ideological tool for negotiating power" or a "socially exhausted idealist claim masquerading as serious theological accounts."[61] Profoundly sobered by the tragedies of past and present, but stubbornly insisting that all is not lost and something survivable and livable has been present and is furthermore newly emerging, I have been scanning several territories on the search for traces and patterns, hints of Spirit and spirits reemerging. The spirit of lament is one of them.

Making Space for Lamenting Loss and Forging Survival

Untold amounts of violence and loss have been the result of imperialism, ancient and modern. Missionary movements have had their share of entanglement in the destruction and exploitation of the inhabitants of the land and indigenous peoples. The loss of cultures of self-knowing especially related to the geography of religiocultural belonging has had many genocidal aspects to it. Indeed, civilizing missions have produced a profoundly destructive impact near and far. Much was lost, much is to be mourned, and much cannot be retrieved. Space must be given to remember, lament, and honor what has been lost, and to name what seeks to reincarnate and survive.

Another danger is the too enthusiastic affirmation of celebratory hybridity. Dominant representations of "pluralism" unaware of their own supersessionisms, and the consumption of exotic cultures through a globalizing economy, including the vagaries of the consumption of exotic theologies—Marcella Althaus-Reid's warnings haunt any such attempts—threaten to yet again engulf what wants to resist imperial assimilation. This dynamic of "inclusivism" often hides a rearticulation of a dominant strand seeking to encompass rather than encounter. Unsurprisingly, for underrepresented cultures threatened by extinction through assimilation, certain forms of compulsory hybridity sound threatening. The instability of identity and the troubles of representation do not foreclose the need to preserve history and knowledge of the more endangered part of the self or community in the onslaught of those many others pushing for assimilation, for supersession, or for consumption, none of which are desirable iterations of salvation.

Lament can create space for the rearticulation of survival and help move towards flourishing. It is important to highlight the adaptability, creativity and resistance, the agency and the ability to invent new forms of identity that show

[61] Willie James Jennings, *The Christian Imgination: Theology and the Origins of Race* (New Haven, CT: Yale University Press, 2010), 10.

incredible resilience, particularly in the face of so much that cooperates to destroy self, community, and earth. Focusing either only on negative effects or, alternatively, on triumphalist accounts of mission falls short of giving a differentiated representation of the many intercoiled dynamics of such intercultural interaction. An exclusively negative evaluation of mission often tends to erase the agency of the persons and converts involved, and instead heightens the impression of a seemingly omnipotent and omnipresent shape of colonial forces. I am here particularly interested in what survives colonial legacies, what creative transformations emerged from it, and what potential for flourishing is present.

Though this book intentionally avoids engagement in contemporary ecumenical controversies around church leadership, and gender and sexuality, it would be hard not to at least point at the underlying connections. Missionary theologies and ethics were expressive of a particular inculturated Christian polity, and intercultural clashes around gender relations paired with colonial disregard of certain sexual practices put many converts and their surrounding societies on the defensive. The need to defend their own sociosexual status over and against an eventually internalized Victorian sexual morality blended with local patriarchalism has in our time contributed to strange rearticulations of the "missionary position" on sex and sexuality. This time from male church leaders in the colonially planted churches toward churches whose theology of sexuality makes room for a greater variety of sexual and gender expressions. A complex history of colonial missions, homophobia, imperialism, and racism are factors in these quarrels around queer sexuality. There are many indications, however, that the struggles are more deeply shaped by contemporary battles between progressive and conservative Christians rather than simply representing a conflict between colonizer and colonized. This has at times been hard to see, as missionary Christianity has often been rigid and conservative, and has generally not represented the variety of positions within the churches of the sending societies. Since many churches planted by missionary movements were planted by more conservative forces within those churches, the conflicts bear more than a passing similarity to conflicts between progressives and conservatives in the north, but from some angles have been represented as conflicts between colonialist and colonized Christians. These representations fade when taking a broader perspective that realizes the influence of American conservative evangelicals in debates over homosexuality in Africa, and, most clearly, in Ghana and Uganda. Rick Warren's explicit and tacit support of homophobic legislation in Uganda[62] is a prominent example of a culture war exported, outsourced, and fought in multiple territories.

---

[62] See Michelle Goldberg's article on the conservative evangelical influence in Uganda and its connection to virulently homophobic legislation in that country. Michelle Goldberg, "Uganda's Radical Anti-Gay Measure and the American Religious Right," *Religious*

Thus, U.S. conservatives appropriated liberal and postcolonial rhetoric that branded the consecration of Episcopal Bishop Gene Robinson as an imperialist move, meant perhaps to trigger liberal white guilt. Yet, the hidden financial support by conservative U.S. Christians to conservative Anglicans worldwide, and their agitation to expel churches that recognize the ministry of Gay, Lesbian, Bisexual and Transgender (GLBT) Christians, and the persecution of GLBT persons in places such as Uganda certainly qualify as a move with its own imperialist impetus.[63] It also highlights the relative absence of moderate and progressive/liberal Christians from mission other than in the form of social service and development, from the study of mission history, and the articulation of missionary theologies.

A resolute articulation of mission in the postcolony seeks to differentiate between cynical instrumentalizations of religious motifs for ends that increase the power, wealth, or public standing of a person or groups and principled and skillful means of encouraging love of God and neighbor in search of justice.[64] All this involves making resolute distinctions between better and worse contextualizations of biblical texts, a process within which Spivak's postulate of a "strategic essentialism"[65] may be of help. Angling for manipulative power occurs in all societies and religions, is hardly unique to Christianity, and should be resisted no matter where it appears.

Instead, the challenge will be to search for polydox rereadings of tradition in the face of the challenges of the context, place, and time. Despite the difficulties involved in any act of interpretation, we cannot but continue in our attempt to make sense of the world as best we can. While apophatic interpretive moves are crucial to a modestly witnessing theology,[66] those hesitant to indicate anything definite about divinity may find themselves ever more compelled to speak as shrill and often rigid, deceptive voices capture the imagination of a public wired for slightly scandalous and sensationalist soundbites. Like Elijah, we might do well to wait for the still small voice of God that is not in the storm or the thunder, but in a light rustling of air. Elijah represents an absent presence, a chair reserved for him at Sabbath, indicating the constant possibility of another presence in our lives. Where loud voices seek to dominate, we are

Dispatches, 30 November 2009, www.religiondispatches.org/archive/religiousright/2070/uganda%E2%80%99s_radical_anti-gay_measure_and_the_american_religious_right/.

[63] Barbara Bradley Hagerty, "Anti-Gay Atmosphere Permeates Uganda," *NPR*, 20 December 2010, www.npr.org/2010/12/20/132147169/anti-gay-atmosphere-permeates-uganda?ft=1&f=1001&sc=tw&utm_source=twitterfeed&utm_medium=twitter.

[64] Though this may be harder to argue in societies where there is not a starkly developed distinction between sacred and secular realms. The more those are blended, the trickier indeed it gets.

[65] Donna Landry and Gerald MacLean, eds, *The Spivak Reader* (New York: Routledge, 1996), 214.

[66] Donna J. Haraway, *Modest_Witness@Second_Millennium. FemaleMan©_Meets_OncoMouse™* (New York/London: Routledge, 1997).

called to be voices that seek to transform fear and anxiety about economic stability, ethnic identity, national boundaries, and the distribution of opportunities. We are to resist radicalized religious sentiments when they foster a culture of fear, and to speak an alternative to them. Speaking with many voices opens up many resolute clusters of un/knowing God.

Pondering Itineraries: A Pilgrim's Guide

Some of the stations on the itinerary of this circumambulation are incidental, as are most travels. They mark places where deepening connections beckoned. Places that have a well-preserved history and culture to be able to explore missionary dynamics and a discourse that is publicly accessible and can be engaged. Trespassing was an attendant danger. At times, I erred on seeking access where refusing it meant to contain the roving eye of colonial research. You might wonder why my wanderings might have to say something to you. I would respond that you might recognize some patterns that are consistent and that might teach you something about the way the gospel travels between and among us. What exactly it might teach you, only you, dear reader, can know.

The first chapter, *Circumambulation*, introduces the reader to the zones of interaction and a particular mode of engagement with encounters in mission. The metaphor of circumambulating a point or place means to suggest the benefit of looking at an instance of interaction from a number of different viewpoints, here supplied by encounters observed in certain select contexts in the history of mission, engaging observations from the conversion of Central and Northern Europe in the early Middle Ages, and juxtaposing them with instances of British Anglican missions in South Africa, New Zealand, and Alaska.

The chapter entitled *Departures* lays out the interdisciplinary, multimodal methodology that informs this circumambulation, and engages the commitments of a polydox constructive theology of missionary encounter. It is followed by *Waymakers*, wherein the attempt is made to articulate possible conceptual frameworks for the observed material within a paradigmatic narrativity, that is, gleaning from the encounters observed patterns that serve to ground a reconstruction of soteriology as missiology. The next part of this book offers three itineraries seeking to explore a number of encounters in mission. Beginning with an exploration of the early post-Roman times of Christian faith, the next two itineraries examine two case studies from the nineteenth century. *Itinerary I* traces heavily contested boundaries, rivers, walls, and forests, in the life of Boniface, "Apostle to the Germans," as he negotiates his Roman papal loyalties with the Frankish dynasty aiming to establish predominance in the area. Foreshadowed by Boniface's destruction of the Oak of Thor in Geismar, Charlemagne's push for radical Christianization according to a Romanized model while asserting Frankish domination in the region, rearticulated earlier missionary theories and perceptions of the relations between Christian and pagan religious practices in more starkly boundaried terms. Contemporary examples from Norway and Greenland map how societies formed by these and subsequent missions struggle to reinhabit this inheritance, theologically, nationally, regionally, politically, and spiritually. *Itineraries II, III,* and *In Transit* bring us to the far ends of the reach of the Church of England and some of the missionary movements that laid the groundwork for the network of Anglican Churches that were established in uneasy concomitance with British imperial structures. Missionaries were deployed to South Africa, New Zealand, and Alaska, locations with large indigenous populations and few, at least, initially, settlers of European extraction. The encounters between missionaries—with scant imperial forces to support their presence—and indigenous peoples give important clues to the possibilities and difficulties of cross-religious encounters, the traps and changes of mutual dependence and the negotiation of land, narrative, relation, and divinity.

These sites serve as theological-hermeneutical case studies; their past, present, and outlook on the future of contextual churches and theologies offer insight for the formulation of a postcolonial theological hermeneutics and missiology. They offer some general coordinates for a re/mapping of spirit and body through (missionary/cross-cultural) encounters and to re/interpret land, time, and the connections between lands and people. In this endeavor, the present inquiry will note the forces of empire, economic and ecological, and how they contribute to shaping how humans interpret divine and human action, but not let overpower the issues at hand. The quasi-omnipotence that has been ascribed to imperial transactions and power seems to me to go strikingly against the first commandment—it has become godlike in the paralyzing fascination it exudes. This obsession with imperial structures has taken for granted empire's omnipotence and posited a level of discontinuity between imperial and colonial cultures that does not bear up to close scrutiny. We will rather aim at resisting the externalizing obsession with the beast of empire while learning enough about its habits within and without to contend with it. *In Transit* briefly engages features of polydox Episcopal-Athabascan Christian faith practice and then asks the question what some of the notable features of indigenizing churches might be.

Holding Patterns plays with the dual interpretive possibilities of that phrase and aims to hold, but hold lightly for closer observation and crosscontextual comparison, some of the patterns observed. At the same time the ongoing polydox process of inculturation manifests in ways that render any articulation thereof as a holding pattern, that is, a process that remains unfinished, is always subject to deferral, impediments, and interruption. *Holding Patterns* attempts to name a number of seeming similarities across differences of time and place as patterns to be held "in the meantime," as we ponder the next incarnations of constructive, polydox Christian mission. Holding patterns, holding them lightly, not as rules set in stone, but as metamorphic yet real iterations, is necessary for developing a good sense of the real layers of religiocultural interaction and what we, as members of certain communities of accountability, may discern as the gospel to speak in particular contexts. They can serve as warnings but also as reminders of the unexpected possibilities for flourishing that can lie hidden in some of the most intractable circumstances.

Aporias concludes the present exploration and reminds of the need to not foreclose the ongoing interactions and encounters by suggesting set routes of travel, itineraries, or patterns. Rather, it exposes the continuing need to engage the paradoxicality of polydox encounters in openness for critical engagement and the necessity to attempt to set out in humble "waylessness", in *aporia*, as we begin rethinking mission, again.

Works Cited

Althaus-Reid, Marcella. *Indecent Theology: Theological Perversions in Sex, Gender and Politics*. London and New York: Routledge, 2001.

Barber, Elizabeth Wayland, and Paul T. Barber. *When They Severed Earth from Sky: How the Human Mind Shapes Myth*. Princeton, NJ: Princeton University Press, 2004.

Beutel, Albrecht, ed. *Luther Handbuch*. Tübingen: Mohr Siebeck, 2005.

Bhabha, Homi. *The Location of Culture*. London/New York: Routledge, 1994.

Breeze, David J. *Edge of Empire: Rome's Scottish Frontier, The Antonine Wall*. Edinburgh: Birlinn, 2008.

Buck-Morss, Susan. *Hegel, Haiti and Universal History*. Pittsburgh, PA: Pittsburgh University Press, 2009.

Caputo, John, and Catherine Keller. "Theopoetics/Theopolitics." *Crosscurrents*, Winter 2007, 105–11.

Derrida, Jacques. *Specters of Marx: The State of Debt, the Work of Mourning & the New International*. Trans. Peggy Kamuf. New York: Routledge, 1994.

ENS Staff. "Virginia: Fire Destroyes VTS Chapel." *Episcopal News Service*, 22 October 2010, www.episcopalchurch.org/81803_125350_ENG_HTM.htm.

Gebara, Ivone. *Longing for Running Water: Ecofeminism and Liberation*. Minneapolis, MN: Fortress, 1999.

Goldberg, Michelle. "Uganda's Radical Anti-Gay Measure and the American Religious Right." *Religious Dispatches*, November 30 2009, www.religiondispatches.org/archive/religiousright/2070/uganda%E2%80%99s_radical_anti-gay_measure_and_the_american_religious_right/.

Grau, Marion. *Of Divine Economy: Refinancing Redemption*. London/New York: T&T Clark/Continuum, 2004.

Greenblatt, Stephen. *Marvelous Possessions: The Wonder of the New World*. Oxford/New York: Clarendon Press, 1991.

Hagerty, Barbara Bradley. "Anti-Gay Atmosphere Permeates Uganda." *NPR*, 20 December 2010, www.npr.org/2010/12/20/132147169/anti-gay-atmosphere-permeates-uganda?ft=1&f=1001&sc=tw&utm_source=twitterfeed&utm_medium=twitter.

Hall, Stuart. "Cultural Identity and Diaspora." In *Theorizing Diaspora*, edited by Nandini Bhattacharya, 233–46. Malden, MA: Blackwell, 2003.

Haraway, Donna J. *Modest_Witness@Second_Millennium.FemaleMan©_Meets_OncoMouse™*. New York/London: Routledge, 1997.

Hatch, Nathan O. *The Democratization of American Christianity*. New Haven, CT: Yale University Press, 1989.

hooks, bell. *Belonging: A Culture of Place*. New York: Routledge, 2009.

Jennings, Willie James. *The Christian Imgination: Theology and the Origins of Race*. New Haven, CT: Yale University Press, 2010.

Keane, Webb. *Christian Moderns: Freedom & Fetish in the Mission Encounter*. Berkeley, CA: University of California Press, 2007.

Keller, Catherine. *God and Power: Counter-Apocalyptic Journeys*. Minneapolis, MN: Fortress, 2005.

—."The Love of Postcolonialism: Theology in the Interstices of Empire." In *Postcolonial Theologies: Divinity and Empire*, Catherine Keller, Michael Nausner, and Mayra Rivera, eds, 221–42. St. Louis, MI: Chalice, 2004.

Keller, Catherine, and Laurel Schneider, eds, *Polydoxy: Theology of Multiplicity and Relation*. London/New York: Routledge, 2010.

King, Richard. *Orientalism and Religion: Postcolonial Theory, India, and 'The Mystic East'*. New York: Routledge, 1999.

Kugel, James L. *How to Read the Bible: A Guide to Scripture, Then and Now*. New York: Free Press, 2007.

Kwok, Pui-Lan. *Postcolonial Imagination & Feminist Theology*. Louisville, KY: WJK, 2005.

Landry, Donna, and Gerald MacLean, eds, *The Spivak Reader*. New York: Routledge, 1996.

Linebaugh, Peter, and Marcus Rediker. *The Many-Headed Hydra: Sailors, Slaves, Commoners, and the Hidden History of the Revolutionary Atlantic*. Boston, MA: Beacon Press, 2000.

Luther, Martin. *On Temporal Authority*. Luther's Works, Volume 45. Edited by Walther Brandt. Minneapolis, MN: Fortress, 1962.

Metz, Johann Baptist. "In Memory of the Other's Suffering: Theological Reflections on the Future of Faith and Culture." In *The Critical Spirit: Theology at the Crossroads of Faith and Culture*, Andrew Pierce and Geraldine Smyth, 179–88. Blackrock: The Columba Press, 2004.

Moltmann, Jürgen. *Theology of Hope: On the Grounds and the Implications of a Christian Eschatology*. Evanston, IL and New York: Harper & Row, 1964.

Nausner, Michael. "Homeland as Borderland." In *Postcolonial Theologies: Divinity and Empire*, Postcolonial Theologies, 118–32. St. Louis, MI: Chalice, 2004.

Rapp, Jennifer R. "A Poetics of Comparison: Euripides, Zhuangzi, and the Human Poise of Imaginative Construction." *JAAR* Vol. 78, No. 1 (March 2010): 163–201.

Reichertz, Jo. "Hermeneutik der Kulturen—Kulturen der Hermeneutik." In *Hermeneutik der Kulturen—Kulturen der Hermeneutik: Zum 65. Geburtstag von Hans-Georg Soeffner*, Jo Reichertz, Anne Honer, and Werner Schneider, eds, 13–15. Konstanz: UVK Verlagsgesellschaft, 2004.

Rieger, Joerg. "Theology and Mission Between Neocolonialism and Postcolonialism." *Mission Studies 21.2* (2004).

Rivera, Mayra. *The Touch of Transcendence: A Postcolonial Theology of God.* Louisville, KY: WJK, 2007.

Rubenstein, Mary-Jane. *Strange Wonder: The Closure of Metaphysics and the Opening of Awe.* New York: Columbia University Press, 2008.

Sandoval, Chela. *Methodology of the Oppressed.* Minneapolis, MN: University of Minneapolis Press, 2000.

Schallmayer, Erich. *Der Limes: Geschichte einer Grenze.* C. H. Beck Wissen. Munich: Verlag C.H. Beck, 2006.

Schneider, Laurel C. *Beyond Monotheism: A Theology of Multiplicity.* London: Routledge, 2008.

Snyder, Gary. "The Circumambulation of Mt. Tamalpais." In *Opening the Mountain: Circumambulating Mount Tamalpais, A Ritual Walk*, Matthew Davis and Michael Farrell Scott. Emeryville, CA: Avalon, 2006.

Stoler, Ann Laura. *Carnal Knowledge and Imperial Power: Race and the Intimate in Colonial Rule.* Berkeley, CA: University of California Press, 2002.

Walls, Andrew F. "Eusebius Tries Again: The Task of Reconceiving and Re-Visioning the Study of Christian History." In *Enlarging the Story: Perspectives on Writing World Christian History*, Wilbert R Shenk, ed., 1–21. Maryknoll, NY: Orbis, 2002.

—.*The Missionary Movement in Christian History: Studies in the Transmission of Faith.* Maryknoll, NY: Orbis, 1996.

Wells, Peter S. *The Barbarians Speak: How the Conquered Peoples Shaped Roman Europe.* Princeton, NJ: Princeton University Press, 1999.

Young, Robert. *Postcolonialism: A Very Short Introduction.* Oxford: Oxford University Press, 2003.

Chapter 2

Departures: Traversing Methodically

Trespassing, Transgressing, Circling, Encountering: Liminal Spaces and Moving Boundaries

The Greek term theorein: a practice of travel and observation, a man sent by the polis to another city to witness a religious ceremony. "Theory" is a product of displacement, comparison, a certain distance. To theorize, one leaves home.[1]

At the beginning of any circumambulation, our steps may be unsure, faltering over faults in the territory, haunted by specters, traps set to explode, always negotiating encounter and relationship with a toxic past and present, skeletons in the ground. A ritual acknowledgment of these haunting present absences occurred at the beginning of a class in Maori theology I took during a two-month research visit in Aotearoa/New Zealand, by way of a creative adaptation of the *powhiri,* a Maori rite of encounter. The *powhiri*—as best as I can discern, as a trespasser on other people's land on this leg of circumambulation—involves several facets of posturing, naming locations, not-so-veiled threats, flexing of muscle, demanding accountability, and finally peacemaking and hospitality, including the sharing of breath and life resources. Certain parts of the ritual encounter are at times performed for tourists, who observe it to get a taste of Maori culture, music, and dance. What we did at the beginning of the class, however, had less performative, and more participatory, functions, the sense of negotiating access and encounter, give and take, in a context where trust and respect had to be earned before strangers could be turned into allies.

Several days earlier, I had spent what seemed like several hours waiting for passport and luggage control after arriving at Auckland airport cramming a book on Maori customs.[2] Providing a sense of how carefully communally owned

---

[1] James Clifford, "Notes on Travel and Theory," *Inscriptions* Vol. 5 (1989).
[2] Hiwi and Pat Tauroa, *Te Marae: A Guide to Customs & Protocol* (Auckland: Reed, 1986).

space was negotiated, protected, and surveyed in Aotearoa/New Zealand,[3] this kind of ritualized first encounter continues to be crucial for the subsequent quality and possibility of reciprocal relationships with a modicum of trust. Needing to turn in my hiking boots for inspection and decontamination of the soles from potential bio-contaminants at customs felt equally puzzling. Though the previous context was that of negotiating intertribal conflict and warfare, it has now taken on a host of other functions, among them being the initiation of colonial inhabitants of the country, as well as a variety of visitors and tourists to the *marae*, the "place to stand" for the local group.[4]

What our teacher Pa Henare Tate's staging of this form of the ritual for our class taught me then and now were several things: access to spaces where people live, move, and have their being is negotiated in particular ways. Unlimited and unaccountable access should not be assumed. Access without accountability was not a possibility here. Trespassers needed to be turned into welcome visitors, based upon their accountability to the hosts of the place, and could not assume access without being questioned about their person, history, assumptions, goals, and intentions. My initial resistance to "giving an account of myself" in the *marae* before the class, and at my first time at the *Te Rau Kahikatea*, the Maori house of study at St. John's Anglican Seminary in Auckland, was a mix of reticence, shyness, resistance, perhaps, and quite likely indignation at having to justify my presence and reveal my intentions publicly to a group of complete strangers. I had come there to observe and learn, not to speak about myself and my background. Yet, as the *powhiri* made clear, my connections to the land and culture that informed me traveled with me, impacting my being there and the relations I would be able (not) to have. In fact, the purpose of the journey had been, among other, an attempt to decenter my location in a place that felt unable to perceive other than for its own purposes, those encountered. The wisdom the ritual brought out in this context was that whatever illusions we might have to want to encounter otherness, we always do so carrying our own family, geographical, and cultural history with us.

As bodies incarnate, we are concrete. Incarnation is nonnegotiable. Escape from incarnation, concreteness, and locatedness into a view from nowhere ultimately denies this at the cost of real relations. Decolonial and postcolonial strategies will fail if they, too, assume some hidden universalist viewpoint. Awareness of my own positionality, intentionality, and the cultural and institutional power I represented through citizenship, education, and employment

---

[3] The term "Aotearoa/New Zealand," a combination of the name given to the land by Polynesian marine migrants and the Anglo name given after settlement by Europeans, represents a transculture in its own way. Aotearoa is often rendered as "Land of the long white cloud" and, according to conflicting versions of Maori mythology, was named either by a principal Polynesian navigator or his wife. Michael King, *The Penguin History of New Zealand* (Auckland: Penguin Books, 2003), 41.

[4] Anne Salmond, *Hui: A Study of Maori Ceremonial Gatherings* (Auckland: Reed, 1975), 31.

were no longer deniable. At least this particular instance of intercultural encounter was predicated on rendering explicit some of its preconditions, rather than leaving all things implied. Others were to follow where implicit and unstated expectations of hosts or guests led to uncomfortable conflict. Thus perambulates circumambulation. The challenge was to find a wobbly balance between the need for greater understanding of indigenous peoples by postindustrial persons and the danger of stealing knowledge for personal gain, and indeed the furthering of one's own career. This circuitous path between seeking at least some degree of understanding of surviving indigenous populations and the exotic accessorizing of tasty morsels of other people's cultures is never clear or easy, and perhaps simply impossible.

Many of the steps of the circumambulation that were to follow involved stumbles and falls over ancient and present boulders of cultural difference, whose size and location I had either overseen or underestimated. Access, trespassing, ownership, and ancestry were some of the forms of boundary negotiation that had to be dealt with between these cultures. Instances of encounter and exchange were highly complex, fraught, loaded, and often unpredictable. It was making me unsure about many things, and therein lay a great opportunity.

Inter/Disciplining Missiology

> *The Western church historiographical tradition was based on a dichotomy with church history on the one side and mission history on the other. Mission history was concerned with Christian activity outside the West. Church history treated the life and work of the church in the West.*[5]

Missiology, or mission studies, has a somewhat odd positionality in places of theological studies. Many mainline seminaries in the United States do not teach missiology as a separate course, having historically been less engaged in the practice of mission themselves, and often quietly embarrassed about the missionary legacy. There, mission studies or missiology tends not to appear in the curriculum at all, or only marginally, under denominational history. Evangelical movements and their schools, historically often on the forefront of missionary movements, generally have a dedicated position in mission studies or missiology, and appear generally more happy to own and engage in study of missions as well as contemporary mission at home and abroad. For the most part, mission studies have not been considered a crucial field for theological thinking within a systematic or constructive framework, with the exception

---

[5] Wilbert R. Shenk, "Introduction," in *Enlarging the Story: Perspectives on Writing World Christian History*, Wilbert R Shenk, ed. (Maryknoll, NY: Orbis, 2002), xvi.

of recent approaches to ecumenical studies or postcolonial theology.[6] David Bosch's challenge to see the study of mission as a vital part of constructive theological enterprises, rather than as an appendage to practical theology, is instructive.[7]

Elsewhere, the study may appear as the background to the study of ecumenism, or interdisciplinary studies, or in the discourse known in some schools as "World Christianity," which often functions separately from systematic or constructive theological conversations. The most relevant contributions from the field of mission studies for the purpose of this book have come from the South African missiologist Robert Bosch, from Robert Schreiter's understanding of inculturation coming out of the Roman Catholic context, and the engaging work of Andrew Walls and Brian Stanley.[8]

Much of the terrain of mission studies has been occupied by David Bosch's *Transforming Mission*. Innovative, expansive and advocating a "'pluriverse' of missiology,"[9] Bosch envisions a mission challenged by multiple factors and needing to respond in a manner that moves beyond narrow, single-issue, ad hoc responses to compound problems. He describes a setting in which Christianities strive for liberation from "what is perceived as the stranglehold of the West," struggle with "racism and sexism," and ask questions about the relation of culture and gospel, technology, development, and the relationship to other religious worlds.[10] Yet, his text addresses none of these in particular, other than in passing. Rather, he presents a dense historical account of the development of missionary paradigms throughout the phases of the Western church in erudite and instructive, if numbing detail. While it provides a helpful history up to the time of its publication, it gives only some very basic, shared contours for mission as a quest for justice, evangelism, contextualization, liberation, inculturation, common witness by all to all, as the call of all of God's people, and as action in hope.[11]

---

[6] See, for example, Joerg Rieger, "Theology and Mission Between Neocolonialism and Postcolonialism," *Mission Studies 21.2* (2004), Kwok Pui-Lan, *Postcolonial Imagination & Feminist Theology* (Louisville, KY: WJK, 2005), Catherine Keller, Michael Nausner, and Mayra Rivera, eds, *Postcolonial Theologies: Divinity and Empire* (St. Louis, MI: Chalice, 2004) and Letty M. Russell, *Church in the Round: Feminist Interpretation of the Church* (Louisville, KY: WJK, 1993).

[7] David J. Bosch, *Transforming Mission: Paradigm Shifts in Theology of Mission* (New York: Orbis, 1991), 489–93.

[8] See Bosch, *Transforming Mission*, Robert J. Schreiter, *Constructing Local Theologies* (Marknoll, NY: Orbis, 1985), and Andrew F. Walls, "Eusebius Tries Again: The Task of Reconceiving and Re-Visioning the Study of Christian History," in *Enlarging the Story: Perspectives on Writing World Christian History*, Wilbert R. Shenk, ed. (Maryknoll, NY: Orbis, 2002), 1–21, Andrew F. Walls, *The Cross-Cultural Process in Christian History: Studies in the Transmission of Faith* (Maryknoll, NY: Orbis, 2002), Andrew F. Walls, *The Missionary Movement in Christian History: Studies in the Transmission of Faith* (Maryknoll, NY: Orbis, 1996).

[9] Bosch, *Transforming Mission*, 7.

[10] Ibid., 188–9.

[11] See chapter 12 in Bosch, *Transforming Mission*.

His account, however, proceeds in a familiar missiological frame, exclusively focusing on the missionaries, the societies and theological movements they were embedded in. The book itself then can hardly be said to participate substantially in a constructive endeavor of shaping a theology of mission that moves beyond the focus on missionaries, and does not yet offer a full reevaluation of missionary theology beyond the above broad list of features. It is also far from clear that he has addressed the heritage of colonial missions and the inherent thought patterns substantially:

> For Bosch['s *Transforming Mission*], the problems of modernity appear to be fading away as we move into postmodernity (Bosch 1991: 349–362). By the same token, colonialism (which in Bosch's narrative is merely a sub-section of his overarching concern with modernity and the Enlightenment) seems to have faded away as well. Mission is thus seen as having found new freedom (and new innocence). Without having to worry about colonialism and the associated (mis)use of power and authority any more, mission and missionary enterprises now seem to be free to reinvent themselves.[12]

Other voices in missiology from Africa have continued the conversation. Lamin Sanneh and Kwame Bediako have expanded the positionality of missiological discourse by raising questions about the cultural ownership of the gospel and post-missionary Christianity in Africa.[13] In a more historical vein, Brian Stanley and Kevin Ward have done important work, tracking the history of Anglican missions under British colonial conditions.[14] Jonathan Draper's and Jeff Guy's work on Bishop John William Colenso and Harriette Colenso has been groundbreaking in helping elucidate the particular lives and relations of the paradigmatic "Colenso Affair."[15]

---

[12] Rieger, "Theology and Mission," 207.

[13] See for example, Lamin Sanneh, *Translating the Message: The Missionary Impact on Culture* (Maryknoll, NY: Orbis, 1989) and Kwame Bediako, *Christianity in Africa: The Renewal of a Non-Western Religion* (Maryknoll, NY: Orbis/Edinburgh University Press, 1995).

[14] See for example, Brian Stanley, *The Bible and the Flag: Protestant Missions and British Imperialism in the Nineteenth and Twentieth Centuries* (Leicester, England: Apollos, 1990) and Brian Stanley and Kevin Ward, eds, *The Church Mission Society and World Christianity, 1799–1999* (Grand Rapids, MI: W. B. Eerdmanns, 2000).

[15] Jonathan A. Draper, "Bishop John William Colenso's Interpretation To The Zulu People Of The *Sola Fide* In Paul's Letter To The Romans," in *SBL 2000 Seminar Papers* (Atlanta: SBL, 2000), 465–93, Jonathan A. Draper, "The Bishop and the Bricoleur: Bishop John William Colenso's Commentary on Romans" and Magema Kamagwaza Fuze's "The Black People and Whence They Came From," ed. Gerald West and Musa Dube (Leiden: Brill, 2001), 415–54, Jonathan A. Draper, "Introduction," in *Commentary on Romans by John William Colenso*, ed. Jonathan A. Draper (Pietermaritzburg: Cluster Publications, 2003), ix–xxxix and Jeff Guy, *The Heretic: A Study of the Life of John William Colenso, 1814–1883* (Pietermaritzburg: University of Natal Press, 1983), Jeff Guy, *The View Across the River: Harriette Colenso and the Zulu Struggle Against Imperialism* (Charlottesville, VA: University of Virginia Press, 2001).

Few missiological accounts pay much attention to the resident culture, and even fewer anthropological accounts include religious histories and concerns on either side of the encounter in any significant depth. Webb Keane's *Christian Moderns: Freedom & Fetish in the Mission Encounter* attempts to more fully overcome some anthropologists' reluctance to substantially engage the interactions between Christian and indigenous history and doctrine. His account assumes that "where postcolonial societies have made Christianity their own, we miss something crucial if we see in their claims only the effects of colonialism," that missionary encounters highlight critical themes of precolonial domestic histories of Christianity, and that one must consider the "particular historical conditions under which the mission operated."[16] Hence, the mission encounter "replays themes of encounter and reflexivity that run through the long history of religious form within the West" well before the colonial and postcolonial eras.[17] At times, the clash "is less one between peoples, or even cultures, than it is between semiotic ideologies," that is, the understanding of how language relates to the experience of reality.[18] Missionary encounters involve a representational economy, where shifts in practices and associated ideologies in one domain, such as biblical interpretation, doctrine, or political affiliations, manifest as shifts in the interpretation and practice of relations, sociopolitical and theological. Hence, missionary encounters are composed of a complex, shifting network of negotiations of the history of bodies and their physical and mental positioning in a variety of places and times. The shape and methods of missiology are rapidly changing. Disciplines such as sociology, anthropology, cultural studies, indigenous epistemologies, postcolonial theories, and pedagogy have been making entryways. Many historians of mission are going about their studies with increased awareness that missionaries relied on the collaboration of "indigenous evangelists, catechists, Bible women, and lay workers,"[19] while mission studies have generally focused on missions and missionaries, leaving today's researcher with a dearth of sources to ameliorate this distorting effect. Ostensibly, this dilemma is similar to that of attempting to rewrite the history of women, of illiterate or poor populations, and slaves within the church: impossible, but necessary for giving a fuller account of all involved.

Circumambulating missionary encounters is much enhanced by anthropological accounts that show a skilled interest in matters of religious culture, such as the work of South African anthropologists John and Jean Comaroff, the American anthropologist Webb Keane and his work in Indonesia, historical

---

[16] Webb Keane, *Christian Moderns: Freedom & Fetish in the Mission Encounter* (Berkeley, CA: University of California Press, 2007), 8.

[17] Ibid., 13.

[18] Ibid., 13.

[19] Shenk, "Introduction," xiv.

and anthropological studies of Maori culture by New Zealand historians Anne Salmond, Brownwyn Elsmore, and Judith Binney, together with vital insights by Maori authors such as Anglican priest Maori Marsden and emerging Zulu and Maori scholars that are only beginning to be more widely known and accessible.

Literary fiction, autobiographies, and novels written by authors responding to missionary and colonial presences are other sources. While, they, too are limited in scope, representing primarily emerging elites, they offer narratives that move beyond academic genres and concerns. Texts such as Witi Ihimaera's *Whale Rider*, and Tsitsi Dangarembga's *Nervous Conditions* thematize theological and religious issues, yet are outside the academic or missionary disciplinary discourses. Despite the known problems of colonial anthropological and missionary accounts, a cautious use of their source material in concert with, when available, material from within local traditions can enhance the pool of resources.

Given the author's limited access, and the continued difficulties for certain subalterns to speak, or be heard, these seem the best resources at hand and available. Much of the oral knowledge that would pertain is often, understandably, closely guarded and can be intentionally obscured, as well as logistically difficult to access to an outsider who is suspect for good reason. Nevertheless, there are times when being an insider to the culture helps, and times when it hinders. There are instances where an outsider can access more information, due to status and connections, than a person from within the culture and vice versa. Within constructive theology, there are a variety of authors who have written on related issues, if not directly on missiology: Marcella Althaus-Reid's indecent theologies, Joerg Rieger's work on liberation theology and missiology, Catherine Keller's work on the theopolitics of empire, Laurel Schneider's work on gender and monotheism, Kwok Pui-Lan's work on postcolonial theory and feminist theology, Mayra Rivera's postcolonial theology of the divine touch of transcendence, and a growing array of polydox theological approaches to think through the multiplicity of faithful commitments within and outside a faith tradition.

Given the limitations of the study of mission, often focused primarily on historical matters and materials that give little in-depth insight into theological approaches and convictions, it becomes important for a constructive theological approach to engage material that allows for deeper engagement with theological questions, culture, and the transmission of religious systems. An interidisciplinary approach offers at least the possibility to move beyond single focus studies. The available archive, at least in much of the past, offers very few significant first-hand accounts of local responses to missionary presence and messages, unless filtered through missionary eyes and often formulated to impress on audiences at home the importance of fund-raising and support for the missionary project. Many of the theological and biblical references involve a discourse that aims to be persuasive to multiple audiences, at the very least supporting communities and authorities in the sending community. Again, we find theological discourse embedded solidly in the everyday concerns of missionaries and church communities.

Sometimes, it is possible to deduce the implied priorities of the missionaries by looking at stated concerns, while at other times, such efforts remain speculative. While single focus studies offer the methodological advantage of seemingly clear parameters, goals, and results, the present study assumes that in order to gain a more well-rounded assessment of what transpires in intercultural theological and missiological encounters, it is not only possible but necessary to include several sets of data. This hopes to help avoid a flat, generalizing account of Christian mission by including economic, social, cultural, and political factors involved where possible and available, rather than assume a theology of mission can be told primarily through institutional histories of mission agencies and missionary correspondence. Upon more closely examining a missionary encounter, I suspect that it is exactly those seemingly extraneous sociocultural and political economic factors that help shape theological and institutional responses, that, in short, shape how the gospel is interpreted and formulated for new audiences and new instances of intercultural encounter. The hope is to choose from the available archive, where information accessible in print is limited in its quality and quantity, many oral accounts have been lost, forgotten, or are not easily accessible.

Nothing approaching a "complete" or even "generalizable" account of missionary encounters can be claimed to be given here. Instead, I propose a form pattern recognition that has a number of similarities to the work of any historian, ethnographer, or anthropologist: The available data is fragmented, displaying perhaps more readily gaps rather than offering solid evidence, and often engaged in a narrative ideology that seeks to provide explanatory and potentially legitimizing force.[20] Neither one of these discourses can provide a "full picture" of anything, and it is best to state that at the outset. The proposed set of itineraries rather offers a series of excursions, pilgrimages, and detours, off the beaten track of several disciplines. Because theology, and in particular its constructive varieties, constitute my home discipline, I will engage the material in its relevance for theological questions; that means questions about the formation, transmission, and adaptation of ideas about God, the sacred, humanity, and society from the vantage point of a sacred universe. I offer the image of circumambulating the fragmented traces of cultures,

---

[20] Andrew Walls argues that in fact there are so many parallels between the early centuries of the formation of Christianity and the growth of Christianity that "we now have better resources for understanding the patchwork of fragments of Christian literature that survived from before the age of the great councils by examining the recent histories of the churches of Africa and Asia than the Bodleian or the Vatican libraries can yield." Walls, "Eusebius Tries Again," 4.

textually, archaeologically, orally, with a sense that aims to be both critically alert and respectful, in a way that can incarnate the relationship described by Joerg Rieger:

> Thinking about mission in terms of building relationships might also prevent us from overreacting against the mission-as-outreach model and falling into the opposite extreme: too often those disappointed by outreach have claimed that instead of trying to help people we should simply get off their backs. Mission as relationship recognizes that we are all connected and must, therefore, not leave people to themselves.[21]

This counteracts the liberal orthodoxy, found among some, that Christians from Western colonizing nations should simply "leave alone" Christians in formerly colonized contexts. But, as they say, "the train has left the station". It is simply not possible, at best, grandiose and at worst—as Christians from colonized nations have pointed out—can represent yet another form of abandonment.

A Polydox Methodology for a Theology of Missionary Encounter

Instead, a study of global connections shows the grip of encounter: friction. A wheel turns because of its encounter with the surface of the road; spinning in the air it goes nowhere. Rubbing two sticks together produces heat and light; one stick alone is just a stick. As a metaphorical image, friction reminds us that heterogeneous and unequal encounters can lead to new arrangements of culture and power.[22]

Accounting for such encounters proves to be as potentially explosive as the terrain of intercultural relations, whether these cultures are among humans or involve human attempts to communicate with or about divinity. Anna Lowenhaupt Tsing describes friction as the "grip of worldly encounter," where cultural diversity "brings a creative friction to global connections" and produces a variety of discourses about the messy zones of interaction between cultures, ecosystems, and peoples.[23] These zones of cultural friction are "transient; they arise out of encounters and interactions," and reappear "in new

---

[21] Rieger, "Theology and Mission," 215.
[22] Anna Lowenhaupt Tsing, *Friction: An Ethnography of Global Connection* (Princeton, NJ: Princeton University Press, 2005), 5.
[23] Ibid., ix–x.

places with changing events."[24] With Tsing, I contend that the "messy and surprising features of such encounters across differences should inform our models of cultural production."[25] This friction is one marker of polydoxy. Layers of meaning intersect, polysemy invades: multiple meaning and many forms of *doxa*, of opinion manifest, of the adoration of "shining beauty" in doxology.[26] The polysemic concept of polydoxy can denote several instances of multiplicity: the simple fact that Christian theology, including its expressions of orthodoxy, has always been multiple. The divine enfolds manifold within itself,[27] the internal paradox of theological language expresses the coincidence of opposites, often having to resort to apophasis, to "critical unknowingness."[28] It may even "release a sense of (interreligious) peace if the doxology of orthodoxy is inherently transformed into a para-doxology of polydoxy," indicates the "divine multiplicity in interreligious entanglement" while it "affirms the unique intuitions of religions as enveloped in a process of the renewal of unprecedented novelty that always is beyond any fixed identities of singular religions and their orthodoxies."[29]

Polydoxy might also make room for the multiple religious belongings that are real in so many people's lives.[30] Therefore polydoxy favors the paradox that resists simple *doxa* (opinion),[31] and glories in the many forms of shining beauty one may discern in the kaleidoscopes of manifoldness. In the gap between supersessionist and pluralist understandings of other religions the category of a "resolute" theology of religions will be important. Moving beyond the polarizations of "the absolute" and "the dissolute," Catherine Keller proposes a resolute positionality that embodies the "practice of discernment, which means to distinguish, to attend to difference, and to exercise good judgment."[32]

I would like to employ this sense of the polydox to the analysis of encounters in mission, and thus expand its meaning to the interactions between multiple socioreligious systems; in the words of Michell Serres, the multiple does not represent "an epistemological monster," but is rather "the ordinary lot of situations."[33] Polydox dynamics are particularly evident in zones of vibrant

---

24 Tsing, *Friction*, xi.
25 Ibid., 3.
26 Roland Faber, "The Sense of Peace: A Paradoxology of Divine Multiplicity," in *Polydoxy: Theology of Multiplicity and Relation*, eds, Catherine Keller and Laurel Schneider (London/New York: Routledge, 2010), 36.
27 Keller and Schneider, "Introduction" in *Polydoxy*, 1.
28 Ibid., "Introduction," 3.
29 Faber, "The Sense of Peace: A Paradoxology of Divine Multiplicity," 49.
30 See, for example, Catherine Cornille, *Many Mansions: Multiple Religious Belonging and Christian Identity* (Maryknoll, NY: Orbis, 2002).
31 Faber, "The Sense of Peace: A Paradoxology of Divine Multiplicity," 45.
32 Catherine Keller, *On the Mystery: Discerning God in Process* (Minneapolis, MN: Fortress, 2008), 2–3.
33 As quoted in Keller and Schneider, "Introduction," 3.

interaction. The friction of "systematic misunderstandings"[34] that mark inter-cultural relationships are a major part of the reality of missionary environments and encounters, that is, encounters where movable concepts and agents interact to articulate, embody, and contest varieties of *doxa*, of opinion, custom, and engaged perspective. Reading polydox encounters as contexts that involve friction, and learning from them, is crucial for a constructive theology that aims to come to terms with the ambivalent heritage of missionary Christianity and seeks a way forward through a complex, circumspect, and resolute progressive missiology. The polydox logic of relational multiplicity that resists predictability, totality, and the idolatry of definitions, complicates rather than simply rejects modes of orthodoxy, trades certainty for trust and anathema for caritas.[35] It occurs wherever "a few us are gathered–in whatever space, medium, or web–seeking understanding,"[36] without presuming answers.

The methodology of such polydox engagement moves beyond the "apart-heid of theory" that defined previous decades of theological engagement, and engages in the fruits of an emerging "coalitional consciousness" under-girded by a "love hermeneutics"[37] that, in these pages, will be resourced through Christian traditions.[38] Thus, a "polydox theology presupposes libera-tion theology's challenge to the privilege of normative statements and, more importantly, it affirms the theological orientation that such debates imply."[39] Methodologically polydox, this study proceeds in ways that hope to model the mission engagement they propose: by engaging interdisciplinary, interreli-gious, intersubjective, intercultural places, words, and practices.

Theologically mobile, like the circuit-riding, nomadic missionary prac-tices, Roland Allen, missionary to China, proposed to replace the unhelpfully static missionary stations that forced nomadic and semi-nomadic peoples to settle down and thus limit their options for survival by subsistence and limit-ing their relationship to the land. This proposal hopes to follow his impulse to remobilize missionary theologies, circumambulating the places of sacred

---

34 Tsing, *Friction*, x.
35 Keller and Schneider, "Introduction," 2, 3, 8, and 13.
36 Ibid., 13.
37 Already Augustine's *On Christian Doctrine* qualifies love as liberative, not oppressive. Chela Sandoval, *Methodology of the Oppressed* (Minneapolis, MN: University of Minneapolis Press, 2000), 71, 10–11.
38 Sugirtharajah argues that universalizing discourses from particular locations having claimed "the mantle to speak for all, have lost their nerve" while "postmodern celebrations of the local and different" can further serve to marginalize theologies from contexts less visible in places of power. It is therefore necessary to make vital, theologically and ethi-cally relevant connections between locations near and far. R. S. Sugirtharajah, *Postcolonial Refigurations: An Alternative Way of Reading the Bible and Doing Theology* (London: SCM Press, 2003), 94.
39 Mayra Rivera, "Glory: The First Passion of Theology?" in *Polydoxy: Theology of Multiplicity and Relation*, eds, Catherine Keller and Laurel Schneider (London/New York: Routledge, 2010), 170.

encounter.[40] There are times when a thinker's method of approaching some-thing changes with the task and circumstance, adapting to contexts and pushed onto us by reality when a combination of several methods necessary to most fully apprehend or comprehend the text, situation, subject, or nexus at hand. Such a combination and interlacing of particular methods can come together to form a methodology, that is an "overall structure and systematic interrelated functioning of a collection of particular methods."[41] The mul-tiplicity of embodied but tentative entanglements in the missionary context can be described as polydox friction positioned, similar to postcolonial dis-course, "between the traps of the universal and the culturally specific."[42] It includes a sense of the apophatic and contingent human, earthly, and divine relations.

If paradox appears to upset, contest, or contradict formed opinions, then polydoxy contains a measure of the paradoxical, by virtue of holding multiple contingencies in tension. It resists claims to strict orthodoxy, if by that we mean the lifting up of one particular opinion as true, but it is engaged in ortho-doxy as a discourse interested in reliable, resolute, and responsible claims to validity and in dynamic tension with orthopraxy. Paradox polydoxy is tuned to the clash of perceptions, lack of cohesion, the recognition of disorienting difference, and the coincidence of (seeming) opposites.[43] Paradox has some of the qualities of the *Unheimlichen* (alien, uncanny, literally un-homelike); it disrupts assumptions about home, perceived securities, and perceptions of the familiar. This paradoxicality, disorienting difference, or friction, necessitates methodological means for perceiving, interpreting, and usefully negotiating fraught encounters. A theological appetite for the polydox may well manifest as "a love for the paradox," which Rebecca Solnit identifies as a needful char-acteristic for any activist.[44] It is also suggestive for theologians contemplating a progressive postcolonial theology of mission.

Missionaries and their interlocutors in native cultures engage in hermetic (sealing) and hermeneutic (unsealing) activities. We explore here a number of instances of polydox friction, using particular examples of missionary-na-tive interaction to help illuminate larger methodological questions that are important for the development of a postcolonial theology of mission. A viable constructive theology of mission must include a robust description of polydox,

---

[40] Bosch, *Transforming Mission*, 379.

[41] Sandra Schneiders offers this useful distinction. Sandra Marie Schneiders, *The Revelatory Text: Interpreting the New Testament as Sacred Scripture* (Collegeville, MN: Liturgical Press, 1999, rev. ed.), 111.

[42] Tsing, *Friction*, 1.

[43] For a discussion of Nicholas of Cusa's sense of the *coincidentia oppositorum*, see Catherine Keller, *Face of the Deep* (New York/London: Routledge, 2003), 206 et passim.

[44] Rebecca Solnit, *Hope in the Dark: Untold Histories, Wild Possibilities* (New York: Nation Books, 2004), 25.

paradoxical friction.[45] Missionaries have long functioned as scholars of religion and heresiologists. They also engage in varieties of comparative theology
and interreligious conversations. Missionaries and their native interlocutors
inhabit a stage of liminality between cultures. They create theological friction in their expressions of faith when communicating across multilayered differences. They negotiate religious, cultural, sociosexual, and socioeconomic
aspects of *doxa* simultaneously.

My employment of the concept of productive friction already signals that
anything resembling perfect coherence in such encounters is neither possible
nor, arguably, desirable. The pathways and crossroads of the "mission field"
are therefore good examples of polydox spaces, and postcolonial discourse
analysis and theories aid in identifying the many folds. Although widely recognized as one of the pioneering postcolonial theorists, few scholars have dealt
with Homi Bhabha's use of missionary sources and scenarios in his writing.
Oddly enough, Bhabha has exemplified a more productive engagement with
missionary texts than some postcolonial biblical scholars and more than most
postcolonial theologians. In a strange displacement, much "metropolitan"
Northern (mostly progressive) postcolonial theological discourses integrate
theories from colonized contexts, but neglect to engage missionary and missiological discourses. While this may follow a widespread tendency in the division between missionary evangelical and liberal mainline theological pursuits,
it is worth reconsidering this opposition, especially in a time when the place,
numbers, and purpose of liberal/mainline/progressive Christian communities are embattled and their sense of explicitly Christian sense of mission and
vision is often hard to locate.

Homi Bhabha's classic essay "Signs Taken For Wonders: Questions of
Ambivalence and Authority Under A Tree Outside Delhi, May 1817" engages
a missionary report of some theological depth, illustrating the concept of
ambivalence and creative friction of authority and identity in an interreligious encounter in colonial India.[46] In the report, Anund Messeh, one of the
first Indian catechists, encounters a group of potential converts in a grove of
trees just outside of Delhi. Bhabha's essay revolves around the fact that native
inquirers confronted with the gospel ask critical questions of a native cat-
echist, manifesting their own cultural assumptions and their sense of polydox
friction in the encounter with a European-inflected Christianity. The people
under the tree ask questions about the provenance of the book they have
read and love, question who can and ought to be the brokers of the Bible,
what terms of conversion they are willing to accept, and what not. They ask

---

[45] Due to spatial constraints, I cannot here discuss in depth African Independent Churches,
which, having moved beyond colonial structures and personnel represent even more
intense forms of polydoxy with very interesting forms of friction.

[46] Homi Bhabha, *The Location of Culture* (London/New York: Routledge, 1994), 102–22.

incisive questions, highlighting paradoxes in the gospel and sacraments as they had received them. At the same time, their questions highlight the clash of worldviews regarding sacrality and purity, challenging the assumptions at work both in their interpretations of the gospel and in their own expressions of culture.

Whereas Bhabha reports on the subarboreal discussion as one in which the European provenance of the Bible, which has been made accessible to residents in translation, is questioned because of a logical difficulty (How can the British, a people of carnivores, produce a book recognized as holy by vegetarian Indians?), Bishop Colenso's Zulu interlocutors question the apparent inconsistency between the British attempts to suppress Zulu polygamy and the fact that the biblical ancestors of faith are shown as righteous and explicitly polygamous men. Bhabha writes, the "institution of the Word in the wilds is also an *Entstellung*, a process of displacement, distortion, dislocation, repetition."[47] The theological friction of missionary encounter is deeply embedded in questions of power, gender, culture, and economics. It is this kind of multilayered friction that must be involved in every step of a postcolonial theology of mission: it must take into account the factors that compound a situation.[48]

Tsing describes friction as something that necessitates two or more surfaces. Tracing friction urges us beyond a static dyad of missionary as privileged narrator and native as informant towards a more complex view that challenges assumptions of hegemony and subalternity, Christian God and Zulu traditions, and competing economic and social systems. Historically, scholars have privileged the missionary voice, and it remains a struggle to encounter a speaking and writing native convert in particular during the times of early modern Christian missions. Many anthropologists and missionaries have preserved indigenous oral traditions while transposing them. Their textual productions are densely interwoven with their own *doxa*, their perspective, and interests. Perhaps, like some women's theologies, a recourse to midrash-like retroactive retellings, reimaginings and retracings will eventually make most sense. Indeed, in postcolonial literature, fiction, and scholarship other voices are increasingly being articulated, through novels, contextual biblical studies, community action, scholarship, and news

---

[47] Ibid., 105.

[48] As such, it could be compared to Tillich's method of correlation where human situations are correlated with Christian theological symbols or concepts. The polydox reality of our world then can be seen as resonating with Tillich's claim that "reality itself makes demands, and the method must follow, reality offers itself in different ways, and our cognitive intellect must receive it in different ways. An exclusive method applied to everything closes many ways of approach and impoverishes our vision of reality." Paul Tillich, "The Problem of Theological Method," in *Paul Tillich: Theologian of the Boundaries*, Mark Kline Taylor (Minneapolis, MN: Fortress, 1991), 128. Kwok Pui-Lan demonstrates a related multi-issue approach in her book on postcolonial theology, calling for the integration of the discourses of gender, race, class, and religion. Kwok, *Postcolonial Imagination*, 7.

media.[49] This expanded, yet fragmentary archive of narrativity shows us that the seemingly incommensurable differences between Zulus and English missionaries can be parabolic for postcolonial socioeconomic and theological reconciliation, "based on negotiating more or less recognized differences in the goals, objects, and strategies of the cause," and a refusal "to homogenize perspectives but rather to appreciate how we can use diversity as well as possible" today.[50]

Polydox hybrid friction illustrates the failure of attempts at distinguishing between "sacred" and "secular" events or realities. In fact, strict separation between these "spheres" disallows theological appreciation of the full scale of realities as entangled.[51] The interpenetration of religious and sociopolitical elements in colonized societies in particular complicates the modern myth that the religious and secular should be separate or at least be separable. This ideologically infused fantasy of separation of church and state turns out to be false not only in postcolonial contexts where religious concerns are manifesting themselves in ever more complex ways within these transforming societies, but also in the return of a repressed (Christian) religious consciousness in Europe in the aftermath of wars of religion and certain rationalist and idealist ideologies in that region of the globe. The openness to a polymorphous methodology and discourses welcomed by polydoxy can help reclaim these multiple, inseparable levels of meaning in life, now organized into separate, false dualisms such as religious and secular, transcendent and immanent, difference and sameness.

Polydoxy is in tension with the modern concept of monotheism, which employs a "logic of the One" that is not false, but rather incomplete. Hence, as Laurel Schneider proposes, a theology of multiplicity seeks company. Multiplicity resists reduction to the one and reduction to the many. It takes incarnation seriously, paying attention to the mutability of bodies.[52] The designation of monotheistic versus polytheistic religious systems increasingly emerges as a reductionist distinction that does not capture the real complexities of each.[53] Schneider argues that the concept of monotheism arose for specific contextual purposes, to secure the dominance of one God in a world of difference, especially in a colonial world of difference, where missionaries

---

[49] I am aware that the resources named here are written only, given the difficulty of accessing more than anecdotal evidence, and can only point to the use of written anthropology as an amelioration of this absence. Some of the novels to give voice to a post-missionary Africa: Tsitsi Dangarembga, *Nervous Conditions* (Oxfordshire: Ayebia, 1988); Ngugi Wa Thiong'o, *Wizard of the Crow* (New York: Anchor Books, 2006); and, more famously, Chinua Achebe, *Things Fall Apart* (London: William Heinemann, Ltd, 1958).

[50] Tsing, *Friction*, x.

[51] Charles Taylor, "The Future of the Religious Past," in *Religion: Beyond A Concept*, ed. Hent De Vries (New York: Fordham University Press, 2008), 180–1.

[52] Laurel C. Schneider, *Beyond Monotheism: A Theology of Multiplicity* (London: Routledge, 2008), 1, 3, 4, 5.

[53] Ibid., 19–20.

must negotiate multiple, competing cultures and gods.[54] A polydox theology
of mission does not offer answers as much as guiding questions, searching
for God in the gaps between the expected, where we might so easily miss the
divine.

Contested Knowledge and Wisdom

*There is a damaging and self-defeating assumption that theory is necessarily the elite
language of the socially and culturally privileged. It is said that the place of the academic critic is inevitably within the Eurocentric archives of an imperialist or neocolonial West. The Olympian realms of what is mistakenly labeled "pure theory" are
assumed to be eternally insulated from the historical exigencies and tragedies of the
wretched of the earth. [. . .] Between what is represented as the "larceny" and distortion of European "metatheorizing" and the radical, engaged, activist experience
of Third World creativity, one can see the mirror image (albeit reversed in content
and intention) of that ahistorical nineteenth-century polarity of Orient and Occident
which, in the name of progress, unleashed the exclusionary imperialist ideologies of
self and other.[55]*

In *Decolonizing Methodologies*, Linda Tuhiwai Smith argues that the other side
of the narrative of colonial research is a story of a great many horrors perpe-
trated on indigenous peoples by colonial science imbued with motives for the
justification of superiority over and exploitation of colonized societies. Despite
these dynamics of epistemological abuse within a discourse of science that
often claimed to be value free, Smith argues that indigenous people can and
should use "Western"-style research methods for the furthering of survival and
thriving of their communities. At the same time, there are many reasons to
distrust researchers from outside, who often appear not unlike a stealing trickster, absconding with other peoples' knowledge and technology, in the pursuit
of fame or personal and corporate gain. Even in postcolonial discourses, she
remarks, there is an ongoing danger for "reinscribing or reauthorizing the
privileges of non-indigenous academics" as even the field of postcolonial discourse can continue to "leave out indigenous peoples, our ways of knowing
and our current concerns."[56]

---

[54] Ibid., 26.

[55] Bhabha, *Location of Culture*, 19.

[56] Reading this could not but concern me, and I quickly abandoned an initial plan to
coauthor anything I might want to write on the intersection of Northern theology with
indigenous theo-cultures, though it seemed convincing to me that such cooperation
was necessary in order to disrupt the gaze of the colonizer and transform it by way of a
more mutual encounter. The systemic disparity of power between a German citizen and
tenured professor in North America and an emerging indigenous scholar with far less

Surely this present essay must negotiate the same danger, and cannot avoid certain degrees of reinscription, unknowingly, or unwillingly. The global hunt for new knowledge to be commercialized brings new threats to indigenous communities, and the classifications of colonial science have established structures used to disinherit the people of the land and establish exploitative class and race hierarchies.[57] The construction of colonial knowledge has often employed hierarchical dualisms of cultured Self and savage Other. Such identity formation, based on reaction formation, has led to mutually distorted constructions of Self and Other, and solidified perceived differences.[58] Likewise, indigenous peoples have often been grossly misrepresented to Self and Other.[59] This project participates in dismantling such reaction formation towards more salutary relational patterns, built not on a denial of tragic history, its present reverberations, or on the perpetual recycling of victim-oppressor dynamics with changing actors. This lack of access to knowing should, however, not preclude the search for wisdom and understanding. Rather, as Gregory of Nyssa's Moses following the ever-receding divine up the mountain, that search must be done with a mixture of humility and persistence, resisting the arrogance of proclaiming a seemingly disinterested truth about the Other or the avoidance of dealing with the unrepresentable Other entirely, a form of misrepresentation by elision. These difficulties share their impossibilities of access with the discourse of theology, which, at its best, negotiates in the creative tension between self-assured assertion about the divine and complete, dangerously quietist, silence in relation to God.[60]

Most reading and interpreting practices involve a version of "intercultural mimesis,"[61] involving the mutual, if differential, interactions and knowledge exchange between cultures, colonized and colonizing forces.[62] The dynamics

---

visibility was another concern, and seemed to render impossible such cooperation in the near future. Various external and internal communal barriers exist also for indigenous scholars. Linda Tuhiwai Smith, *Decolonizing Methodologies: Research and Indigenous Peoples* (London: Zed Books, 1999), 24.

[57] Ibid., 25.

[58] Ibid., 26.

[59] Ibid., 51.

[60] For a development of this notion of negative theology, see for example, Keller, *Face of the Deep*, 200ff.

[61] King borrows Charles Hallisey's term "denoting the cultural interchange that occurs between the native and the Orientalist in the construction of Western knowledge about 'the Orient.'" Richard King, *Orientalism and Religion: Postcolonial Theory, India, and "The Mystic East"* (New York: Routledge, 1999), 148ff

[62] The study of such intercultural mimesis helps deflect monocausal and short-sighted interpretations of actions or patterns, and can have major effects on the perception of, analysis of, and reaction to certain phenomena. Consider, for example, what it might mean that the Spanish *reconquista* was in part also an imitation of Islamic jihad, as Robert C. Young suggests. See Robert Young, *Postcolonialism: An Historical Introduction* (Oxford: Blackwell, 2001), 16.

of such interactions are often multilayered, and while major power differences shape these interactions, their effects are multifarious and often resemble dynamics observed in chaos theory more than deterministic directionalities.

᠌Some commonly articulated Maori epistemologies speak about an epistemological framework of three baskets of knowledge: *Tua-uri* (knowledge of the structure and processes of the cosmos and life energy), *Aro-nui* (the things before our senses), and *Te Ao Tua-atea* (the world beyond space and time, infinite and eternal).[63] This knowledge is traditionally fostered in the *whare wananga* (house of learning). Today, many learning institutions, such as universities are tagged in the bi-cultural mode of Aotearoa/New Zealand as *whare wananga*, thus signaling a certain kind of continuity as well as adaptation of Maori and European learning styles. Tuhiwai Smith stresses her intent on preserving knowledge of the ancients for the purposes of survival and flourishing, and insists that the primary goal is knowledge with communal purpose.[64]

Each of these epistemological frameworks and educational modes features a number of disciplinary elements. Contrary to some romantic perceptions, indigenous knowledge and learning frameworks and institutions engage in hazing, limit access, and create distinctions among members of the community, just as in "Western" educational frameworks. Lost knowledge vanished not only due to colonial influence, but, as some report, also due to the unwillingness of elders to pass on their knowledge. While elders were "storehouses for the knowledge" and "guardians of the tikanga for their people," many did not disseminate their knowledge, "human nature what it is, they were jealous of their positions," and did not fulfill their duty of passing this knowledge on, and so future generations were deprived of their heritage.[65]

Some young Maori scholars can be hamstrung by research that must benefit their immediate community in perhaps somewhat narrow ways: by establishing proof that lands and rights were taken against the conditions of the Treaty of Waitangi, by discussing land use rights and the difficulties of reestablishing Maori language teaching in primary schools. While much of this is certainly necessary and crucial for the restoration of land use and means of survival and profit to Maori *hapu* and tribes, the Waitangi tribunal has also spawned its own cottage industry of research as evidence for real and can seem as bizarre and arcane as the U.S. legal system with its self-propelling tendencies, ironies, and inconsistencies. As elsewhere, adaptation to capitalistic economic structures

---

[63] Te Ahukaramū Charles Royal, ed., *The Woven Universe: Selected Writings of Rev. Māori Marsden* (Masterson, NZ: The Estate of Maori Marsden, 2003), 60–2.

[64] Likewise, Maori Marsden states that "the route to Maoritanga through abstract interpretation is a dead end. The way can only lie through a passionate, subjective approach." Ibid., 2.

[65] Te Ahukaramū Charles Royal, "Editor's Introduction," in *The Woven Universe*, xxxvii.

carries the danger of the ravaging of tribal lands and profitmaking at any cost. When knowledge is structured to benefit only one's own community, and the community becomes open to capitalistic profit-driven economics, then it is hard to see how subversive or transformative such practice is. It may benefit the particular community, but without attending to the needs of a larger whole that is also global.

Smith sees the work of history as a crucial technique for understanding the present and a significant contribution to the process of decolonization.[66] For her, decolonization does not imply a complete rejection of all theory or research or Western knowledge, but rather sets out criteria that structure and inform the process of indigenous research. Smith insists on using the master's tools in combination and bricolage with indigenous tools, while setting out guidelines for how knowledge should be applied. Likewise, she proposes that the cultural archive of colonial science should not be rejected as a unitary system of knowledge but rather should be conceived as containing multiple traditions. Thus, Smith suggests engagement with the ambivalent, mixed heritage of educational systems, where modes of thinking, writing, and evaluation are continually contested.[67] Survival, adaptation, and flourishing can occur by taking charge of research and using methods that shift power and knowledge. Smith proposes a four-directional indigenous research agenda that is emphatically aiming towards self-determination, of the pursuit of knowledge of self as a form of survival, rather than claiming to be "disinterested."[68] She uses the metaphor of rising and falling ocean tides as a metaphor for the method and shape of the research. As the ocean is giver of life, always in process, and changing, so the research represents a nonsequential process, with all four directions representing a nonteleological process where all pieces inhabit the same degree of priority.

Thus healing, decolonization, transformation, and mobilization (each in one of the four directions) are not stages, but can and should occur at the same time, and are "not goals or ends in themselves," but processes that "connect, inform, and clarify the tensions between the local, the regional, and the global."[69] The research projects fostered by such an approach, and particularly resonant with the present project, include the celebration of survival rather than documenting demise,[70] remembering, intervening, and changing institutions,[71] making connections through reestablishing healthy nested identities within the land,[72] critically rereading Western history and

---

[66] Linda Tuhiwai Smith, *Decolonizing Methodologies*, 30, 34.
[67] Ibid., 39, 42, 64–5.
[68] Ibid., 117, 116.
[69] Ibid., 116.
[70] Ibid., 145–6.
[71] Ibid., 147.
[72] Ibid., 148.

indigenous presence,[73] gendering, and reframing.[74] Such pursuit of knowledge can, in Maori terms, be framed as the *atua* (deity) Tane's "research method" involving three baskets of knowledge, which contain highly specialized forms of knowledge, but where each aspect of knowledge is sought "on behalf of everyone else," and essential to the collective well-being, and hierarchical.[75]

That is, it was gained by select persons through "observation, practice, and the guidance of kaumatua" (elders), who did not tolerate sloppiness, laziness, or unfinished projects.[76] That such communal enforcement and discipline of research goals, methods, and practices can be beneficial for the community, by resisting exploitative and destructive scientific projects, is very likely, but the shadow side is that it can hamstring indigenous researchers and, ironically, give outside researchers more access than those accountable to their tribal and family communities in such a direct way.[77] While not intended for either the discourse of mission, theology, or perhaps for persons shaped by hegemonic life in colonial powers, Linda Tuhiwai Smith's *Decolonizing Methodologies: Research and Indigenous Peoples* is a *taonga*/treasure for many researchers, no matter where they hail from. As she points out, the pursuit of knowledge involved in what many know as "research," has a troubling entanglement with colonial patterns. Thus, for example, she states, adapting the work of a number of postcolonial theorists, that "the critique of Western history argues that history is a modernist project which has developed alongside imperial beliefs about the Other."[78]

That is, history (and, *mutatis mutandis*, church history) is far from a neutral enterprise. If, indeed, "the principal function of history within a theological curriculum is to keep the theologians honest,"[79] what does a postcolonial reconstructed history of Christianity mean for the articulation and the teaching of theologies? Andrew Walls states that "general" church history itself has the character of "European clan history,"[80] which becomes problematic in a colonial context where it has been promulgated as universally relevant, and is reflected in church history syllabi beyond where that clan history is central to

---

[73] Ibid., 149.

[74] Ibid., 151, 153.

[75] Tane also allows for life in the known world by separating sky father Ranginui and earth mother Papatuanuku with his tree trunk legs.

[76] Ibid., 173.

[77] Thus Sinclair observes that she "as an American anthropologist" has had "far greater access to the accumulated written records of the movement than any member." Karen Sinclair, *Maori Times, Maori Places: Prophetic Histories* (Lanham: Rowman & Littlefield, 2003), 7.

[78] Linda Tuhiwai Smith, *Decolonizing Methodologies*, 30.

[79] Walls, "Eusebius Tries Again," 18.

[80] Ibid., 11. Hence, for Walls, one of the tasks of the historian of Christianity has to do with expanding the syllabus of church history. The same applies to syllabi in theology.

Christian experience. This is not to say that the history of the church should not be taught outside the lands that shaped many centuries of Christian theology and practice, and informed successive missionary movements, but these clan histories cannot be the only ones, as each new community brings its own *sensus communis* to bear on the incarnation of the words of the biblical texts— for better, and for worse.

> Churches struggled with the issue that has faced migrant or exilic communities throughout history, "how do you sing the Lord's song in a strange land." The tendency was to sing it in exactly the same way as you had in the places from which you came.[81]

The next question then, it seems to me, ought to be how can we reevaluate each of these tribal histories in relationship to each other, rather than simply excluding the one from the other. Rather than continuing to concede superior status to Western European-based histories, and hence to continue to treat them as universal in their power to destroy (rather than, as previously claimed, to save), it is necessary to provincialize Europe[82] rather than giving it the status of theological superpower, or to declare its contribution as outdated and bankrupt in the aftermath of a Christianity dominated by the global South.[83] This might mean to consciously "re-indigenize" theologies that have been given lofty status elsewhere. For indigenous peoples, Tuhiwai Smith suggests, the pursuit of knowledge is significantly different from the pursuit of colonial knowledge and, at its best, a strategy for survival, with the goal of self-determination. Departing from the claim of impartiality in many "Western" research projects, indigenous research states as its goal the survival and flourishing of indigenous peoples. This raises, however, the question of whether "Western" research strategies ever were impartial, or not simply partial to other goals. The famous adage regarding history, which is "written by the winners of history," clearly indicates an ideologically focused project promoting the centrality of dominant culture and status. Such "interest" certainly renders this point of distinction between indigenous and "Western" research questionable. If, as Donna Haraway and other feminist critics of science have suggested, all research is partial and interested,[84]

---

[81] Allan Davidson, "The Interaction of Missionary and Colonial Society in Nineteenth Century New Zealand," *Studies in World Christianity* Vol. 2, No. 2 (1996): 156.

[82] Dipesh Chakrabarty, *Provincializing Europe: Postcolonial Thought and Historical Difference* (Princeton, NJ: Princeton University Press, 2000).

[83] The narrative of the supersession of global Christianity over European-based forms of Christianity is itself not without ideological infusion. It often becomes harnessed in old disputes between evangelical and liberal theology, accusing Christian liberalism and secularization of being responsible for the decline of average Sunday attendance in weekly church services, as well as church membership in many regions in Europe.

[84] See, for example, Donna J. Haraway, *Modest_Witness@Second_Millennium. FemaleMan©_ Meets_OncoMouse*™ (New York/London: Routledge, 1997).

that is, cannot help being contextual, it makes sense to inquire into the kinds of commitments and communities of accountability that stand behind such partiality. It becomes further necessary to consider the values, technologies, and goals of each research project, as well as the attending tensions between being centered and thus partial to one's home tradition/s and a sense of accountability to global issues and community. The assertion of essentialist politics of identity hinders rather than helps in the need for advocacy and search for greater justice. Rather, some suggest replacing a "politics of authenticity" with a "politics of belonging and connection." Thus,

> indigeneity is not primarily an individual biological or cultural identity; it is a mode of belonging to places, communities and nations. It is also a type of connection between people who belong to these places, communities and nations in indigenous ways.[85]

One of the most pressing concerns in the decolonization of theological studies then has to do with expanding the canon to include varieties of Christian expressions, telling the story of Christian faith through a variety of methods and discourses, and integrating a wider sense of cooperative mission work, including resistant readings and critical interlocutions.

Mission and Mimicry

Christians, so Andrew Walls states, have "an adoptive past" and are therefore already profoundly intercultural, though we tend to forget this under the umbrella of the "universalizing factor."[86] Thus,

> the history of Israel is part of Church history, and all Christians of whatever nationality, are landed, by adoption with several millennia of someone else's history, with a whole set of ideas, concepts, and assumptions which do not necessarily square with the rest of their cultural inheritance; and the Church in every land, of whatever race and type of society, has this same adoptive past by which it needs to interpret the fundamentals of the faith.[87]

This past tells Christians who they are; "without our past, we are lost."[88] And yet, what the central terms of a theology are at a given time and place may

---

[85] Jeffrey Sissons, *First Peoples: Indigenous Cultures and Their Futures* (London: Reaktion, 2005), 58.
[86] Walls, *The Missionary Movement in Christian History*, 9.
[87] Ibid., 9.
[88] Ibid., 13.

differ widely. And that, exactly, may be one of the purposes of a history of Christianity, the understanding that at any given time, "things which we think are vital points of principle will seem as far away and negligible to African theologians as those theological prize fights among the Egyptian monks now seem to us."[89] Indeed, mimesis and its close cousin mimicry are deeply involved in human existence and inform exchange between colonizer and colonized, in intercultural mimesis.

Thus, Gananath Obeyesekere, attempts to decode how cannibal talk, that is, the discourse about cannibalism by colonial voices, is related to the actual human flesh-eating practices of Maori and other Polynesians. How much of the "we will eat you" incantations was hyperbolic Maori bluster, indeed a "weapon of the weak,"[90] and a ritualized performance of shock and awe against enemies, rather than a reliable indication of the actual practice of devouring the flesh of one's enemies, may never be resolved. The hermeneutics of interpreting the discourse of cannibalism is tricky, as Europeans of the time were greatly obsessed with the practice, real or imagined, and often linked it to human sacrifice, which was indeed something that was part of Polynesian cultures.[91] What did not exist was the habitual, quotidian consumption of human flesh, which at times was imagined in European artists' depictions of butcher shop-like scenarios, something that did not easily fit into the ritual worlds of the peoples involved in the practice, and would have been unsustainable for any human population. Obeyesekere contends there are times when indigenous people play with and feed the rapacious imagination of the inquiring visitor and greatly enjoy doing so, so that "the Maori are at great pains to prove that not only are they cannibals, but also they are truly horrible ones."[92] This appears especially when the visitors' hermeneutic ensures that they are being tricked by their tendency to literal-mindedness over against what seems to them exotic and mysterious: In the case of cannibal talk, it is possible that indeed "British discourse [. . .] literalizes Maori speech."[93]

Hermeneutics emerges as a crucial component to intercultural, and hence missionary, encounters. When European cultures are deeply enmeshed in a ritual practice that uses the terminology of human sacrifice, and, in fact of the consumption of human body parts and blood in the Eucharist; when they manifest deep-seated fears around this practice, articulated, among others, in accusations against Jews of blood libel and profanation of the host, there are complex underlying conceptualities that inform the interpretation of what European observers think they see. Intercultural mimesis thus informs hermeneutics.

---

[89] Ibid., 11.
[90] Gananath Obeyesekere, *Cannibal Talk: The Man-Eating Myth and Human Sacrifice in the South Seas* (Berkeley, CA: University of California Press, 2005), 52ff.
[91] Ibid., 58.
[92] Ibid., 53.
[93] Ibid., 107.

Relating these practices becomes a forcefield of possible misunderstandings, stereotyping, and narcissistic mirroring. Such hermeneutically unstable zones are profoundly dangerous but bear the possibility of seeing commonality, connection, and can enable mutual learning and creative adaptation. Yet, rendering such zones of interaction safe remains impossible. Rather, at the "edge of chaos"[94] of intercultural communication, at the cusp of the next form of structural exchange emerging, things are permanently poised to break loose again when least expected. It may remain impossible to unearth reliably the motivations, extent, and function of the actual practice of anthropophagy (the eating of human flesh), as distinguished from the performance of cannibal talk.[95] In the end, Obeyesekere admits that "however rigorously we formulate our thinking, interpretation remains a vulnerable exercise, not only because of the difficulty of verification, but also because some texts are simply impossible to interpret."[96] The sheer impossibility of adequate interpretation may resign some to apophatic silence. While that is often an important discipline, there comes a time when, despite the great impossibility of speaking, something needs to be articulated, but with circumambulatory gestures of respect.

> While the archaeologist is able to help date the arrival of the first settlers and describe their way of life, the nature of Maori religion before European contact is much more difficult to discern. Just as the European reconstruction of Maori discovery and migration has shaped people's perception of the prehistory of Aotearoa, so Eurocentric views of Maori religion and the influence of Christian and other theological categories have ordered for many the nature of precontact religion. In particular the debate over the place of Io as a "Supreme Being" in the Maori cosmology raises many questions about these influences.[97]

Access to precolonial practices and knowledges is virtually impossible. This is not so very different from the hermeneutic sealing of many religious texts whose meanings we simply cannot disentangle once and for all, but which remain powerfully resplendent in their polysemy. Such obscurity can also affect contemporary attempts to write indigenous history, as "Maori like other subaltern peoples might come to accept the colonial interpretation of their traditional past."[98] Obeyesekere mentions the curious fact that colonial visitors

---

[94] Keller, *Face of the Deep*, 198.
[95] These are the distinctions Obeyesekere uses, following Peter Hulme's work, while allowing that they overlap. Obeyesekere, *Cannibal Talk*, 14.
[96] Emphasis in original. Ibid., 267.
[97] Allan Davidson, *Christianity in Aotearoa: A History of Church and Society in New Zealand* (Wellington: Education for Ministry, 1991), 2–3.
[98] Similarly, European nations have internalized the values and views of Roman and Greek thinkers, lifted them up as ideals, and proceeded to strive to be considered cultivated nations according to their terms. Obeyesekere, *Cannibal Talk*, 75.

tended to assume that skulls and bones displayed in Hawai'ian and Tahitian shrines were the result of a cult of human sacrifice, while one could, using the same logic, assume that European Christians' obsession with saints' relics and the public display of monks' bones in some of Rome's churches were the result of such practices.[99] There are many more reasons to display ancestral or enemy bones, and far from all of them have to do with a logic of sacrifice. Likewise, much ink has been spilled on the question of whether the drastic warfare measures described in some of the Pentateuch and Joshua books were to be read as literal historical descriptions, or can be decoded as mystification of an imagined past.

Cooperative Interpretations: Bible Translations and Local Intellectuals

Yet within imperial space allergy may also turn into attraction; alien traditions may collude and mingle, birthing all manner of strange religio-cultural hybrid.[100]

Accounts of missionary activity have traditionally focused on the missionaries, while the "natives" form the backdrop for a story that is perhaps innocently, but certainly focused on a colonial audience that either needs to be convinced missionary work is successful or worth being funded. Much missionary writing is directed toward audiences that were supporting or evaluating missionary work from afar, and therefore much of it is apologetic, if not propagandistic and intent on showing a certain side of it, presenting graspable results and identifying needs for further support. These particular needs produced genres of missionary writing (translation, letters, educational texts, lectures, books explaining or defending their work) that tended to de-emphasize, overlook, or obscure the agency, thought, and contributions of local contacts, unless they showed the efficiency of missionary work.

When reading those accounts, as with any historical writings, it is important to also understand the setting and context of the missionaries, their theology, and their state of mind as they write. As with the gospel writers, missionaries can stand between us and a desired, or at least imagined, *ipsissima vox* of Jesus, or the precolonial native. As in biblical studies, the search for the original, authentic voice may be not only without hope, but also built on an illusion of precontact purity. And as with biblical studies, this inability to access "pure"

---

[99] Ibid., 256.
[100] Catherine Keller, "The Love of Postcolonialism: Theology in the Interstices of Empire," in Postcolonial Theologies: Divinity and Empire, Catherine Keller, Michael Nausner, and Mayra Rivera, eds, (St. Louis, MI: Chalice, 2004), 222.

voices—if there is such a thing—does not forestall that important wisdom and important witnesses can be transmitted by other means. The colonial "experts" on indigenous cultures could not have been seen that way without the cooperation and often buried and unrecognized contribution of their native informants. This invisibility haunts any attempt to rewrite such accounts, though such problems of subalternity are not unknown to theologians as well. Those who contributed oral narratives and knowledge to the writings of biblical texts will often continue to remain obscure, despite the many techniques designed to peel away layers, interpret motifs, rhetorical forms, grammar, word history, and imagery. That is, as theologian, I already participate in a tradition of im/possible discursivity, that has its own silences, ghosts, and loudly clamoring dominant voices. A widened notion of divine multiplicity aims to perceive in greater detail the "fluidity, porosity, and interconnection"[101] of realms of existence and experience, paying attention to context while resisting the temptation of irrelevance of other contexts to one's own.

At the same time, much depended on the particular shape of the missionary enterprise. The development of a settler society, the scenario and the support and strategy of their sending agents can aid or impair missionary work. At the early stages of many missions, missionaries were at the whim of the waxing and waning of institutional support from the sending agency dependent on establishing protective and mutually beneficial connections with local ruling classes. They needed to learn the language, and at the same time secure means of survival, protection, economic sustainability, and human connection.

Over time, some missions recruited and educated indigenous translators for translating biblical texts, for example, into Zulu:

> Those who in missionary discourse are characteristically called "informants," in addition to being the actual missionaries in many cases, are also the ones responsible for our missionary-translators or translation consultants' acquaintance with native languages; it is only unfortunate that in its Western wrappings Christian historiography could not escape the tendency to credit individuals for what are in fact products of collective activity.[102]

John William Colenso seems to have implicitly acknowledged the translators' agency by not claiming the translation as his own, but rather as appearing as something perhaps closer to a compiler. It is also significant to note that these translations, or renderings, were occurring at the same time as many

---

[101] Thus Laurel Schneider proposes to conceptualize divine multiplicity. Schneider, *Beyond Monotheism*, 164.

[102] Maarman Sam Tshehla, "Colenso, John 1.1–18 and the Politics of Insider- and Outsider-Translating," in *The Eye of the Storm: Bishop John William Colenso and the Crisis of Biblical Interpretation*, ed. Jonathan A. Draper (London/NY: T&T Clark International, 2003), 30.

indigenous languages found a written form facilitated through the terms of colonial English.[103] Native translators participated in these projects, and research is underway to try to articulate the contributions of these translators and conversationists, who were indeed in many cases hermeneutic agents interpreting their own and the other culture to suggest equivalents and discourage the use of certain words or phrases.[104] Subalterns speak, argue, and translate, but remain hidden from the vision of theological discourse.

The Passions of Postcolonial Hybridity

In speaking of cultural hybridity, it is crucial to consider the location of those who seek to either promote or resist it, in particular, their location in terms of cultural power and status. It is a very different thing for a relatively large and dominant group to attempt to recommend an embrace of hybridity in order to deconstruct its sense of purity, universality, and power, and instead to emphasize commonality and bonding. This can occur after great injuries, such as colonialism, genocide, slavery, Holocaust, and similar situations of hegemony. But that same promotion of hybridity can have a very different ring for the minority group that fears being forced into a hybridity that equals loss of identity or assimilation. Contested identities who feel under threat of assimilation and eradication (perhaps by way of a voracious hybridity) are less able and willing to engage as peers—whatever that would mean—in a conversation that also critiques that minority identity while appreciating it. Thus it is helpful to distinguish different kinds of hybridity: the case can be made that minorities need a certain degree of hybridity for survival's sake; that converts live notoriously as hybrid entities; that there are chosen and non-chosen forms of hybridity in the case of intermarriage, colonial rape, and abuse. For those who resist hybridity, what does it mean to respect hybridity in others? What is the difference between hybridity, appropriation, and borrowing? There can be situational or strategic hybridity, during times when one wants to affirm it, and other times when it is important to reject it.[105]

---

[103] This is a problem in all of the case studies mentioned here: Gwich'in was to a large part preserved from looming language death through its use in hymnody and Bible/prayer book translations. Maori knew a form of writing in the art of carving and *Moko*/tattoo, and perhaps their appreciation for literacy has to do with having a comparative practice, despite the obvious representational differences. As concerns spoken Maori expressed in the form of Roman letters, the first texts were biblical translations. This is similar for the first written and printed forms of *isiZulu*.

[104] See, for example, Hlonipha Mokoena, "The Queen's Bishop: A Convert's Memoir of John W. Colenso," *Journal of Religion in Africa* Vol. 38 (2008): 312–42, and Martin Ngodji, "The Story of the Bible Among Ovakwanyama: The Agency of Indigenous Translators" (University of KwaZulu-Natal, Pietermaritzburg, 2004).

[105] I am indebted here to Devorah Schoenfeld and Julia Watts Belser for offering these distinctions from a Jewish perspective during a discussion at the AAR/Luce Seminar on

Gendering Mission

One integral facet of a polydox methodology is the attention to gender and the repression of women and sexual minorities. Rather than providing a historical trajectory, here we can only point out some gaps and patterns. This will include new tasks, such as "resignifying gender", and "requeering sexuality,"[106] addressing the "interlocking nature of oppression,"[107] and rethinking our economic and ecological embeddedness in the communal construction of theology in the postcolony. In short, such theology aims to be accountable to the fullness of life on this planet in relationship with the divine. This includes pushing inquiries into the sexual perceptions of religious groups further: beyond analyzing the frameworks under which some persons' sexuality becomes problematic to "querying religion" why such sexuality becomes associated with idol worship and otherwise disloyal practices.[108]

It is of key importance to represent the internal complexity of communities in their interpretive and agential practices. In patriarchal societies, missionary and metropolitan theologies generally preferred men as missionaries. After the initial house churches, where women of substance had some sense of leadership, the *ekklesia* left the private spaces of the feminine domain to enter the public spaces of the male domain, where women's leadership roles are diminished and lost.[109] They remain active as widows and patrons of congregations bishops, priests, and theologians.[110]

After the demise of the Roman Empire and through the Reformation, the presence of nunneries created a space for a variety of women, some wealthy, some not, to receive education and live a life somewhat more removed from the sphere of male dominance. Occasionally, women were recognized as prophets, teachers, and saints of the church. The secularization of monastic communities that followed the Reformation in some locations eroded that space and recast women as wives and mothers first and foremost, yet in some contexts, also with new authority to speak not only to women, but also to men. It would be centuries until women would take on leadership roles outside the realm of positions subordinate and controlled by men. Some of these moves into new, yet old positions of agency—after all, Leoba could be a missionary

Theologies of Religious Pluralism and Comparative Theology, Cohort 1, Summer 2010.

[106] Kwok, *Postcolonial Imagination*, 128.
[107] Ibid., 130.
[108] Ibid., 140.
[109] See Karen Jo Torjesen, *When Women Were Priests: Women's Leadership in the Early Church and the Scandal of Their Subordination in the Rise of Christianity* (New York/San Fransisco: Harper, 1995).
[110] See the deprecatory hints in some patristic writing regarding women congregating around Arius and other so-called heretics. For example, Virginia Burrus, *The Making of a Heretic: Gender, Authority and the Pricillianist Controversy*, The Transformation of the Classical Heritage (Berkeley, CA: University of California Press, 1995), 146–7.

nun in the realms of the Franks and Saxons at the time of Boniface and centuries later groups of nuns sailed to North-American colonies for mission—of
single non-monastic women (women married to a missionary were expected
to participate in his work, but in limited capacity) occurred during the nineteenth century. Unless they were members of a religious order, and vowed
to be celibate, Protestant missionary societies in the nineteenth century preferred their men married, or at least engaged to be married to women who
would support or share their mission. Thus, the roles of women in mission
have been limited and securely prescribed ones. Women were not only secondary as missionary agents, but also as missionary targets. A number of common
missionary strategies targeted upper or ruling-class males engaged by a class
of priest-monks or bishops. This strategy can be observed from the time of
the missionaries that worked throughout Western Europe aiming to convert
and lead the likes of Chlovis, Aethelbert, and Charlemagne, to the work of the
Jesuits with Brahmins in India. When women participated more substantially
in the ventures of colonial mission they, too, became part of, entangled in,
and to varying degrees complicit with imperialist missionary ventures, often
quite consciously so. Their own oppression as women was at times internalized and manifested in their complicity in the patriarchal ruling structure in
colonies or missionary societies. In many Protestant missionary settings in the
nineteenth century, wives were expected to participate in the vocation of their
husbands, without remuneration. Their work as schoolteachers, in gathering
women around them, often took the form of Mothers' Unions whose purpose
it was, among others, to reinforce "the strong sense of Christian duty associated with home and family," often inducing women to live lives of sacrifice, to
construct, in keeping with Victorian ideas of femininity, the home as a "sanctuary" and the "centre of love, tenderness, and purity."[111]

These unions have at times morphed from being institutions inculcating
Victorian mores and reinforcing local gender roles to the centers of power
in colonially founded churches. Women's participation in mission carries the
potential for domestication as well as for subversion of gender and colonial
regimes. At times, women missionaries broke new molds in settings that gave
them complex levels of agency, while their empowerment could come at the
cost of local peoples.

The Maori Women's Welfare League, under the leadership of Roman Catholic
laywoman Whina Cooper, was able to improve things notably for Maori women.
As the first national Maori organization, it was able to speak with a national
voice, promoted fellowship and understanding, voiced a variety of social and cultural concerns, and worked hard to improve Maori health, housing, education

---

[111] Davidson, *Christianity in Aotearoa*, 141. See also Rosemary Radford Ruether, *Christianity
and the Making of the Modern Family: Ruling Ideologies, Diverse Realities* (Boston: Beacon
Press, 2001).

and welfare.[112] If, with Christine Lienemann-Perrin, the Swiss missiologist, we count their work as mission work both within the church and as a witness without, the scope of mission becomes larger, more complex, and, of course, also ambiguous, depending on what notions of womanhood, agency, and advocacy are being lifted up. Many women have been abused through the organs of missionary work, and the "missionary position" has too often included sexual and emotional violence towards the recipients of such mission.[113]

These abuses continue to infect and affect possibilities of healthy relations and emotional survival in indigenous as well as in seemingly "secular" countries, where people turn away from churches in droves, upon the waves of revelations of pervasive cover-up of clergy sexual abuse in the Roman Catholic Church. Priest and clergy abuses occur in missionary settings as well as in seemingly "civilized" urban and rural settings, and the silences are only slowly receding. Such abuses can undo and render suspect the work of many decent missionaries. We may never know what the extent of abuse was in certain missionary contexts, or the sexual violence of past centuries. The number of Catholic hagiographies involving women saints defending their virginity could be an indicator for the constant threat of sexual violence and the precariousness of young women's lives in these circumstances. A crucial issue for rethinking mission is the implementation of structures of transparency, prevention, accountability and clear processes for the legal and institutional prosecution of such violations. While sexual and emotional violence are certainly not the sole province of religious institutions and groups, the combined spiritual, emotional, and structural power of sexually abusive practices has been extraordinarily destructive.

The picture fills out and the narrative of women's marginal role in mission shifts, when one rethinks what counts as missionary agency. Consider an analogue: In many cultures, trickster figures are primarily masculine, if not hypermasculine, at times caricatured as a laughable version of a man driven by his impossibly large genitals. Lewis Hyde has argued that because the criteria were based on tricksters with dominantly male features, such as for example itinerancy, female tricksters remain invisible, as they do not fit the categories of male tricksters. Female tricksters tend to be marked by different characteristics. Thus, in order to recognize female tricksters, the criteria for trickster agency need to be revised and expanded.[114]

Lienemann-Perrin argues something similar for women and mission. In the first and second centuries, she writes, "just as the idea of being church was

---

[112] Davidson, *Christianity in Aotearoa*, 149.
[113] See, for example, Andrea Smith, *Conquest: Sexual Violence and American Indian Genocide* (Cambridge, MA: South End Press, 2005).
[114] Lewis Hyde, *Trickster Makes This World: Mischief, Myth, and Art* (New York: Farrar, Straus and Giroux, 1998), 335–6.

still in a state of flux, so too was the idea of what we today call 'mission'."[115]
Therefore, the biblical foundations for mission are complex, and should
include various versions of local leadership in gatherings, care for the needy
and for itinerant apostles. Despite a male-dominated missionary history, some
feminist missiologists have argued that women were in fact the first missionaries. According to the Gospel of John, Mary Magdalene was the first witness of
the resurrection, sent by the risen Christ to tell other disciples of her discovery. Hence she can be named the Apostle to the Apostles or "mother of the
church,"[116] and can be seen as the first missionary. This would have been possible at the same time as other communities had far more restrictive views of
women's agency in the gatherings.[117]

Subsequently, women's roles generally became reduced, resulting in certain biases: (1) Seeing mission almost uniformly as sending people out and
winning new members at the expense of service, participation, and just gender relations; (2) prioritizing control, regimentation, and discipline in local
churches at the expense of the diverse moves of the Spirit; (3) prioritizing the
training of men for church offices at the expense of participatory concepts
of ministry that could include women.[118] Lienemann-Perrin's articulation of
"feminist, participatory missiology" uses Galatians 3:26–28 as a hermeneutical
key, intentionally choosing a strand of tradition that obliterates arguments for
the separation of sexes, ethnicities, and cultural obstacles among Christians.[119]
Such a missiology widens the understanding of the type of activities considered "mission-critical." For Lienemann-Perrin, the particular circumstances
and contexts in which mission occurred include an "oikos-missiology," a missiology of the house that rebuilds home and church for equitable and just
relationships.[120]

Lienemann-Perrin argues that the Samaritan woman, Junia and Prisca,
Mary Madgalene, Thecla, and others were pioneering missionaries, early
adopters of messages too strange to believe for male disciples.[121] It is with the
Pastoral Epistles, and more particularly with the movement of *ecclesiae* congregations from *oikos* to basilica, into the male-dominated public spaces of
the Roman Empire that "gendered mission," that is, patriarchally dominated

---

[115] Christine Lienemann-Perrin, "The Biblical Foundations for a Feminist and Participatory
Theology of Mission," *International Review of Mission* Vol. 95, No. 568 (January 2004): 17.
[116] Ibid., 20, 27–9.
[117] Incidentally, this is no different from today, where, at the time of writing, a congregation
led by a woman can be expelled from the Southern Baptist Convention in the United
States, the Episcopal Church in the United States and the German Protestant Church
can elect a woman as the national bishop, and the Episcopal Diocese of Los Angeles can
elect a lesbian bishop, while elsewhere women can be neither priests, nor deacons, nor
serve close to the altar.
[118] Lienemann-Perrin, "Biblical Foundations," 27.
[119] Ibid., 22.
[120] Ibid., 31.
[121] Ibid.

mission becomes forcefully instituted. In the societies that sent missionaries in the modern Protestant movements, women were the most numerous and faithful supporters. They founded societies, collected monies, and moved from initial "auxiliary" work that served as support and help to the missions of men, to Protestant wives that accompanied their missionary men and single Protestant women joining the female missionary orders of the Roman Catholic Church during the nineteenth century.[122] Women were thought to be crucial in many ways: to keep their missionary husbands from taking fleshly advantage of native women, to educate native women—which would have been improper for males to do—as well as children, to create a settler culture and model the heterosexual, monogamous households natives were induced to assimilate into. While there have been a few historical accounts and missiological histories of women in mission, even less has been done in feminist missiology as a part of a constructive theological project.

Civilizing Ad/Missions: Some Thoughts on the Cultural Location of the Gospel

A central question of missiology, as of constructive theology, is the relationship of the gospel to culture, to power, to the complexities of differential embodiment, and vested interests. If one key ambivalence of Christian existence consists in the tragic entanglement with empire, the search for access to power, the propagation of the rights of nations, and extension of their understanding of "civilization," then the progressive Christian tendency to drop anything overtly "Christian" or that might seem "evangelical" out of its vocabulary and articulation of faith is its reaction formation overreaction. Ironically, decommissioning "mission" from "civilizing mission" for shame of such entanglement can leave progressives with promoting what likely is the more problematic part: civilizing.

If mission becomes reduced to civilizing, it can become the carrier not of good news, but of the tragic flattening seen by the end of the social gospel movement: social salvation means increasing access to and consumption of goods, and the salvific progress turns into giving more people access to consumption and comfort. It is, of course, never quite that simple, but the tendency has been consistent and no less troubling. Regardless of their background, conservative, evangelical, or liberal missionaries will filter an already contextualized reading of the gospel through additional civilizing hermeneutical strategies. In many postcolonial contexts, where neocolonial global market policies are

---

[122] See Robert Pierce Beaver, *American Protestant Women in World Mission: History of the First Feminist Movement in North America* (Grand Rapids, MI: Eerdmanns, 1980), 35.

pushed along with conservative Christianities, we have seen instantiations of a rather ancient, tried and true missionary strategy: the promise of prosperity, wellbeing, and power through adoption of the gospel.

It stands to reason that each incarnation of the gospel has its own version of civilizing. What it civilizes towards depends on the hermeneutical preferences of the interpreting community and the way it filters the home culture to another culture. Thus, each expression of the gospel comes in civilizing garb, disciplining disciples towards a particularly angled enfleshment. This gives rise to multiple reactions and interpretations as filtered and incarnated in yet other settings, not unlikely each civilizing the gospel, rendering more acceptable in hegemonic cultural terms, while also being civilized by it—adopting values where they were not previously central to the understanding of self in community. This process of inculturating gospel becomes even more complex if we concede that the myth of a secular imaginary—seemingly untrammeled by Christian values—has been a persistent but self-defeating illusion. In fact, one might consider such an illusion—found in some versions of Enlightenment thought—a self-deluded "prejudice against prejudice,"[123] as if there were such a thing as speaking and thinking "from nowhere."

If mission cannot be reduced to being about the promise of a better life either here and now, or about pie in the sky, how might we conceive it? What difference does the gospel—whatever it means—make, to a life, or to a community? Certainly, there will be no one answer to that question, but it can provide a heuristic approach to investigating the relations. The proliferation of consciously local theologies may be pointing a way to a refocusing on theology as an occasional enterprise, that is, one dictated by circumstances and immediate needs rather than the need for system-building.[124]

Initially local and occasional theologies have a way of becoming permanent and, rather than fading away, forming a deep layer in the sediment that informs new layers.[125] How much may a structural setting, a hegemony, a colonial system, trade and political concerns impact, influence, inform, and undermine any such ethical goal? What is freeing for some can be predicated on the disenfranchisement of others. Moves against oppression may reincarnate as repression.

---

[123] Hans-Georg Gadamer, *Wahrheit und Methode: Grundzüge einer Philosophischen Hermeneutik* (Tübingen: Mohr Siebeck, 1960), 276ff.

[124] Schreiter, *Constructing Local Theologies*, 23.

[125] Thus, in contemporary Maori politics in Aotearoa/New Zealand, the concerns of *tangata whenua* (the concerns of the inhabitants of the land) overrule the more cosmic gene-aology of *Papatuanuku* (earth mother) and *Ranginui* (sky father) in struggles around land-use and environmental protection.

Works Cited

Beaver, Robert Pierce. *American Protestant Women in World Mission: History of the First Feminist Movement in North America.* Grand Rapids, MI: Eerdmanns, 1980.

Bediako, Kwame. *Christianity in Africa: The Renewal of a Non-Western Religion.* Maryknoll, NY: Orbis/Edinburgh University Press, 1995.

Bhabha, Homi. *The Location of Culture.* London/New York: Routledge, 1994.

Bosch, David J. *Transforming Mission: Paradigm Shifts in Theology of Mission.* New York: Orbis, 1991.

Burrus, Virginia. *The Making of a Heretic: Gender, Authority and the Pricillianist Controversy.* The Transformation of the Classical Heritage, Berkeley, CA: University of California Press, 1995.

Chakrabarty, Dipesh. *Provincializing Europe: Postcolonial Thought and Historical Difference.* Princeton, NJ: Princeton University Press, 2000.

Clifford, James. "Notes on Travel and Theory." *Inscriptions* Vol. 5 (Santa Barbara: Center for Cultural Studies, 1989).

Cornille, Catherine. *Many Mansions: Multiple Religious Belonging and Christian Identity.* Maryknoll, NY: Orbis, 2002.

Davidson, Allan. *Christianity in Aotearoa: A History of Church and Society in New Zealand.* Wellington: Education for Ministry, 1991.

—."The Interaction of Missionary and Colonial Society in Nineteenth Century New Zealand." *Studies in World Christianity* Vol. 2, No. 2 (1996): 145–66.

Draper, Jonathan A. "*The Bishop and the Bricoleur: Bishop John William Colenso's Commentary on Romans and Magema Kamagwaza Fuze's The Black People and Whence They Came From,*" eds, Gerald West and Musa Dube, 415–54. Leiden: Brill, 2001.

—."*Bishop John William Colenso's Interpretation To The Zulu People Of The Sola Fide In Paul's Letter To The Romans.*" In SBL 2000 Seminar Papers, 465–93. Atlanta: SBL, 2000.

—."*Introduction.*" In Commentary on Romans by John William Colenso, edited by Jonathan A. Draper, ix–xxxix. Pietermaritzburg: Cluster Publications, 2003.

Faber, Roland. "The Sense of Peace: A Paradoxology of Divine Multiplicity." In *Polydoxy: Theology of Multiplicity and Relation*, eds, Catherine Keller and Laurel Schneider, 36–56. London/New York: Routledge, 2010.

Gadamer, Hans-Georg. *Wahrheit und Methode: Grundzüge einer Philosophischen Hermeneutik.* Tübingen: Mohr Siebeck, 1960.

Guy, Jeff. *The Heretic: A Study of the Life of John William Colenso, 1814–1883.* Pietermaritzburg: University of Natal Press, 1983.

—.*The View Across the River: Harriette Colenso and the Zulu Struggle Against Imperialism.* Charlottesville: University of Virginia Press, 2001.

Haraway, Donna J. *Modest_Witness@Second_Millennium.FemaleMan©_Meets_OncoMouse™.* New York/London: Routledge, 1997.

Hyde, Lewis. *Trickster Makes This World: Mischief, Myth, and Art.* New York: Farrar, Straus and Giroux, 1998.

Keane, Webb. *Christian Moderns: Freedom & Fetish in the Mission Encounter.* Berkeley, CA: University of California Press, 2007.

Keller, Catherine. *Face of the Deep.* New York/London: Routledge, 2003.

—."The Love of Postcolonialism: Theology in the Interstices of Empire." In *Postcolonial Theologies: Divinity and Empire*, Catherine Keller, Michael Nausner, and Mayra Rivera, eds, 221–42. St. Louis, MI: Chalice, 2004.

—.*On The Mystery: Discerning God in Process*. Minneapolis: Fortress, 2008.

Keller, Catherine, Michael Nausner, and Mayra Rivera, eds, *Postcolonial Theologies: Divinity and Empire*. St. Louis, MI: Chalice, 2004.

Keller, Catherine, and Laurel Schneider, eds. "Introduction." In *Polydoxy: Theology of Multiplicity and Relation*, 1–15. London/New York: Routledge, 2010.

King, Richard. *Orientalism and Religion: Postcolonial Theory, India, and 'The Mystic East'*. New York: Routledge, 1999.

Kwok Pui-Lan. *Postcolonial Imagination & Feminist Theology*. Louisville, KY: WJK, 2005.

Lienemann-Perrin, Christine. "The Biblical Foundations for A Feminist and Participatory Theology of Mission." *International Review of Mission* Vol. 95, No. 568 (January 2004): 17–34.

Mokoena, Hlonipha. "The Queen's Bishop: A Convert's Memoir of John W. Colenso." *Journal of Religion in Africa* Vol. 38 (2008): 312–42.

Ngodji, Martin. *"The Story of the Bible Among Ovakwanyama: The Agency of Indigenous Translators."* Pietermaritzburg, University of KwaZulu-Natal, 2004.

Obeyesekere, Gananath. *Cannibal Talk: The Man-Eating Myth and Human Sacrifice in the South Seas*. Berkeley, CA: University of California Press, 2005.

Rieger, Joerg. "Theology and Mission Between Neocolonialism and Postcolonialism." *Mission Studies* 21.2 (2004): 201–27.

Rivera, Mayra. "Glory: The First Passion of Theology?" In *Polydoxy: Theology of Multiplicity and Relation*, eds, Catherine Keller and Laurel Schneider, 166–85. London/New York: Routledge, 2010.

Royal, Te Ahukaramū Charles, ed. *The Woven Universe: Selected Writings of Rev. Māori Marsden*. Masterson, NZ: The Estate of Maori Marsden, 2003.

Royal, Te Ahukaramū Charles. "Editor's Introduction." In *The Woven Universe: Selected Writings of Rev. Māori Marsden*, Woven Universe. Masterson, NZ: The Estate of Maori Marsden, 2003.

Russell, Letty M. *Church in the Round: Feminist Interpretation of the Church*. Louisville, KY: WJK, 1993.

Salmond, Anne. *Hui: A Study of Maori Ceremonial Gatherings*. Auckland: Reed, 1975.

Sandoval, Chela. *Methodology of the Oppressed*. Minneapolis: University of Minneapolis Press, 2000.

Sanneh, Lamin. *Translating the Message: The Missionary Impact on Culture*. Maryknoll, NY: Orbis, 1989.

Schneider, Laurel C. Beyond *Monotheism: A Theology of Multiplicity*. London: Routledge, 2008.

Schneiders, Sandra Marie. *The Revelatory Text: Interpreting the New Testament as Sacred Scripture*. Collegeville, MN: Liturgical Press, 1999, rev. ed.

Schreiter, Robert J. *Constructing Local Theologies*. Maryknoll, NY: Orbis, 1985.

Seidman, Naomi. *Faithful Renderings: Jewish-Christian Difference and the Politics of Translation*. Chicago, IL: Chicago University Press, 2006.

Shenk, Wilbert R. "Introduction." In *Enlarging the Story: Perspectives on Writing World Christian History*, Wilbert R Shenk, ed., xi–xvii. Maryknoll, NY: Orbis, 2002.

Sinclair, Karen. *Maori Times, Maori Places: Prophetic Histories.* Lanham, MD: Rowman & Littlefield, 2003.

Sissons, Jeffrey. *First Peoples: Indigenous Cultures and Their Futures.* London: Reaktion, 2005.

Smith, Andrea. *Conquest : Sexual Violence and American Indian Genocide.* Cambridge, MA: South End Press, 2005.

Smith, Linda Tuhiwai. *Decolonizing Methodologies: Research and Indigenous Peoples.* London: Zed Books, 1999.

Solnit, Rebecca. *Hope in the Dark: Untold Histories, Wild Possibilities.* New York: Nation Books, 2004.

Stanley, Brian. *The Bible and the Flag: Protestant Missions and British Imperialism in the Nineteenth and Twentieth Centuries.* Leicester, England: Apollos, 1990.

Stanley, Brian, and Kevin Ward, eds, *The Church Mission Society and World Christianity, 1799–1999.* Grand Rapids, MI: W. B. Eerdmanns, 2000.

Sugirtharajah, R. S. *Postcolonial Refigurations: An Alternative Way of Reading the Bible and Doing Theology.* London: SCM Press, 2003.

Tauroa, Hiwi and Pat. *Te Marae: A Guide to Customs & Protocol.* Auckland: Reed, 1986.

Taylor, Charles. "The Future of the Religious Past." In *Religion: Beyond A Concept*, edited by Hent De Vries, 178–244. New York: Fordham University Press, 2008.

Tillich, Paul. "The Problem of Theological Method." In *Paul Tillich: Theologian of the Boundaries*, Mark Kline Taylor, 126–41. Minneapolis, MN: Fortress, 1991.

Torjesen, Karen Jo. *When Women Were Priests: Women's Leadership in the Early Church and the Scandal of Their Subordination in the Rise of Christianity.* New York: HarperSanFransisco, 1995.

Tshehla, Maarman Sam. "Colenso, John 1.1–18 and the Politics of Insider- and Outsider- Translating." In *The Eye of the Storm: Bishop John William Colenso and the Crisis of Biblical Interpretation*, ed. Jonathan A. Draper, 29–41. London/NY: T&T Clark International, 2003.

Tsing, Anna Lowenhaupt. *Friction: An Ethnography of Global Connection.* Princeton, NJ: Princeton University Press, 2005.

Walls, Andrew F. *The Cross-Cultural Process in Christian History: Studies in the Transmission of Faith.* Maryknoll, NY: Orbis, 2002.

—."Eusebius Tries Again: The Task of Reconceiving and Re-Visioning the Study of Christian History." In *Enlarging the Story: Perspectives on Writing World Christian History*, Wilbert R Shenk, ed., 1–21. Maryknoll, NY: Orbis, 2002.

—.*The Missionary Movement in Christian History: Studies in the Transmission of Faith.* Maryknoll, NY: Orbis, 1996.

Young, Robert. *Postcolonialism: An Historical Introduction.* Oxford: Blackwell, 2001.

Chapter 3

Waymarkers: Pattern Recognition Along the Way

As we amble along our itineraries, we discern cairns and waymakers left by those that have come before us. They may orient us, we may stumble over them, we may overlook them. With ambiguous meanings, without clear authority, the marked landscape is open for many readings. The present chapter circumambulates some of the notoriously complex, fraught, ill-used, and misappropriated terms and concepts that affect discussions around mission, missiology, comparative theology and intercultural theological work. The relationship between gospel and culture, between imperial polytheisms and monotheisms, the problematic mirroring of Christian identity on a Jewish Other, and the projection of this relationship onto Christian–"heathen" relations accompanies us throughout. As colonial travelers encounter previously unknown populations, they look to their cultural archives both religious and scientific to render the terms of relation and encounter. As ancient biblical tropes like the ten lost tribes, Babylon, and Noah are deployed alongside notions of evolution and historiography, projection and intercultural hierarchies inform the revised genealogies of humankind.

The question of what constitutes a "religion," what its nature might be, what counts as one, and how it might be related to other aspects of a community's lifeworld attends many negotiations of the relationship between indigenous life narratives and Christian narrativity. The limitations of the employment of a culturally specific category to describe an experience across cultural difference remain with each attempt to transcend context. Linguistic and economic crossroads continue to be haunted by difference and deferral.[1] The im/possibilities and dangers of translation, of rendering across linguistic and conceptual difference, the question of ancestry and identity, the question of conversion and its ties to power, health, and wealth—the slippage between the economic moves of cargo cult, projections of colonial observers in an economy

---

[1] Derrida's notion of différance serves well as a "nonsynonymous substitute" for encounters inherent with slippage and misunderstanding in the context of mission. Jacques Derrida, *Margins of Philosophy*, trans. Alan Bass (Chicago, IL: University of Chicago Press, 1981).

of excessive differentiation, desires of entry into a globalizing economy of exchange, medicine, power, and prosperity, and Christian conversion—haunt the encounters between itinerant missionaries and local peoples across time and place. Attempts to neatly separate sacred and secular spheres are increasingly recognizable as failing, and require new negotiations beyond simple conflation or separation.

The Relationship Between Gospel, Culture, and the Cultures of the Gospel

The faith of Christ is infinitely translatable, it creates "a place to feel at home." But it must not make a place where we are so much at home that no one else can live there. Here we have no abiding city.[2]

What is the "gospel," the "good news"? Is it transhistorical, or does it change with geography, time, language, and culture? What good news is, and how it is delivered, is informed by the context. Agrarian metaphors may mean little to hunter-gatherers, or to suburban dwellers. Hermeneutical gaps may widen, translation and interpretation may attempt to close them. As biblical texts are translated into other languages, into other cultural frameworks, how should they engage the language and culture of the previous rendering as well as the following? What are useful parameters to determine such creative transmission, friction, and adaptation? What Babylonian captivities are risked, what subversions of the status quo are possible? How are sociocultural identities affirmed, denied, and rearticulated? Given these circumstances, what constitutes proclamation? What form does it take? What factors are involved?

If religions often travel along trade and migration routes, what does the experience of migration and trade contribute to the transformation of religious systems? If these experiences are layered and intertwined, how can any "mission" avoid being "civilizing" given that it is embedded in and transformed along with other conceptual and material practices?[3] This coalescence of forces in a colonial missionary context is powerfully stated below not by a theologian, but by a thinker of postcolonial conditionality:

For at the same time as the question of cultural difference emerged in the colonial text, discourses of civility were defining the doubling moment of the emergence of Western modernity. Thus the political and theoretical

---

[2] Andrew F. Walls, *The Missionary Movement in Christian History: Studies in the Transmission of Faith* (Maryknoll, NY: Orbis, 1996), 25.

[3] Above, I name both aspects not because they are separate, but because they may have to be named in order to be considered present and effective.

genealogy of modernity lies not only in the origins of the idea of civility, but
in this history of the colonial moment. It is to be found in the resistance of
the colonized populations to the Word of God and Man—Christianity and
the English language.[4]

Bhabha hints here at the theory that the emergence and shape of Western
modernity is a result of the "doubling moment" of "discourses of civility," that
is, forms of communication between colonizer and colonized that induced
both sides to transform their thinking and speech in response to the "Word of
God and Man." One could read these sentences also to indicate that the issue
of cultural difference and the issue of what constitutes "civilized" human cultural expressions co-occur, and that these differentiations have to do with the
way in which the "English word", and the "divine Word" seem, initially at least,
to appear to be hard to distinguish. Resistance to the one cannot be easily separated from resistance to the other, but what interests us here are in particular instances where such resistance was complex, adaptive, and moved beyond
attempting complete rejection or complete assimilation (though either one
would be hard to pursue in purity) towards survival and flourishing of both
the indigenous and Christian cultural elements.

There is some controversy about whether "the gospel"—whatever good news
that may be—is itself culturally constructed. Positions range from postulating
the gospel as absolute and transhistorical to rubbing oneself raw on the "scandal
of particularity." Universality and particularity both risk irrelevance—whether
to any concrete context from a seemingly unconditioned message, or any other
context than the one out of which it arose. Whether or not the gospel is "transhistorical," its expression, translation, and thus missionary discourse, certainly
are not. Some of the factors involved in these transmissions are: the theological underpinnings of a missionary movement, group, or the particular missionary group/family. Not all Christian communities have seen the so-called Great
Commission (for which communities is it central, for which not? When does this
happen?) as central to their existence, or even part of their existence. Those
who saw it as important and central tended to send out most of the missionaries.
Their theologies became highly influential to the developing churches in these
regions. Can there be too much inculturation, verging on assimilation? Do
revitalized indigenous faiths indeed "endanger their overall enterprise by seeking a mode of 'being *in* the world' that risks becoming indistinguishable from
'being of the world,'"[5] and if so what disciplines expressions of "the gospel"?

---

[4] Homi Bhabha, *The Location of Culture* (London/New York: Routledge, 1994), 32–3.
[5] Jean Comaroff, "Uncool Passion: Nietzsche Meets the Pentecostals" (Forthcoming),
7 referring to Birgit Meyer, "Religious Revelation, Secrecy and the Limits of Visual
Representation," *Anthropological Theory* 6 (4) (2006): 11.

What versions of orthodoxy and orthopraxy are mustered for contestations of Christian faith and practice? How might polydox expressions trace both expansions and limitations of Christian narrativity?

The transformative potential of some Christian principles and cultural practices can be profound and quite attractive in the perspectives for community they confirm, and enhance.[6] In other cases, certain concepts and principles can tend towards repression, especially in cohesion with imported or local hierarchical traditions or developments in response to colonial presences. Each situation requires critical evaluation, including an assessment of what the interests of interpreters of these encounters, both missionary and indigenous, might have been. Ambivalent as ever, on occasion a pacifying effect can be observed that cannot be reduced to submission, but can function as an intervention in self-destructive behavior following great losses of cultural coherence and sense of place in the world. Adaptations range from the extremes of triumphalist attempts to justify the "greater good" of mission, to hypercritical anticolonialist dismissals of missionary endeavors, along the continuum of accounts of material exchanges without attention to the theological content and critical theological appraisals of missionary efforts. Though the source archive is generally limited, especially when attempting to find records of the perspectives of local peoples on missionary encounters, it would be hard to maintain that there is only one particular effect that missionary encounters had, that they were uniform or monolithic. Rather, dissemination eludes any attempts at control, and theories postulating a tightly controlled or controllable hegemonic regime may be going too far.[7]

Economies of Rendering: Things Lost and Gained in Translation

The written authority of the Bible was challenged and together with it a post-enlightenment notion of the "evidence of Christianity" and its historical priority, which was central to evangelical colonialism. The Word could no longer be trusted to carry the truth when written or spoken in the colonial world by the European missionary. Native catechists therefore had to be found, who brought with them their own cultural and political ambivalences and contradictions, often under great pressure from their families and communities.[8]

---

[6] I am assuming here that it is preferable first to assert and affirm similarities that reinforce constructive tendencies in the local culture that aid in survival, and an adaptation of identity that can aid transition into the challenges that a global cultural scenario brings with it.

[7] Peggy Brock, "Introduction," in *Indigenous Peoples and Religious Change*, ed. Peggy Brock, (Leiden: Brill, 2005), 2.

[8] Bhabha, *Location of Culture*, 33–34.

Homi Bhabha here observes the difficulties of rendering English theological concepts in terms already occupied within the native signifying system as described in the Scottish Presbyterian missionary Alexander Duff's influential text *India and India Missions*. Not only does language become more noticeably unstable, but the worry about what happens through the cultural ambivalence of translation and the reinterpretation by local converts is palpable.

> The process of translation is the opening up of another contentious political and cultural site at the heart of colonial representation. Here *the word of divine authority is deeply flawed by the assertion of the indigenous sign, and in the very practice of domination the language of the master becomes hybrid—neither the one thing nor the other.* The incalculable colonized subject—half acquiescent, half oppositional, always untrustworthy—produces an unresolvable problem of cultural difference for the very address of colonial cultural authority.[9]

A crisis of translatability opens anew as texts are rendered in languages beyond the Latinate. Translations open themselves up to the signifying systems of the indigenous language, and import the terms and traditions resident. In this exchange at the limits of languages, much secret and sometimes not so secret contraband traverses.

In the modern European context, comparative religious studies as a discipline emerges alongside missionary thought and colonial science. Missionaries are often poised between two places, neither here nor there. They interact with peoples from their home contexts, while they compare and contrast language and culture with the help of native interlocutors, servants, catechists, printers, and converts. Some of them communicate with their missionary peers in other parts of the empire, some with scholars to exchange experiences and information, and write to missionary boards and publications for support and funds. They function as informants also for the colonial society on the cultures and texts of colonized societies. Missionaries were some of the main cultural mediators as they translated texts hitherto unknown to Europeans in the emerging university disciplines of Indic Studies, Oriental Studies, African Studies, Ethnography, and Anthropology. Scholars in these disciplines begin to interact with new texts in ways that have deeply shaped European philosophy and cultural self-understanding.[10]

> Missionary translations had made foreign literatures, such as the literature of the East, available to British readers. But translation also required extensive

---

[9] Emphasis mine. Bhabha, *Location of Culture*, 33.
[10] The dynamics include the acquisition of local culture by the dominant culture through religious interaction and vice versa. In some cases the boundaries between who appropriates whom become blurred. For an exploration of such dynamics, see J. J. Clarke, *Oriental Enlightenment: The Encounter Between Asian and Western Thoughts* (London: Routledge, 1997).

knowledge on the part of missionaries since every field of knowledge [. . .] was required to make successful translations.[11]

Translations, and hence transformations, extend into multiple directions. Such translations are interesting reiterations of the translations of Hebrew texts into the Septuagint and later Latin Christian idiom. What makes a "faithful" translation or an unreliable, dangerous one, can be a matter of great complexity and remains a contested field among biblical scholars and between interpreting communities, both within and among different religious traditions. In fact, as Naomi Seidman has suggested, any translation is a "faithful rendering," that is, rendered through the eyes of a particular faith, and therefore always already inherently suspect.[12] Rendering in Christian idiom then could mean both conversion and translation. Both terms, Seidman argues, "related etymologically and, as we have seen, historically, emerge in medieval Europe as closely allied if not parallel operations." Furthermore, "medieval conversion from Judaism to Christianity (and vice versa) implied the move to a new language, and conversion testimonies [. . .] simultaneously served as evidence of a spiritual rebirth and a linguistic transformation—the Latin exam passed."[13]

F. D. E. Schleiermacher, a highly competent translator and interpreter of classical texts, profoundly influenced the development of the academic discipline of hermeneutics. He urged interpreters to acquire the capacity to fully explicate the grammar and meaning of a text, to "pursue understanding in the light of a negative goal: that misunderstanding should be avoided," and toward achieving a "precise understanding."[14] Such linearity can devolve into linguistic reductionism, ignoring that knowing the language does not mean one knows the soul of a people. All the grammatical skill in the world alone will not help us understand another. Even if we could perfectly understand others, each person in community only holds part of the story, sometime overlapping, sometimes not. Yet, the reciprocity involved in some of the translation processes means that the cooperation and the use of indigenous terms enabled

---

[11] David Chidester, *Savage Systems: Colonialism and Comparative Religion in Southern Africa* (Charlottesville, VA: University of Virginia Press, 1996), 89.

[12] Cf. Naomi Seidman's work on the use by Christians of Jewish "native informants" for the translation of sacred texts. Though they were assumed to have both greater expertise and skill, Christian interpreters often felt at greater risk of missing the "hidden transcript" of an interested translation. The history of Christians employing Jews for translation purposes is full of fears of concealed and shifted meanings in those who consider themselves reliant on a reliable translation. Naomi Seidman, *Faithful Renderings: Jewish-Christian Difference and the Politics of Translation* (Chicago, IL: Chicago University Press, 2006), 133ff.

[13] Ibid., 141.

[14] From the 1819 Lectures on Hermeneutics. See Gayle L. and Alan D. Schrift Ormiston, eds, *The Hermeneutic Tradition: From Ast to Ricoeur* (Albany, NY: SUNY, 1990), 92.

"many peoples to acquire pride and dignity about themselves in the modern world, and thus opening up the whole social system to equal access."[15]

The Scottish missiologist Andrew Walls states one of the functions of theology arises out of the need to explain the faith to outsiders, out of "situations that actually happen, not from broad general principles."[16] This also means that missionaries cannot help but respond to questions and produce theologies out of their own contextual and epistemological framework. And without a clear sense of what the context of the situation encompasses, the theological narrative produced is like a tool that does not fit. It is like using a hammer to try and saw something in half. While translation is a large and important part of communication and Christian mission—and endless energies and monies have been spent in the process—the assumption that translation is an unambiguous vehicle is bound to fail.

Walls sees missionary theology as having to negotiate between two principles, the "indigenizing principle" and the "pilgrim principle." An indigenizing process "associates Christians with the particulars of their culture and group," whereas the pilgrim process, "in tension with the indigenizing," associates the (indigenized) gospel "with things and people outside the culture and group." Hence, the pilgrim principle functions to bridge cultural experiences (of the gospel) or as a "*universalizing* factor."[17]

Similarly ambivalent dynamics permeate missionary acts of exchange and translation. The Gambian missiologist Lamin Sanneh has argued that while it may look like the missionary is in control of the dynamics of cultural transmission, in fact they (for a long time it was primarily a "he") have to submit themselves and their language, theology, and culture to the language, theology, and culture of the location in which they are working: "if people are trying to learn your language, then they can hardly avoid striking up a relationship with you however much they might wish to dominate you."[18] The relationship between missionaries and Africans, he argues, then would in fact constitute a form of "reciprocity" that goes beyond the assumptions that "Africans" are merely "victims of missionary oppression, either because they were forcibly converted or because missionary contact proved fatal to indigenous originality."[19] Sanneh claims that translation breaks what feels like a stranglehold of Western culture,[20] yet this claim raises further questions about

---

[15] Lamin Sanneh, *Translating the Message: The Missionary Impact on Culture* (Maryknoll, NY: Orbis, 1989), 172.

[16] Walls, *The Missionary Movement in Christian History*, 11.

[17] Ibid., 9.

[18] Lamin Sanneh, *Translating the Message: The Missionary Impact on Culture* (Maryknoll, NY: Orbis, 1989), 173.

[19] Ibid., 173.

[20] Lamin Sanneh, *Whose Religion is Christianity? The Gospel Beyond the West* (Grand Rapids, MI: Eerdmanns, 2003), 130.

what the culture of the "gospel" is and what "Western" culture is. We may think we know exactly what those terms mean, but if the "West" has, certainly imperfectly, but in its own way, both been transformed by and inculturated features of "gospel culture," certainly enough to institute central elements inspired by Christian values in day-to-day life (a basic, but often unconsidered example is the absence of kosher or halal ways of slaughtering animals and the availability of pork in countries that were and are shaped by Christian culture, or the work-free Sunday), the distinction between "Western" and "gospel" values becomes a bit more difficult, and requires more careful exegesis.[21] Neither is the "West" thinkable without some measure of "gospel" culture or values, nor is the gospel, as Sanneh claims, somehow free of culture, as the diverse library of biblical texts comes loaded with many cultural assumptions. As soon as such complexities are admitted, the importance of a thoughtful, complex hermeneutics of culture and biblical text moves into focus. Whether the sheer fact of translation itself can be claimed as uniquely Christian is questionable.[22]

In the cross-cultural communication process, translation can switch grammatical gender around, erase or add it. In some indigenous languages there is no grammatical gender, so the learning of another language changes the ways in which the genders of beings and gods are conceived, perceived, and encountered. How much grammatical gender informs relationships, and vice versa, remains a contested subject. Male-centered power structures also pertain in cultures where language is not grammatically gendered. While Elizabeth Johnson rightly holds that "the symbol of God functions,"[23] language structures alone do not determine practice but rather have to be embodied to affect and transform relations. Hence, Kwame Bediako's claim

---

[21] What "gospel" culture means depends on place and culture, and generally presumes a number of shared assumptions when invoked, assumptions that may or may not actually be shared. Indeed, as is well known, "gospel values" appear to have little trouble with slavery, female submission, and other values many do not or no longer consider Christian in the sense that they do not represent the deepest Christian values (as perhaps then represented by Galatians 3:28) as many understand them today.

[22] As a convert from Islam, the missiologist Lamin Sanneh has claimed that reformed Christianity has an advantage over Islam in lowering the threshold of access by "translating the message," while, as he claims, translations of the Qur'an are still questionable and do not replace learning the Arabic verbatim whether or not one understands it. Sanneh, *Translating*, 175. Sanneh's often undifferentiated claims about the superiority of Christian vernacularization ignore the fact that both biblical texts and Qur'an have been translated in many places and times. W. Jennings sees in this a lingering supersessionism in both Walls and Sanneh. Willie James Jennings, *The Christian Imagination: Theology and the Origins of Race* (New Haven, CT: Yale University Press, 2010), 159. Language barriers were more significant in early Christianity, but Latin, the language of the empire, remained solidly in place in Western Europe before Protestantism, and there continue to be persons who hold that Latin should remain the language of the Roman Catholic liturgy due to its special status.

[23] Elizabeth Johnson, A. *She Who Is: The Mystery of God in Feminist Theological Discourse* (New York: Crossroad, 1992), 2.

that "in many African languages, God talk is non-sexist"[24] if offered as evidence that therefore patriarchal structures in Africa are less problematic than elsewhere, is as questionable as some feminists' claim that gender-differentiated language is particularly determinative of patriarchal structure. Language structures here may be less determinant of religiosocial structures than often assumed.

Christian supersessionism comes here in the form of overly simplistic juxtapositions between Western inculturations of the gospel that position African localizations as qualitatively superior, but are suspiciously congruent with a conservative agenda aiming to delegitimize progressive Christian options.[25] Certainly, it is not desirable to mimic colonial forms of Christianity, but since Christianity is indeed an "adoptive tradition," and carries innumerable layers of inculturation, some layers are less culturally specific than assumed when they come with missionaries.

The response to translations into native languages and the availability of Bibles to natives, engendered a multiplicity of responses, some of which were misinterpreted by missionaries. The Bible was often considered to be an object of power that was highly desirable to obtain, whether one could read or not; apart from its content, it was and is a symbol of cultural force. As perceptions of the sacral power of an object or a text change, shifts in attraction follow:

> The decline in Bible sales seems to have come from a realisation that it was not a magical volume, from some disillusion with the Christian message, and a significant decline in the number of missionaries.[26]

Thus, the Bible as an object can be an indicator of a number of things, such as the kind of esteem Christianity holds, the importance of literacy, and access to colonial culture. Some venture that "Maori people reverenced the Bible perhaps with something of a sense of a *tapu* volume and were most interested in its recitation virtually as incantation."[27] Some thus considered the biblical text a sacred object, in this particular form, as *karakia,* solemn sung prayers or incantations that continue to have a great importance in many Maori settings. For those accustomed to more modernist notions of textuality and mate-

---

[24] Kwame Bediako, "'Whose Religion is Christianity?' Reflections on Opportunities and Challenges in Christian Theological Scholarship: The African Dimension," in *Mission in the 21st Century: Exploring the Five Marks of Global Mission*, eds. Andrew Walls and Cathy Ross (Maryknoll, NY: Orbis, 2008), 116.

[25] Bediako, "African Dimension," 112.

[26] Peter Lineham, "This is My Weapon: Maori Response to the Maori Bible," in *Mission and Moko: Aspects of the Work of the Church Missionary Society in New Zealand, 1814–1882,* ed. Robert Glen (Christchurch: Latimer Fellowship of New Zealand, 1992), 173.

[27] Ibid.,174.

rial realities, such layers of meaning and numinous power are challenging, especially in increasingly post-secular settings. Many interpretations of the biblical texts seemed to the missionaries starkly literalist, in that some Maori took certain passages very seriously, such as in some instances literally anointing heads, and strictly observing the Sabbath. Each sociocultural community brings certain sensitivities to the biblical text and develops greater responses to some aspects of biblical culture than others. Thus, Zulu in particular felt that Christians were unfaithful to scripture because they did not wear garments made of animal hides and fur.[28] Of course, elsewhere biblical narratives mention the use of woven garments. Thus, we may wonder if the claims being made have more to do with binding one's own cultural identity to the text and finding resonances and claiming authoritative readings over against those of cultural others, rather than suspecting random, uninformed readings by illiterate peoples, not having enough information about the text and context of the Bible. Indeed, are such reading practices so very different from what we know of the history of biblical interpretation elsewhere? Selective literalisms are quite common in the history of biblical interpretation, including practices like snake-handling, or the extensive focus on sexual practices to the exclusion of the far more prominent prophetic denouncements of greed. Rather than denouncing selective reading practices *per se*, we might consider what parts of the biblical texts resonate "literally" with a community, and what this reveals about their motivations, sorrows, and commitments and struggles of identity. This does not make selective readings less problematic, especially when claimed as exclusively authoritative over against others, but it does allow for seeing not only textual, but cultural motives as part of such hermeneutic processes.

A parabolic story about the transition between the Bible as a powerful object (South African biblical scholar Gerald West calls this the "closed bible") and the "open bible," that is the Bible as regards its transformative content, is that of Tarore, the daughter of a Tainui leader. She had been given a copy of the CMS printer William Colenso's 1835 edition of the Gospel of Luke, and was murdered by rivaling Maori after an ambush when traveling with her father.[29] The gospel was taken as booty and led to the conversion of the son of a prominent chief, whose community later sought peace with their previous enemies.[30] Having a copy of the Bible or prayer book also transferred authority from the

---

[28] Sanneh, *Translating*, 176.

[29] William Colenso is the cousin of John William Colenso, the Bishop of Natal. William Colenso worked as a printer for the Church Missionary Society in New Zealand. They were close contemporaries. A. L. Rowse, *The Controversial Colensos* (Trewolsta, Trewirgie, Redruth, Cornwall: Dyllansow Truran, 1989).

[30] Allan Davidson, *Christianity in Aotearoa: A History of Church and Society in New Zealand* (Wellington: Education for Ministry, 1991), 18. Elsewhere, the story is told in more personal terms. See Lineham, "This is My Weapon," 176–7.

missionaries to the catechists, and enabled Christian practices and thought to be received on a more independent basis, sometimes even leading to the death of some of the native missionaries in revenge for intertribal killings.[31]

Moving from orality to literacy for a previously oral people has consequences for how text is perceived. Bible and hymn translations can have a strong effect on the development of the written form of a language, and can be one reason subsequent revisions of Bible translations and liturgies are extremely unwelcome among many church folk.

> As the revisers discovered, Maori people soon turned traditionalists about the scripture, and objected to any changes, even of format, in later editions of the Bible.[32]

Since the first translations were not always the best, and mistakes were made, this can be a significant problem. Older translations, faulty though they may be, can acquire an uncanny authority, in a dynamic that reminds of the struggles around the King James Version, or liturgical revisions.

Nervous Boundaries with "Jews" and "Pagans"

> *Conquest and colonization created on the frontiers of Latin Christendom societies in which different ethnic groups live side by side, and everywhere in the frontier zone of Latin Europe race relations were thus a central issue. It is worth stressing at the outset that, while the language of race—gens, natio, "blood," "stock,"and so on—is biological, its medieval reality was almost entirely cultural.*[33]

> *Race was invented as a modulation of culture, and the term "race" was often used in place of "culture" in nineteenth-century tracts. Races, moreover, were not defined by their immutability, but were viewed as fragilely vulnerable to alteration and destruction, particularly through miscegenation. Within Christian theology, supersessionism provided the model for Judaism's infiltration and the cultural dangers of religious "mixed breeding."*[34]

A primal boundary negotiation and circumambulation for Christians has been the contested, wildly negotiated, often violent and hardly simple relationship with perceived and real aspects of Judaism and its adherents. Christian

---

[31] See Davidson, *Christianity in Aotearoa*, 18 and Lineham, "This is My Weapon," 177.

[32] Lineham, "This is My Weapon," 174.

[33] Robert Bartlett, *The Making of Europe: Conquest, Colonization and Cultural Change 950–1350* (Princeton, NJ: Princeton University Press, 1993), 197.

[34] Susannah Heschel, *The Aryan Jesus: Christian Theologians and The Bible in Nazi Germany* (Princeton, NJ: Princeton University Press, 2008), 29.

hermeneutics of Hebrew scriptures distinguished many ways in which divine action and presence were seen and understood, and informed the faith and action of both communities. Both were thrown into radical turmoil with the destruction of the temple in Jerusalem through Roman imperial occupation forces crushing local resistance, and forged identities in increasingly distinct, if related, and continually entangled ways.

The Roman imperial setting informed an artful and artificial construction of boundaries, a border "partition" of Christianity and Judaism: "Rather than a natural, inevitable 'parting of the ways,' such as we usually hear about with respect to these two 'religions,'" Daniel Boyarin suggests what occurred was "an imposed partitioning, much as India and Pakistan, and Israel and Palestine [. . .] artificially positioned by colonial power."[35] Such boundaries, like the Roman *Limes* in Germania Superior, are often "imposed by strong people on weaker people."[36]

Discourse about differences between the emerging Christian faith within and among other Jewish groups first manifests itself in writing with the first Apostolic texts and continues with the heresiological texts of the patristic writers. Boundaries are drawn, first between "those other Jews," then "Jews," and those who recognize messiah in Jesus of Nazareth.[37] Boundaries are also access points for traders and smugglers, some of whom smuggle across heavily policed boundaries with their goods hidden in plain sight.

Imagined Ethnogeneses: The "Lost Tribes" Option

Modern racism, although dismissed for its philistinism, was actually the product of scholars working in a range of academic disciplines, to which theology was no exception. [. . .] Race began its appearance with a theological challenge: monogenesis, the biblical idea that all humans were created by God, was thrown into question by the "discovery" of different races. The problem for Christian theologians, [. . .] was that if humanity was not united as a single creation, then original sin could not be universally transmitted to all people and Christ's death would not bring atonement to all human beings. Yet while the discovery of races initially seemed a threat to Christian

---

[35] Daniel Boyarin uses an anecdote of smuggling across the U.S.-Mexican border in Tijuana to illustrate some of his observations about the emergence of Jewish and Christian differences. While the customs inspector is focused on the content, in the end, we learn that it was the wheelbarrows used for transporting across the border that were smuggled, not that which may have been stored inside them. That is, the means of transport, rather than the content, for the smuggling of goods between "religions," here emerging Judaism and Christianity. Daniel Boyarin, *Borderlines: The Partition of Judaeo-Christianity* (Philadelphia, PA: University of Pennsylvania Press, 2004), 1.

[36] Ibid., 1.

[37] John Dominic Crossan, *Who Killed Jesus? Exposing the Roots of Anti-Semitism in the Gospel Story of the Death of Jesus* (San Francisco, HarperSanFransisco, 1995).

doctrine, theological responses were formulated to defend against it or arrive at a compromise with it. Scriptures came to be used to justify racist but also antiracist claims, especially around slavery and monogenesis.[38]

One hermeneutic strategy to conceptualize the religioethnic identity of newly "found" tribes encountered by colonial scientists or missionaries, officials, and theologians was to speculate that they were related to the "(ten) lost tribes" of the biblical northern realm of Israel.[39] The understanding was that the "Lost Tribes" had to have migrated due to their exile and had been forgotten by history, and perhaps lost their own historical identity. The term Israel had been reassigned and redefined since the northern kingdom was destroyed by the Assyrians.[40] What was left after the first exile was the southern kingdom of Judah/Judaea. Yemeni Jews and Ethiopian Jews have existed for centuries in Africa, but lost tribes were also assumed to be in other areas inhabited by Ashkenazi Jews. Theories are proffered about Maori Jews, Zulu Jews, Native American Jews—the ten lost tribes are suspected to be located in a variety of colonial locations. In fact, "the ten tribes story is present among the many other features that meet, clash, and intersect in colonial 'contact zones,' " and are invoked by countless missionaries and colonial officials in their attempts to locate descendants of the biblical tribes.[41] The relation to the lost tribes has perhaps more to do with seeking to define and relate one's own identity and heritage to an untraceable, but haunting absent presence from the texts and stories that inform a community's identity. The particular ways in which these searches for identification and association work are certainly quite distinct for Jewish communities and Christian historiographers.

For Christian missionaries, anthropologists, and historiographers, the assumption that biblical texts had something historically reliable to offer for the history of peoples was quite common, especially as dispersion theories (imagining a common geographical origin of humanity from which they later

---

[38] Heschel, *The Aryan Jesus*, 29.

[39] These were the tribes that were brought into exile after the destruction of the northern kingdom of Israel, but ceased to leave a historical trail, and are widely assumed today to have merged and vanished into the populations among which they were placed. The Second, Babylonian Exile, however, left a far larger and ongoing historical imprint in terms of ethnogenesis, historical and ethnic consciousness of the Jewish people and religion.

[40] Daniel Boyarin has argued that Paul, through his renegotiation of the identity of Israel, creates new Jews or redefines Israel: "Post-Pauline Christianity, with its spiritualizing allegorization of these signifiers, was universalizable but paid the enormous price the suppression of cultural difference." Daniel Boyarin, *A Radical Jew: Paul and the Politics of Identity* (Berkeley, CA: University of California Press, 1994), 24–5, 26. This already occurred with the loss of the ten Northern tribes whose corporate identity became layered with that of Judah. Zvi Ben-Dor Benite, *The Ten Lost Tribes: A World History* (Oxford: Oxford University Press, 2009).

[41] Benite, *Ten Lost Tribes*, 6.

"dispersed") were wildly popular. Biblical historiography and dispersion theories helped fill in the gaps, for example, of a virtually nonexistent or limited ethnogenesis of the Zulu as described in Magema Fuze's *The Black People and Where They Came From*, who reports his frustration on attempting to write a communally compiled history.[42] The brief and perhaps untrammeled story that the Zulu came "from the north" or "out of the reeds" were unsatisfying answers to the probing questions of diffusionist theorists and theologians who were interested in ethnographic genealogies.[43]

The deluge narrative was used by missionaries, among others, as a key event to link to and to attempt to reinterpret the chronologies and historiographies of other peoples.[44] Bishop Colenso advocated letting the Zulu know about suspicions of the lack of historicity of biblical narratives such as the flood narrative.[45]

In the nineteenth century, narratives of origin continue to be reworked to answer questions about identity and difference heightened through colonial encounters, biblical criticism, and the emergence of evolutionary theories. Thus, David Chidester suggests that in Africa, "indigenous myths of sea and land were recast to make sense out of the strange encounters and violent oppositions of colonial contact."[46]

Thus, while missionaries and colonialists wrestled with scientific theories and the questions they raised for theories of biblical history, Africans cast colonial encounters "in terms of the mythic opposition between sea and land." Thus, the Xhosa chief Ngqika observed that Europeans as "natives of the water" had no business on the land and a Zulu emergence myth was later reworked in terms of this juxtaposition of land and sea:[47]

In the beginning, uNkulunkulu created human beings, male and female, but also black and white. Whereas black human beings were created to be naked, carry spears, and live on the land, white human beings were created to wear clothing, carry guns, and live in the sea.

---

[42] Fuze had urged "our people to come together and produce a book about the black people and whence they came, but my entreaties have been to no avail." Magema Magwa Fuze, *The Black People And Whence They Came* (Pietermaritzburg: University of Natal Press, 1979), v.

[43] Colin Kidd, *The Forging of Races: Race and Scripture in the Protestant Atlantic World, 1600–2000* (Cambridge: Cambridge University Press, 2006), 152–6.

[44] William Jones arbitrarily fixed a universal deluge as the starting point of human history, because he felt it was documented in various ancient writings, among them the Bhagavata Purana, which features a story similar to the Genesis creation narrative. R. S. Sugirtharajah, *The Bible and Empire: Postcolonial Explorations* (Cambridge, MA: Cambridge University Press, 2005), 149.

[45] Ibid., 611.

[46] David Chidester, "Colonialism and Postcolonialism," in *Encyclopedia of Religion*, 2nd edn, ed. Lindsay Jones (Detroit, MI: MacMillan Reference, 2005), 1854.

[47] Ibid., 1854f.

For these African religious thinkers, therefore, the mythic origin—the primordium—was clearly located in the new era that opened with the colonial opposition between people of the sea and people of the land. By appropriating foreign religious resources and recasting local religious resources, indigenous people all over the world struggled to make sense out of colonial situations.[48]

The notion of indigenous peoples as "Jews" may, among others, have to do with the notion that many scientists and missionaries, still operating with at least a partially biblical historiography, were seeking for ways to account for these tribal groups within a biblical historical metanarrative, as "in the early nineteenth century, biblical scholars still saw the Old Testament as an account of universal human history."[49] One of the few ways previously unknown peoples could be epistemologically slotted in known frameworks was under the trope of the "lost tribes of Israel."

We can observe this by noting an example from the Natal region in South Africa. Though the Zulu had not converted to Christianity they had "a kind of recognizable religious life that could be distinguished from other religions." Hence, the Zulu were "represented as people living a relatively stable life like ancient Israelites"—an ethnographic argument—that could be "contained, and perhaps even ghettoized, under a system of Christian rule"—a political argument, as they had been "contained by annexation and the location system." Furthermore, according to one observer, the Zulu "had not been corrupted by the superstitions of West Africa. Avoiding both idolatry and superstition, the Zulu practiced a type of religion found in ancient Israel." Thus, the Zulu were consistently depicted as "the Jews of Natal."[50] What is more, historical Israel was thought to represent the "gradual development of human society", so that Jews—and other indigenous peoples—represented the "earliest stages in the advancement of comparative civlization."[51] However, such links were more than ambiguously read, as

[r]ooting Zulu ancestors in Palestine did not elevate their descendants to a privileged race. That Elohim's lost tribe could have been in South Africa might have confirmed assumptions of early nineteenth-century comparative philologists who reputedly traced "physiological classification of racial difference" through "historical linguistics." [. . .] While both Jew and Aryan supposedly had "pure bloodlines" that flowed back to one "Adamic" source,

---

[48] Ibid., 1854–5.
[49] Chidester, *Savage Systems*, 141.
[50] Ibid., 125.
[51] Chidester here portrays the approach of Henry Hart Milman, a nineteenth-century historian. Ibid., 141.

Semites were supposed to have degenerated into "darkness" for they no longer saw the light of Christian truth.[52]

Some of these early perceptions of Zulu religions were thus informed and symbiotic with antijudaistic stereotypes, in addition to being particularly slanted by settler interests and assumptions, and portrayed the Zulu, and in particular the larger-than-life visions of the Zulu king Shaka, as degenerate and ready for the arrival of a "superior race."[53] Three European colonial scholars, adopting the emerging university disciplines of linguistics, historical critical studies, and ethnography, were to change these perceptions, and claiming to give, due to a more critical and less biased study of their subjects, a more just account of native culture and religion: John William Colenso, Wilhelm Bleek, and Henry Callaway.[54] Chidester suggests that Colenso's universalism and positive reading of a natural theology or religion can be seen as a "general theory of comparative religion." Chidester argues that Bishop Colenso made a "significant contribution" to comparative religion, as he "anticipated a new comparative strategy by which the universal history of religion could be reconstructed, not from records found in the Hebrew Bible, but by evidence drawn from reports about the Zulu."[55]

Missionaries and Europeans often used the histories and narratives they had at hand to make connections to societies and groups unknown to them. How they did this was starkly different and crucial for the relationships that developed. We should not be surprised that incarnate persons and groups employ what they already know to make sense, associate that which is similar, and then assimilate, subvert or resist something that appears new and different. Over time, additional adjustments are made, as new epistemological frameworks become available.

In New Zealand, too, we find attempts to identify Maori as a hidden and lost part of the biblical Israel.

Among the missionary ethnologists, the most able and sympathetic, the Reverend Richard Taylor, advanced the synthetic concept of the Semitic Maori. Like Thomas Kendall, he viewed them as one of the lost tribes of Israel.[56]

---

[52] Benedict Carton, "Awaken *Nkulunkulu*, Zulu God of the Old Testament: Pioneering Missionaries During the Early Age of Racial Spectacle," in *Zulu Identities: Being Zulu, Past and Present*, eds. Benedict Carton, John Laband, and Jabulani Sithole, PL (Scottsville, South Africa: University of KwaZulu-Natal Press, 2008), 143–4.

[53] Chidester, *Savage Systems*, 120.

[54] Ibid., 128.

[55] Ibid., 140.

[56] Jane Simpson, "Io as Supreme Being: Intellectual Colonization of the Maori?" *History of Religions* Vol. 37, No. 1 (August 1997): 59.

Another biblical template for these relations is identifying the native peoples as "children of Noah," or a colony of Egyptians that were "Ham's sons" who, having abandoned the one God, continue to sink lower on the "scale of existence."[57]

Such creative relocation could include the integration of a number of smaller groups, such as the example of "Hopification" and Zulufication. In the case of the Navajo, this remapping involved smothering the land with stories.[58]

> Although the thirty or more in-migrating clans that constitute today's Hopi Indian tribe, for example, originated from every conceivable direction and showed up in their Arizona mesa lands at different times, through the process of selective adaptation [. . .] they congealed into a hierarchy of clan groups dispersed into separate villages, each retaining, however, its own migration stories and hallowed sites of arrival.[59]

It would be hard for anybody with any familiarity of biblical history and the ethnogenesis of the biblical Israel and Judah not to sense a degree of recognition. Similar ethnogenetic traces can be found in the mythic creation of the Zulu nation. The amaZulu, people from the sky, according to a creation narrative, indicate a divine descent of the Zulu ruling class. The account also employs as elements of creation those images that are central to Zulu culture: an ox, reed, bovine intestines as rope to descend from the skies onto the earth, the stars of the Milky Way as the hoofprint holes through which the perpetual light from the sky shines onto the earth. Other Zulu creation stories hold that the people emerged from the reeds, or connect fertility to banana plants.[60] Some missionaries and scholars assumed that the Zulu had no concept of a supreme deity. However, this may be due to a kind of *via negativa* theology that considers it disrespectful to speak of the deity. Thus, some Zulu state that the "Lord-of-the-sky" would deem it a sign of "bad manners" to "speak of him as if he were our acquaintance. So we simply keep quiet and say nothing." Similar to the avoidance of enunciating the divine name by many Jews, it is then not a sign of lack of knowledge of the deity, but a sign of respect for the deity's integrity and power.[61] Instead, mediating "shades," the deceased intercede with the deity on behalf of the living, unless the need is so severe and desperate that petitioners address the deity directly.[62]

---

[57] Judith Binney, *The Legacy of Guilt: A Life of Thomas Kendall* (Wellington: Bridget Williams Books, 1968), 132–3.

[58] Peter Nabokov, *Where The Lighting Strikes: The Lives of American Indian Sacred Places* (New York: Penguin, 2006), 91.

[59] Peter Nabokov, *A Forest in Time: American Indian Ways of History* (Cambridge: Cambridge University Press, 2002), 140.

[60] Axel-Ivar Berglund, *Zulu Thought Pattern and Symbolism* (Bloomington, IN: Indiana University Press, 1989), 33–4.

[61] Ibid., 42.

[62] Ibid., 43, 46.

A narrative of creation would be told with different assumptions under-girding it. While many traditions in the Western Latin stream became focused on explaining an ex nihilo creation, there are many other interests in telling a story. Thus, for example, "In the popular Maori creation stories recorded by [Peter S.] Buck there is no supreme deity. The concern in these stories is not creator and creation but the ancestral link through time from the beginning."[63] A suspected interpolation of a supreme creator has been controversial:

> Whether Io is an ancient concept or a post-Christian construct is an area of theological contention in Maoridom today. The Io concept is regarded by many Maori as authentic tradition and it becomes increasingly popular among Maori nationalists as a statement of self-determination. But the con-cept, as in the biblical tradition, sets Io apart from creation. This is problem-atic and inconsistent with the usual pattern of emergent creation stories.[64]

The emergence of the known world is, in many creation narratives, intimately connected to the emergence of the people of the land, as they know them-selves within all their relations.

> Within Scripture, moreover, there is an important text that mixes ethno-graphic and linguistic concerns with an account of human descent from a single point of origin. This is Genesis 10, which traces Noah's lineage through seventy-six patrilineal descendants, many of whom are transpar-ently the founding ancestors of foreign nations. . . . For by disclosing the deep similarities of languages that lie beneath their superficial differences, one can restore the unity people enjoyed in Noah's time.[65]

Mythic origins and historical accounts find new and creative synthesis in colo-nial encounters. New nations and tribes needed to be written into the emerg-ing world-scale map. The ancient world map and its storylines are stretched to the breaking point with histories that, it is only slowly recognized, were simply not part of it. But what are the alternatives? Monogenesis, the theory of the descent of all of humanity from the same ancestors, or polygenesis, humanity's descent from different ancestors? Which is the more correct and meaningful theory? These questions deeply occupy not only the missionaries struggling to integrate narratives, but also scholars in the European metropoles, attempting

---

[63] Moeawa Callaghan, "A Reflection on Creation Stories in Maori Tradition," *First Peoples Theology Journal* (September 2001): 79.

[64] Ibid., 82.

[65] Ibid., 80.

to digest and integrate information that is brought back from the colonies and that propels and founds a number of modern disciplines. The links between colonies and metropole are not always fully recognized, and it is important to try to show the interdependence of European modernity, Reformation, Enlightenment, and Romanticism with the anthropological and historical sciences emerging.

"Imagine There Is No Religion": When Visitors Misrecognize Other "Religions"

I believe that they would easily be made Christians, because it seemed to me that they belonged to no religion.[66]

How do the manyness, ambiguity, and changeability of everyday experience actually fit into an ultimate frame of One? If all of reality must fit the laws of the One God and/ or the laws of the One Nature, then those things that confound either or both present problems for faith. And indeed, they do, over and over again.[67]

Moving from one misidentification to another, from ethnic identification, we move to religous practice. What does it take to imagine that somebody does not have a religion? As we have seen, not much. Columbus was neither the first nor the last to have made the claim that the natives he encountered had no recognizable religion and therefore should be easy to convert. What are the circumstances under which these people, carrying certain variations of Christian understandings of divinity in their mind, cannot or will not recognize other religious practices? What are they looking for, missing, and what do they find? And what are the circumstances when missionaries or scientists resist some of their cultural formation and are cautiously open to difference, appreciate similarities, and embody an ethos in their comparative venture that is respectful of the articulations of divinity they encounter?

In *Savage Systems*, David Chidester reports on the search for the unknown god of the Zulu.[68] Multiple missionaries and colonial officials report that there is no concept of, or only a vanishing memory of, something like a creator God. This does not, however, mean that these societies were devoid of ritual (especially around agriculture, fertility, and transitions in social rela-

---

[66] From the diary of Christopher Columbus of the Second Voyage, Eliot Samuel Morison, *Journals and Other Documents on the Life and Voyages of Christopher Columbus* (New York: Heritage Press, 1963), 65. Quoted in Catherine Keller, *Apocalypse Now And Then: A Feminist Guide to the End of the World* (Boston, MA: Beacon, 1996), 155.

[67] Laurel C. Schneider, *Beyond Monotheism: A Theology of Multiplicity* (London: Routledge, 2008), 80.

[68] See especially Chapter 4. Chidester, *Savage Systems*, 75ff.

tions) or certain practices intended to influence or control weather, events, and relationships. Whether or not this vanishing—or retained knowledge— was due to the beginning transformation of local societies or represented, as the missionaries might have wished, a convenient and providential opening for their message of a universal God remains unclear:

> Beginning with an indistinct belief in a Supreme Being, a belief that was remembered by some but forgotten by most in the course of the degradation of the Zulu people, belief in God was being recovered under colonial influence. Gardiner asserted that "since their recent intercourse with Europeans, the vague idea of a Supreme Being has again become general."[69]

Colenso argued for the use of Zulu terms of a locally expressed version of a "universal natural religion" and the creator God. Thus, he put elements of indigenous religion into the service of Christian proclamation.[70] Thus, depending on the observer, the Zulu have no religion, practice superstition, ancestor worship, or witchcraft, exemplify a "primitive universal religion," or, so Colenso, have a "natural theology."

There are indeed curious instances in which Europeans postulate an original indigenous monotheism, which, according to best evidence, reflects a post-contact indigenous cosmology, that is, a state after missionaries had begun speaking about a supreme deity they called Jehovah. In New Zealand's North Island, the first written reference to "Io" occurs in 1876 and is widely considered to be an interpolation. Yet historian Judith Binney reports that in CMS missionary Thomas Kendall's writings, the "earliest account of Maori religion written by a man who penetrated deeper than almost any other European into the mysteries of the Maori world, is a hint of a monotheistic cult."[71] His material is the only one taken "from conversations with men who had not been converted to Christianity, who had not forgotten or deliberately cast aside their knowledge."[72] Kendall carried his own theological assumptions with him, assuming a natural theology that manifested as "an inherent adoration for the Supreme Being," and the love for that which "was expressed in every culture, no matter how corrupt the form." Kendall described this natural theology in the language he knew, using biblical language from the Gospel of John and the Apocalypse of John. His only frame of reference for Maori religion was Old Testament idolatry.[73] This is hardly surprising, though Binney remarks on the reality that his comparisons were deeply informed by

---

[69] Ibid., 122.
[70] Ibid., 129.
[71] Kendall wrote his materials in 1814, 1815, and 1820. Binney, *Legacy of Guilt*, 131.
[72] Ibid., 131.
[73] Ibid., 132.

his own theology and his own cultural context, as if it were not only puzzling but indeed flawed. Though Binney is quite clear that Kendall did not have any other resources, an undertone of reproach seems to persist throughout her narrative, though quite what the alternative to it would have been remains unclear. Indeed, Binney suggests that a broadening education, respect for cultural difference that could not simply be rendered in the terms of one's own, and a sense of generous conceptions were starkly absent from Kendall's anti-intellectual, evangelical cultural and theological resources, while the lack of a unified "system" of Maori thought would have rendered any kind of "accurate" representation questionable.

> Maori religion was not a well-defined system of beliefs or observances, and legends of one tribe were by no means necessarily those of another. Internal contradictions are many. At the most it might be argued that religious practices were regionally consistent, but it is clear that there was a wide range of choice for the individual. It is also certain that a great deal of lore has gone, which has added to the general confusion.[74]

Later ethnographers drew on Christianized Maori for their information about religiocultural practices. Thus, the curious case of the ethnographic postulation, popularized by colonial anthropologist Elsdon Best, of a "secret" supreme deity "Io"—which could simply be a contraction of "Jehovah."[75] The reason put forward for why this deity was "discovered" and written about so late was that only an intellectual and priestly elite had access to it in the *whare wananga*— the house of teaching. Many scholars, however, consider it more likely that the reason for the absence of mention of this deity had to do with its nonexistence within the precolonial Maori context. Another reason for the promulgation of this theory may have been the thesis of "romantic decline" of the "Maori race," which was prevalent among ethnographers at the time. Some saw it as their province to "rescue" the Maori past to ease assimilation of the past into a colonial present.[76] The thesis that there was an "original" monotheism underlying the Maori religiocultural framework then was repeated by colonial scholars, seeped into reputable sociology, and is repeated by writers aiming to promote the formation of indigenous theologies. It may now have become impossible to retract, passing as unassailable truth.[77]

---

[74] Ibid., 157.
[75] Simpson, "Io," 51.
[76] Ibid., 58.
[77] It is repeated, Simpson argues, even by Jonathan Z. Smith, and by theologians like C. S. Song, from where it is then picked up by Pakeha New Zealand theologians writing in favor of an inculturation of indigenous theology. Ibid., 52–3. See also Maori Marsden in *The Woven Universe: Selected Writings of Rev. Māori Marsden* ed. Te Ahukaramū Charles Royal (Masterson, NZ: The Estate of Maori Marsden, 2003), 16–18.

Likewise, the African theologian John Mbiti's claim that all African religion is ultimately monotheistic strikes one as being a more politically motivated—resisting colonial scientists and theologians that claimed otherwise and hence saw African religious systems as on a "lower rung" of civilization—than realistic claim. The inability of ethnocentric scientific systems—and what would indeed be the alternative to that for those skeptical of the possibility of a "universal" science or system—to capture other forms of religious consciousness in a way that did not insert them into a hierarchical system, where one's own always comes out on top, was only slowly challenged and relativized. These efforts to find an *Urmonotheismus* are a cautious tale about the dangers involved in comparing cultural phenomena and the importance of considering motives and guiding questions the researcher has.

In some African contexts, the supreme deity needs mediation by ancestors, who can function as the mediating force between the remote (bi-gendered) deity and the lifeworld of humans. Charles Nyamiti and others then proceeded to propose a christology of Jesus the ancestor, highlighting in particular the mediating function between God and world.

I hope here to question narratives of romantic idealism, noble savagery, and "romantic decline," and to propose instead a greater recognition of the mutuality of encounters and the multiple agencies and factors involved. Ethnographers' claims about what phase of "religious consciousness" Maori "religion" belonged to were highly contested: Maori were either "savage", "barbaric" or—apparently a step up from savage— "neolithic" and "primitive."[78]

> For all their protestations of advanced mentality, postmythopoeic thinking, objectivity, and impartiality, these text makers show themselves to be both myth creators and myth sustainers of the highest order. Their derived authority and outwardly impressive modes of discourse in an apparently "religionless" context render this mythmaking all the more subtle and pervasive.[79]

Other questions can be raised regarding the absoluteness of the category of temporality. If the concern of colonial scientists had not been so thoroughly filled with issues of temporal succession and the assumption that such succession and sequence prove something about a cultural system, things might have been very different. It appears that, unlike the colonial scientists, the Maori involved in the oral transmission of these concepts simply did not consider either the origin or the sequence of the tradition of importance. Adaptation at times overrides and accessorizes easily, in ways that could have been familiar from the emerging research on biblical texts. Where modern readers of biblical texts were interested in factual chronology and distinction of sources, most

---

[78] Simpson, "Io," 70–71.
[79] Ibid., 84.

editors of biblical material were less so. Hence, somebody like Maori Marsden, who does not problematize Io[80] and sees it as an authentic feature of Maori religion, could be seen to simply continue the adaptation of various concepts into Maori religious thought. Thus, adaptation can indeed produce a new authenticity, no matter whence the concept or the thought adapted. Ultimately, the search for a "pure" and "untouched" tradition of any kind is a fruitless search, unfortunately involved in constructing categories of "authentic" and "inauthentic" identity and practice. Ignoring the adaptive processes of cultural narrative in this way can indeed function as a form of disinheritance of the past, present, and future of others. Jane Simpson ends up arguing, somewhat unfortunately, that yet again Maori have been victimized. She identifies them as the newly primitive, that is, after having been duped by colonial scientists who projected their own struggles onto their religious world, now being potentially the only community (because scholars now know better) to continue believing in the existence of a precontact Maori notion of a supreme deity. Once the need to defend oneself against having had a "primitive" religion wanes, perhaps the strained need to assert evidence to the opposite will dissipate. Yet, as the concept of colonial mimicry could suggest, the effects of mimicry outstrip the intentions of the colonial mind, generate surprisingly resistant options, and building blocks of religiocultural creativity.

There is, to take a different take on the heading of this section, "no religion" in the sense that the very term is notoriously slippery and when applied to other cultures' notions of ritual, divinity, and spirituality (none of these terms solve the issue of terminology, but rather simply transfer it onto another fraught term), it can have two strangely different, but related functions: the misrecognition of religiocultural practice and the universalization of it.

Boundaries between Religions, Real and Imagined

In the postcolonial aftermath of British presence, India descended into a civil war, partly alongside religious communities and regions. Eventually India and Pakistan are separated, partly along religious faultlines that had, throughout a long history, been insignificant enough to enable a largely peaceful coexistence. The second installment of Deepa Mehta's films on the elements, "Earth," presents us with a personal take on how people and land are torn apart by emerging, heightened aggressive attention to their differences that pulls them apart. The men's friendly rivalry for the young servant woman for whose attention they compete descends into betrayal and murder. The close-knit suitor-friend community and its collapse might be read as a metaphor for the distintegrating relationship

---

[80] Ibid., 84.

of what was then becoming India-Pakistan. On the eve of the partition, the separation of peoples into distinct, demarcated "religious traditions" looms. Uncomfortable and unstable nation states emerge that continue to be highly volatile. As in this case, the fateful introduction of sharper contours between religious and ethnic communities through colonial presences marks new formations of postcolonial power relations. The reality of India and Pakistan now means living with the divisions and differentiations that have occurred. For the conversations in comparative and postcolonial theologies attempting a "general recall" of the category "religion" risks a maneuver as colonialist as its imposition was in the first place—and—profoundly unrealistic.

Indeed, the term religion as it is often used today can be seen as "entirely the product of Christianity," while others have argued that "Christianization and [. . .] the emergence of religion as a discrete category of human experience—religion's *disembedding*," that is the invention of Christianity, also invents religion as a discrete category of human experience.[81]

In the Middle Ages, the distinction between *religio* and *superstitio* provided a basic framework of distinction, which endured into early modernity. Some credit the Anglican theologian Richard Hooker with introducing the use of the plural, "religions," referring to the Roman Catholic and Protestant forms of Christianities.[82] If missionaries and colonialists were operating with this kind of distinction, they may not find among indigenous peoples what they would recognize as "religion," namely orthodox Christianity as defined by the respective church authorities. The shifts in meaning of the term religion continue to manifest themselves in comparative "religion" or theology and inter-religious dialogue, where unstated or unrecognized assumptions continue to manifest themselves. The future study of "religion" requires great care in devising its definition, subject, and in how the boundaries between religious systems are framed and negotiated. One of the most important tasks of comparative studies in religion and theology will be to challenge the "secularist and Eurocentric foundations"[83] of the study of religion. The redefinitions and remappings of these fields are also crucial for the study of missionary interaction, for the comparative theological studies that, however misguided, have been a consistent feature of missionary interactions.[84]

Comparisons between religions were also part of medieval Islamic thinking, especially in the work of two Persians, the philosopher and mystic Al-Ghazali

---

[81] Boyarin here summarizes the contribution of Maurice Sachot and Seth Schwartz to this issue. Boyarin, *Borderlines*, 11.

[82] David Chidester, *Christianity: A Global History* (San Francisco, CA: Harper San Francisco, 2000), 345.

[83] Richard King, *Orientalism and Religion: Postcolonial Theory, India, and 'The Mystic East'* (New York: Routledge, 1999), 61.

[84] Francis X. Clooney, *Comparative Theology: Deep Learning Across Religious Borders* (Chichester, West Sussex, UK; Malden, MA: Wiley-Blackwell, 2010).

and the mathematician and philosopher Ibn Ahmad Biruni.[85] Perhaps these hermeneutical movements are less systematic and less recognizable to the eyes of new observers, but the danger is that the perspectives of scholars who legitimize their own discipline as something new and specific to one particular cultural spacetime prove to be "theorieverhaftet"—caught in the hermeneutical frameworks of their own preconceptions. Rather, evidence is plentiful that many cultures, and perhaps especially those with a history and experience of migration, nomadic existence or travel, or shifting relationships and trade with neighbors led to a variety of discourses that processed, through story, song, tale, and writing, the cultural "friction" that occurred.[86]

In the tradition of documents as loaded as Justin Martyr's *Dialogue with Trypho*, Pseudo-Dionysious, and philosopher theologians of the Middle Ages like Ramon Lull, Peter Abaelard (*Collationes Sive Dialogus Inter Philosophum, Iudaeum, et Christianum*)[87] and Nicholas de Cusa (*Dialogus de Deo Abscondito*) penned writings that stylized and staged stock arguments that might come up in interreligious conversations. Since these works are in essence apologetic, the arguments were more or less heavily weighted on the Christian side.

In Victorian England, Frederick Denison Maurice suggested that the development of the study of comparative religion was a "colonial imperative," arguing that the British nation needed a greater knowledge and sensitivity toward other religions. Thus, "political changes at home, as well as the extension of political rule abroad, required new attention to the role of faith in the religions of the world." Maurice, however, resisted the classification of religions, and preferred dialogue as a way of engagement, displaying a kind of intersubjective sensibility in arguing that a dialogue partner "will not really be intelligible to you [. . .] if instead of listening to him and sympathizing with him, you determine to classify him."[88]

The challenge posed by Martin Luther to the medieval conception of the *sacrum imperium*, as manifested in the Holy Roman Empire of the German

---

[85] Hamid Reza Yousefi, *Grundlagen der Interkulturellen Religionswissenschaft* (Nordhausen: Verlag Traugott Bautz, 2006), 14–15.

[86] The Dine Bahane, the Navajo ethnogenesis, at Alaskan tales of travel and migration, are just a few Pacific Coast and Mountains examples. See Paul G. Zolbrod, *Diné Bahane: The Navajo Creation Story* (Albuquerque: University of New Mexico Press, 1984) and Velma Wallis, *Bird Girl and The Man Who Followed the Sun: An Athabascan Indian Legend from Alaska* (HarperPerennial, 1996).

[87] Abaelard uses the term *fides sectae* to distinguish between Jew, Christian, and pagan. This term does not avoid carrying a Christian sensibility about the kind of relationality to the divine, and hence considers them comparable with the Christian internal conceptual system. Peter Abailard, *Gespräch Eines Philosophen, Eines Juden und Eines Christen*, ed. and trans. Hans-Wolfgang Krautz (Frankfurt/Main: Wissenschaftliche Buchgesellschaft, 1995), 10.

[88] Chidester, *Savage Systems*, 131–2. See F. D. Maurice's *The Religions of the World*, as well as Schleiermacher's speeches *On Religion*.

Nation,[89] threatened to disintegrate the "mittelalterliche geistlich-weltliche Einheit," so that the traditional bond of emperor and empire to the Roman Church was beginning to dissolve. As a result, the political system of the empire itself became unstable, until the *Augsburger Religionsfrieden* of 1555 created a structure that allowed for different religious options to be held in different spheres of authority, depending on the confession chosen by the various princes (*cuius regio eius religio*).[90]

It has been claimed that high medieval and Reformation Christianity moved from a more external focus on collective rituals and group participation toward a more internal focus on "taking religion seriously" as an internal commitment, with internal discourses that became externalized in the confessional and as personal devotion. The coexistence of different levels of commitment and practice were moved toward a priesthood of all believers, where "all Christians were expected to be fully committed."[91] This would suggest that the move toward a secular society, rather than being a move away from religion, is a move from within a particular religious impetus, namely a "drive toward personal religion." The move against ancestral links and magical practices in the Reformation and counter-Reformation can be seen as part of this drive. The repression of these elements has been described as "disenchantment" of the world, a "great disembedding of the merely human," away from great chains of being toward smaller scale universes.[92] Taylor postulates a contrast between "the modern, bounded self," a "buffered" self, and the "porous self of the earlier, enchanted world" that influences, among others, how people see cause and effect, and the forces that determine life. In this distinction, the "modern self" is able to "take a distance from, to disengage from, everything outside the mind," and the "crucial meanings of things are defined in my responses to them."[93] Manipulation of these responses can occur through counter-manipulation, such as avoiding certain experiences or substances. The boundary of the self here becomes "buffer" rather than entry point.[94]

The vulnerable, if not volatile, self may simply manifest itself in different ways, but, as Taylor cedes, while analogous, these dynamics are seen as "coded manifestations of inner depths," as dynamics within the person, and hence deals with them differently.[95] The contamination of violence in urban gangs,

---

[89] This term had become common in the fifteenth century. See Albrecht Beutel, ed., *Luther Handbuch* (Tübingen: Mohr Siebeck, 2005), 70.

[90] Ibid., 82.

[91] Charles Taylor, "The Future of the Religious Past," in *Religion: Beyond A Concept*, ed. Hent De Vries (New York: Fordham University Press, 2008), 178–9.

[92] Ibid., 180.

[93] Ibid., 183.

[94] Ibid., 184.

[95] Ibid., 184.

the domino dynamics and instant communication, the opinion and information exchange of social networking, the corporate impact of work done in
common and enjoyment had in common indeed suggest a morphing of social
permeability rather than a fading. The "porous" self's vulnerability to "spirits,
demons, cosmic forces" is reinterpreted as internal or socially psychological.
These selves are simply porous or bounded to different things, but, on a closer
look, things that are not as different in their social function as this potentially
overly dualistic view proposes.

Yet, to some degree these dynamics within European Christianity inform and
infuse the Christian missionary movements. In fact, one might wonder what
missionary activity would have looked like without these dynamics. Within the
context of Eastern Orthodox churches, mission has little or nothing to do with
external mission, but rather consists in the life of the church itself.[96] There are
instances of a new "buffered identity," which shows a greater insistence on personal devotion and discipline, and "increased distance from, disidentification
with, even hostility to the older forms of collective ritual and belonging."[97] This
hostility can be directed against one's own past belongings and that of current
belongings of newly encountered selves and collectives.

One of the most tempting fallacies of "Western historiography" including
religious comparisons is the problematic negotiation of boundaries: sometimes underappreciated and trespassed, at other times overemphasized and
lifted up to absolutes.[98] This obscurity is heightened by a tendency in historio-
graphical framing of accounts of history or religion. If there is "no evidence"
then the tendency can be to deny the existence of religion and culture in
a society. The often brief sections on precolonial peoples and cultures in
most modern historical books on a geographical region such as Alaska, New
Zealand, and South Africa can reinscribe the silencing with their own silence.
This leads to blank pages, to elision, and compression, whereas cultures with

---

[96] See Richard E. Sullivan, "Early Medieval Missionary Activity: A Comparative Study of
Eastern and Western Methods," *Church History* Vol. 32 (March 1954): 17 More recently,
"Western" missiologists like Christine Lienemann-Perrin want to correct what is seen
as mission: It consists as much of the internal nodes and networks of service as in exter-
nal preaching and teaching. See Lienemann-Perrin, "The Biblical Foundations for A
Feminist and Participatory Theology of Mission," *International Review of Mission* Vol. 95,
No. 568 (January 2004): 17–34.

[97] Taylor, "The Future of the Religious Past," 189.

[98] Thus, for example, medievalist Chris Wickham critiques the misreading and underap-
preciation of the "medieval," the "in between" age, read most often from the vantage
point of either the age prior to or following those centuries. He particularly lifts out
the self-congratulatory nature of medieval historiography: "Early medieval history thus
becomes part of a teleology: the reading of history in terms of its (possibly inevitable)
consequences, towards whatever is supposed to mark 'why we are best'—we English, or
French, or (western) Europeans, or at least, for less self-satisfied communities, 'why we
are different'." Chris Wickham, *The Inheritance of Rome: A History of Europe from 400 to 1000*
(London: Allen Lane ; New York: Penguin Group, 2009), 3.

written records and extensive imperial histories (such as in India and China) are lifted up as more "civilized."

> Sponsored and propagated by the [British] Raj, [historiography] has had the effect of replacing the indigenous narratologies of precolonial times with ones that are typically modern and Western.[99]

Contrary to many Enlightenment philosophers, Schleiermacher held that there is "no universal natural or rational religion that alone is true and that is applicable to all,"[100] though that did not keep him from exhibiting some of the same stereotypes about other religions, and in particular Judaism, his contemporaries articulated.[101] The term "religion," even after Schleiermacher and others attempted to delink it from referring to Christianity alone, thus remains culturally located and originally a specific rather than a universal term.[102] Its roots describe the state cult of the city of Rome and its empire. Postcolonial critics and some comparative religion scholars point out that the term, used universally, remains problematic, and assumes certain philosophical and religious categories, features, and contents.

The postcolonial situation serves to interrogate, often in rather unpleasant ways, the hard-won attempts to separate state and religious affiliation and values in nations from Europe to New Zealand and South Africa. Jean Comaroff's research in the public development of secular-religious boundaries reveals a postcolonial collapse of the lines of demarcation as the breakdown of both colonial and indigenous epistemes of order, law, and any sense of peaceful social coexistence to occur in South Africa.[103] The disintegration of such boundaries also encompasses a more publicly visible reemergence of indigenous forms of

---

[99] Ranajit Guha, *History at the Limit of World-History* (New York: Columbia University Press, 2002), 5.

[100] As quoted in Kwok Pui-Lan, *Postcolonial Imagination & Feminist Theology* (Louisville, KY: WJK, 2005), 191.

[101] Ibid., 192.

[102] See Richard King's lucid genealogy of the term in his second chapter. King, *Orientalism and Religion*, 35ff.

[103] See Jean Comaroff's chapter "Detective Fictions" in the forthcoming *The Metaphysics of Disorder: Policing the Postcolony*. There she discusses three instances of "divining detectives", the entanglement of faith and law. One of them, a post-Apartheid Special Investigations crime unit, a police force that uses both religious and forensic methodologies to diagnose and engage in crime combat, claiming high levels of sovereignty and mythic status as would-be saviors of postcolonial South African civic society. Elsewhere, one can observe the collapse of a conservative Christian diagnosis of satanism with indigenous categories of witchcraft and the dangerous conflation in conservative Christian policing. These instances, among others, mark the nervous boundary between inquisition and what Foucault describes in Christian reformers and prisons, and the prison industrial complex. Crime moves from an expression of iconoclasm against an idolatrous regime to postcolonial random violence and disintegrating society despite a progressive and inclusive South African constitution.

"religious" practice and exercise of authority, such as traditional healers despite a number of challenges.[104] The nervous boundaries between sacred and secular, which were never impermeable, are also reconfiguring North America and Europe.

Artificially imposed boundaries also occur in the genealogy of academic disciplines and within schools of thought. Hence, modern Western academic discourse can articulate itself as superseding, even erasing contributions distant in time and place in its claims for the "foundation" of a discipline and its "fathers," as Christianity toward Judaisms, Islam toward Christianities, and Mormons toward other religious discourses. The socio-religious system out of which a religious option emerges is often overridden and claimed as superseded, while the relations between traditions may resemble an underground network of roots that subterraneously connects traditions without easily visible, forgotten, or repressed connections.[105]

Overly determined distinctions between sacred/secular, sacred/profane, religious/secular, and so forth manifest their own forms of hermeneutical and methdological tyranny. Saba Mahmood has lucidly demonstrated the irony of the operative assumptions embedded in a "project of secular hermeneutics."[106] Such a project has identified Islam uniformly as an ill-conceived conflation of religion with irrationality and lack of tolerance that can only be "redeemed" if Muslims adopt a particular kind of reading of the Qu'ran. Consequently, it furthers a certain politico-ideological agenda to promote so-called moderate, "reformed" forms of Islam. Mahmood raises the question whether such quasi-missionary attempts to further a particular "reformed," or rather, a particularly conceived form of "secular" consciousness deemed expedient to particular politio-economic motives do not carry their own ideological determination. And though the intent may be to supersede previous interventions in Middle East nations, and pursue more "enlightened" strategies, it is in danger of functioning as a more slickly disguised cultural imperialism unaware of its inherent hermeneutical preconceptions. Hence, "contrary to the normative understanding of secular-

---

[104] It is questionable whether these practices ever entirely vanished, or merely went underground as traditional healers were decried as evil and "agents of moral backwardness."

[105] Likewise, "comparative theology" can present itself as a modern discipline, "founded" by primarily white male Roman Catholic thinkers. In that, ironically, it is both an accurate account of the particular history of a discipline, as well as a potentially exclusionary delineation. See Chapters 2 and 3 in Clooney, *Comparative Theology: Deep Learning Across Religious Borders*. While it is important indeed to culturally locate contexts that shape the discourse of a discipline, on the other side of this owning may be a disowning of other times, places, and agents who have engaged in equally valid, if not identical practices. Similarly, the discipline of hermeneutics is often described as having been "fathered by" Schleiermacher and others, erasing and superseding other cultures' hermeneutical and interpretive traditions.

[106] Saba Mahmood, "Secularism, Hermeneutics, and Empire: The Politics of Islamic Reformation," *Public Culture* 18:2 (2006): 342.

ism today, its force seems to reside not in neutralizing the space of politics from religion but in producing a particular kind of religious subject who is compatible with the rationality and exercise of liberal political rule."[107] Certain hermeneutical gaps between Islamic and critical Christian readings of sacred texts are thus redrawn as enlightened secular versus benighted irrational, misunderstanding and underestimating both traditions in the bargain.

Ancestry, Ethnicity, Identity: On the Genealogy of Genealogy

Ethnogenesis, the emergence of an ethnic group, is a process of the present and the future as much as it is of the past.[108] Much of the consciousness of distinct ethnicity has less to do with common ancestry than with a common experience and a common narrative. Recollections of stories of origins, of defeats, victories, struggles, migrations, gatherings, and foundations of cities constitute and reconstitute narratives of belonging, identity, and social culture of a group. Ancestry can comprise descent in terms of knowledge, survival skills, wisdom, valued habits, resources, ethos, and practices passed down through generations of learners, and thus intellectual as well as physical descent.

Following a number of ancient bone findings by British and American palaeontologists, contemporary South Africa has been reconceived as the "cradle of humankind," the genetic garden of Eden where remains of primates close to human ancestors continue to be unearthed. These findings have challenged earlier attitudes that saw Africa as a "dark continent," in Joseph Conrad's famous idiom, and certainly marginal to what many Europeans considered cultured or civilized. Ironically, these findings, based upon Charles Darwin's observations about the evolutionary logic of lifeforms, could undermine some of the racialized Social Darwinisms that have sprung up as a result of Darwin's quest for the way life on earth emerges and changes. The implications of a monogenesis of all humanity, in symmetry to Augustine's sense that all living humans were "derive[d] from the original and first-created man," no matter how bizarre their embodiment,[109] seem to render ambivalent any sense of racial superiority just as much as

---

[107] Ibid., 344.
[108] Patrick J. Geary, *The Myth of Nations: The Medieval Origins of Europe* (Princeton, NJ: Princeton University Press, 2002), 174.
[109] Augustine of Hippo, *The City of God Against the Pagans*, trans. R. W. Dyson (Cambridge, UK: Cambridge University Press, 1998), 708, Book XVI, chapter 8.

anti-judaistic supersessionism remains ambivalent in its dependence on the ancestral religion or ancestral conceptual "gene pool."

Some of the first articulations of the theory that humankind originated in Africa did not come from archaeological evidence, but from scholars like the German philologist Wilhelm Bleek, who was introduced to Bishop Colenso by their common friend F. D. Maurice. In contrast to the assumptions that the Zulu religion represented a degeneration of Jewish religion, he argued that it represented religion in its most original and primitive form, that he had discovered the "original religion—not merely of Africa but of all humanity."[110]

> While Colenso reread the Old Testament under Zulu influence, Bleek turned the oral testimony he had gathered in Natal into the chapters and verses of a Zulu bible.[111]

In ancestor worship, Bleek thought to have found the original religion of the Zulu, and potentially one of the most ancient forms of religion of humankind. Bleek conjectured that reference back to the Zulu ancestors was an active resistant strategy deployed by native informants, and designed to resist and counteract the presence and influence of European settlers in Natal. In addition, he saw in it a powerful and primal religious force. Certainly, he also observed that ancestors were preeminent in Zulu worldviews, far beyond a more subdued awareness of a more "unknown" and remote creator god.[112] Instead, David Chidester argues, Bleek encountered Zulu myths that represented attempts to make sense of the encounter between Zulu and colonial presences. They represent a "creative improvisation on colonial conflict," that "manipulated contemporary, historical oppositions that defined the modern world of Zulu religion in the middle of the nineteenth century."[113] Since Bleek assumed that Hottentots displayed a complete absence of ancestral veneration, and instead appeared to venerate the moon, he hypothesized that a parallel religious origin could be found in the worship of heavenly bodies.[114]

---

[110] Chidester, *Savage Systems*, 144.

[111] Ibid., 145.

[112] Berglund reports that there is neither worship nor prayer directed to the "Lord-of-the-Sky" and little attention is generally given to him. Some of his informants reported that "we do not speak much about him. That is true. It would be bad manners to speak of him as if he were our acquaintance. So we simply keep quiet and say nothing." Others see this "apophatic" approach more as a response to the lack of trustworthiness attributed to this high deity: "We do not know what next he will do to us. So I speak correctly when I say that one cannot love one who is not trustworthy. He is not trustworthy in that we do not know what to expect of him." See Berglund, *Zulu Thought Pattern and Symbolism*, 42.

[113] Chidester, *Savage Systems*, 146.

[114] Ibid., 147.

Cause for Conversion: Missionary Strategy, Promises of Power, Wealth, Health, and Progress

And while the [Christians] possess lands rich in wine and abounding in other resources, they have left to the [pagans] lands stiff with cold where their gods, driven out of the world, are falsely supposed to rule. They are also frequently to be reminded of the supremacy of the Christian world, in comparison with which they themselves, very few in number, are still involved in their ancient errors.[115]

That break was from a conception of time /space in terms a history of salvation to one that ultimately resulted in the secularization of Time as natural history . . . . In the medieval paradigm, the Time of Salvation was conceived as inclusive and incorporative. . . . The naturalization of Time which succeeded to that view defines temporal relations as exclusive and expansive. The pagan was always already marked for salvation, the savage is not yet ready for civilization.[116]

Thus writes bishop Daniel of Winchester to Boniface in Francia in the ninth century, urging him to continually remind those pagans of the cold North "of the supremacy of the Christian world." When German theologian Friedrich Schleiermacher utters close to identical sentiments to Daniel's, it raises questions about how thoroughly the pagans of the North had internalized these messages and projected them onto the "pagans" of their own times. Such statements thus may reflect a stock, retooled and internalized Christian theory of culture rather than simply Schleiermacher's personal theology—presenting the reader with an uncritical repetition of an ancient intertext of mission rhetoric:

> In view of the great advantage in power and civilization which the Christian peoples possess over the non-Christian . . . the preachers of today do not need such signs [i.e., miracles].

Joerg Rieger comments:

> The proof of the power of the colonialist nations was ultimately seen as stronger than the reference to the authority of the miracles of Christ. In other words, the power differential between the colonizers and the colonized was also perceived as an authority differential: God was on the side of the missionaries.[117]

---

[115] Ironically, this remark was written at the time when the Iberian peninsula was only recently lost to Christian rule. Letter XV (23) Saint Boniface, *The Letters of Saint Boniface*, Introduction by Thomas F.X. Noble, trans. Ephraim Emerton (New York: Columbia University Press, 2000), 27–8.

[116] Johannes Fabian, *Time and the Other: How Anthropology Makes Its Object* (New York: Columbia University Press, 1983), 26.

[117] Schleiermacher's upper middle class confrontation with Judaism in Berlin's salons did, however, serve as a way of beginning to question the complete supremacy of Christianity, in the context of what the position of Jews was within Prussia. Joerg Rieger, *Mission Studies*, 201–27.

We find plentiful examples of missionaries concocting various stews of civilizing mission. Even honest efforts to separate the two may only serve to further demonstrate the illusory separation between sacred and secular, if secular is assumed to mean a space where theological or spiritual discourse exists in abstraction from the realities of material life. We do better to distinguish among different forms of the sacro-secular than condemning the unavoidable mingling *per se*, as our "theological souls are also economic souls,"[118] and our faith cannot be but embodied.

The entanglement of sacred and secular raises with even greater urgency the uncomfortable question of what a conversion actually is and what compels people to convert. We have evidence of ancient religious and missionary references to promise of health and wealth, backdating that theology far beyond Kenneth Hagin, Joel Osteen, and Creflo Dollar.[119] And then, as now, a particular population, with particular concerns finds such promises, realistic or not, appealing.

When aware of this ancient, tried and—well, successful—strategy, there is nothing particularly surprising in the fact that conversion to what is becoming a culturally dominant religion involves mixed motifs, guns, for example, a technology mediated by early modern Christian peoples, were attractive to the Maori, Hawai'ians, Native Americans, and Zulu, among others, to be able to gain an edge in the ongoing saga of internecine tribal warfare and as modes of defense against colonial intrusion. The following interaction provides an example:

> [. . .] when Colenso and Shepstone finished their theological lectures, the chief demonstrated his more immediate concern in the political and military relations of the region. European teachings about uNkulunkulu might be interesting, but, as Pakade asked, "How do you make *gunpowder*?"[120]

The power or powder talk both links and contrasts spiritual and material forms of biopower. Products and technology, gospel and discourses of civility, encountered through separate persons, but linked with the colonial experience, offered access to greater power for native leaders. What it offered the women and children may have been very different: literacy, a different sense of selfhood and agency, travel, access to goods, spiritual, cultural, and emotional sustenance.

---

[118] Marcella Althaus-Reid, *Indecent Theology: Theological Perversions in Sex, Gender and Politics* (London and New York: Routledge, 2001), 194.

[119] I will not here rehearse again the entanglement of discourses of salvation with discourses of poverty, wealth, riches, and the abandoning of riches, except to say that these dynamics are related. For that see Marion Grau, *Of Divine Economy: Refinancing Redemption* (London/New York: T&T Clark/Continuum, 2004).

[120] Emphasis in original. Chidester, *Savage Systems*, 135.

As cargo and conversion transform peoples, questions about the nature of cultural and religious difference, and about constructions of self and other rise to the surface:

> To be sure, if African villagers now found their heroes in American soap operas rather than in primordial myths, if their rituals had come to be as much about shopping as making sacrifices, if their music was mingling with ours to yield a ubiquitous "world beat," wherein lay the cultural contrasts, the practices of "otherness," that we had hitherto spent so much time analyzing—and squabbling about?[121]

The negotiation of material and spiritual benefits and wealth is a crucial factor in conceptualizing and negotiating putative meanings of encounters in mission. Most religious systems have to negotiate the relationship between divine favor, sacred allies, and human material and event-based, historical flourishing. For some of the coastal indigenous societies of the Pacific Northwest "wealth came from having powerful spiritual helpers," and the access of Europeans to powerful and new goods and technologies led to the conclusion that they had very "powerful spiritual allies."[122] Narratives delineating such connections between matter and spirit could be described by Western observers as the idolatrous "monstrosity" of a cargo cult, that is the putative "worship" of material objects as an expression of sacred and material power.

Yet, the cargo cults of "other peoples" are not as exotic and far from more seemingly "cultured" mores as we might want to imagine. Jared Diamond begins his *Guns, Germs and Steel* by repeating to his audience a question that came to inform the inquiry of his book: a Papua New Guinean inquired of him, the U.S. American user of many tools and gadgets, how it came to be that the white people have all the cargo.[123] Diamond does not make an explicit connection to what in anthropological discourse is called a "cargo cult," a religious expression that seems to ask the very same question that Diamond seeks to answer in terms of historical and geographical difference.[124] The question raised, however, also goes to the heart of what constitutes mission and conversion.

An anthropologist from Papua New Guinea in New York might find that several of its residents practice an odd kind of cargo cult called consumer capi-

---

[121] John Comaroff and Jean Comaroff, *Ethnography and the Historical Imagination* (Boulder, CO: Westview Press, 1992), x.

[122] John Sutton Lutz, "First Contact as a Spiritual Performance: Encounters on the North American West Coast," in *Myth and Memory: Stories of Indigenous-European Contact*, John Sutton Lutz (Vancouver/Toronto: University of British Columbia Press), 44.

[123] Jared Diamond, *Guns, Germs, and Steel: The Fates of Human Societies* (New York: W. W. Norton & Company, 1997), 14.

[124] For an exploration of cargo cults and its links to capitalism, see Chidester, *Christianity: A Global History* (New York: HarperCollins), 471–90.

talism that locates value and sacrality as emitting from various sacred spaces, among them Wall Street's Federal Treasury and New York Stock Exchange, fashionable boutiques and restaurants, and the quasi-sacral remains of the World Trade Center. Max Weber's momentous study in *Protestant Ethic and the Spirit of Capitalism* outlines just one of the forms of the matrices of sacred materiality possible in a far broader matrix of possible configurations at times described by anthropology, theology, as well as sociology, but often lacking in interest or expertise in theological concepts, the history of their development, attendant epistemologies, and cultural contexts. If no clear, well-defined, and final barrier can be articulated between sacred and secular, spiritual and material forms of power, wealth, favor, and benefit, tangible or intangible, then this coagulation of energy, spiritual and material, should neither surprise nor shock.

Cargo cults would also no longer be reducible to the powerful corrupting effect of European forms of merchant and industrial capitalism and its interpretive, epistemological distortions of identifying wealth with spiritual power and divine access (i.e., a version of prosperity theology), but also an interpretive response from within a system that (1) did not have identical boundaries, if any, between spiritual and material power/knowledge regimes as colonizing societies, and (2) had differently structured and applied ways of interpreting spiritual and material wealth depending on values and situation. On both sides of the encounter, in different ways, mythic and historical modes of consciousness complement each other,[125] and raise with new urgency questions about what kind of good life is sought through a particular religiocultural engagement.

We now proceed with a closer walk in "pagan lands stiff with cold," where Jewish and Christian communities settle along the Rhine, where Boniface and the author of the *Heliand* renegotiate the meaning of pagan, Christian, Roman, and Saxon, reinterpreting pagan symbolism of tree and cross, of the sacrifice of Christ and of Odin, and contemporary Scandinavians seek to negotiate and recapture forgotten Christian pasts and recreate new paths to old pilgrimage sites.

Works Cited

Abailard, Peter. *Gespräch Eines Philosophen, Eines Juden und Eines Christen*. Hans-Wolfgang Krautz. Frankfurt/Main: Wissenschaftliche Buchgesellschaft, 1995.

Althaus-Reid, Marcella. *Indecent Theology: Theological Perversions in Sex, Gender and Politics*. London and New York: Routledge, 2001.

---

[125] Lutz, "First Contact," 45.

Augustine of Hippo. *The City of God Against the Pagans.* Trans. R.W. Dyson. Cambridge, UK: Cambridge University Press, 1998.

Bartlett, Robert. *The Making of Europe: Conquest, Colonization and Cultural Change 950–1350.* Princeton, NJ: Princeton University Press, 1993.

Bediako, Kwame. " 'Whose Religion is Christianity?' Reflections on Opportunities and Challenges in Christian Theological Scholarship: The African Dimension." In *Mission in the 21st Century: Exploring the Five Marks of Global Mission*, Andrew Walls and Cathy Ross, 107–17. Maryknoll, NY: Orbis, 2008.

Benite, Zvi Ben-Dor. *The Ten Lost Tribes: A World History.* Oxford: Oxford University Press, 2009.

Berglund, Axel-Ivar. *Zulu Thought Pattern and Symbolism.* Bloomington: Indiana University Press, 1989.

Beutel, Albrecht, ed. *Luther Handbuch.* Tübingen: Mohr Siebeck, 2005.

Bhabha, Homi. *The Location of Culture.* London/New York: Routledge, 1994.

Binney, Judith. *The Legacy of Guilt: A Life of Thomas Kendall.* Wellington: Bridget Williams Books, 1968.

Boniface, Saint. *The Letters of Saint Boniface.* Introduction by Thomas F. X. Noble. Trans. Ephraim Emerton. New York: Columbia University Press, 2000.

Boyarin, Daniel. *Borderlines: The Partition of Judaeo-Christianity.* Philadelphia, PA: University of Pennsylvania Press, 2004.

—.*A Radical Jew: Paul and the Politics of Identity.* Berkeley, CA: University of California Press, 1994.

Brock, Peggy. "Introduction." In *Indigenous Peoples and Religious Change*, Peggy Brock, ed., 1–11. Leiden: Brill, 2005.

Callaghan, Moeawa. "A Reflection on Creation Stories in Maori Tradition." *First Peoples Theology Journal*, September 2001, 77–83.

Carton, Benedict. "Awaken *Nkulunkulu*, Zulu God of the Old Testament: Pioneering Missionaries During the Early Age of Racial Spectacle." In *Zulu Identities: Being Zulu, Past and Present*, edited by Benedict Carton, John Laband, and Jabulani Sithole, PL, 133–52. Scottsville, South Africa: University of KwaZulu-Natal Press, 2008.

Chidester, David. *Christianity: A Global History.* San Francisco: Harper San Francisco, 2000.

—."Colonialism and Postcolonialism." In *Encyclopedia of Religion, 2nd edn*, edited by Lindsay Jones, 1853–60. Detroit: MacMillan Reference, 2005.

—.*Savage Systems: Colonialism and Comparative Religion in Southern Africa.* Charlottesville, VA: University of Virginia Press, 1996.

Clarke, J. J. *Oriental Enlightenment: The Encounter Between Asian and Western Thoughts.* London: Routledge, 1997.

Clooney, Francis X. *Comparative Theology: Deep Learning Across Religious Borders.* Chichester, West Sussex, UK; Malden, MA: Wiley-Blackwell, 2010.

Comaroff, Jean. "Uncool Passion: Nietzsche Meets the Pentecostals," Online at: http://cadmus.eui.eu/bitstream/handle/1814/9928/MWL_2008_10.pdf?sequence=1.

Comaroff, John, and Jean Comaroff. *Ethnography and the Historical Imagination.* Boulder, CO: Westview Press, 1992.

Crossan, John Dominic. *Who Killed Jesus? Exposing the Roots of Anti-Semitism in the Gospel Story of the Death of Jesus.* San Francisco: Harper San Fransisco, 1995.

Davidson, Allan. *Christianity in Aotearoa: A History of Church and Society in New Zealand.* Wellington: Education for Ministry, 1991.

Derrida, Jacques. *Margins of Philosophy.* Trans. Alan Bass. Chicago, IL: University of Chicago Press, 1981.

Diamond, Jared. *Guns, Germs, and Steel: The Fates of Human Societies.* New York: W. W. Norton & Company, 1997.

Fabian, Johannes. *Time and the Other: How Anthropology Makes Its Object.* New York: Columbia University Press, 1983.

Fuze, Magema Magwa. *The Black People And Whence They Came.* Pietermaritzburg: University of Natal Press, 1979.

Geary, Patrick J. *The Myth of Nations: The Medieval Origins of Europe.* Princeton, NJ: Princeton University Press, 2002.

Grau, Marion. *Of Divine Economy: Refinancing Redemption.* London/New York: T&T Clark/Continuum, 2004.

Guha, Ranajit. *History at the Limit of World-History.* New York: Columbia University Press, 2002.

Heschel, Susannah. *The Aryan Jesus: Christian Theologians and The Bible in Nazi Germany.* Princeton, NJ: Princeton University Press, 2008.

Jennings, Willie James. *The Christian Imgination: Theology and the Origins of Race.* New Haven, CT: Yale University Press, 2010.

Johnson, Elizabeth, A. *She Who Is: The Mystery of God in Feminist Theological Discourse.* New York: Crossroad, 1992.

Keller, Catherine. *Apocalypse Now And Then: A Feminist Guide to the End of the World.* Boston, MA: Beacon, 1996.

Kidd, Colin. *The Forging of Races: Race and Scripture in the Protestant Atlantic World, 1600–2000.* Cambridge: Cambridge University Press, 2006.

King, Richard. *Orientalism and Religion: Postcolonial Theory, India, and 'The Mystic East'.* New York: Routledge, 1999.

Kwok Pui-Lan. *Postcolonial Imagination & Feminist Theology.* Louisville, KY: WJK, 2005.

Lienemann-Perrin, Christine. "The Biblical Foundations for A Feminist and Participatory Theology of Mission." *International Review of Mission* Vol. 95, No. 568 (January 2004): 17–34.

Lincoln, Bruce. *Theorizing Myth: Narrative, Ideology, and Scholarship.* Chicago, IL: Chicago University Press, 1999.

Lineham, Peter. "This is My Weapon: Maori Response to the Maori Bible." In *Mission and Moko: Aspects of the Work of the Church Missionary Society in New Zealand, 1814–1882*, Robert Glen, ed., 170–8. Christchurch: Latimer Fellowship of New Zealand, 1992.

Lutz, John Sutton. "First Contact as a Spiritual Performance: Encounters on the North American West Coast." In *Myth and Memory: Stories of Indigenous-European Contact*, John Sutton Lutz, 30–45. Vancouver/Toronto: University of British Columbia Press.

Mahmood, Saba. "Secularism, Hermeneutics, and Empire: The Politics of Islamic Reformation." *Public Culture* 18:2 (2006): 323–47.

Meyer, Birgit. "Religious Revelation, Secrecy and the Limits of Visual Representation." *Anthropological Theory* 6 (4) (2006): 431–53.

Morison, Eliot Samuel. *Journals and Other Documents on the Life and Voyages of Christopher Columbus.* New York: Heritage Press, 1963.

Nabokov, Peter. *A Forest in Time: American Indian Ways of History.* Cambridge: Cambridge University Press, 2002.

—.*Where The Lighting Strikes: The Lives of American Indian Sacred Places.* New York: Penguin, 2006.

Ormiston, Gayle L. and Alan D. Schrift, eds. *The Hermeneutic Tradition: From Ast to Ricoeur.* Albany, NY: SUNY, 1990.

Rieger, Joerg. "Theology and Mission Between Neocolonialism and Postcolonialism." *Mission Studies 21.2* (2004), 201–27.

Rowse, A. L. *The Controversial Colensos.* Trewolsta, Trewirgie, Redruth, Cornwall: Dyllansow Truran, 1989.

Royal, Te Ahukaramū Charles, ed. *The Woven Universe: Selected Writings of Rev. Māori Marsden.* Masterson, NZ: The Estate of Maori Marsden, 2003.

Sanneh, Lamin. *Translating the Message: The Missionary Impact on Culture.* Maryknoll, NY: Orbis, 1989.

Schneider, Laurel C. *Beyond Monotheism: A Theology of Multiplicity.* London: Routledge, 2008.

Seidman, Naomi. *Faithful Renderings: Jewish-Christian Difference and the Politics of Translation.* Chicago, IL: Chicago University Press, 2006.

Simpson, Jane. "Io as Supreme Being: Intellectual Colonization of the Maori?" *History of Religions* Vol. 37, No. 1 (August 1997): 50–85.

Sugirtharajah, R. S. *The Bible and Empire: Postcolonial Explorations.* Cambridge, MA: Cambridge University Press, 2005.

Sullivan, Richard E. "Early Medieval Missionary Activity: A Comparative Study of Eastern and Western Methods." *Church History* Vol. 32 (March 1954): 17–35.

Taylor, Charles. "The Future of the Religious Past." In *Religion: Beyond A Concept,* ed. Hent De Vries, 178–244. New York: Fordham University Press, 2008.

Wallis, Velma. *Bird Girl and The Man Who Followed the Sun: An Athabascan Indian Legend from Alaska.* 1996: HarperPerennial, 1996.

Walls, Andrew F. *The Missionary Movement in Christian History: Studies in the Transmission of Faith.* Maryknoll, NY: Orbis, 1996.

Wickham, Chris. *The Inheritance of Rome: A History of Europe from 400 to 1000.* London: Allen Lane; New York: Penguin Group, 2009.

Yousefi, Hamid Reza. *Grundlagen der Interkulturellen Religionswissenschaft.* Nordhausen: Verlag Traugott Bautz, 2006.

Zolbrod, Paul G. *Dine Bahane: The Navajo Creation Story.* Albuquerque: University of New Mexico Press, 1984.

Chapter 4

Itinerary I:
Converting Rome's Successors

If Berlin were to meet the fate of Rome, Hitler wrote in 1925, only the department stores of some Jews, and the hotels of some corporations would be left for future generations to admire. These tawdry commercial buildings, he believed, accurately reflected the Weimar Republic's political corruption and social disintegration. One day, the Führer was determined, Germany would have a capital worthy of its imperial destiny; when distant generations visited the remains of his Thousand-Year Reich, they would find ruins to rival Rome's. Of course Hitler's empire lasted only a few years, not a thousand; it left behind only piles of rubble.[1]

By the Rivers of Babylon—Converting German-Jewish Identities

Heinrich Heine, a German Jewish writer, reimagined life at the boundary of the empire. He rearticulated German Jewish identity at the Rhine as by the rivers of Babylon. In his novelistic fragment *Der Rabbi von Bacherach*, he reminds his German readers that Jewish communities had made a home at the banks of the Rhine since the times of the *Limes*. He maps the "Rhineland's—and by extension Germany's—Jews, as a community that dates back to Roman times."[2] In Heine's fragment, Rabbi Abraham and his wife Sara flee their hometown Bacherach on the Rhine, avoiding anti-Semitic attacks,[3] and travel up the River Rhine toward Frankfurt, a city in which they hope to be safe from the riots against Jews in the Rhineland. Rising from the fog and traveling along the River, Sara perceives the ghostly memory of the generations of Jews who had

---

[1] Quoted from a review of Mark Mazover's, *How the Nazis Ruled Europe.* James J. Sheehan, "Lebensraum," *New York Times* (September 19, 2008).

[2] Aamir Mufti, *Enlightenment in the Colony: The Jewish Question and the Crisis of Postcolonial Culture* (Princeton, NJ: Princeton University Press, 2007), 84.

[3] Bacharach is a small town set on the Rhine. Some of its inhabitants engaged in notorious blood libel rumors that had attached themselves to the cult of a Saint Werner, a child supposedly killed by Jews. The town features a church dedicated to this fictional saint whose cult was only denounced in the 1960s.

been murdered in pogroms near the River's banks, or drowned within its waves during the first crusade. But as Sara, the Rabbi's wife, sees these specters, a mythic Father Rhine—*sagenumwoben*—a large "repository of German national culture, seeks to comfort his *Jewish* children with tales from Germanic mythos. The treasures of the *Nibelungen*, in other words, are as enchanting and comforting for the Jews as they would be for the River's non-Jewish children[.]"[4] Children of this earth now, where they had migrated, the River adopts as its offspring all those who live on it, whose dust and ashes rise and return from, no matter what their ethnic or cultural practices.

Heine's imagery is even more poignant after the Holocaust and could appear frighteningly prescient of it. The "ghostly procession along the Rhine is a figure for the history of violent persecution of the Jews in German history," as the "heimlich pleasures of national belonging are disturbed by the unheimlich recollection of violent exclusions and discordant histories."[5] Heine invokes the ambivalence of assimilation, of opening oneself to another culture, another soil, of the pressures and passions of hybridity, the twists and turns of identity assertion and denial of descent. Heine reimagines the Rhine as the source of memories of different communities:

> The Rhine is thus portrayed here as the source not only of Germanic fables but also of the stories of the Hebrew Bible, a narrative move that parallels Heine's inclusion of Spinoza in the history of philosophy and religion in Germany in his famous long essay from the early 1830s. National culture, in other words, is seen by Heine not as singular trajectory at whose beginning is the image of the Germanic tribe but rather as a historically contingent articulation of different cultural claims. The culture of the modern nation, therefore, has both "Jewish" and "Germanic" roots; it is at the strange intermixing and blending of these images and memories that culture is located and produced.[6]

Near this boundary of the Roman Empire, Heine warns his German compatriots against tendencies to deny or erase such memories. Disaporic Jewish communities were planted along the Rhine long before impulses to form a German nation were even perceived. Quite likely, the first Christian communities in the area were not far behind them. Traders bring with them their religious beliefs, establishing communities of exchange replete with ambiguous characters: merchant, missionary, imperial soldiers and concomitant entourages, crusader, Jews, peasants, burghers, women and men of diverse commitments.

---

[4] Mufti, *Enlightenment in the Colony*, 85.
[5] Ibid., 86, 87.
[6] Ibid., 86.

While the Brothers Grimm anxiously attempt to narrate a fictive, indeed a "märchenhafte" purity of the well of German folktales, Heinrich Heine's *Rabbi von Bacherach* contests this narrative by showing that Jews have not only been part of the narrative stream, but have populated the Rhineland's landscape since ancient times. The Rhine's flow, Heine suggests, "may not be unidirectional, its volume not as self-contained, and its very source perhaps not as pure" as the Grimms maintain.[7] Heine's novelistic fragment reveals also that diasporic communities are caught between the twin pressures of assimilation and hostility, with their own preoccupations about the preservation of a pure tradition, passed down through the generations. Rabbi Abraham and his wife Sarah "epitomize the Jewish community's anxious commitment to a purely Jewish way of life to the exclusion of all that is perceived as foreign."[8] Heine juxtaposes the Passover Haggada with the "Grimms' depiction of the domestic transmission of German Märchen," as narrative that counters the fairy tales told by the children's German nurse and recalls the Jewish ancestry. Thus, "the Jews of Bacherarch exhibit a concern for purity that resembles that of the dominant German population," though in the case of oppressed people, these discourses represent a survival strategy in the arsenal of the weapons of the socially disenfranchised.[9] Heine argues that "German and Jewish history and cultural traditions cannot be separated from one another, but rather are interwoven, integrated on the level of memory, on the level of landscape."[10] This cultural hybridity interweaving "the melodies of the Haggadah with the murmuring of the Rhein is thus by no means consoling, but rather deeply disturbing."[11] Schreiber suggests that "Heine's text presents hybridity as neither a strictly positive nor a strictly negative phenomenon; indeed, by its very mixed, ambiguous nature, it eludes any attempt to categorize it in terms of pure dichotomies."[12] Such ambivalence is a feature of the frontier/boundary/liminal encounters we are interested in here.

Heine intervenes in the Brothers Grimm's attempt to repristinate German traditions, revealing how they are related to the ongoing populist attempts to cleanse "the German community, through bloodbaths or baptisms, or a marginalized Jewish population suspected of having tainted the town wells."[13] And despite the "vigilance of the community elders," the folktale tradition of the Jewish community is "continually contaminated by the German tradition."[14]

---

[7] Elliott Schreiber, "Tainted Sources: The Subversion of the Grimm's Ideology of the Folktale in Heinrich Heine's *Der Rabbi von Bacherach*," *The German Quarterly* 78.1 (Winter 2005): 27.

[8] Ibid., 33.

[9] Ibid., 33.

[10] Ibid., 35.

[11] Ibid., 36.

[12] Ibid., 37.

[13] Ibid., 40.

[14] Ibid., 40.

The waters of the Rhine have seen peoples and traditions migrate, fabled treasures sunk. During the First Crusade in 1096, the Jews of Worms were drowned by Christians in contests over purity, identity, pollution, religious and cultural differences.[15] Heine began writing *The Rabbi* in 1824 but abandoned it until 1840. That year a pogrom occurred in Damascus, provoked by a French Consul who had propagated the unfounded accusation of Damascene Jews for the supposed ritual murder of a Capuchin priest.[16] Heine commented on the terrible irony that while the Grimm Brothers collect fairy tales, sagas, and *Märchen*, in a society transitioning towards modernity, stories like these are read as entertainment rather than inducing fear and violence. Blood libels and tales of profanations of hosts, Heine argues, should be taken seriously, because *they are tales that kill*. While readers of Grimms' fairy tales laugh and forget the tales of witches, werewolves, and Jews, elsewhere, in the Orient, those old lies continue to maim.[17]

Indeed, the Grimms' own body of research and the comparisons with Chinese, French, and other folktales indicate, despite their own worries, an "original contamination," meaning that "the wells of any particular folkloric tradition are always already contaminated by other wandering traditions."[18] This original contamination can be seen even within the work of the Grimm Brothers, as scholars have pointed out that "many of the tales that the Grimms collected were French in origin" because many of the tellers were, though living in German lands, of Huguenot extraction.[19] Still, the Grimms were influenced by the then relatively recent theory of an Indo-Germanic family of language developed by the philologists Franz Bopp in 1816 and Rasmus Rask in 1818. They expanded these theories to folk tales, arguing that the "Indo-Germanic inheritance paradigm accounts for the connections not only between German folktales" but with Scandinavians, the English, Welsh, Slavs and "oriental peoples." The adoption of this theory widens the Grimms' very tightly German frame of traditioning, while they continue to resist allowing for a full acknowledgement that stories migrate and are shared between cultures.[20]

Mission to Jews and Mission in the Colonies

In early modern Germany, Pietist missionaries "who were becoming ever more focused on Jewish conversion" were a greater challenge for "the rabbis

---

[15] On the First Crusade, see Daniel Josyln-Siemiatkoski, *Christian Memories of The Maccabean Martyrs* (New York: Palgrave Macmillan, 2009), 126.

[16] Schreiber, "Tainted Sources," 30.

[17] Ibid., 31.

[18] Ibid., 40.

[19] Ibid., 38.

[20] Ibid., 39.

across Germany" than the waning differentiation between Germans Jews and Christians in terms of dress and talk.[21] Some of these missionaries particularly targeted vagabond Jewish peddlers.

> For them, peddler Jews represented "a unique combination of all those forms of marginality" which they desired to "redeem and integrate." [. . .] Across the German lands we find growing numbers of illegal Jews "on the road," without residence rights in any one town.[22]

This focus on Jews marginalized within their own communities is a key feature of conversion activity.

> Throughout the medieval centuries it had typically been the most desperate Jews, who were facing excommunication by the rabbis, who chose to convert. Accused criminals, for instance, often chose conversion. But now those Jews tempted by life's fate to become Christians could receive considerable practical aid from the missionaries. [. . .] Conversion was therefore the rare chance to make a dramatic change in one's life circumstances.[23]

For a Jew to become a professor and teach at a university, baptism would be required,[24] even after the Edict of 1812 which brought about a "special time for a handful of lucky Jews in Berlin, who had found a way to combine Jewish renewal and avid participation in high culture."[25] The poet and author Heinrich Heine took the baptismal name Christian Johann, and remarked about the reason for his baptism that it was the "entrance ticket to European culture."[26]

> Because of their high-culture accomplishments, converts such as the Rahel Levin Varnhagen, Eduard Gans, Heinrich Heine, and Felix Mendelssohn were watched from near and far with a huge range of feelings, from admiration to jealousy to critique. Sometimes those facing similar predicaments found ways to support each other. But Heine's poem about Gans shows clearly, parallel predicaments did not always lead to solidarity.[27]

In *Enlightenment in the Colony: The Jewish Question and the Crisis of Postcolonial Culture*, Aamir Mufti probes the links between Ashkenazi Jewish and European

---

[21] Deborah Hertz, *How Jews Became Germans: The History of Conversion and Assimilation in Berlin* (New Haven: Yale University Press, 2007), 30–1.
[22] Ibid., 31.
[23] Ibid., 31–2.
[24] Ibid., 198.
[25] Ibid., 179.
[26] Ibid., 199.
[27] Ibid., 201.

Christian identities. He suggests that the negotiation of religiocultural identity, nation, state, and citizenship that occurred between these two populations informed the colonial relations of empires—and traces the particular in the way in which British negotiations of Jewish identity and citizenship have informed British governance in India.[28]

Retracing the *Limes*

In such a cosmos lines must be clearly drawn. Civic officials may physically set up and maintain boundary stones with inscriptions proclaiming, "I am the border." Cartographers may draw maps which show the boundaries of the world polis, with border people (Scyths, Indians, Celts, and Ethiopians) who are not like us, their strangeness expressed in either their idealization as "noble savages" or their denigration as monsters.[29]

Conversion and mission have ancient history along the liminal regions of Roman imperial presence. The River Rhine functioned as part of the Roman *Limes*; alongside it Roman cities were erected and migrant populations from around the Roman Empire settled there. The post-Roman Rineland became the heartland of Ashkenazi Jews, place of diaspora and tenuous home.

Modern German obsessions with establishing Germanic origins, national identity, and boundaries were supplemented by a passionate literary relationship to Tacitus' *Germania* and its ambivalent discourse of the Germans as indigenous noble savages, as the "better Romans" of the time.[30]

> For though Tacitus makes them ferocious primitives, he also invests them with natural nobility through their instinctive indifference to the vices that corrupted Rome: luxury, secrecy, sensuality, slavery. They were, in strong contrast to the Romans, bereft of wine and letters, a "people without craft or cunning."[31]

In tropes now familiar as the rhetoric of the "noble savage," Tacitus uses the Latin term *indigenus* to describe people who are from a particular region, where they have been for many generations and who do not intermarry with other ethnic groups. In fact, Tacitus' unproven and unprovable conjecture at the lack of intermarriage among the *Germanii* with other tribal or ethnic identities, "a race unmixed by intermarriage with other races, a peculiar people

---

[28] Aamir Mufti, *Enlightenment in the Colony: The Jewish Question and the Crisis of Postcolonial Culture* (Princeton, NJ: Princeton University Press, 2007).

[29] Jonathan Z. Smith, *Map is Not Territory: Studies in the History of Religions* (Chicago, IL: University of Chicago, 1978), 136–7.

[30] For an exploration of the Nazi obsession with finding the manuscript of Tacitus' Germania in the last days of the war, see Simon Schama, *Landscape and Memory* (New York: Alfred E. Knopf, 1995), 76 ff.

[31] Schama, *Landscape and Memory*, 77.

and pure, like no-one but themselves,"[32] was later seized upon by Nazi ideologues desperate to find traces to claim a pure ethnic identity.

There is a dearth of information about pre-Christian Germanic religions and attempts to deduce them from Icelandic Nordic myths ignore the fact that those represent a far later and geographically distant version, committed to writing in an already Christian nation.[33] The modern notion of indigenous is related, but distinguished from the Roman expansion around the Mediterranean and into Northern Europe by expansive settlement and migration patterns of Europeans to colonized locations, something which has remained somewhat more limited during antiquity.

In both antique and modern colonial cultural hegemony, colonial language, trade, and materiality impacted and shaped the interaction between the societies. While cultures were hardly strictly separate in pre-modern times, imperial intrusions, if they included strong cultural programs for the imposition of colonial culture, resulted in cultural loss of language, as well as the clash and mutual interpretation of narratives and technologies. Most modern European languages have been transformed by Latin and Greek in some way, and Graeco-Roman ideas have permeated into religiocultural systems that are now considered part of resident ethnic and cultural identities themselves. Yet, what we know about ancient Angles and Saxons and pre-Christian Germanic peoples and their experiences of colonization is notoriously vague, and consists, for the most part, of bits and pieces, scraps, and genealogies. Tacitus remains one of the few reports, and is of questionable reliance. His *Germania* has incited a proliferation of searches for origins rather than an ability to rest with the traces of a largely mute past: multiethnic groups of people with both large continuities and discontinuities with their neighbors mixed multiply throughout the ages of migration.[34]

Indigeneity and Identity

In a sense then, religion must relate to the land, and it must dominate and structure culture. It must not be separated from a particular piece of land and a particular community, and it must not be determined by culture.[35]

---

[32] Ibid., 82.

[33] John Lindow, *Norse Mythology: A Guide to the Gods, Heroes, Rituals and Beliefs* (Oxford: Oxford University Press, 2001), 10, 17, 23.

[34] Patrick Geary's excellent examination of Central European tribal cultures gives evidence of the hybrid histories and intermingling of these peoples and their migrations, as well as the futility of delineating them by names and designations, tribal, national, or racial designations in a misled search for essential national or racial identities in more recent times. See Patrick J. Geary, *The Myth of Nations: The Medieval Origins of Europe* (Princeton, NJ: Princeton University Press, 2002).

[35] Vine Jr. Deloria, *God is Red: A Native View of Religion* (Golden, CO: Fulcrum, 1994), 202.

There is a dangerous consequence of attaching identity to territory: When a people imagines itself as the people of a given land, the obvious threat to its identity is loss of that land.[36]

What are the relations between land, culture, religion, identity, and indigeneity? What does inhabiting land, losing land, exploring and settling land, migrating to and from land mean for how people engage and change local and adopted traditions? How do spatiotemporal identity formation, sedentariness and migration, interacting at the boundaries of religiocultural and political economic practices and identity formation inform and transform? The polydox environment of worlds both ancient and contemporary continues to challenge identity formations that have blended and will continue to blend various pieces of self-fashioning and identity.

Traveling missionaries, whether moving with colonial forces or without them, engage with indigenous peoples whose identities and religiocultural systems are strongly connected to the land, and who are exposed to narratives that have grown in other indigenous soils, or have adapted their existential narratives to locations they have migrated to. Navajo and Maori both exemplify indigenous peoples whose narratives of place remember quite consciously a migration or canoe voyage that brought them to their present sacred geography. The creation story of the Bible refers to certain geographic locations and imagines, for example, the ability to walk naked in a garden, something which is only possible in certain regions of the globe. For many Christian peoples, Christians for centuries, local sacred geographies have been overwritten by a narrative that has been adopted, decontextualized and recontextualized. Here, the narrative migrated, as much as the people.

Laurel Schneider writes of God (or, alternatively, the divine, sacred) as a "subaltern" who "cannot speak, so to speak" its reality "wholly inacessible to the master tongues,"[37] but for whom an army of translators, hermeneuts, prophets, and spin doctors offer to speak, rendering widely different accounts. Incarnate cogitation renders sacredness, geography, and divinity in ways that speak, articulate, and ritualize, negotiating multiple forms of cultural belonging. Missionary encounters constitute one site of heightened intercultural exchange, cultural conflict, often involving the real possibility of irrevocable loss to cultural identity, as well as creative adaptation. This difficult economy of exchange can be found not only in the modern period, but also in times of ancient missionary action. There are significant differences between these periods, not the least in terms of the technological aspects of transformation, forms

---

[36] Regina Schwartz, *The Curse of Cain: The Violent Legacy of Monotheism* (Chicago, IL: The University of Chicago Press, 1997), 44.
[37] Laurel C. Schneider, *Beyond Monotheism: A Theology of Multiplicity* (London: Routledge, 2008), 129.

of power, and the context in which missionary action occurred. In ancient and medieval times, generally pioneering Christian missionaries were not followed by colonial settlement patterns. That does not mean there were not substantial pressures and incentives to enter the church or to become a Christian nation, assuming the mantle of the heritage of imperial Rome, which had become internalized and functioned, among others, to associate one's own polity with a powerful past and its cultured succession. Many polities in Eurasia were deeply informed with the cultural and religious impact of Rome, of *Romanitas*. Former "barbarians" competed about who could best emulate Rome or Troy in terms of polity, legal system, religious authority, and military prowess. The colonized refashioned themselves into the faded image of the glory of the colonizer, whose identity had become part of their own identity. Cultural mimesis infuses traditions that pass on practices, including reading and relational practices across generations and spatial extension. The cosmos that exists at these intersections bounds psychospiritual energies, incarnates them in versions of similarity and difference, encoding the genetic code of bodies, practices, traditions, while mutating in space and time.

Colonial Conversions among Angles, Saxons, and Germans

Who the ancient people called "Germans" were has been a notoriously vexed issue. The different designations given to "Germanic peoples" by their neighbors —Frisians, Germani, Saxons, Angles, Franks— remind us that this region has been and is profoundly multiethnic: "Deutsche," "Teutonen," "Tyskere," "Allemands," "Tedesci," "Germans."

Anglo-Saxons, being some of the seafaring folk adjacent to the Channel in the North Sea for whom the Sea was a highway of connection rather than a divide, settled further along both of its coasts and gave their names to the southern parts of Britain (East Saxons of Essex, South Saxons of Sussex, and the West Saxons of Wessex) and in the areas around Boulogne, Bayeux, and the mouth of the Loire.[38] A pocket of rural Christians had built a church near Canterbury during Roman times. When the Anglo-Saxon Ethelbert of Kent wed his Frankish wife Bertha, who came with her own bishop, he put this church at their disposal. In some ways, the pattern of Ethelbert's conversion fits with that of Clovis:

A Germanic king, ruling a sub-Roman kingdom in which a little Christianity survives, enjoying close relations with Christian neighbors, married to a Christian wife, becomes a Christian.[39]

---

[38] Ibid., 109.
[39] Ibid., 111.

As early as 595, Pope Gregory the Great intended to send a mission to convert Anglo-Saxons, the only successor state to the Roman Empire whose ruling elite had not yet converted to Christianity.[40] In the wake of Ethelbert's conversion, Canterbury rose to prominence as a Christian, royal city, and today remains the seat of the Archbishop of Canterbury, the spiritual head of the Church of England, and the so-called Anglican Communion, the extension of the Church of England through the means of modern colonial missions. Thus, post-imperial churches grew as Roman military influence wanes. Rome's religiocultural influence remained powerful and helped form a sense of identity at least for the ruling classes and literate elite of former Roman territories. However, what the content of the "gospel" was for these elite men is less clear. Certainly their own status and claim to power was a factor in their conversion. Their honor, fame, and power would have increased through conversion. This represents an early form of what is today called "prosperity theology," as effective then as today, showing that conversion was generally infused and motivated multiply, a consideration for all aspects of life. Thus, we read such statements as these: As soon as "the orthodox faith had enlightened their darkened minds . . . God willing, the power of the Goths now thrives."[41] Indeed, conversion could inaugurate "royal actions which marked entry into the orbit of *Romanitas*."[42] The cooperation of the local aristocracy was necessary to create a widespread acceptance of Christianity, as they were "the people who had the local influence necessary to diffuse the faith among their dependants."[43] The missionary pattern then was to engage the local powerful in relationship, so that the noble conversion may trickle down to the subjects. That is, a seemingly reverse movement from the times of early Christianity, where dissemination occurred from many different entry points, but primarily among the colonized, a few key local leaders (Nicodemus) and occupation personnel (various Roman soldiers), seemingly more from the bottom up.

In the fourth and fifth centuries the Germanic invasions into Roman influenced territories let to a collapse of the Roman ecclesial structures and the seat of government was moved from Trier to Arles, further west.[44] In an instance of civilizing mission, important cathedrals and monasteries like Cologne and Trier had to be reestablished and the surrounding areas were rechristianized.[45] At the Synod of Whitby, Anglo-Saxon Christianity became more strongly in line with Rome, changing the date of the celebration of Easter from that proposed by Iona to that held in regions further to the south and in uniformity with Rome.

---

[40] Ibid., 114.
[41] Ibid., 122.
[42] Ibid., 124.
[43] Ibid., 130.
[44] Ibid., 131.
[45] Ibid., 134.

This change marked a certain realignment of loyalty and union with other regions in Europe.[46]

The work of the Anglo-Saxon missionary Wynfrith-Boniface continues in this direction, aiming to transform Iro-Scottish presences west of the Rhine into greater alliance with Rome and *Romanitas*, further blurring the lines between barbarians and Romans.

> From the start, the barbarian peoples across the Rhine and the Danube were never homogeneous language and cultural groups, bound together by ancestry or even by common tradition. Instead, they were every bit as complex as the Roman people itself. As the boundaries between Roman and Barbarian dissolved, what today is called "identity politics" became one way of organizing and motivating followers: New constellations claimed names of "ancient" peoples.[47]

While Roman soldiers from across the empire built the *Limes* to ward off tribes of barbarians, Roman writers like Tacitus imagined "Germanic" tribes as red-haired, handsome, rugged, hardy noble savages. Most likely the "Germanic tribes" Tacitus mentioned were not the Frisians, Angles, or Saxons further to the north and east, but it is those to which Wynfrith felt an ancestral connection, and felt sent to, as they were not Christian. Wynfrith-Boniface was an Anglo-Saxon monk, teacher, missionary, ecclesial intellectual, and bishop who struggled to organize Germanic churches in the Hessian-Saxon borderlands.[48] He is often referred to as the "apostle of the Germans," though this title is somewhat misleading. While he did in some sense function as apostle or missionary, his main work was in the reorganization of the church in an emerging Carolingian Francia rather than in introducing Germanic peoples to Christianity.[49] Hence, much of his work consisted in teaching, fortifying a Roman-centered monastic infrastructure, enforcing Roman ecclesiastical canons, church discipline, synods, annual episcopal visitations, and the general disciplining of laity, clergy, and nobility.

---

[46] Peter Brown describes the importance of this shift and the changes in hairstyles of monastics as marking allegiance, loyalty, and honor, rather than being merely outward marks. In a society of mostly illiterate populations, the calendrical count of Easter would shift a major unifying event by which time and seasons were tracked. Peter Brown, *The Rise of Western Christendom: Triumph and Diversity, A.D. 200–1000. Second Edition* (Malden, MA: Blackwell, 2003), 361.

[47] Geary, *Myth of Nations*, 173.

[48] He was born as Wynfrith in Wessex in 675, spent most of his first 40 years in monasteries there, and the next 36 years as missionary and reformer on the European continent in the Frankish church. He took on the name Boniface later in his life. When he was 74, he and his companions were killed by robbers in 754 in Dokkum, Frisia.

[49] Brown, *Rise*, 420.

What the Romans called *Germania* was located predominantly east of the Rhine, between the Northern Sea and the Danube to the south.[50] Hence, his sphere of influence did not correspond to any of the incarnations of modern Germany, but rather primarily to central Germany and the regions of Hesse, East-, and Westphalia. Other Irish and Anglo-Saxon missionaries worked in adjacent areas on the continent.

The Europe of the time saw the slow decline of the Roman Empire only temporarily delayed by the unifying influence of the Christianization of the empire. The empire had exposed much of Western and Central Europe to Christianization by a slow and partial assimilation that had allowed for a variety of hybrid versions that combined local religious sensitivities with Christian practices. The age of migrations had started with the pushing of a variety of peoples into Western Europe, ceding to the pressures of central Asian steppe people pushing west.[51] Migrating Visigoths and Ostrogoths had become Christian centuries before Boniface's time and had created an indigenized version of vernacular Gothic Christian culture with the help of the Gothic bishop Wulfila (d. 383). Doctrinal and creedal developments had overtaken some of these peoples remote to the centers of imperial power and they were retrospectively declared "Arian" and hence effectively "heretics" or "pagans."[52] The Frankish lineage of the Merovingians had been brought into increasing conformity with the Roman Catholic version after the baptism of Clovis and his army in 508.[53] In Boniface's time, the Frankish rulers like most peoples located within the direct Roman sphere of influence claimed at least nominal allegiance to the Christian God and the terms of Nicene-Chalcedonian orthodoxy. Hence, the Romanization promoted by Boniface had much to do with the extension of Frankish power toward the east.[54]

Prior to the Anglo-Saxon missions, Iro-scottish monasteries had sent numerous missionaries to the continent, and had many points of presence in Alamannia and Bavaria, south of where Boniface migrated to. The age of migrations had sped the decline of the Roman Empire—but not of *Romanitas* as the cultural ideal to aspire to—and sped the splitting of the Christian lands into two distinctly separate regionally dominant cultures, the Western Latin tradition and the eastern Greek Byzantine tradition. Over time, the close ties with the Greek

---

[50] Herwig Wolfram, *The Roman Empire and Its Germanic Peoples* (Berkeley, CA: University of California Press, 1990), 247, 11.

[51] Dates given for the migrations vary quite widely. This is the wave relevant to us here. Other migrations are dated later and at times are considered in some places to have continued into early medieval times.

[52] See Augustine's designation of the invading Arian Visigoths in the *City of God Against the Pagans*.

[53] Brown, *Rise*, 137.

[54] Lutz E. von Padberg, *Bonifatius: Missionar und Reformer* (München: C. H. Beck Wissen, 2003), 35.

East had been lost, due to increasing theological differences and rivalries but also due to the beginning invasions of Arabic peoples which diverted much of the attention and energy of Byzantium. The invasions of Arab armies into Southern Europe and northern Africa led to the fall of Visigothic Spain to the Umayyad dynasty in 711. By 718 most of the Iberian peninsula was under Muslim rule and in 733 Charles Martel ("the Hammer") stopped a Muslim raiding party on its way to loot Tours. Subsequently, he gave new meaning to the expression "terror of the Franks" as he embarked on a series of invasions into areas around and south of Tours and Poitiers and with much violence imposed his hegemony over local people.[55] Under Charles Martel and his successors the Frankish warlords of his fledgling dynasty began to command increasing power beyond their traditional tribal lands. They were the rising regional power to reckon with. Since the emerging Carolingian dynasty lacked dynastic legitimation once they finished off the shadow reign of the Merovingians, they offered themselves as supporters to the papacy in return for its willingness to recognize their claim to rule and for endowing it with sacral qualities. This bond led to a realignment of the papacy towards the West, and towards the rising imperial powers to its north.[56] Boniface was a crucial broker in solidifying and extending this bond as the papacy found itself in need of powerful military supporters to shield it from the threat of invading peoples such as Lombards and Muslims.[57] This tie was sealed in 751 through the crowning of Pippin the Younger (III) as the first "king" of the Franks with the consent of Pope Zachary.[58] Consequently, Boniface sought papal recommendation letters that would secure the protection and support of the Frankish kings for his plans to convert the "savage" Saxons. The military expansionism of the Franks led to the establishment of Charlemagne's (747–814) Frankish kingdom only a few years after Boniface's death and inaugurated a long-lasting, if vigorously embattled, Frankish-Germanic Christian monarchical rule that was expanded throughout the following centuries. Charlemagne's eventual crowning as "imperator augustus" and protector of the Western church by Pope Leo II paved the way to a "Holy Roman Empire" (later with the addition "of the German nation") that lasted for many centuries in its various incarnations. It is this second *Reich* that Hitler aimed to tragically and perversely recreate in the third *Reich*.

---

[55] Brown, *Rise*, 408.
[56] Lutz E. von Padberg, *Christianisierung Im Mittelalter* (Darmstadt: Wissenschaftliche Buchgesellschaft, 2006), 67.
[57] Brown, *Rise*, 429.
[58] Assumptions vary as to whether Boniface or a local, Frankish bishop crowned Pippin. Padberg argues for a Frankish bishop loyal to the king and makes the case that the aging Boniface had become frustrated and withdrew from the Carolingians after Pippin had put the ecclesial reforms he had pushed on the back burner. Lutz E. von Padberg, *Christianisierung*, 68–69. Pippin is the first "king" of the Franks, previous rulers in his line had the title of *maior domus*, the mayor of the palace.Theodor Schiefer, *Winfrid-Bonifatius und die Christliche Grundlegung Europas* (Freiburg: Herder, 1954), 258.

Genealogy and Mission: Mission as Connection to Ethnic Roots

This agglomeration which was called and which still calls itself the Holy Roman Empire was neither holy, nor Roman, nor an empire.[59]

When Anglo-Saxon missionaries crossed the North Sea toward the European mainland they were motivated by an Irish ascetic ethos of spiritual pilgrimage. They felt a call to return to the places where their ancestors came from and to share their Christian religion with those now living there. Monastics often functioned as cultural brokers traveling and settling abroad. The people of temperate Europe both gained and lost cultural expressions during these transformations. They lost so much that the closest written record of their religiocultural worldviews was preserved by Icelandic sources that were not written down until Iceland's population converted, at least on the surface, to Christianity. Various attitudes toward these cultural transformations, these losses and gains can be observed: While the consciousness of what may have been lost, or even that something has been lost may not strike most Central Europeans as something of concern, others feel a loss and are trying to retrieve Germanic cultural elements, often under the label of "Neopagan," an identity that is virtually irretrievable and impossibly made up of fragments of ancient European and Scandinavian lore. These attempts at retrieval raise questions about the possibility of a return to "origins" and the problem of what constitutes "authenticity." The transformative effect of some Christian principles, if effectively applied, can be profound, just as others can become very oppressive. Each situation requires critical evaluation, including an assessment of what the interests of interpreters of these encounters might have been. They range from the extremes of triumphalist attempts to justify the "greater good" of mission, to hypercritical anti-colonialist and dismissals of missionary endeavors, along the continuum of materialist accounts for exchanges without attention to the theological content and critical theological appraisals of missionary efforts. Though the sources are generally limited, especially when attempting to find records of the perspectives of local peoples on missionary encounters, it would be difficult to suggest there is only one effect that missionary encounters had and that they were monolithic. Rather, dissemination eludes any attempts at control, and theories postulating a simple hegemonic regime that guides and informs all actions of the colonized like a jealous, omnipotent deity often succumb to fatalistic determinisms. When one considers the complex interactions between colonial churches, indigenous churches, and syncretic prophetic movements, which appear, for example, both in South

---

[59] Voltaire, *The General History and State of Europe* (1756), chapter 70.

African and New Zealand contexts as a response to the restrictive hierarchies and theologies of colonial churches, the picture resembles less hegemony but rather evokes descriptions of chaos and complexity theories.[60]

Centuries after the arrival of Irish and Anglo-Saxon missionaries, the descendants of converted Germanic peoples faced the return of their own repressed pagan past as they encountered indigenous peoples in other continents. Often, the "internal others"—Jews, heretics, and women—were conquered and subjected along with the colonial "external other." Internalized ethnocentrism within the colonized, deployed against them centuries earlier in missionary theologies and ideologies, became something they seemed programmed to inflict on other indigenous peoples. Certain groups of people, such as the Irish, Scots, Welsh, and in many cases Jews, were induced toward assimilation into a succession of empires or nation states at home and ironically became the operators of civilizing mission abroad. The return of the repressed indigenous person found voice in the numerous postcolonial discourses that manifest a recognition of complexity at the heart of each culture, including those previously thought to be superior and reflecting universal values. The present analysis attempts to move beyond the separation of self and other, assuming that there is a repressed part of the self that is being rejected.[61]

The blending of religiocultural traditions makes it a tender and complex task to distinguish and impossible to surgically separate religious symbol-systems with long histories of cohabitation and encounter, hostile or friendly. Syncretism happens, but it also raises concerns in many quarters, and at the very least begs the question of where and how to make useful distinctions.

The production of hagiographies has to do with recreating a sacred geography, of naming a powerful presence, and locating it permanently. They inscribe a location with numinous presence bringing power and economic leverage to a community that can regulate access to such sites. Sites of contested political and religious power sought to associate themselves with the spiritual power of saints and relics.[62] Samaritan worship on the mountain of Garizim claims sacred power for a social group in the north rather than going south for worship in Jerusalem. Religious practices express sociocultural formations of populations exiled under empire. The importation of sacred power into a site

---

[60] Peggy Brock, "Introduction," in *Indigenous Peoples and Religious Change*, Peggy Brock, ed. (Leiden: Brill, 2005), 2.

[61] This would be not unlike Frantz Fanon's creative reappropriation of C. G. Jung: "In the degree to which I find in myself something unheard-of, something reprehensible, only one solution remains for me: to get rid of it, to ascribe its origin to someone else." Frantz Fanon, *Black Skin, White Masks* (New York: Grove Press, 1967), 190.

[60] See, for example, the struggle around the final resting place of St. Boniface's bones, or the claims that Trier had a piece of the Holy Garment of Christ, while Cologne had the bones of the Three Kings and Edinburgh a piece of the cross at Holyrood Palace. For an exploration of the significance, trade, and theft of relics, see Patrick J. Geary, *Furta Sacra: Thefts of Relics in the Central Middle Ages* (Princeton, NJ: Princeton University Press, 1978).

via relics both overwrites and recreates a genealogy of sacred ancestry, both genetic and spiritual.

Daniel of Winchester's letter to Boniface outlines a dangerous missionary economy: the assumption and promise of a prosperity theology that is still with us and wreaking havoc, especially in a climate of hypercapitalism and enduring poverty in Africa and Latin America.[63] Some evangelists and preachers still try to win converts by promising a better life. This age-old argument of rivaling religions persists, despite traditions, equally time-tried, that warn of linking the favor of the Divine with wellbeing: The book of Job and the Psalms speak about the suffering of the righteous, the gospels about the reality of Christ's suffering and death.

Wynfrith-Boniface's Ambivalent Position in the Frankish World

Boniface, having sought and received both a blessing and letters from the Apostolic See, was sent by the blessed pope to make a report on the savage peoples of Germany. The purpose of this was to discover whether their untutored hearts and minds were ready to receive the seed of the divine word.[64]

The written sources on Boniface's life and mission are limited. The main source about the dates and events of his life is the biography written by the monk Willibald a few years after his death. At the behest of Lullus and Megingoz, his former proteges and now successors as bishops in Mainz and Würzburg, Willibald committed to writing the life and events so that later generations may be "instructed by Boniface's model and led to better things by his perfection."[65] Also preserved is a collection of his correspondence with abbesses, bishops, Frankish rulers, monks, nuns, and popes.[66] Both sources are laced with numerous conventions of time, place, and genre. His hagiography repeats previous models of sanctity, and embellishes when portraying him as

---

[63] For Daniel's letter to Boniface, see J. N. Hillgarth, ed., *Christianity and Paganism, 350–750* (Philadelphia, PA: University of Pennsylvania Press, 1969), 172–4. Anglican priest and ideologue of colonial expansion into the Virginia colonies, Richard Haklyut, and others use the image of their ancestors, the Picts, to argue that being christianized and civilized improves the lot of natives. Peter C. Mancall, *Haklyut's Promise: An Elizabethan Obsession for an English America* (New Haven, CT: Yale University Press, 2007), 206–7.

[64] Thomas F.X. and Thomas Head Noble, eds, "The Life of Saint Boniface," in *Soldiers of Christ: Saints and Saints' Lives from Late Antiquity and the Early Middle Ages*, Soldiers of Christ (University Park, PA.: Pennsylvania University Press, 1995), 121.

[65] Noble, "Life of Saint Boniface," 110.

[66] For an English edition of his letters see Saint Boniface, *The Letters of Saint Boniface*, Introduction by Thomas F.X. Noble, trans. Ephraim Emerton (New York: Columbia University Press, 2000).

"having brought light and order to a wild country." This grandiose contrast was far from reality, as "what he found, instead, was much Christianity, and almost all of it the wrong sort."[67]

Wynfrith grew up in monasteries and made a name for himself as a talented grammarian and teacher, knowledgeable in matters of scripture and doctrine. He gained some popularity among the ecclesiastical elite there, including a number of nuns and abbesses who formed part of his spiritual and material support system during his time abroad. To flee his increasing popularity, he crossed the Channel in 718 and attempted to convert the Frisians of the northern coastal plains. The Christian Anglo-Saxons of his time thought of the continental Saxons as their relatives, close enough to feel sent to bring them the faith.[68] After a year of laboring without social standing and support, Wynfrith gave up and returned to Britain. From there he departed to Rome in order to beg the current pope for support and recommendation letters to the representatives of the rising power of the region, the Frankish rulers.

During his first visit to Rome, Pope Gregory II asked him merely to "make a report on the savage peoples of Germany."[69] While Christian missionaries were ready to go to the "savage peoples" at the boundaries of Frankish rule, they did not entertain thoughts about moving to Arab-Islamic religions. The same was true of Muslim missionaries. Despite the tempestuous expansion of both religions in the early Middle Ages, they did generally not compete on the same territory. Rather these religious worlds remained largely separate.[70]

After challenges to his mission in Frisian and Saxon territories proved insurmountable at this point in time, his main goal became to uproot the various kinds of symbioses between indigenous and Christian beliefs and practices he found in places where Christianity had been present for some time. Pope Gregory II, who was little aware of the regions north of the Alps, took note of these circumstances as he endowed the new Bishop with a new name and a mission:

> Hearing, to our great distress, that certain peoples in Germany on the eastern side of the Rhine are wandering in the shadow of death at the instigation of the ancient enemy and, as it were, under the form of the Christian faith, are still in slavery to the worship of idols, while others who have not as yet any knowledge of God and have not been cleansed by the water of holy baptism but as pagans, to be likened unto the brutes, do not acknowledge their Creator, we have determined to send the bearer of these presents, our

---

[67] Brown, *Rise*, 420.
[68] The terms Wessex, Sussex, and Essex refer to Westsaxon, Southsaxon, and Eastsaxon regions in Britain.
[69] Noble, "Life of Saint Boniface," 121.
[70] Lutz E. von Padberg, *Christianisierung*, 66.

brother the reverend Bishop Boniface, into that county, for the enlightenment of both classes, to preach the word of the true faith [. . .] If perchance
he shall find there some who have wandered away from the true faith or
have fallen into error by the cunning persuasion of the devil, he is to correct
them and bring them back into the haven of safety, teach them the doctrine
of this Apostolic See and establish them firmly in that same catholic faith.[71]

Hence, Boniface set about to remedy the undereducation of clergy and the
decline of the catechumenate for laity, and disciplined several bishops and
clergy that had overstepped their bounds of authority. Others he denounced
as heretics and apostates to the papacy. His stridency, obsessive adherence to
canon law, and willingness to publicly criticize anybody, including popes, who
would not adhere to Christian law and values as he understood them, assured
that he was a controversial figure. While some of his critiques may seem justified and even courageous as they challenged the status quo, many saw him as
an interloper who habitually interfered with local authorities. Many Frankish
and Bavarian bishops resented his tendency to run interference with the pope
and overriding others' areas of power, at worst.[72] It seems, however, that he
chose to refrain from interference in some other regions, such as that of the
Iro-scottish monk Pirmin in Alamannia, presumably out of respect for his
work.[73]

Boniface had grown up in a British monastery influenced by the venerable
iro-scottish tradition of the *peregrinatio* that motivated many of the Anglo-
Saxon and Irish intellectual elite to travel abroad to found new monasteries
and spread Christian life practices. The particular shape of Christian practices Boniface knew were those of an Anglo-Saxon Christianity that had kept
close ties with Rome since Gregory the Great (540–604) had sent the monk
Augustine (d. 605) to become the first Archbishop of Canterbury. The resulting cultural clash between local iro-scottish indigenized Christianities and the
exported local Roman traditions had been shifted toward Roman liturgical
and canonical traditions through a synodal decision at Whitby (644) and the
solidifying influence of the archbishopric of Theodore of Tarsus (668–690) at
Canterbury. The bond to Roman tradition and influence was dominant and
travels to Rome were becoming more frequent.[74] Subsequently, Roman liturgical and canonical traditions came to dominate, though some Irish elements

---

[71] Letter IX. Boniface, *Letters*, 20.
[72] Nikola Proksch, "The Anglo-Saxon Missionaries to the Continent," in *Monks of England: The Benedictines in England from Augustine to the Present Day*, ed. Daniel Rees (London: SPCK, 1997), 47.
[73] Gert Haendler, "Bonifatius," in *Mittelalter (Gestalten der Kirchengeschichte)*, ed. Martin Greschat (Stuttgart, Germany: Kohlhammer, 1983), 78.
[74] Compare Nicholas Howe, "Rome: Capital of Anglo-Saxon England," *Journal of Medieval and Early Modern Studies* Vol. 34, No. 1 (Winter 2004): 147–72.

endured. It is during one of these travels that he was consecrated bishop
by Pope Gregory II and renamed Boniface.[75] His oath of loyalty tied Bishop
Boniface closely to Rome, with an oath that omitted the oath of allegiance to
the Eastern emperor.[76]

Like any monastic, missionary, or church official of the time, Boniface
needed to secure the favor of the powers that be in the region he intended
to work in. Those powers were less and less those of the Roman Empire, but
rising regional powers. The Franks had strong ties to Rome that preceded
Boniface, and hence it is between both of these centers of worldly and sacral
power that he had to map out his role and function.[77] For the next decades
he worked under the protection of Charles Martel, Pippin, and Carloman.
Consequently, his work among Saxons and Frisians was quite limited, as they
were resisting these Frankish rulers' expansionism and considered the fact
that Boniface received their protection and support as an impediment to their
adoption of the Christian faith. It is perhaps also because of this ambiguous
alliance with Frankish power that we hear virtually nothing from Boniface
about the atrocities they committed in war or their treatment of the populace. On the contrary, Frankish expansion was expected to lay open "heathen"
lands (the lands of the heath dwellers) to Christian mission and hence was
both in Boniface's and in the papacy's interests. Difficult negotiations with the
Frankish rulers and the needs of the local churches were a constant factor in
Boniface's long presence in Francia, especially since the Franks focused their
Christian adherence on cultic reverence and tribal loyalty to a powerful deity,
rather than on ethical behaviors emphasized by church officials at the time,
such as monogamy, for example.[78] When it comes to the sphere of church canons, correct doctrine and marital ethics, however, Boniface showed no incli-
nation to hold back in his duty as disciplinarian empowered not least by his
ordination to the episcopal office by Pope Gregory II himself during his journey to Rome in 722. Boniface's critique of Frankish rulers' behavior, it seems,
was mostly limited to a critique of adultery and other personal habits, rather
than their treatment of subjugated peoples or slaves. In the texts and sources
that remain today, the subaltern, whether "pagan" or subaltern of any other
sort, cannot speak. The borderlines between Christian Francia and the tribal
religions of the Saxons also demarcated the boundary between civilization
and savagery in some of Boniface's rhetoric, even though his letters and hagiography show that a hybridized Christianity remained intermingled with local
religious loyalties to sacred springs and trees both in Boniface's native lands

---

[75] Noble, "Life of Saint Boniface," 126.
[76] John Seville Higgins, "The Ultramontanism of Saint Boniface," *Church History* Vol. 2,
      No. 4 (December 1933): 203.
[77] John Michael Wallace-Hadrill, "A Background to Boniface's Mission," in *England Before
      the Conquest*, England (Cambridge: Cambridge University Press, 1971), 38.
[78] Schiefer, *Winfrid-Bonifatius*, 57.

and in Franco-Germanic regions for centuries to come. Yet, for Boniface, a recognizably Christian life and worship had in some places, as in Thuringia, been repressed by negligence and oppressive rulers. When Boniface arrived there

> he addressed the elders and the chiefs of the people, calling on them to put aside their blind ignorance and to return to the Christian religion that they had formerly embraced. [. . .] Thus, when the power of the leaders, who had protected religion, was destroyed, the devotion of the people to Christianity and religion died out also, and false brethren were brought in to pervert the minds of the people and to introduce among them under the guise of religion dangerous heretical sects.[79]

This powerful statement about the connection between a ruler's patronage of Christianity and its proper shape and strength illustrates well the concerns of Boniface. In the wake of the declining Roman Empire, power had increasingly returned to more local entities. Many of the semi-romanized societies throughout Europe at the time showed increasing community formation around charismatic individuals enforced by strong bonds of honor and shame. Some of the culturally specific Germanic customs included a "sacral kingship" that required as its highest value an unquestioned loyalty to the military leader of the community.[80] Loyalty to a male charismatic leader in war often transitioned toward a permanent rule over increasing facets of life, attempts to establish a dynastic rule, and attempts to emulate the greatness of the Roman Empire through the local adaptation of romanesque customs and laws. These military leaders united several offices in them, including some forms of religious leadership. Their conversion had been a main objective of missionaries.[81] Since these were men who knew best how to respect a coercive power that was greater than theirs, and, what is more, could potentially crush theirs, missionary rhetoric focused on demonstrating the superior power of the Christian God. Hence, much of the missionary tactics presented a version of "muscular Christianity," emphasizing a strong, male God and targeting an audience of military rulers who needed to be convinced that shifting allegiances both politically and spiritually would enhance their power, welfare, and influence. The problem can become replicated in other inculturated christologies, where Christ becomes

---

[79] Noble, "Life of Saint Boniface," 127.

[80] Later missionaries and teachers attempted to harness this mindset and produced texts like *The Heliand*, and the *Dream of the Rood*, which depicted Christ as a tribal leader and the disciples as a loyal group of brothers in arms. Others tried to remake feuding warriors into Christian knights, with highly problematic outcomes, such as the crusades.

[81] Proksch writes: "A common feature of the mission to the Germanic peoples—whether in Merovingian Gaul, Anglo-Saxon England, or in northern Germany—was the initial acceptance of Christianity by leading figures of high social standing. Often their entire clan-group would follow them in the new allegiance." Proksch, "Anglo-Saxon Missionaries," 49.

likened to the African chief or priest. Similar problems obtain with this meta-phor as with the Christ the king metaphor.[82] What is understood as conver-sion of the heart in the history of missions occurs in a tangled symbiosis with conversions on the plane of the representational economy of power, influence, and status.

Boniface, as obsessive in seeking advice from ecclesial mentors and power holders as in attempting to discipline each expression of Christianity he encountered, did eventually adopt a missionary strategy of gradualism as pro-posed by Gregory the Great in his letter to the Abbot Mellitus. The pope had recommended

> [. . .]that the temples of idols in that nation should not be destroyed, but that the idols themselves that are in them should be. Let blessed water be prepared, and sprinkled in these temples, and altars constructed, and rel-ics deposited, since, if these same temples are well built, it is needful that they should be transferred from the worship of idols to the service of the true God; that, when the people themselves see that these temples are not destroyed, they may put away error from their heart, and knowing and ador-ing the true God, may have recourse with the more familiarity to the places they have been accustomed to. [. . .] For it is undoubtedly impossible to cut away everything at once from hard hearts, since one who strives to ascend to the highest place must needs rise by steps or paces, and not by leaps.[83]

What we read here manifests a marked shift in the mental horizons of the Church. Boniface is a representative of what took place during his time: Christianization was less and less perceived as a clash between supernatural powers as the victory of Christianity over the gods was taken for granted.[84] Peter Brown asserts that the "real task of the Church" was a *mission civilatrice* where "education was as important as miracles."[85] The letter Boniface received from his episcopal mentor Daniel of Winchester thus encourages him to employ the following missionary apologetic:

> [I]f the gods are all-powerful, beneficent, and just, they not only reward their worshipers but punish those who reject them. If, then, they do this

---

82 Some may argue that there is a difference in the authority of a chief, which exists only by consensus from the people. That may be in the ideal, but the same could be said about a warrior king or a king or emperor, who cannot rule with loyal subjects and needs their cooperation to exercise any power.

83 Gregory the Great, Epistle LXXVI. To Mellitus, Abbot. NPNF 213. Hillgarth, *Christianity and Paganism, 350–750*, 152–3.

84 See, for example, Virginia Burrus' rendering of the hagiography of St. Martin of Tours. Virginia Burrus, *The Sex Lives of the Saints* (Philadelphia, PA: University of Pennsylvania Press, 2003), 100.

85 Brown, *Rise*, 427.

in temporal matters, how is it that they spare us Christians who are turning almost the whole earth away from their worship and overthrowing their idols? And while the [Christians] possess lands rich in wine and abounding in other resources, they have left to the [pagans] lands stiff with cold where their gods, driven out of the world, are falsely supposed to rule. They are also frequently to be reminded of the supremacy of the Christian world, in comparison with which they themselves, very few in number, are still involved in their ancient errors.[86]

The "civilizing mission" loomed large in the modern history of Western Christianity and its reach around the globe. The most remembered and depicted event in Boniface's life was his well-orchestrated felling of an ancient sacred oak tree at an intertribal sanctuary on the border between the nominally Christian Hesse and pagan Frisians. Boniface's publicity stunt in felling the sacred Oak of Geismar exemplifies this "shock and awe" missiology. At the same time, the incident at Geismar is an exception to his generally more realistic stance, likely enforced by encountered reality and necessity. A more regular sight would have been the missionary entering the market places, delivering a standardized sermon in the local language. This occurred with the support of the local power holders and included attempts to reform the local clergy and monasteries.[87]

From what we can tell, the event represents the challenge of Christianity to the local powers of life and strength as experienced by locals especially in old, large trees. The incident was intended to demonstrate the impotence of local deities and spiritual presences in nature and claim omnipotence and universal presence and relevance of the Christian deity. It was located in a liminal space, an intertribal sanctuary at the boundary between the nominally Christian Hesse and the pagan Saxons to the north.[88] Willibald, the writer of his hagiography, indicates that many of the Hessians who had acknowledged the "Catholic faith" continued, secretly or openly, "to offer sacrifices to trees and springs," and engaged in divination, incantations, and "other sacrificial rites; while others, of a more reasonable character" had abandoned these activities. Boniface, "with the counsel and advice of the latter persons" attempted to cut down "a certain oak of extraordinary size called in the old tongue of the pagans the Oak of Jupiter."[89]

Taking his courage in his hands (for a great crowd of pagans stood by watching and bitterly cursing in their hearts the enemy of the gods), he

[86] Letter XV (23) Boniface, *Letters*, 27–8. Ironically, this remark was written at the time when the Iberian Peninsula was only recently lost to Christian rule.

[87] Lutz E. von Padberg, *Christianisierung*, 65.

[88] Brown, *Rise*, 421.

[89] The Germanic deity referred to here may have been Odin or Tyr. Noble, "Life of Saint Boniface," 126.

cut the first notch. But when he had made a superficial cut, suddenly the oak's vast bulk, shaken by a mighty blast of wind from above, crashed to the ground shivering its topmost branches into fragments in its fall. As if by the express will of God (for the brethren present had done nothing to cause it) the oak burst asunder into four parts, each part having a trunk of equal length. At the sight of this extraordinary spectacle the heathens who had been cursing ceased to revile and began, on the contrary, to believe and bless the Lord. Thereupon the holy bishop took counsel with the brethren, built an oratory from the timber of the oak and dedicated it to Saint Peter the Apostle.[90]

Though the hagiographer heightens the dramatic effect by stressing the anger of the "pagans," the Frankish garrison nearby would have been enough of a presence to keep Boniface safe without direct divine intervention.[91] Much could be said about this highly loaded passage, and much of what seems to carry significant spiritual meaning can only be guessed at due to our ignorance about pre-Christian Germanic religions. Simon Schama's reading points to a theological reinscription, a wooden palimpsest, inscribed on material too valuable to destroy:

It is often said that the source of Boniface's determination was his own native landscape of Devon, dotted with obstinate tree cults, not least that of the Celtic yew, which still decorates Devonian churchyards as an emblem of immortality. But it is at least as plausible to offer an opposite interpretation, namely that his familiarity with local animism may have given him a healthy respect for its power. After all, Willibrord's story, ostensibly a conversionary miracle, actually demonstrates the ways by which pagan beliefs could be turned to Christian ends. The "divine blast" that helped Boniface fell the oak is identical with the pagan lightning bolts which in Celtic and Germanic lore mark the tree as the tree of life. [. . .] So Boniface's axe transformed rather than destroyed. The spiritually dead pagans were turned into living believers. The rotten (perhaps hollow) trunk of the idolatrous tree was turned inside out to reveal four perfect, clean timbers, from which a house of the reborn and eternally living Christ could then be constructed.[92]

Schama sees the felling of the oak as a transformation rather than as a destruction, and makes much of the seasonal life cycles of a tree and their similarity to the life of Christ and the ensuing iconography of the verdant cross, symbolizing the death as well as the resurrection of Christ. However, the continuation of

---

[90] Noble, "Life of Saint Boniface," 126–7.
[91] Lutz E. von Padberg, *Christianisierung*, 64.
[92] Schama, *Landscape and Memory*, 217.

place and substance of the wood also irrevocably indicates the merging rather than the outright replacement of a tradition that would continue to contribute its own share of meaning and symbolism to the mix. Boniface was unable to avoid the mutual transformation of Christian and pagan practices that had been ongoing in the centuries before his arrival, as well as in his homeland, where many famous monasteries and churches were located on sites of pagan reverence. This repressed history of their own tradition's "symbioses" haunted Boniface and many modern European missionaries that would follow in his ideological footsteps.

Others see this meeting of metal and wood as the prelude to the clear-cutting of Germanic forests that heretofore had been left untouched because of their sacral quality.[93] This episode is also symbolic for the foundations of monasteries Boniface induced throughout his area of influence. At least some of them seem to have been intentionally built in sacred groves or clearings and the logged timber made use of to erect the monasteries. Hence, there is more than an exchange of spiritual economies at work here. This event also symbolizes the beginning change from forest foraging economies to expanding agricultural societies. With the *Concilium Germanicum*, in 742, Boniface was able to step up the reform program. Boniface and Carloman rewrote the Frankish Church in the Anglo-Saxon image, reorganizing it as a Rome-oriented episcopal union. Yet, eventually, his reform program was slowed down by the resistance of the locals to the "recovery" of church property and the gradualist policy of the king. Frustrated, Boniface removed himself from this particular context, and headed off to Frisia.[94]

Boniface's relationship to women was, unsurprisingly, ambiguous. In some ways his activities contributed to the further marginalization of women in Europe, as he was intent on enforcing the papal tradition of monastic, and hence celibate, clergy. Yet monastic women were arguably some of the closest friends and supporters of Boniface. The abbess Eadburga sent him important supplies for this work, for which an exhausted Boniface shows himself very grateful:

> To his beloved sister, the abbess Eadburga [. . .] May he who rewards all righteous acts cause my dearest sister to rejoice in the choir of angels above because she has consoled with spiritual light by the gift of sacred books an exile in Germany who has to enlighten the dark corners of the Germanic peoples and would fall into deadly snares if he had not the Word of God as a lamp unto his feet and a light upon his path.[95]

---

[93] Large-scale deforestation, however, does likely not occur until the late Middle Ages and the beginning of the transformation towards capitalism and industrialism.
[94] Lutz E. von Padberg, *Christianisierung*, 67–8.
[95] Letter XXII. Boniface, *Letters*, 38–39.

Furthermore, he assigned some of his female relatives to posts on the continent. Thus he called on the noble woman Saint Leoba of Wessex (702–782) to become the abbess of the German nunnery of Tauberbischofsheim. Thecla (d. 790) became the abbess at Kitzingen and Ochsenfurt and Walburga (d. 790) in Heidenheim.[96] Toward the end of Boniface's life, as he left toward Frisia, he entreated Leoba to stay in her adopted land and gave orders that "after his death, her bones should be placed next to his in the tomb, so that they who had served God during their lifetime with equal sincerity and zeal should await together the day of resurrection." He left her with his cowl, making her his delegate in his absence. She was in charge of all the nuns that worked for Boniface, and was the only woman with access to male monasteries in Fulda, where monks consulted her advice.[97] Hildegard, the wife of Charlemagne, considered her a friend, and she was held in high esteem at the court of Frankish ruler Pippin III. The presence of Leoba, Walburga, Thecla, and others on the continent emphasize the important role played by women in the establishment and management of monasteries.[98] Hence, Boniface's mission was not only partly funded and supported by Anglo-Saxon women, but they themselves were crucially involved in bringing Anglo-Saxon Christian practices to women in Germanic territories. There, along with other Anglo-Saxon abbots and bishops, they formed and educated a literate diasporic elite.

Traveling in Frisia, his earliest missionary field, where "the faith had been planted strongly [. . .] and the glorious end of the saint's life drew near," he and his party were killed, most likely in order to access potential valuables they carried. Though his companions aimed to defend themselves against the attackers, Boniface is reported to have encouraged them "to accept the crown of martyrdom":

> Sons, cease fighting. Lay down your arms, for we are told in Scripture not to render evil for good but to overcome evil by good [. . .] brethren, be of stout heart, fear not them who kill the body, for they cannot slay the soul, which continues to live forever.[99]

A box they had carried was found broken, and its content, perhaps some of the "sacred books" Eadburga had sent him in years past, were found strewn around

---

96 Other clan members include Willibald and Hugeburc. Lutz E. von Padberg, *Christianisierung*, 65.

97 Thomas F. X. and Thomas Head Noble, eds, "The Life of Saint Leoba," in *Soldiers of Christ: Saints and Saints' Lives from Late Antiquity and the Early Middle Ages*, Soldiers of Christ (University Park, PA.: Pennsylvania University Press, 1995), 272–73. See also Proksch, "Anglo-Saxon Missionaries," 45.

98 Thomas F. X. and Thomas Head Noble, eds, "Introduction," in *Soldiers of Christ: Saints and Saints' Lives from Late Antiquity and the Early Middle Ages*, Soldiers of Christ (University Park, PA: Pennsylvania University Press, 1995), xxxv.

99 Boniface, *Letters*, 135.

and torn apart. One, in particular, known as *Codex Ragyndrudis* (its contents are a collection of mainly anti-Arian texts), sustained a severe cut and was thought to be the book Boniface used to protect himself from the sword of his killer. Some hagiographic depictions from the ninth through the twelfth century show him with a book in his hand as the sword comes down on his head. Others show him with a book only, or with a sword in one hand and a book in the other. Sometimes, he holds a sword with a book impaled upon it.[100]

His hagiographer reports that at least two monasteries, Mainz and Fulda, contended for Boniface's relics, as they represented a powerful local presence of sacrality.[101] For a church or monastery to have its own relics gave it significance and meaning in the local sacral landscape. Rome continued to solidify its own power by piling on relics as gifts for Rome-travelers that these deposited in local sanctuaries upon their return.

The Anglo-Saxon and Iro-scottish traveling monks and nuns represented a subset of voluntary diasporic intellectuals of their time. Their willingness to travel to the liminal spaces of Christian influence made them powerful brokers between local and Christian cultures, indigenous power holders and the claims to the power of Christian God and church, and the founders of centers of education for royalty, nobility, and other local elites. As foreigners they were infused with an understanding of a universal Christian community that transcended numerous ethnic boundaries. What is the position of contemporary post/colonial intellectuals, writing in a time, outside of their homelands, ambivalently placed in positions of power and privilege, estranged from the populace by in-group language, culture, education. What is their "mission" within the world?[102]

Boniface's presence has likely meant the loss of more indigenized religious options. This loss of a pre-Christian past in Europe has sparked a variety of movements. Among the more harmless are neo-pagan attempts to resuscitate an imagined past Germanic religion. However, the focus on local, tribal, and supposed national pasts has also resulted in nationalist and xenophobic attempts to recover a figment of an essential tribal, national, or racial identity. Boniface's context reopens for us the possibility of reconstructing our own ideas of mission,

---

[100] Lutz von and Hans-Walter Stork Padberg, *Der Ragyndrudis-Codex Des Hl. Bonifatius* (Fulda: Verlag Parzeller, 1994), 17 and images throughout.

[101] See Schiefer, *Winfrid-Bonifatius*, 59.

[102] Valuable future explorations of this topic could be an investigation of how Christianity benefited from the unifying aspect of empire which facilitated Christianity's transethnic shape and development, and how Christian theology today can be shaped to avoid the false alternatives of the universalism of an imperial Christianity and of xenophobic ethnocentrisms that must dismiss, dominate, or destroy the other. How can we facilitate the many spaces for Christian theologies that each uniquely combine aspects that are translocal and transcendent of each particular context, while constructing relevant local theologies respectful and inclusive of the sacred truths and sites of all our ancestors?

inculturation, the relation between Christians and power, and the attendant ambivalence of trying to negotiate these economies of exchange. The symbolic event of the felling of the oak at Geismar contributed to shaping later missionary attitudes towards indigenous peoples of the land and sacred groves during the times of European colonial empires. Hence, Nobel laureate Wangari Maathai has argued that missionary policies against sacred groves are part of the cause of deforestation in Africa.[103] Fears of "syncretism" and "nature worship" are hardly issues of the past. The resurgence of neo-pagan practices and the violent fear of some Christians that environmental action and protection equals nature worship, feed on ancient stereotypes of iconoclast missionaries that with their actions also solidify a growing split between nature and culture, with "nature-worshipping pagans" as the paradigmatic uncultured human. As these conceptions were internalized, hostility to nature religions often accompanied ecocidal tendencies, prying the people of the land away from the land and toward a God that was claimed to be both universal and hence placeless and omnipresent, and present in all places. Might the strong stress on divine power and transcendence have to do with the suppression of native healers, worries about witchcraft, and old pre-Christian wells, tree sanctuaries, and the like?

Remembering the wisdom of indigenous peoples throughout the world as one related to that of European ancestors could be a far more helpful reconnection to a lost past than xenophobia and ethnic violence. Contemporary reconstructions of transcendence and immanence and the rise of ecological theologies are attempting to mend this split in the Western mindset. As theologians rediscover the local and contextual nature of all theology, a reassessment of intercultural encounter between gospel, the culture of the missionary, and local religious culture becomes crucial. Some of the heuristic epistemology that might accompany such investigations center around what appropriate mixtures of local and translocal culture might be: what practices can bear compromise (*adiaphora*), what pieces can take local shape, and who decides what these are?

The Heliand as a Saxon Indigenization of the Gospel Narratives

In the thousand-year history of Christianity's missionary efforts in Europe, I doubt if there is any page as brutal as that of Charlemagne's thirty-three year war of conversion and conquest of the Saxons in northern Germany.[104]

---

[103] See http://speakingoffaith.publicradio.org/programs/plantingthefuture/transcript.
shtml

[104] G. Ronald Murphy, *The Saxon Savior: The Germanic Transformation of the Gospel in the Ninth-Century Heliand* (New York/Oxford: Oxford University Press, 1989), 11.

The question of translation, indigenization, and inculturation of cultural artifacts, oral, literal, and material, continues to perplex us. While it may seem that Boniface and Charlemagne succeeded, if with profoundly undesirable methods, in imposing and more or less enforcing a Catholic uniformity of practice and doctrine within the Frankish domain, the Saxons Boniface initially felt called to convert remained, even as a conquered and defeated people, resistant and recalcitrant to an imperially imposed narrative and its cultural implications. *The Heliand,*[105] a Saxon-styled rendering of gospel narratives overlaid with the values and idiom of Saxon warrior culture, represents an attempt to allow a highly patriarchal, military culture to adopt Christianity as their own. Saxon social values were in tension with the cultural values of the gospel or Frankish Christian culture. The writer of the *Heliand* seemed to aim to allow a defeated culture to find images of victorious, warlike masculinity in a narrative that had arrived with and that had been imposed by its conquerors. It may not be all too untoward to compare this literary product to a contemporary attempt to frame the gospel within the values of, say, gang warfare in Los Angeles. An apologetic retelling of the gospel attempts to make the argument that Christ, and therefore Christianity, requires "true," deeper, and less randomly violent forms of masculinity than may be proposed by past and present honor-shame patriarchalities.

The masculinity of colonizer and colonized appears central to these reconstructions of Frankish adoption of Christianity and the colonization, suppression, and forcible conversions of the Saxons. Stereotypically masculine characteristics are associated with the construction of Christian discipleship. The conversion was imposed by Frankish military victory, helped by the Saxon Capitulary laws designed to force conversion and enforce certain Christian customs such as Lenten fasting.[106] Saxon resistance to conversion before Frankish conquest was tied in with the preservation of Saxon indigenous cultural— that is, here, political and religious—independence. Thus, the audience of the *Heliand* might well primarily have been located in a "poetic environment in order to help the Saxons cease their vacillation between their warrior-loyalty to the old gods and the 'mighty Christ.' "[107] Likely composed by a Saxon monk in sympathy with the losses his fellow countrymen had experienced, the text attempts to combine honoring a culture with its ultimate transformation into a form of Christianity that could be accommodated to the Roman Catholic Frankish imperial realities. The *Heliand*'s author used Tatian's Syrian *Diatessaron*, a gospel harmony from around A.D. 170, as a guide. The rendering that ensued may best be understood as "an intercultural poetic translation

---

[105] *The Heliand: The Saxon Gospel,* trans. and ed. G. Ronald Murphy (New York/Oxford: Oxford University Press, 1992).
[106] Fletcher, *Barbarian Conversion,* 215.
[107] *The Heliand: The Saxon Gospel,* xvi.

of the Gospel created by an epic poet,"[108] rather than simply a translation. Despite the author's frequent exhortations to leave behind doubts and believe the Christian message within the pages of the epic, he incorporated some of the "most profoundly pagan beliefs into his gospel epic."[109]

One theological difference from the Gospel of John is expressed in the assertion that the world and humans are already of light, and that John the Baptist's words or Christ's presence represents an additional light, rather than a light that "shines in the darkness."[110] Despite the recontextualization in a milieu of Saxon nobility and its military allegiances, the writer "consistently presents Christianity as a mild and peaceable faith."[111] This is in stark contrast to the forcible means by which the Saxons were pressured to convert. The Saxon main god Wodan/Odin, who in Roman times in Germano-Gallic regions appears to have been associated with Mercury/Hermes,[112] shares with his Greek and Roman incarnations the function of teaching the arts of writing, here "the runes and magic." Yet the divine agency in the *Heliand* is reframed within the concept of a monotheistic Creator-God rather than a powerful, but mortal Germanic deity, based on a four-gospel inspired canon (to the exclusion of other gospels), and pagan traditions.[113]

Such gospel renderings were to be imagined as sung, as was central to the Saxon culture. Corporately performed sung pieces appear to have been more esteemed than spoken and written. The victory of Rome is interpreted as given and granted by the Christian God and circumstances of the Roman occupation of Judaea are compared to the situation of the Saxons under Charlemagne.[114] The *Heliand* offers a synthesis of warrior virtues of "treuwa," the unquestioning loyalty and obedience to one's chieftain and the principal characteristic of the Christ: the angel Gabriel announces obedience to Christ who will be "the

---

[108] Murphy, *Saxon Savior*, 28.
[109] Ibid., 33.
[110] *The Heliand: The Saxon Gospel*, xvi.
[111] Fletcher, *Barbarian Conversion*, 267.
[112] With Mercury as an ongoing recognizable label for this force or agency in these lands, one could say that some sense of Wotan survived, or that a messenger god's characteristics were shaped to accommodate a mediating Christ who knows powerful words and speech acts, rather than, as Murphy claims, representing an accommodation to a "Celto-Germanic world" and its notions of "magic power." This exoticization of Celtic-Germanic notions of powerful words as "magic" seduces too easily into an opposition of *logos* and *semeion* as essentially different and sequesters pagan notions of powerful language and action into the realm of myth. Certainly there are distinct cultural practices regarding such forms of speech and agency, but overly exoticizing them raises suspicions as to the presence of a polemic against continuing local practices associated with magic, rather than marking actual distinctions between cultures. Similar concerns around practices of naming can be found in biblical traditions around the issues of the divine name as unspeakable, of numerology, of blessings and curses as powerful speech that is connected to change in life substance.
[113] *The Heliand: The Saxon Gospel*, xvii.
[114] Ibid., 6.

chieftain of mankind" born in "David's hill-fort" as the primary trait of John the Baptist.[115]

But one of the biggest hurdles to tackle was that of class and of cultural difference: The author struggles to "show that Joseph and Mary are upper class, of good family . . . born inside the hill-fort." The no-room-at-the-inn scene is avoided, and Jesus the chieftain is portrayed as if born as a cherished, expected ruler child.[116] Shepherds were presumably socially unacceptable and hence the sheep and shepherds present at Christ's birth are transformed into horses and horse-guards.[117] Charlemagne forbade burials in grave mounds and ordered bodies to be buried in church cemeteries. Thus the *Heliand*'s locating of Christ's body under a wooden plate evokes a mound grave burial.[118]

As Robert Bartlett suggests, social barriers in what is becoming Europe are not conceived according to skintone, but rather in terms of custom, law, and power, that is, social and cultural status.[119] It is therefore perhaps not just a general Germanic warrior ethos that is being suggested here, but it is worth remembering here that this was a gospel addressed to those of high standing in society, not to the poor and outcast that have a place in the biblical narratives. The author's strategy appears primarily to have been one that made it socially acceptable for high-class Saxons to show loyalty and faithfulness to a "chieftain" rather than to a lowly poor peasant child.[120]

Apologetic renderings of Christ within a frame of "muscular Christianity" are more familiar to contemporary U.S. audiences, most recently through movements such as the Promise Keepers, one of the more recent incarnations of the desire to win men in particular for a gospel that appears to suggest a Christ that does not fit the resident image of masculinity in a culture. Hence, Christ is depicted here as a "Germanic chieftain gathering young noblemen

---

[115] Ibid., 15. Many Central European seats of local power, dating back at least to the Celtic La Tène the period, were located on the top of hills, overlooking the surrounding landscape. Enclosed by stone palisades they provided some degree of defense.

[116] Mikhail Bakhtin, *The Dialogic Imagination: Four Essays*, ed., trans. Carl Emerson and Michael Holquist (Austin, TX: University of Texas, 1981), 17, fn. 26.

[117] See footnote 25, *The Heliand: The Saxon Gospel*, 16.

[118] Murphy, *Saxon Savior*, 95.

[119] He writes that "while the language of race—*gens, natio*, 'blood', 'stock', and so on—is biological, its medieval reality was almost entirely cultural." See Robert Bartlett, *The Making of Europe: Conquest, Colonization and Cultural Change 950–1350* (Princeton, NJ: Princeton University Press, 1993), 197.

[120] One might wonder, then, how prevalent a missionary strategy was that emphasized power as something that a large group of socially upper-class families were unwilling to either concede or needed evidence of to consider submitting themselves to such higher divine powers, as well as a strategy to convince groups of lower status that the divine chieftain commanded the same or more loyalty as their earthly chieftains. Though it is tempting to read this also as a manifestation of patriarchal power and a strong preoccupation with the maintenance of such power patterns, another layer is the concern with a power that is effective in the face of cosmic fate.

to be in his private retinue," offering the cloak of face-saving masculine virtues.[121] The intercultural synthesis involves religious motifs and as cultural
expressions of masculinity as the *Heliand*'s author initiates a "new Germanic-
Christian synthesis of the ideal man: a composite of personal strength and
interior gentleness," thus recontextualizing a mythic divinized masculinity
that persisted into the Middle Ages and informed knightly virtues.[122] This
theological gender reassignment dynamic is familiar from earlier doctrinal
transformartions in Roman imperial contexts. Virginia Burrus has made
more fully visible the "(re)conceptions of manhood" in the development of
creedal orthodoxy, and thereby offered "deeper insight into the powerful
paradox of God's singular multiplicity," that is so often articulated as a "sub-
lime patriliny," as "fourth-century trinitarian doctrine both pervades and is
pervaded by late-antique claims for masculinity."[123] Set on a theological track
that Mary Daly has called out as reifying masculinity as divine "if God is male,
then the male is god,"[124] even such reformed and disciplined masculinity does
little more than recommend a type of love patriarchalism.

At what point this message goes from anti-imperial, because suspicious of
Frankish power designs, to being recontextualized as a narrative that empow-
ers the merging of military endeavors and crusades is hard to say. A form of
andragogy aimed at reformable male subjects, it helps create an imaginary in
which masculinity and warrior culture can be resymbiotized within a new cultural setting, beyond the initial imperial synthesis of Rome. As a strategy for
missionary apologetics, such renderings are quite obviously problematic when
we remember the resulting synthesis of Christianity and medieval warrior culture. Though rendering an African Christ as chief, ancestor, or warrior, when
missiologists make arguments for more deeply indigenized gospels, may not
get the same attention.

The saving power of the *Heliand* is associated with overcoming the ends
associated with Thor and Wotan by countering them with Christ's resurrection and the calming of the storm. In the "twilight of the gods" Wotan the
Wise was to be devoured by the great wolf Fenrir, whose maw is like the "emptiness of the abyss," while Thor was killed by a Leviathan-like poisoned great
serpent associated with the depths of the ocean whose coils represent the edge
of the universe. In the *Heliand*, hence, the story of Christ's calming of the sea
renders the water as fearsome and dangerous and the resurrection as coming
back from the abyss were particularly highlighted. Christ is portrayed as the

---

[121] Murphy, *Saxon Savior*, 58.
[122] Ibid., 86–7.
[123] Virginia Burrus, *Begotten, Not Made: Conceiving Manhood in Late Antiquity* (Stanford, CA:
        Stanford University Press, 2000), 3.
[124] Mary Daly, *Beyond God the Father: Toward a Philosophy of Women's Liberation* (Boston, MA:
        Beacon, 1973), 19.

divine mediator who survived the end of the Germanic mortal gods.[125] The cross might have its own resonance with the mythical meaning of the sacred cosmic tree of life where Wotan/Odin sacrificed himself, hanging and piercing himself (symbolically) to gain knowledge of the sacred runes that would give hidden knowledge. One of the central narratives around Wotan/Odin is the "woodland sacrifice," possibly a "ritual of collective rebirth" in which Wotan/Odin "hanged himself on the boughs of the cosmic ash tree Yggdrasil (the Nordic symbol of the universe) for nine days and nights, in a ritual of death and resurrection."[126] He saved himself by raising a pile of stone runes, lying below the tree, through the force of his will, to help him step down from the tree, with greater power and strength.[127] Echoes with the story of Christ's crucifixion would have been impossible to ignore and might have factored into the rise of the portrayal of Christ as crucified, which had not previously been common. Odin's self-sacrifice here is associated with Christ's self-sacrifice. In the case of Odin, the runes do not signify merely the power of word and writing, but the mysterious powers over life. The purpose of their sacrifice differs, however: While Christ's sacrifice was to bring the relationship between humans and God into balance, Odin's sacrifice turns on the search for knowledge, which is a central theme in Nordic mythology.[128]

Research into Nordic religious pasts comes from a number of motivations. For one of the most respected scholars, Gro Steinsland, the impulse is not to romantically reimagine, create, or recreate a religion that fits a culture that no longer exists, but to employ it to understand the present.[129] As best as can be discerned, Germanic-Nordic cosmologies were centered around the world ash tree Yggdrasil, the *axis mundi* around which the world revolved. The tree connects the powers of destiny, humans, divine, and chaos forces. From it the power to order and create radiates forth in widening circles, each like a ring around this source. In the outer circle are chaotic forces, demons, and strange entities that give rise to fear in humans. Humans are located between the circle of the deities Åsgård, and Utgård. Midtgård literally means the home in the middle (elsewhere rendered as Middle-earth). The image of the tree for all these forces shows a sense in this cosmology of the deep interrelation between all these forces.[130] These relations are in a tender balance that will unravel in Ragnarok. The world ash will be felled by way of a parasitic growth on it, a mistletoe branch, killing the god Balder, and threatening the core of this cosmos.

---

[125] Murphy, *Saxon Savior*, 76.
[126] Schama, *Landscape and Memory*, 84–5.
[127] Ibid., 85.
[128] Gro Steinsland, "Fra Yggdrasils Ask Til Korsets Tre—Tanker Om Trosskiftet," in *Fra Hedendom Til Kristendom: Perspektiver På Religionsskiftet i Norge*, ed. Magnus Rindal (Oslo: Ad Notam Gyldendal, 1996), 29.
[129] Ibid., 21.
[130] Ibid., 23.

With the shift to a Christian worldview, this sense of complex forces at odds with each other was replaced, often by force from powerful men and institutions, with a christocentric image of the world. And, as before, this sense of the enthroned ruler of heaven, was often used to promote the power of rulers on earth who claimed the mantle of divine sovereignty. At least three Norwegian kings returned from foreign lands with plans to both assume power and Christianize the country, and would have learned about the Christian royal ideology while abroad. Thus, a new ideology of royal power and Christian faith was the dual basis for the shift in religion and of the creation of a nation.[131]

In terms of imagery, the cosmic tree—with its microcosmic representation in the tree that stood at the center of settlements—resonates deeply with the symbolism of trees in the garden of Eden and its Christian interpretations. The cross of Christ becomes the new tree of life and is often shown with branches of new life shooting from it. As Yggdrasil stood at the center of the cosmos, so now the Cross did. Likewise, sacred springs are reinterpreted and linked with the waters of baptism and the baptismal font, the new source of life.[132] The most powerful spring in Norway lay at the sanctuary of St. Olav in Nidaros (today Trondheim), where the image of female Norns' water feeding the world ash was replaced with a male sainted king at whose grave forgiveness and healing could be found. This shift also signified a stronger emphasis on the life of the individual over against the concerns of the community.[133] None of this was absolute, of course, especially since the new Christian affiliation was bolstering a new sense of nation and community, but there are rituals and narratives that emphasize the individual in new ways.

In the *Heliand* Christ knows the secret runes and teaches the knowledge to his disciples.[134] Ultimately, the death of Christ is, similarly to Gregory of Nyssa's *Catechetical Oration*, a divine trickster chief escaping as a "prisoner of war from his captors," and the resurrection becomes the "return of the warrior leader to his own people."[135] Meanwhile, the poem "deliberately visualizes the resurrection of Christ in a manner that is in violation of the Carolinginan law against burial in pagan (Saxon) mound graves, thus creating an image of Christ risen that gives a clear hope of Saxon resurrection."[136]

Brock and Parker reinterpret the *Heliand* as a resistive text that has at its center a vision of paradise on top of a mountain.[137] This vision of paradise combines Hebrew and Germanic images, the Genesis narrative, and the motif

---

[131] Ibid., 25.
[132] Ibid., 27.
[133] Ibid., 28.
[134] Murphy, *Saxon Savior*, 77.
[135] Ibid., 110.
[136] Ibid., 113.
[137] Rita Nakashima Brock and Rebecca Ann Parker, *Saving Paradise: How Christianity Traded Love of This World for Crucifixion and Empire* (Boston, MA: Beacon, 2001), 244.

of Valhalla.[138] The author of the *Heliand* inserts a number of resistant elements into its retelling of the gospel stories: Herod appears to be identified with Charlemagne and the strong critique of Herod's genocidal measures at eradicating Hebrew children seems to be directed at Charlemagne's actions against the Saxons.[139] The Eucharistic rite described in the text continues in the Gallican rite that focused on resurrection versus the accommodation to the Roman rite.[140] While Charlemagne may have attempted to shift the visual and theological focus of Frankish Christianity to a tortured dead body, it may not have succeeded in dominating as completely as Brock and Parker imagine.

What, in pursuing these indigenizations, should be some of the precautions we might take? Ironically, as in modern indigenizing theological interpretive moves, the specter of an internal colonial narrative threatens. Thus, in the nineteenth century, moves were made to claim the *Heliand* as proposing a "pan-Germanic ideal" with the attendant nationalist flavor and tone of cultural superiority.[141] The adaptation of an external narrative, though several centuries later, when the narrative has lost some of its local and particular ethnic associations, its "dark tones of dissatisfaction with the 'pan-Germanic' Frankish power in Aachen,"[142] that is with Charlemagne's rule over the defeated and demoralized Saxons, is ignored and forgotten and the piece is recast in a different sociopolitical context, again by interested upper-class parties as a pan-ethnic myth and employed to promote one's own cultural superiority and a pan-ethnic nationalist narrative. Countless examples of this dynamic of narrative recasting can be named across the world.[143]

To counteract Boniface's hatchet job on the oak, in the aftermath of "Waldsterben"—the dying forest—in Germany, avant-garde artist Joseph Beuys began planting 7,000 oaks to ameliorate the results of deforestation and environmental degradation in twentieth-century Germany.[144] In recent years, a revival of religious consciousness has taken the form of reestablishing a pilgrimage path that follows the path on which his relics were moved from where he died to Fulda. Today, around 25,000 persons make the pilgrimage to the site of Boniface's death and his relics each year. For the anniversary of his death in 2004, a musical was created and performed.[145]

---

[138] *The Heliand: The Saxon Gospel*, 103, fn 145.

[139] Brock and Parker, *Saving Paradise*, 242.

[140] Ibid., *Saving Paradise*, 247.

[141] Murphy, *Saxon Savior*, 3.

[142] Ibid., 4.

[143] See, for example, Geary, *Myth of Nations*; see also Elizabeth Wayland Barber and Paul T. Barber, *When They Severed Earth from Sky: How the Human Mind Shapes Myth* (Princeton, NJ: Princeton University Press, 2004).

[144] Kai Uwe Schierz, ed., *Von Bonifatius Bis Beuys—oder: Vom Umgang mit Den Heiligen Eichen* (Erfurt: Druckhaus Gera, 2004).

[145] It appears that the growing together of Europe does not always erase local traditions and specificities but, *au contraire*, revives local traditions in a search for one's own particularity.

Popular opinion of Boniface has varied between outright hagiography and cult for his efforts in "converting the Germans," to criticism for bringing Christianity at all (from the neopagan proponents of Nazism), or for bringing a nonindigenous ultramontanist version of Rome-enslaved Christianity (opinions predictably more prevalent on the Protestant side of things, as well as among German Christians during the Nazi reign). The changes wrought by the rise of industrial capitalism and fears of modernity's challenges led, in some German contexts, to the desire for a nationalist romantic recovery of an imagined pure Germanic past, or a particular contribution to Christianity that could be accredited to Germans.[146] Religiocultural identity is complexly interwoven with political and social forms of life, and can become unstable under the force of social changes.

Andrew Walls' warning that the more successful the indigenization, the more problematic the missionary expression of this indigenized gospel to another culture comes to mind. Walls' comment seems to assume that there is a translocal and transcontextual gospel to be passed from culture to culture, and that there can be greater or lesser loyalty to some kind of core sense of the gospel. Yet, determining what this core is, continues to divide communities. Seeking to embody a strategic essentialism, following Gayatri Spivak's suggestion, can be a way to avoid the dissolution of specificity while resisting a "misplaced concreteness"[147] that results in claiming reductionistic limitations for what the gospel can and might mean. Far from enabling a romanticization of embodiment, with the flesh and soul in spirit the datum of our lives, our preconditions and limitations will always function as both lifegiving form and restricting mold—the ambiguity of embodiment and the reality of our social and personal fragility and damage.

From the British Isles to Scandinavia—Migration, Secularization, Re/Christianization

Naval traffic between the British Isles, North and Central Europe, and Scandinavia was lively and frequent. With these trade and exchange routes, slowly, Christian

---

There is a marked increase in redeveloping pilgrimage routes throughout Europe, in the aftermath of the great popularity of Santiago de Compostela. And as in the *Canterbury Tales*, the destination of the pilgrimage, Canterbury, becomes lost in the stories told along the way. Then and now, pilgrimage was often undertaken for more than religious reasons. www.bonifatius-musical.de/go.php

[146] See Friedrich Wilhelm Graf, "Germanisierung Des Christentums," in *Religion in Geschichte und Gegenwart, 3rd Edn.*, Hans Dieter Betz, et al. (Tübingen: Mohr Siebeck, 1998), 754 and James C. Russell, *The Germanization of Early Medieval Christianity: A Sociohistorical Approach to Religious Transformation* (Oxford: Oxford University Press, 1994).

[147] Alfred North Whitehead. *Process and Reality* (New York: Free Press, 1978), 93.

missionaries made it further north. Trade routes from Norway to the Hebrides to Scotland and Ireland were frequently sailed. How was Christian faith and practice introduced and transformed in these locations, then and now? In Iceland, the entire people decided that all had to convert, lest the body of the people break asunder, or battles are fought that imply both kingly power and religious adherence. Some of the pre-Christian culture was irretrievably lost, and much of what is extant now is post-Christian, written by Snorre Sturlason, who wrote it past conversion, in order to preserve it.[148] Similar critical issues apply as do with modern missionary anthropologists who have turned out both the destroyers and keepers of indigenous socioreligious traditions.

Back in Britain, another group of Christian travelers make their way across another sea, following ancient trade and migration routes along the way north, and the coast of Norway. Lisbeth Mikaelsson's essay on "Locality and Myth: The Resacralization of Selja and the Cult of St. Sunniva"[149] presents us with a fascinating case study of how in the present day, an old legend is used to reimagine pre-Christian, Catholic, and hence pre-Protestant spiritualities in a society where the Lutheran national church has been in a position of seemingly unchallenged hegemony. Free-floating forms of spirituality and a revival of pilgrimages as unstructured and unrestricted forms of quasi-religiosity throughout Europe are attaching themselves to contrapuntal reemergings of regional and local identity in a Europe that has become more unified than ever before.

The recapturing of a legend of a female figure is particularly interesting in a Protestant Norway whose shaping figures are first and foremost male. Women are writing themselves back into Norwegian church history through reconstruction and adoption, albeit of a nonhistorical figure. Historical factuality, in resistance to a long emphasis on historicality and factuality, are secondary here. What seems primary is the reconstruction of identity through a figure that allows reentry into lost streams of tradition.

The holy men of Selja, an island with a monastery that had hosted monks from the British Isles (testifying to the strong British influence on early Christianization in Norway), were revered in the Middle Ages, and iconographic representations of them were found throughout the land. Protestantism had done away with these old memories of the first Christian presences in the country, and so a piece of identity and history was lost, along with the association with Christianity's first entry into Norway through an "Irish princess." The island of Selja itself had long been seen as a "thin space," a numinous location, where ships waited for better weather going north, also by pilgrims on their way north to the tomb of St. Olav in Nidaros, the most important northern

---

[148] Brown, *Rise*, 472–3 and Gro Steinsland, *Norrøn Religion: Myter, Riter, Samfunn* (Oslo: Pax Forlag, 2005), 53.

[149] Lisbeth Mikaelsson, "Locality and Myth: The Resacralization of Selja and the Cult of St. Sunniva," *Numen* Vol. 52 (2005): 1.

pilgrimage site in Scandinavia. This made the island relatively central to traffic routes, contrary to today.[150] Long traditions of associations of Celtic saints with caves are also echoed here.[151] Olav Tryggvason, the first Christian king in Norway, who traveled to Selja, is said to have built a small church to Sunniva's memory (probably the Irish monastery was really the first site there). The saint's shrine was later moved to Bergen and she became the city's patron. The shrine remained in the cathedral there until it was destroyed during the Reformation.[152] Having undergone conversion abroad through contact with Anglo-Saxon England, he later "imposed Christianity with great violence on the Trondelag, the region around Trondheim," breaking the will of "an entire society of independent farmers."[153] In response to such events, Icelanders, who had left Norway because they did not want to be subject to kings, decided that if they were to convert, it would be "entirely on their terms." Before their society would be split through the influx of Irish slaves and influential landowners who moved from Ireland to Iceland, they decided, via pagan divination, that the entire society should adopt Christianity.[154]

Some scholars assume there is no historical kernel to the Sunniva legend, but that it represents a version of the Ursula legend (attached to Cologne) and a specimen of the lore around devoted virgins.[155] Layers of religious meaning were attributed to Selja: in many places of pilgrimage, when a number of different elements coalesce, it is highly likely that the location was considered holy in pre-Christian times and has become multiply overwritten: a mountain spring by a curative well, a sacred tree hanging over a holy well by a sacred stone.[156] Selja's connection with royalty and the early Christianization process makes it a national symbol for a country with a fusion of national and Christian inheritance, perhaps especially in a time when this heritage is being reexamined. The violent transformation of Norway into a Christian country under King Olav Haraldsson and his transformation into a saint by his enemies continue to manifest an ambivalent heritage that produced other colonial formations.[157] Sunniva, on the other hand, is the only female figure of great importance in Norwegian church history besides the virgin Mary.[158] The many layers of the site open it up to many interpretations. Spirit/s rest and inspire here, haunting and vying for a place in the reconstruction of Christian cultural heritage.

[150] Mikaelsson, "Locality and Myth," 193.
[151] Ibid., 195.
[152] Ibid., 199.
[153] Brown, *Rise*, 471–2.
[154] Ibid., 472–3.
[155] Mikaelsson, "Locality and Myth," 200.
[156] Ibid., 201.
[157] Ibid., 205.
[158] Ibid., 208.

In many ways, the gods could never be put entirely in the past, unless that past itself was appropriated on Christian terms.[159]

The old gods remain stubbornly present. Histories often show centuries of the coexistence of and integration of varieties of pagan and Christian practices with each other. Under conditions of empire, the next phase of conversion generates further complexities: those converted under pressure in the past may show little concern for the forcible conversion of others.

Another curious twist on Scandinavian colonial histories and the rethinking of Christianity comes from Denmark. In her essay *Moses and Abraham Go Arctic*, Christina Petterson reminds fellow Danes that Denmark's colonial history tends to be remembered selectively. While colonization of the West Indies, Norway, and Iceland are indeed in the past, and there is no longer a formal colonial relation with Greenland, it remains a Danish territory.[160] In a paradigmatic narrative illustrating the layers of Christian identity negotiation, she describes a very particular, profoundly revealing struggle about who can speak authentically for Christianity in Greenland. Given the history of colonial Greenland, there are great tensions around the identity of Greenlanders, Inuit, and Danish. Some see Christianity as Greenland's only true religion while others see it as a problematic colonial influence.

In 2005, the official website of the Lutheran church in Greenland, which had previously been located as a subsite of the Danish Lutheran National Church, presented itself as independent on the site. This despite the fact that there had been no changes in the legal or ecclesial relations to match this changed online profile. The female Danish bishop of Greenland, commenting on such insubordination, emphasized her authority over the Greenland church, by claiming to represent the Holy Spirit in the controversy. This she juxtaposed by questioning the spiritual motivation of Mannuaq Berthelsen, the Inuit woman associated with the changes in affiliation, identifying her with troublesome Inuit spirits. Berthelsen, however, sees herself as a Christian in good standing with God, and, what is more, claims access to the correct understanding of divine nature and purpose. Indeed, she calls on Moses and Abraham as guiding (ancestral) spirits to the promised land. Berthelsen identified one particular Inuit spirit as encouraging her to lead the people of Greenland to their "correct spiritual identity,"[161] out of exile under the Danish National Lutheran Church.

Petterson observes that the verbal retaliation of the Danish church echoes rhetorical elements from how the Gospel of John describes and labels

---

[159] Brown, *Rise*, 481.
[160] Christina Petterson, "Moses and Abraham Go Arctic," *Biblical Interpretation* 16 (2008): 366.
[161] Ibid., 369.

its opponents, as mad, as seeing themselves as equal to God, and, finally, as witches. Meanwhile, the Inuit shaman draws on her spiritual insight and a form of Inuit nationalism for the reinterpretation of the gospel and the designation of the Danish church as colonial and misguided. Berthelsen further draws upon Moses and Abraham, as Petterson notes, in similar ways as the prologue of John does, by subverting them and reintegrating them into a new narrative where they come to highlight the function of the Johannine logos and, in Berthelsen's case, by assimilating them with Inuit spirits to undermine the claims of the state church.[162] Petterson concludes that at the very least hegemonic interpretations of the Gospel of John are undermined and the text reappears as newly ambivalent.

Multiple Religious Identities, or "Secular Europe" and "Religious Africa"?

European and Scandinavian societies are undergoing vast transformation as they negotiate the changed and changing nature of religious and national identity. Germany's population, though being an amalgam with near untraceable roots of ethnic diversity—distinguished primarily by customs and language rather than pigmentation—had in modernity perceived itself as an ethnic nation-state, not a destination for migration and immigration. As it negotiates the integration of large and diverse minorities from Africa, other parts of Europe, and especially the large Muslim minority that has been present since the end of World War II, new challenges have emerged, and Jewish presences have resurged. Though sometimes described as thoroughly secularized, Germany remains a society based on implicit, if not explicit, German Christian values—of course in an "indigenized" expression—and cultural assumptions. Questions of sacred and secular, of religious culture and civic law, of what makes or breaks a nation, and under what circumstances ethnic groups, local and relocated, can negotiate identity of difference are paramount.

Only initially then can it seem surprising that many regions in the European Union are experiencing forms of new regionalisms: the retrieval of regional dialects, local religious sites, sanctuaries and saints, foods, histories, garments, traditions, music, and so on. While among other a function of setting oneself apart in a sea of globally mediated sameness, inviting travelers, tourists and pilgrims to regions extolling their deep histories, can these new "soft" regionalisms represent a viable option for the negotiation of self and other? Where do these expressions fit in this particular historical moment and what do these particular *Völkerwanderungen*—this particular age of migrations—mean

---

[162] Ibid., 371.

theologically, for the production and formation of polydox theologies of mission that can address intercultural issues with the strength of the critical reception of the theological tradition? Of great value in such negotiations is the ability to affirm and creatively maintain one's ethnic heritage, while being permeable, transformable, and flexible to others. Cultural exchange, migration, interpretation, and translation, far from being new experiences, have been the reality of human life on this earth, and it is important for the negotiation of peace and reconciliation to find a way that does not unduly restrict either.

Many nations in Europe, whatever, wherever, and whoever "Europe" may be, are struggling with regional, national, and European layers of identity and belonging, with the reality of cultural diversity, not merely its ideal. The specter of world wars and Holocaust still looming, real and imagined fears of Islamization, fired up by political ideologies fostering islamophobias,[163] complicate the real complexities of religiocultural integration. New frontiers of ethnocentrism, citizenship, religious, and cultural identity are being explored in tenuous settings, settings reminiscent of ancient histories of the landmass and the tenuous Christianization of its own population, as well as its modern involvement in spreading Christianity in other continents, and the developing relationship to Judaism and Islam in particular.

Other nations renegotiating their identities along a Secular-Christian continuum, are attempting to come to terms with the way they negotiate their groundedness on historical Christian formations. The secular expression of many nations increasingly becomes visible as an inculturated form of Christianity that integrated, over centuries, forms of government with religious values and beliefs and assumptions. Over time, events occur that shatter the existing order and unveil it as no longer sufficient.[164] The seeming secularisms worked well enough for a time, but are now challenged by the presence of Muslim immigrants. Similar discourses are occurring across Europe, and to some degree, in the United States. Even in the discussion of what happens, however, inculturated Christian enlightenment values hover in plain sight, if not always recognized, and, indeed, not always negotiable.

Philip Jenkins suggested in his first major book *The Next Christendom: The Coming of Global Christianity* that the new epicenter of Christianity lies in the—predominantly conservative—Christianities of Africa. This claim overlooks

---

[163] Philip Jenkins, *God's Continent* (New York: Oxford University Press, 2007).

[164] The Comaroffs suggest that something similar is happening in post-Apartheid South Africa, where the colonial imposition of a "secular" society is being severely challenged and the sense of distance, if not separation of religion and state, is shrinking, for better and for worse. Though, as in the case of the United States, it is hard to see how this "separation of church and state" is anything but a fiction, if understood as absolute, but rather speaks about the need for the state not to impose on religious bodies. The discussion of Christian values as foundational for the states in the United States, however, is rather different, historically, from many European nations that predate modern Enlightenment secular visions.

the degree to which such a thesis is ideologically loaded in its polemic against liberalizing forms of Christianity, while it assumes that forms of African Christianity, for example, are overall presumably less compromised than, say, the British Church of England. A closer look reveals, as so often, that these juxtapositions are hard to maintain, and their dynamics involved far from simple. One might, for example, argue that each of these expressions of Christianity displays forms of utilitarian and syncretic features. Jenkins' later work, responding to criticism, corrects these gross overgeneralizations, and further elucidates some of the dynamics of where Christian faith and culture is growing, how it is changing, and reemerging.[165]

This has the potential to move at least this particular discussion beyond the ghost of the ancient trope of the noble savage. In his *Germania*, he used the image of noble Germanic Barbarians to direct a stark critique against his Roman contemporaries, describing them as decadents and weaklings. The device employs a projected "uncivilized" ethnic "Other" to level a critique at its real target: tendencies toward decline in the writer's own civilization. In one of its post-modern incarnations, the narrative goes like this: The Christian from the Southern hemisphere is truly noble, or here, truly Christian, while the supposed culture- or gospel-bringer has left civilization—or Christianity— behind. In this romantic narrative, the Christian noble savage from the South lifts up "true faith" and will now come to re-civilize, or rechristianize "formerly" Christian cultures. There are a number of problems with this narrative. It fits all too well the evangelical legitimization narrative that "liberal" theology has sold out the faith and has caused a decline of Christendom in the former "heartland" of Christian faith, Western Europe, and North America. It is all too convenient in its often facile indictment of attempts of theologians to take seriously the *sensus communis* of a populace coming to terms with changing understandings about the world and how God works within it. It resembles a reverse triumphalism that ignores the history, complexity, and indeed contextuality of Christian roots, practices, and institutions in areas where it has long been established. What can seem like an effort to claim a supersession of Western Latin Christianity and its cultural expressions by a seemingly discontinuous and purified "African Christianity" overemphasizes the seeming differences and thereby veils some of the more significant distinctions. The pathos of a mighty, but somehow kinder, gentler African Christianity hardly corresponds to the complex reality on the ground, where acts of misogyny, xenophobia, and homophobia can be tolerated, if not encouraged. Hence ideologically loaded and triumphalist utterances betray theological stereotypes about the "Western Christian paradigm," where there is apparently

---

[165] Philip Jenkins, "Godless Europe?" *International Bulletin of Missionary Research* Vol. 31, No. 3 (2007): 115–20 and Jenkins, *God's Continent*.

little that a Christian theologian can say about his or her faith to a person of another faith without becoming adversarial, while a person of another faith cannot encounter the Christ of Christianity, except on the terms of a Christian theology whose categories have been established with little reference to the faiths of others.[166]

Beyond the unhelpfulness of such crude generalizations, upon a closer look, we find they extend rather openly the cultural conservativism of U.S. theologians such as Stanley Hauerwas. Bediako's reference to Hauerwas, invoked here as a critic of natural theology and therefore frowning upon "Christian theology's false humility" in allowing its "social contribution to be shaped and defined by the secular disciplines of political science, economics, and sociology,"[167] suggests his impetus is in fact an internal critique of rival theological traditions such as a network of radical orthodox and theologically conservative thinkers who find a common foil in any theology that smacks of what they consider "liberal" or "liberation".[168] Hence, this jab points less to the claimed Africanization of Christianity than the attempt to recast African Christianity in the image of U.S. Christian conservatives.

Meanwhile, beyond exporting U.S. culture wars between conservative evangelicals, moderates, and liberal progressives, to other regions, it makes sense to perform a deeper archaeology and consider what might be the underlying questions, those around divine agency and human freedom, the use of reason and confidence in it that inhere already ancient forms of Christianity and are indeed old problems,[169] at the very least since patristic writers used the "natural theology" and "science" of their time, various versions of Platonism and Greek philosophy to articulate the terms of human-divine relations. Indeed, secularist hostility towards Christianity can be a powerful factor in Western societies, and in some circles it seems that such "secular disdain gives fodder for an awakened Islam."[170]

Yet, the reduction of nonconservative forms of Christianity as either "Western" or "secular" is neither accurate nor helpful for thinking through

---

[166] Kwame Bediako, "'Whose Religion is Christianity?' Reflections on Opportunities and Challenges in Christian Theological Scholarship: The African Dimension," in *Mission in the 21st Century: Exploring the Five Marks of Global Mission*, eds. Andrew Walls and Cathy Ross (Maryknoll: Orbis, 2008), 110.

[167] I am referring here to Bediako's reading of Katongole's reading of Hauerwas in Bediako, "African Dimension," 112.

[168] See John Milbank, ed. *Radical Orthodoxy: A New Theology* (London: Routledge, 1999), and so on.

[169] So argued in booklong form by Michael Allen Gillespie, *The Theological Origins of Modernity* (Chicago, IL: University of Chicago Press, 2008).

[170] Lamin Sanneh, "The Church and Its Missionary Vocation: The Islamic Frontline in a Post-Christian West," in *Mission in the 21st Century: Exploring the Five Marks of Global Mission*, Andrew Walls and Cathy Ross, eds, (Maryknoll, NY: Orbis, 2008), 146.

what the future of Christianity may be in historically dominantly Christian-inflected societies. Secularism is not just a missionary challenge, it is also a response to mission: It attempts to protect, with all its inherent contradictions and problems, the existence and relative freedom of religious minorities.

The narrative of Christian decline in the "West" also assumes that areas that have been Christianized in the past will somehow magically stay so consciously and explicitly, and that church attendance and fervent expression in worship are reliable signs of the deep penetration of Christian faith or culture. This is, however, problematic for a number of reasons. While Sunday attendance may be low, comparatively, in many European nations, those numbers are not the only data available, nor perhaps a reliable indicator of religious inclinations and commitments, at least not one that looks at the larger picture. Churches in Africa, for example, provide a great number of social services, and are thus much more part of the social fabric, in the absence of other societal agencies. Over time, many hospitals, orphanages, kindergartens, and schools in Europe have become less directly or visibly aligned with churches, and charitable organizations form their own structures rather than being directly administered by denominations. This structural difference means that church attendance and social services became somewhat more separate than is currently the case in many developing countries. Even in Africa, the side benefits of attending churches offering access to health care and help with economic issues directly are a significant factor for the patronizing of ecclesial bodies. The delinking of charitable institutions from ecclesial bodies in other parts of the world has been both a blessing and a bane: less external pressure but also incentives to attend churches, and sinking attendance as churches become primarily providers of liturgical worship rather than complex social institutions. The resulting distance between liturgical faith expressions, that is, practiced faith in ecclesially mediated ways, and a more generalized "NGO" culture, between "religious Christians" and "secular" or "cultural Christians," often with atheist expressions and multiple religious belongings has resulted in circumstances where "Christians" might benefit from the arguably tenuous distinction of the oft-named difference between "religious Jews" and "cultural Jews," despite the obvious differences between the communities.

Many secular thinkers engage these questions of underlying moral or religious values, analyzing them from the perspective of theorists like Schmitt, Agamben, Nancy, and others. Yet these theorists' theological and religious illiteracy deprives them of crucial tools to engage and contribute constructively to such struggles. Here is where historical, systematic, and constructive theological studies are sorely needed, having kept alive the knowledge and practice of epistemologies of the sacred. The challenges of encounters between modern secularized societies with Muslims highlights the different ways in which sacred-secular dynamics are experienced and negotiated. The increasing visibility of Muslims in Western societies raises the question of what grounds culture and identity. At the same time, the seeming secularism of U.S. foreign policy in the Middle East, and in particular the U.S. government's "project to reshape and reform Islam on a global scale"[171] is revealed as deeply informed by Christian values, revealing secularism as tightly linked to the societies it emerged in: nations that were deeply informed by deep relation with Christian churches, values, and indeed "the religious sensibility the traditionalist Muslim is beckoned to embrace (with its attendant scriptural hermeneutics)" is a (post-)Christian one. The Rand corporation, for example, has been drafting documents that witness of intentions to pacify Islamic societies by attempting to foster and encourage in Muslims a "critical hermeneutics":

> The recalcitrant Muslim is faulted for his inability to recognize that the truth of Quranic scripture is grounded not in its theological claims but in culture and history. The Quran, like the Bible, should therefore be appreciated for its cultural significance, as an object of aesthetic, poetic, and spiritual appreciation, rather than treated as a source that can guide one through the problems of contemporary existence. In this view, a correct interpretation is neither allegorical nor literal; it is based instead on an empiricist notion of history in which the particularity of the Quranic verses is rooted but from which their true meaning must be abstracted through the poetic resources of human labor.[172]

As much as some would like to deny the cultural, religious, and indeed hermeneutical and methodological heritage of Christian inculturation, it is harder to conceal in interreligious interaction. Indeed, Michael Gillespie argues that the very questions that governments informed by these narratives were seeking to solve can be traced to ancient theological problems, such as the unresolved question of the relationship between divine power and agency, human free will, nature and perfectability.[173]

This dynamic manifests and illustrates the inherent ambivalence of separating sacred and secular—and the impossibility of doing so. Each structure a society produces for the intersection between religion and public life produces regimes of proper knowledge and behavior, no matter what legitimation and form are chosen. The key question is not *whether* technologies of disciplining knowledge are executed, but *how they are legitimated, what form they take, and what values they restrain and shape.*[174]

---

[171] Saba Mahmood, "Secularism, Hermeneutics, and Empire: The Politics of Islamic Reformation," *Public Culture* 18:2 (2006): 328.

[172] Ibid., 326.

[173] Gillespie, *The Theological Origins of Modernity*.

[174] As Foucault and Agamben (Homo Sacer)—reading Carl Schmitt—have amply reminded us, there is no sphere of neutrality when it comes to power, and with it, the forcefulness with which it structures realities and bodies. Theologically this might be expressed in

The South African anthropologist Jean Comaroff describes the postcolonial breakdown of colonially imposed separations between sacred and secular through a case study on the "detective fictions" of a post-Apartheid crime unit that includes "diviner detectives" in an attempt to reintegrate the priestly functions of healing minds and bodies after a crime has been committed.[175] Detectives knowledgeable and skilled in recognizing and interacting with spiritual underpinnings of crimes and violence were able to cut through to a level of detection that was unparalleled by apartheid or post-Apartheid "secular" police forces, albeit with a level of crusading machismo that integrated the secular crime series of U.S. TV whodunits with traditional divining and auguring practices. In postcolonial South Africa, as in other societies transitioning from colonial to postcolonial rule, the deferred productive integration of indigenous and colonial cultures approximates a "return of the repressed" as multiple legitimating narratives compete with each other, endangering the populace and rewriting social forces. In a strange reversal, this reemergence of sacred facets of crime response evokes a Victorian move from priestly detection narrativity to the modern crime novel:

> A Victorian detective was a secular substitute for a prophet or a priest. In a newly uncertain world, he offered science, conviction, stories that could organise chaos. He turned brutal crimes—after the vestiges of the beast in man—into intellectual puzzles.[176]

The postcolonial and the postmodern moment here seem to overlap, both manifesting a return of the religious. Many anthropologists, taking for granted an internalized ideology of secularist bourgeois senses of law and nation, are struggling to contribute to such troubles with anything more than liberalist humanist descriptions, while indigenous and Pentecostal churches, which in many instances articulate themselves as postcolonial churches, rival and often surpass the colonial churches in responding with spiritual warmth and hands-on, comprehensive care. Meanwhile, the colonial churches can tend to limit their public ministrations to Sunday services, as is secular practice, where Sunday is church day, the rest of the week is workweek. While a historical development with its own kind of logic, this reality does little to address the spiritual

---

terms of the totality of power claims made upon the world. Much theological narrativity strives to comprehend and structure how humans engage divine power, divine word and commandment toward creative and destructive ends.

[175] Unpublished manuscript, "Detective Fictions and Sovereign Pursuits: Adventures in Policing the Postcolony," forthcoming as a chapter in *The Metaphysics of Disorder: Policing the Postcolony*, by Jean Comaroff.

[176] See also preface in Kate Summerscale, *The Suspicions of Mr. Whicher: A Shocking Murder and the Undoing of a Great Victorian Detective* (New York: Walker & Company, 2008), XII, which indicates that detectives took over priestly functions and were part of the secularization, and so on of British society.

and human needs of young people in a national transition. The increasing marginalization of colonial churches in certain locations of postcolonial Africa and elsewhere appears to highlight a strange amalgam of unarticulated anticolonial sentiment that undermines their influence while being replaced with the more emotive, evangelical, and personable impetus of Pentecostal churches. Ironically, of course, many "independent" Pentecostal theological expositions are based in yet another colonial logic, that of prosperity gospel, a spiritual articulation of and response to global capitalism, offering little protection from exploitation and abuse of power through spiritual leadership.[177]

Many in what counts as the "poor South" by the standards of developmental theories, have embraced Christianity, and increasingly a gospel of prosperity. If, indeed, "the poor themselves may prefer prosperity and so desire a theology of prosperity," theology "has the option of following these desires of the poor and so of rewriting its agenda along secular lines, or else of discerning here a heresy, which therefore gives theology an important task."[178] Though the lines between secular and sacred cannot be that clearly drawn, and, as we have been arguing, the "secular" is deeply related and entangled with the sacred, these two theological possibilities are the most widely represented. It is the repetition of a different gospel that appeals to the poor while the repetitions of different gospels in the North receive a colder shoulder by comparatively rich Westerners, whose ambivalence to Christianity has many facets, but among them a declining religiosity that may be related, in some cases, to their relative prosperity and the fact that Northern churches supply less vital health and social services than previously.

Prosperity gospels are often too easily dismissed from the vantage point of seemingly more secular societies, perhaps because within them the pursuit of wealth came to be seen as a secular pursuit, not acknowledging the scandalous sacrality of money, wealth, property, and products. Though "the line between Ponzi schemes and evangelical prosperity is very thin indeed,"[179] some forms of prosperity theology function for their constituents by announcing a different theological anthropology: spiritual empowerment for colonized subjects whose sense of self has been that of black poverty. The speech act announcing power and promise for each person, lifting them out of a global narrative that has often forgotten them, despite its very limited likelihood, provides tools for a transformed self-perception and sense of identity.[180] The global growth

[177] Jean Comaroff, "Uncool Passion: Nietzsche Meets the Pentecostals," European University Institute, Max Weber Lecture, No. 2008/10, 7–8. http://cadmus.eui.eu/bitstream/handle/1814/9928/MWL_2008_10.pdf?sequence=1 and Paul Gifford, *Ghana's New Christianity: Pentecostalism in a Globalizing Economy* (Bloomintgon & Indianapolis: Indiana University Press, 2004): only online.

[178] Bediako, "African Dimension," 117.

[179] John Comaroff and Jean Comaroff, "Millennial Capitalism: First Thoughts on a Second Coming," *Public Culture* Vol. 12, No.2 (2000): 291–343, 313.

[180] Gifford, *Ghana's New Christianity*, 52–3.

of phenomena like this, and the rise of "occult economies," the Comaroffs argue, represent

> a response to a world gone awry, yet again: a world in which the only way to create real wealth seems to lie in forms of power/knowledge that transgress the conventional, the rational, the moral—thus to multiply available techniques of producing value, fair or foul.[181]

The quasi-religious functions of consumer capitalism are perhaps less easy to distinguish from cargo cults than one might assume. Even after the markets crashed in 2008, the lack of a full examination of the religious qualities of belief in markets, currencies, and other financial "assets" helps to prevent more extensive rethinking of economic belief systems and their hegemonic invisibility. The layers of material and spiritual meaning implied here pose a key challenge to the articulation of polydoxy missiologies.

Works Cited

Bakhtin, Mikhail. *The Dialogic Imagination: Four Essays.* Holquist, Michael, ed. Trans. Carl Emerson and Michael Holquist. Austin, TX: University of Texas, 1981.

Barber, Elizabeth Wayland, and Paul T. Barber. *When They Severed Earth from Sky: How the Human Mind Shapes Myth.* Princeton, NJ: Princeton University Press, 2004.

Bartlett, Robert. *The Making of Europe: Conquest, Colonization and Cultural Change 950–1350.* Princeton, NJ: Princeton University Press, 1993.

Bediako, Kwame. "'Whose Religion is Christianity?' Reflections on Opportunities and Challenges in Christian Theological Scholarship: The African Dimension." In *Mission in the 21st Century: Exploring the Five Marks of Global Mission*, Andrew Walls and Cathy Ross, 107–17. Maryknoll: Orbis, 2008.

Boniface, Saint. *The Letters of Saint Boniface.* Introduction by Thomas F. X. Noble. Trans. Ephraim Emerton. New York: Columbia University Press, 2000.

Brock, Peggy. "Introduction." In *Indigenous Peoples and Religious Change*, Peggy Brock, ed., 1–11. Leiden: Brill, 2005.

Brock, Rita Nakashima, and Rebecca Ann Parker. *Saving Paradise: How Christianity Traded Love of This World for Crucifixion and Empire.* Boston: Beacon, 2001.

Brown, Peter. *The Rise of Western Christendom: Triumph and Diversity, A.D. 200–1000.* Second Edn. Malden, MA: Blackwell, 2003.

Burrus, Virginia. *Begotten, Not Made: Conceiving Manhood in Late Antiquity.* Stanford: Stanford University Press, 2000.

—.*The Sex Lives of the Saints.* Philadelphia, PA: University of Pennsylvania Press, 2003.

---

[181] Comaroff and Comaroff, "Millennial Capitalism," 316.

Comaroff, Jean. "Uncool Passion: Nietzsche Meets the Pentecostals," forthcoming.

Comaroff, John, and Jean Comaroff. "Millennial Capitalism: First Thoughts on a Second Coming." *Public Culture* Vol. 12, No. 2, (2000): 291–343.

Daly, Mary. *Beyond God the Father: Toward a Philosophy of Women's Liberation*. Boston: Beacon, 1973.

Deloria, Vine Jr. *God is Red: A Native View of Religion*. Golden, CO: Fulcrum, 1994.

Fanon, Frantz. *Black Skin, White Masks*. New York: Grove Press, 1967.

Fletcher, Richard. *The Barbarian Conversion: From Paganism to Christianity*. Berkeley, CA: University of California, 1999.

Geary, Patrick J. *Furta Sacra: Thefts of Relics in the Central Middle Ages*. Princeton, NJ: Princeton University Press, 1978.

—.*The Myth of Nations: The Medieval Origins of Europe*. Princeton, NJ: Princeton University Press, 2002.

Gifford, Paul. *Ghana's New Christianity: Pentecostalism in a Globalizing Economy*. Bloomington & Indianapolis: Indiana University Press, 2004.

Gillespie, Michael Allen. *The Theological Origins of Modernity*. Chicago, IL: University of Chicago Press, 2008.

Graf, Friedrich Wilhelm. "Germanisierung Des Christentums." In *Religion in Geschichte und Gegenwart, 3rd Ed.*, Hans Dieter Betz, et al., 754. Tübingen: Mohr Siebeck, 1998.

Haendler, Gert. "Bonifatius." In *Mittelalter (Gestalten der Kirchengeschichte)*, edited by Martin Greschat, 69–86. Stuttgart, Germany: Kohlhammer, 1983.

Heine, Heinrich. *Zur Geschichte der Religion und Philosophie in Deutschland*. Stuttgart: Philipp Reclam Jun., 1997.

The Heliand: The Saxon Gospel. Trans. and edited by G. Ronald Murphy. New York/ Oxford: Oxford University Press, 1992.

Hertz, Deborah. *How Jews Became Germans: The History of Conversion and Assimilation in Berlin*. New Haven: Yale University Press, 2007.

Higgins, John Seville. "The Ultramontanism of Saint Boniface." *Church History* Vol. 2, No. 4 (December 1933): 197–210.

Hillgarth, J. N., ed. *Christianity and Paganism, 350–750*. Philadelphia: University of Pennsylvania Press, 1969.

Howe, Nicholas. "Rome: Capital of Anglo-Saxon England." *Journal of Medieval and Early Modern Studies* Vol. 34, No. 1 (Winter 2004): 147–72.

Jenkins, Philip. *God's Continent*. New York: Oxford University Press, 2007.

—."Godless Europe?" *International Bulletin of Missionary Research* Vol. 31, No. 3 (2007): 115–20.

Josyln-Siemiatkoski, Daniel. *Christian Memories of The Maccabean Martyrs*. New York: Palgrave Macmillan, 2009.

Keller, Catherine. *On The Mystery: Discerning God in Process*. Minneapolis, MN: Fortress, 2008.

Lindow, John. *Norse Mythology: A Guide to the Gods, Heroes, Rituals and Beliefs*. Oxford: Oxford University Press, 2001.

Mahmood, Saba. "Secularism, Hermeneutics, and Empire: The Politics of Islamic Reformation." *Public Culture* 18:2 (2006): 323–47.

Mancall, Peter C. *Hakluyt's Promise: An Elizabethan Obsession for an English America.* New Haven, CT: Yale University Press, 2007.

Mikaelsson, Lisbeth. "Locality and Myth: The Resacralization of Selja and the Cult of St. Sunniva." *Numen* Vol. 52 (2005).

Milbank, John. ed. *Radical Orthodoxy:A New Theology.* London: Routledge, 1999.

Mufti, Aamir. *Enlightenment in the Colony: The Jewish Question and the Crisis of Postcolonial Culture.* Princeton, NJ: Princeton University Press, 2007.

Murphy, G. Ronald. *The Saxon Savior: The Germanic Transformation of the Gospel in the Ninth-Century Heliand.* New York/Oxford: Oxford University Press, 1989.

Noble, Thomas F.X. and Thomas Head, eds "Introduction." In *Soldiers of Christ: Saints and Saints' Lives from Late Antiquity and the Early Middle Ages,* Soldiers of Christ, xiii-xliv. University Park, PA.: Pennsylvania University Press, 1995.

—,eds "The Life of Saint Boniface." In *Soldiers of Christ: Saints and Saints' Lives from Late Antiquity and the Early Middle Ages,* Soldiers of Christ, 107–40. University Park, PA.: Pennsylvania University Press, 1995.

—,eds "The Life of Saint Leoba." In *Soldiers of Christ: Saints and Saints' Lives from Late Antiquity and the Early Middle Ages,* Soldiers of Christ, 257–77. University Park, PA.: Pennsylvania University Press, 1995.

Padberg, Lutz E. von. *Bonifatius: Missionar und Reformer.* München: C. H. Beck Wissen, 2003.

—.*Christianisierung Im Mittelalter.* Darmstadt: Wissenschaftliche Buchgesellschaft, 2006.

Padberg, Lutz von and Hans-Walter Stork. *Der Ragyndrudis-Codex Des Hl. Bonifatius.* Fulda: Verlag Parzeller, 1994.

Petterson, Christina. "Moses and Abraham Go Arctic." *Biblical Interpretation* 16 (2008): 363–74.

Proksch, Nikola. "The Anglo-Saxon Missionaries to the Continent." In *Monks of England: The Benedictines in England from Augustine to the Present Day,* ed. Daniel Rees, 37–54. London: SPCK, 1997.

Russell, James C. *The Germanization of Early Medieval Christianity: A Sociohistorical Approach to Religious Transformation.* Oxford: Oxford University Press, 1994.

Sanneh, Lamin. "The Church and Its Missionary Vocation: The Islamic Frontline in a Post-Christian West." In *Mission in the 21st Century: Exploring the Five Marks of Global Mission,* Andrew Walls and Cathy Ross, eds Maryknoll: Orbis, 1989.

Schama, Simon. *Landscape and Memory.* New York: Alfred E. Knopf, 1995.

Schiefer, Theodor. *Winfrid-Bonifatius und die Christliche Grundlegung Europas.* Freiburg: Herder, 1954.

Schierz, Kai Uwe, ed. *Von Bonifatius Bis Beuys—oder: Vom Umgang mit Den Heiligen Eichen.* Erfurt: Druckhaus Gera, 2004.

Schneider, Laurel C. *Beyond Monotheism: A Theology of Multiplicity.* London: Routledge, 2008.

Schreiber, Elliott. "Tainted Sources: The Subversion of the Grimm's Ideology of the Folktale in Heinrich Heine's *Der Rabbi von Bacherach*." *The German Quarterly* 78.1 (Winter 2005): 23–44.

Schwartz, Regina. *The Curse of Cain: The Violent Legacy of Monotheism.* Chicago, IL: The University of Chicago Press, 1997.

Sheehan, James J. "Lebensraum." *New York Times* September 19 (2008).

Smith, Jonathan Z. *Map is Not Territory: Studies in the History of Religions.* Chicago, IL: University of Chicago, 1978.

Spivak, Gayatri. *A Critique of Postcolonial Reason: Toward a History of the Vanishing Present.* Cambridge: Harvard University Press, 1999.

Steinsland, Gro. "Fra Yggdrasils Ask Til Korsets Tre—Tanker Om Trosskiftet." In *Fra Hedendom Til Kristendom: Perspektiver På Religionsskiftet i Norge,* edited by Magnus Rindal, 20–30. Oslo: Ad Notam Gyldendal, 1996.

—.*Norrøn Religion: Myter, Riter, Samfunn.* Oslo: Pax Forlag, 2005.

Summerscale, Kate. *The Suspicions of Mr. Whicher: A Shocking Murder and the Undoing of a Great Victorian Detective.* New York: Walker & Company, 2008.

Voltaire. *The General History and State of Europe,* 1756.

Wallace-Hadrill, John Michael. "A Background to Boniface's Mission." In *England Before the Conquest,* England, 35–48. Cambridge: Cambridge University Press, 1971.

Wolfram, Herwig. *The Roman Empire and Its Germanic Peoples.* Berkeley, CA: University of California Press, 1990.

Chapter 5

Itinerary II:
Going South:
The Zulu, the Colensos, and
the Hermeneutics of Salvation

Ethnic Loyalties and Interethnic Alliances in
Contexts of Mission

Ethnicities, so states Benedict Anderson, can be seen as "imagined communities."[1] They have often been successfully deployed to make "claims for unity under leaders who hoped to monopolize and to embody the traditions associated with these names," while "appropriating disparate traditions and inventing new ones."[2] This could be said for the apostle Paul, the church fathers, Frankish leaders, as well as Shaka, the Zulu king. Ancient Roman writers often misidentified, collapsed, or simply "did not distinguish clearly between ethnic, political, and territorial terminology," and there were times when peoples were seen as "territorial units of geographical and political organization, not social or cultural groups."[3] Hence, *Germania* and *Franchonoland* could at times be identified. The Carolingian dynasty in particular, needing to establish its legitimacy over against the Merovingians, created an identity that was being "forged even as it was projected backwards onto a distant, mythic, past in order to confer legitimacy on it by infusing it with an ancient aura."[4] Then and now, the key to imperial rule includes techniques of co-opting the local elites. Carolingian regional policy "guaranteed them a public place and a separate law while planting imperial agents throughout a vast Empire," thereby creating a "new kind of European ethnicity," grounded in legal privilege rather than ancestry or culture. Demythologizing the "myth of nations," of ethnic

---

[1] Benedict Anderson, *Imagined Communities: Reflections on the Origin and Spread of Nationalism* (London: Verso, 1983).
[2] Patrick J. Geary, *The Myth of Nations: The Medieval Origins of Europe* (Princeton, NJ: Princeton University Press, 2002), 155–6.
[3] Ibid., 151.
[4] Ibid., 153.

purity or even basic ethnic consistency in political configurations then and now, Patrick Geary deflates nationalisms old and new, those that manifested in the modern world, both in the North, and the postcolonial nationalisms in the South. Rather, he argues that "the history of European peoples in Late Antiquity and the early Middle Ages is not the story of a primordial moment but of a continuous process," so that "the peoples of Europe are a work in progress and always must be."[5] Geary compares Zulu and Frankish, Gothic and Serbian ethnogenesis to illuminate how we think of European peoples and European consciousness no longer "as historical reconstructions but rather as self-evident and essential components of national identity."[6] Indeed, he proposes that the classic story of Zulu ethnogenesis "includes the same mythical, literary, and classical motifs that we find in European history,"[7] that is, they were written under similar influences of "Judeo-Christian and classical traditions." The myth-shattering potential is powerful:

> Some Europeans may bristle at seeing the origins of their own ethnic and political groups equated to those of a southern African people. For many, the reason may be less specifically racism than the deeply held belief that while the "history" of an African people may be a mere cultural construct, their own past is somehow "real."[8]

It may not be as strange as it seems to "entertain the possibility that they are no different from the millions of South Africans who trace their origins to Shaka KaSenzangakhona, the founder of the Zulu nation, who shares the same place in his people's history as does Clovis for the French, Chrobatos for the Croats, and Isperikh for the Bulgarians."[9] Just as in the history of these European peoples, Geary suggests, an outsider, in this case A. T. Bryant, a Christian missionary, became the "collector of Zulu 'history.'" Similar to foreign or colonial writers of history such as Tacitus or Bede, he assumed and hence created what he thought had to be a "single 'correct' version of the Zulu past," rather than allowing for the complexity of different accounts from different angles and interests, seeing his task as filling in the gaps and to "harmonize discrepancies." While he may have been motivated by a sense of "altruistic duty 'to our unlettered Negro brother to rescue for him from final oblivion, before too late, such of his simple traditions as are still recoverable, whatever be their worthlessness to us,'"[10] his positionality defines his account. Like many of his contemporaries, Bryant recast the "Zulu history into a Hebrew or European ethnogenesis, as he understood it" while "the manner in which

5 Ibid., 155–6.
6 Ibid., 157–8.
7 Ibid., 158.
8 Ibid., 159.
9 Ibid., 159.
10 Ibid., 161–2.

he assigned motivation and meaning likewise mirrored European traditions," partly, as other colonial writers, to make the material seem more familiar to their European readers by "drawing constant parallels to European cultural traditions."[11] Predictably, like most of the authors "at the end of Antiquity and in the early Middle Ages did," he drew "explicit parallels between the Zulu and both the Hebrew people's wanderings in *Exodus* and the legendary wanderings of the Lombards, the Goths, and the Slavs in the early Middle Ages."[12] Though migration narratives like these "may indeed be a fiction," often the "individual fragments are not," and it may be possible to draw from them kernels of insight into the dynamics of ethnogenesis and its narrative iterations.[13] In reexamining the evidence, Geary suggests it is possible to postulate a narrative "radically different from that created by Bryant," where "*Nguni* [or Zulu], rather like *Germans*, has meaning only as a linguistic designation, never as a political, cultural, or social grouping."[14]

The archaeological record and close reading of Zulu legends provide no evidence of long-distance population movements in the seventeenth and eighteenth centuries, any more than one can accept the legends of Gothic migrations from Scandinavia or Frankish wanderings from the Danube to the Rhine. Rather, the groups that would, in time, become Zulu emerged from the indigenous population of the area. These narratives of migration are thus means of projecting mythic "founding charters" onto nineteenth-century polities.[15]

As historians assume with Arminius, Geary suspects that a similar dynamic, generated by the presence of imperial trade, was a major factor in helping Shaka consolidate a "system of political control" due to "weakened ties uniting young men with older generations," binding them instead to his own person as the Zulu king. In the forcefield of empire, a local power figure can use certain advantages to expand their own often starkly repressive power.[16] Thus, these versions of Zulu history ring familiar to Europeans for at least two reasons: (1) their writers shared a very similar subject position as ancient and medieval historians such as Gregory of Tours, Bede, and (2) these accounts were attempts to incorporate new peoples into a greater narrative of "history," a history that "for them could only mean the history of Rome."[17] Ironically, it is through a closer look at the presumed mythical origins of European peoples, the "constructs of European ethnic mythology," that more complexity has been brought to the understanding of the complex emergence of the Zulu.[18] Geary concludes that

---

[11] Ibid., 163.
[12] Ibid., 162–3, 164.
[13] Ibid., 165.
[14] Ibid., 166.
[15] Ibid., 166–7.
[16] Ibid., 169.
[17] Ibid., 171.
[18] Ibid., 171.

"a history that does not change, that reduces all the complexities of centuries of social, political and cultural change, to a single, eternal moment, isn't history at all."[19] It is perhaps no coincidence that many supporters of the Zulu cause were recruited from among Irish, Welsh, and Scottish nationalists, who, one would assume, had a keen consciousness of having been colonized by the English themselves.[20]

Re/Visions of the Terrible Warrior and the Noble Savage

The question of what the Zulu chief Shaka's role before the colonization of Natal was is complex. Revision piles upon revision. On his first trip through Natal as the area's new Anglican bishop, John William Colenso initially adopted the received narrative, which held that

> [a]bout thirty years ago, Natal was almost emptied of its inhabitants, owing to the continual ravages of the great Zulu chief, Chaka, who then lived in the Zulu country, to the north of our colony, and made himself a very notorious name by devastating conquests abroad, and deeds of brutality and bloodshed at home.[21]

The Colenso family, who later came to support the notion of a Zulu kingdom, appears to have rejected a version of its history as that "of the tyranny of the Zulu royal house over the people of Zululand"[22] as propagated by colonial brokers such as Theophilus Shepstone, or at least to have taken a kinder view of its potential for the preservation or survival of Zulu identity, a complex phenomenon to begin with. The term "Zulu" was initially associated with a clan. Over time, through Shaka's resistance against the overpowering Mthetwa kingdom and his subsequent defeat and subjection of several other kingdoms, the term Zulu came to stand for the political, rather than ethnic, formation that resulted from his conquests.[23] Colonial historical revisionism tended to justify its own existence in part by pointing to the less than pure history of the colonized. Thus, Theophilus Shepstone in a nineteenth century version of "political correctness" gone awry and put in the service of oppression,

---

[19] Ibid., 173.
[20] Jeff Guy, *The View Across the River: Harriette Colenso and the Zulu Struggle Against Imperialism* (Charlottesville, VA: University of Virginia Press, 2001), 319.
[21] John William Colenso, *Ten Weeks in Natal: A Journal of a First Tour of Visitation Among the Colonists and Zulu Kafirs of Natal* (Cambridge: MacMillan & Co., 1855), vii–viii.
[22] Guy, *The View Across the River*, 12.
[23] John Parker and Richard Rathbone, *African History: A Very Short Introduction* (Oxford: Oxford University Press, 2007), 40.

argues that "the Zulu kingdom was an aberration," and that its founder "had terminated African chiefly rule and replaced it with autocracy, supported by a military system which oppressed its people and terrrorized its neighbors."[24]

A common colonial hermeneutic strategy—long before the postmodernity that is now commonly blamed for such moves—is the repositioning of history with bias toward colonial designs, manifesting a reckless desire for power and a need to appear magnanimous to a certain public. Similar to Shepstone's stories about Shaka and his claim that the Zulu chiefs are simply cruel tyrants, early New Zealand Pakeha historians have argued that some Maoris' cruelty toward the Chatham Islanders justified their subjugation and the colonization of Aotearoa/New Zealand. Both Maori tribal groups and Zulu kingdom were, contrary to some romanticized visions of indigenous societies, highly stratified, including concepts of serfdom, slavery, and marginal humans. The Bushmen, for example, were considered barely human by the Zulu. Of course, we know about such stratifications partly because they were noticed by missionaries and settlers and at times used in an arsenal to justify conversion both spiritually and economically.

> The history of the peoples of Europe in the early Middle Ages cannot be used as an argument for or against any of the political, territorial, and ideological movements of today, any more than the future of KwaZulu-Natal can lie with the "correct" interpretation of the life of King Shaka.[25]

That the colonial domestication of indigenous peoples in numerous places involved a conscious conversion of household and spiritual economies into European-centered ones is no longer a surprise. But some of the questions the Comaroffs raised in the early 1990s still bear further and closer investigation:

> Precisely *which* Western models of domesticity, for instance, were imported to the colonies? How stable and consensual were they in their own societies? Were they merely vehicles of European "family ideology" or did they implicate more thoroughgoing social and cultural forces? Most significantly, was this imperialist gesture a simple act of domination of the "periphery" by the "center" or were the changes wrought on the colonial fringe also entailed in the making of the world from which they came?[26]

The Comaroffs here point to the mutual generation of colonial and colonized societies. David Livingstone claimed that "the promotion of commerce

---

[24] Guy, *The View Across the River*, 50.

[25] Geary, *Myth of Nations*, 173.

[26] John Comaroff and Jean Comaroff, *Ethnography and the Historical Imagination* (Boulder, CO: Westview Press, 1992), 266.

[among African natives] diminishes the sense of isolation which heathenism engenders." Leaving aside for a moment the question of why and how heathenism would have been particularly isolating, strikingly, Livingstone continues in tropes that still inform some developmental and nongovernmental agendas: "to promote the preparation of the raw materials of European manufacturers in Africa, for by that means we may not only put a stop to slave-trade, but introduce the negro family into the body of corporate nations."[27] The increase of global trade is lifted up as the beginning of liberation and a move toward nationhood.

Signs Taken for Polydoxy in a Zulu Kraal

Money and commodities, literacy and Christendom challenged local symbols, threatening to convert them into a universal currency. But precisely because the cross, the book, and the coin were such saturated signs, they were variously and ingeniously redeployed to bear a host of new meanings as non-Western peoples—Tswana prophets, Naparama fighters, and others—fashioned their own visions of modernity.[28]

There was never a complete hegemony within British political culture. That culture was nothing if not conflictual, and increasingly so. It is as simplistic to assume that the colonizers were uniformly pro-colonization as it is to assume that those being colonized were uniformly against it—many of the latter's upper classes and comprador bourgeoisie did very nicely out of colonialism.[29]

The emergence of the Zulu kingdom around the time of first colonial presences, the interactions with colonials and missionaries in the nineteenth century, and its twentieth century repackaging as a developmental cause, cultural tourist spectacle and ethnic identity presented as commodity, invite a study in the dynamics of ethnic, religious, and national identities in colonial and intercultural encounter. The sociosexual and economic organization of this Zulu kingdom was challenged by confrontation with Victorian Christian mores, sexually transmitted diseases, resource exploitation and family breakdown, a long history of racial apartheid and socioeconomic marginalization. Post-Apartheid South Africa struggles mightily to move beyond the problematic aspects of reemerging tribal ethnocentrism, reiterations of repressive indigenous and colonial patriarchal masculinities, and socioeconomic disparities redistributed through global capitalist adaptations by a local elite. The opening of this society toward consumer capitalism and U.S.-spread prosperity

---

[27] Ibid., *Ethnography*, 145.
[28] Ibid., 5.
[29] Kwame Anthony Appiah, *Cosmopolitanism: Ethics in a World of Strangers* (New York: W. W. Norton & Company, 2006), 74.

theologies represents merely the latest wave of highly ambivalent colonial cultural influences. It is precisely such formations of postcolonial and post-missionary dynamics we must circumambulate to move toward articulating a viable polydox theology of mission.

Don't Mess with the Missionary Clan!

A general willingness to adapt, to opt for a syncretic approach to the task of Christianization, is always going to raise the question: how far down that path may any missionary venture? When does compromise become surrender? Is "syncretism" just a sophisticated way of saying that almost anything will go? This question in its various forms is always going to be at its most insistent when a structure of the ecclesiastical authority is barely existent. Almost by definition, is in the mission field that this state of affairs is likely to be found. There is plenty of scope for disagreement between missionaries and the home church, or between different missionaries, about the issues that will arise. The anguish of the misunderstood or misrepresented has been a feature of missionary history from Patrick to Bishop Colenso of Natal—and beyond.[30]

The Anglican Church in South Africa started as a settler church, and initially had no bishopric. With the foundation of the Church Missionary Society in 1799, this began to change. The Cornish mathematician, schoolbook author, and cleric John William Colenso (1814–1883), deeply influenced by his friend the Anglican evangelical Frederic Denison Maurice and the poet Samuel Taylor Coleridge, was recruited as the Bishop of Natal in Pietermaritzburg in South Africa. Over the course of his tenure there, his engagement with the Zulu around issues of biblical truth claims, as well as economic and sociosexual realities, increasingly alienated him and his family from the growing white settler population. He was tried for heresy and henceforth severely impaired in his function as a bishop. His legacy was carried on after his death most prominently by his daughter Harriette (1847–1932), who worked tirelessly to defend and support Zulus who had gotten tangled up in colonial law while advocating the recognition and repatriation of the Zulu king after his banishment to St. Helena by the Crown.

The issues brought to bear in the heresy trial of Bishop John William Colenso deeply informed the self-understanding of the Church of England and the Anglican Church of Southern Africa, as well as the formation of the beginnings of what is now called the "Anglican Communion." Colenso provides a compelling case study of the collision of a number of factors: The Church of

---

[30] Richard Fletcher, *The Barbarian Conversion: From Paganism to Christianity* (Berkeley, CA: University of California, 1999), 271.

England and attempts to disestablish it; conservative, dissenting, and evangelical movements within Britain; the Oxford Movement; attempts at ecumenical cooperation, and the rise of German historical criticism and liberal theologies. In addition, British colonialism and the emerging thought of Charles Darwin complicated conflicts, along with challenges to previous theories of history and historiography. Benjamin Disraeli, a Jewish convert and himself suspect to British society, remarked on the Colenso affair, "They defeat our generals, they convert our bishops" and thus suggested that Colenso, the missionary trickster, was tricked by his own so-called converts.[31] But the story was by far not as simple as this mot suggests.

John William Colenso held controversial opinions before he left Britain. He was a mathematician, open to new developments in Western science, and interested in Darwin's theories and observations. Darwin, in return, was a supporter of Colenso's during the church controversy attacking the bishop's views. In South Africa, the Colensos engaged in a "long conversation"[32] that transformed Zulu communal ideas and the missionary family's self-understanding. Colenso's encounter with Zulu cultural values, and his support of Zulu independence meant that "his converts and scholars from [the mission station] Ekukhanyeni were among the vanguard of a new Zulu consciousness, known early on as the 'Bishopstowe faction,' after his house in Ekukhanyeni."[33] The term "cool conversion" is a good descriptor for the "Colenso effect." Sugirtharajah names as Colenso's three exegetical ambitions: he wanted to change missionary misperceptions of Africans; speak the truth about the Bible, even if inconvenient; and offer an "exegesis of practical engagement."[34] Colenso thus became a "dissident" reader of biblical texts. Though "located within and co-opted by the colonial system," dissident readers, in their own way "caused unsettlement, dislocation, and placed a question mark over territorial and cultural expansion."[35]

The Colensos practiced a liberal optimism that believed if people acted according to their best knowledge they would be just and truthful at all times. They assumed that if people gave others a fair chance and respected the law

---

[31] Cited in Magema Magwa Fuze, *The Black People And Whence They Came* (Pietermaritzburg: University of Natal Press, 1979), 154.

[32] This term, introduced by the Comaroff's into ethnographic study, has become widely used for the ongoing nature of cultural encounters. John Comaroff and Jean Comaroff, *Of Revelation and Revolution: Christianity, Colonialism, and Consciousness in South Africa, Vol. 1* (Chicago, IL: Chicago University Press, 1991), 200.

[33] Jonathan A. Draper, "Bishop John William Colenso's Interpretation To The Zulu People Of The *Sola Fide* In Paul's Letter To The Romans," in *SBL 2000 Seminar Papers* (Atlanta: SBL, 2000), 491.

[34] R. S. Sugirtharajah, *The Bible and the Third World: Pre-colonial, Colonial, and Postcolonial Encounters* (Cambridge: Cambridge University Press, 2001), 128–31.

[35] R. S. Sugirtharajah, *Postcolonial Criticism and Biblical Interpretation* (Oxford: Oxford University Press, 2002), 44.

given by God and held up by the Queen, then God would approve the colonial situation. They explicitly critiqued British colonial authorities, but appealed, somewhat ironically, to the Queen to discipline British colonial functionaries and to defend them against the Church of England who had expelled Colenso. Many settlers in the Bishop's diocese interpreted the Colensos' critical attitude toward colonial practices, racial discrimination and their willingness to consider Africans as fully capable human subjects as a betrayal. The settlers were also suspicious of a "conversion" Bishop Colenso had supposedly undergone.

The Divine Economy as Mission and Missionary Economies

The intersecting economies of conversion bring together layers of civilizing mission with the mixed motifs for conversion or affiliation with a mission. The economic implications of the term conversion are far from incidental. A trade and a trade-off are often involved in converting. Thus, in nineteenth century Zululand,

> the initial converts to Christianity were largely the despised, the disparaged, and the disaffected, drawn to the mission stations by the prospects of land and security. By far the largest category was homeless refugees, the product of Shakan wars, which ravaged southeast Africa in the nineteenth century in the wake of the rise of the Zulu kingdom.[36]

The dynamic of attracting physically or socially orphaned persons, the disenfranchised, women, and persons of lower class or status, toward missionary institutions is well established. External pressure on a society adds to this forcefield. In fact, "the rise of the Zulu empire had the same sort of effects upon nearby peoples such as the Sotho as the rise of the Hun empire had upon the German peoples in the fourth and fifth centuries."[37] Ethnic groups under pressure established their own polities, forming a more centralized rule united around one leader. There are distinct echoes of the "close spatial association of royalty and mission so often found in early medieval Europe."[38] In other cases, male missionaries approached powerful men in the culture they

---

[36] Shula Marks, *Ambiguities of Dependence in South Africa: Class, Nationalism, and the State in Twentieth-Century Natal* (Baltimore, MD: Johns Hopkins University Press, 1986), 45 See also Comaroff and Comaroff, *Of Revelation and Revolution*, 261.

[37] Fletcher, *Barbarian Conversion*, 126.

[38] Ibid., 126.

were aiming to connect to and engage in Christian faith and treat them as a beachhead, following the tried formula of top-down evangelization that was prevalent in the conversion of European peoples to Christianity: Constantine, Clovis, Charlemagne, and was also attempted, with varying degrees of success in modern colonial missions, by Jesuits in India and by Protestant missionaries seeking to form close relations with tribal leaders.

At the edges of societies, individuals who seek transformation, spiritually, socially, and economically, can become attracted to what manifests itself as an opening in the density of established relationality. Whether it is young nobles who seek education from the likes of Boniface and Leoba in Charlemagne's Frankish realm or women missionaries in interior Alaska who find that their teaching labors are most successful among orphans, the transitional status of the bi-culturally perched is peculiar, unstable, and thus highly ambivalent. Because of the disintegration that occurs simultaneously with a transformation, the psychological and physical effects of moving from one disciplinary system to another are often profoundly dislocating, especially if they occur within a setting where new kinds of violences manifest themselves.

In Europe, the top-down approach to collective religious identity manifested during the Reformation as *cuius regio, eius religio*, the region took on the religion of the ruler. These forced religious allegiances led some to question whether European lands could indeed be said to be converted, and if so, what that may have meant. We may raise similar questions about conversions under colonialism, in Africa, Asia, and elsewhere. As early Christianity became somewhat more upperclass and fashionable in Late Antiquity, it enticed the literate elite who converted not without importing previous cultural presuppositions and practices. Converts notoriously display multiple religious identities and incremental conversions. Alongside "sanctioned" expressions of missionary Christiantiy, forms of religiosity far and beyond the intentions of the missionaries manifest themselves: African Independent Churches, and varieties of prophetic movements constitute only some of them. Converts, manifesting a hybrid identity, can create varieties of quasi-orthodoxies, with multiple effects. For example, Justin Martyr's "intellectual argument of mimicry to subvert philosophical authority necessarily led to the subversion of orthodox Christianity itself"[39] At the same time, Justin's logic restricts access for the next generation into territories still accessible to him. Conversions in all their complexity manifest not either a simply liberating nor solely oppressive process, but provisionally as a transition between disciplinary regimes, either one of which comes with conveniences and disadvantages.

[39] See Rebecca Lyman, "The Politics of Passing: Justin Martyr's Conversion as a Problem of Hellenization," in *Conversion in Late Antiquity and the Middle Ages: Seeing and Believing*, eds Anthony Grafton and Kenneth Mills (Rochester, NY: University of Rochester Press, 2003), 45.

Colenso addressed the status of converts to Christianity prominently in his 1862 letter to the Archbishop of Canterbury. Colenso argues that even though polygamy was not considered a sin anywhere in the scriptures, while adultery and slavery were, "the practice of polygamy is at variance with the whole spirit of Christianity, just as much as that of slavery is, and must eventually be rooted out."[40] This overlooks the biblical support for slavery, so Colenso is adopting somewhat of a double standard. One might argue, that he had to choose between the greater evil of pushing away potential converts by making pre-baptism requirements that tear apart families and remove the children of such unions from Christian teaching. The lesser evil would then consist in allowing polygamous men (there is little mention of the agency of women and children apart from what the agency of men could mean for them) to become Christians in the hope that future generations might be transformed toward monogamous marriages. Colenso argues that "polygamy was practised by eminently pious men," and was not against the law.[41] Yet, the same could be said about slavery. It appears Colenso considered polygamy to be in a different state of abolition than slavery, which was abolished throughout the British Empire in 1833, only about 30 years prior, but still within proximity of memory. This practice makes most sense from the point of view of a male missionary who considers, as Colenso does, primarily, if not only, the agency and life world of the men involved in this practice and its legality. The economic situation of women and children appears only as an appendix. Colenso appears to promulgate Victorian mores with little or no room for women's agency apart from home and hearth, even as the women in his family were far from constricted to the privacy of the home. All of the women in his household led active intellectual and writing lives and engaged the public powerfully. While polygamy was forbidden in the Roman Empire, Colenso finds, the ancient Christian authorities see little reason to condemn a practice that was not considered to be against biblical law.[42]

While the integrity of patriarchal property (including women and children) is protected by these laws as well as Zulu laws, the economic ruin of women through frivolous divorce and widowhood is not against biblical law, even as it is critically engaged in biblical narratives of women like Rahab, Tamar, and Ruth, who had to work the patriarchal system for survival. The practice is judged or accepted based on ethnocentric criteria, Colenso submits, as "polygamy was abhorrent to the habits of the Romans (and to those of almost all the nations of Europe, as the Greeks, Gauls, and Germans) in their heathen state,

---

[40] John William Colenso, *A Letter to His Grace the Archibishop of Canterbury Upon the Question of the Proper Treatment of Cases of Polygamy, as Found Already Existing in Converts from Heathenism* (London: Macmillan and Co., 1862), 2.

[41] Ibid., 4–5.

[42] John William Colenso, *Polygamy*, 25.

and was ultimately forbidden by law, when Eastern practices began to creep among them," while it continued to be tolerated among Jews, even under the Roman empire, as a national custom.[43] Yet, Colenso, far from arguing divine origin for any of the social sexual organizations, attributes the suppression of polygamy among Jews in Europe to the

> influence of Roman laws, customs and opinions, that would naturally take effect upon them, and the practice of polygamy altogether die out among them, as among the Jews of modern Europe. Indeed, it is possible that the extreme dislike which an European feels to the very idea of a polygamist being recognized as a true Christian, may be partly attributable to our Western habits and education, as well as to religious feeling.[44]

Colenso states quite strongly that "believing as I do, [. . .] polygamy as found among the untaught heathen, is not [. . .] in fact, a sin at all."[45]

Colenso's overall argument tends toward a sense of gradualism in mission, similar to the practice of medieval missionaries, rather than an overall acceptance of polygamy, which he states in the beginning of his document, is not the ideal imagined in the gospel. However, so he quotes Theophilus Shepstone, the Secretary for Native Affairs in Natal "to say that the married native women of this country are slaves, or sold as such, is to betray utter ignorance of the social condition of the natives."[46] Rather, the cattle given to their families are a "guarantee for their good treatments by their husbands, and a perpetual security for their being cared for, and protected by their parents and blood-relatives."[47] Shepstone continues that "a native woman is in this respect, more protected than her English neighbour," and to persons who argue that a native woman is the equivalent of slaves, "because she is compelled by her position to work as one," he replies that "almost every English lady in this colony is as much a slave, and for the same reason."[48] Indeed, both systems are patriarchal in the sense that they require the unremunerated work of a wife for her husband's household. Colenso bluntly states that "there may be virtual 'buying and selling' in a nominally Christian land, and under a law of monogamy, as well as among these natives."[49] Monogamous heteronormativity, despite its own propensity to the exploitation of women, is generally promoted as the "missionary position." Colenso objects to an outright rejection of polygamy as that there are several misperceptions about its history and practice, and ignorance about the violence

---

[43] Ibid., 25.
[44] Ibid., *Polygamy*, 26.
[45] Ibid., 75.
[46] Ibid., 89.
[47] Ibid., 90.
[48] Ibid., 90.
[49] Ibid., 39.

that would be inflicted on entire communities if polygamous marriages had to be dissolved. There are instances where he makes unfortunate comparisons with slavery, for example, that one should "not refuse to a man the Christian sacraments, simply because he had a number of slaves,"[50] as if the practices stood at similar levels, where elsewhere he distinguishes them quite strongly.

Con/Versions of Narratives: Can the Subaltern Conversion Narrative Write?

Any doubts in Christian teachings that might be cloaked by living in a predominantly Christian society can arise ever more forcefully if a missionary enters into conversation with natives and prospective converts whose view of the world does not easily accommodate some of the more questionable elements of a religious system. The accounts we have from many missionaries focus primarily on the activities of the missionaries and therefore often do give the impression that missionaries were the dominant agents in missionary encounters. This perception disregards that the "missionaries were only ever partially in control of the process of evangelization, whatever they themselves imagined." Beyond the political, economic, and ecological circumstances that shaped and restricted missionary movement, native peoples were hardly "passive victims of European aggression, but purposive participants in events," engaging in "resistance and negotiation."[51] Certainly the economic and military power balance was far from equal, but the progress of negotiation was in many ways dialectical and had more intricate, contested, and mutual aspects.[52] In addition, it is key to remember that missionaries were often drawn from lower social classes and came from societies themselves in transition, such as for example an "England in acute intellectual and social crisis" with new ideas, philosophies, historical, and critical biblical studies emerging, and a rising industrial capitalism. It can be argued that at least Nonconformist missionary efforts are an attempt to resolve internal contradictions by the "creation of a new world in their image in the 'blank spaces' of Africa." The Comaroffs suggest that the emerging gap between religious and political dominion led to a growing insecurity of British forms of Christianity and led in some ways to a recreation of the kingdom of God at the "fringes of the European world."[53] With both social universes disrupted by colonial

---

[50] Ibid., 46.
[51] Jonathan A. Draper, "The Bishop and the Bricoleur: Bishop John William Colenso's Commentary on Romans and Magema Kamagwaza Fuze's The Black People and Whence They Came From," ed. Gerald West and Musa Dube (Leiden: Brill, 2001), 415.
[52] Ibid., 416.
[53] Comaroff and Comaroff, *Of Revelation and Revolution*, 77–8.

encounters, the mutual process, bricoleurs on both sides sort through the "debris of the two collapsing social universes for usable odds and ends of culture."[54]

When one considers the question of conversion in terms of Magema Fuze and Zulu intellectuals like him, the inseparability of motives for "conversion" manifests itself: Since the mission system was offering an education in Christian faith and in European culture, the exchanges involved are multiple. In Tsitsi Dangarembga's postcolonial novel *Nervous Conditions* the female main character Tambu's motivation in getting educated at the mission blends motifs of hunger for education, for transcending the patriarchal and chauvinist world of her village and family, her own growing contempt for her native context, learning, and language, as well as an ambivalent attraction to the seductions of material comforts, internalized cultural preferences, and access to an exotic-seeming privileged colonial cultural world.[55] Tambu comes to the mission only after the untimely death of her brother that opens up an opportunity to escape the patriarchal grasp for her, highlighting from the beginning how gender functioned in this particular social economy. Attempts to locate religious intervention in a sociocultural and economic vacuum continue to be self-deluding, if not strategically disingenuous.

Outside the "colonial churches" independent African churches formed in ways that allowed some Africans to encounter and develop forms of Christianity that allowed them greater agency and functioned as institutions whose independence from colonial oversight and missionary leadership represents an "act of resistance," perhaps more concretely a form of resistance by adaptation and appropriation.[56]

Many persons were nurtured on missionary stations and had their own conversions, sometimes multiple ones, throughout their lives. The transformative nature of encounters, of language and sign, made syncretic negotiations a part of the technologies employed to broker relationships. Meanwhile,

> the crisis was not one-sided, since the missionaries themselves also came from an England in acute intellectual and social crisis, arising out of the related phenomena of the Enlightenment and industrial capitalism [. . .][57]

John William Colenso matches some of the characteristics observed in Nonconformist missionaries as "persons caught between the rich and the

---

[54] Draper, "Bishop and the Bricoleur," 418.
[55] Dangarembga, *Nervous Conditions* (Oxfordshire: Ayebia, 1988), 38, 53,94.
[56] Linda Thomas, "Survival and Resistance In An African Indigenous Church," *Journal of Theology For Southern Africa* No. 98 (July 1997): 19.
[57] Ibid., 468.

poor, either indeterminate in their class affiliation or struggling hard to make their way over the invisible boundary to the bourgeoisie."[58]

He found that questions he had entertained himself but had avoided confronting were reopened, and he found himself questioned by his native informants, in particular his language teacher and translator, the convert and teacher William Ngidi.[59] The missionary bishop did not react to questions and doubts by insisting on the need to believe without proofs or logical assent, but instead saw the questions as needing to be answered in good faith, and with the best of biblical exegetical scholarship that was at hand. This included a method that had recently been pioneered in German lands, but still viewed with much skepticism in the British Isles—historical biblical criticism.[60]

Like any traveler to a different context, Colenso—and in an expanded sense the women in his life—represented a very specific embodiment of the church. Rather than succumbing to doubt or resorting to the absolutisms of scriptural literalism, he was interested in freeing the gospel message from convention and pushed for "a new mission to replace the old," in some ways a typical liberal theological impulse. "The old" for him meant propositions of inerrancy, insistence on conscious and professed Christianity as the only way to salvation, clinging to a biblical rather than a scientific historiography, and greater openness to the diversity of ethical social systems.

In the history of missionary encounters where most of the focus has been on the missionary, their struggles, their accomplishments, their theologies, and their failures, it is often difficult to access the converts' own perspectives, even in their own written words.[61]

In this regard, the history of South African missions is proof that few if any converts wrote about their relationships with missionaries or their life on mission stations. Where autobiographical and conversion narratives do

---

[58] While Colenso was from the lower middle class rather than the peasant class, he is clearly an upwardly mobile person and his family struggles financially even before the controversies. Comaroff and Comaroff, *Of Revelation and Revolution*, 85.

[59] Guy, *The View Across the River*, 21.

[60] James Long, working as a missionary in Bengal, in a quite different context, found it unhelpful to discuss the emerging modern criticism with the Bengal indigo workers he engaged. He hoped that Colenso, whose critical work on the authorship of biblical texts he thought was damaging to the missionary enterprise, would do the right thing and resign to avoid becoming a liability to missionaries. Long appears to have avoided introducing Jewish or Roman historical temporalities and spatialities in the missionary context and focused instead on images and illustrations in biblical texts. R. S. Sugirtharajah, *The Bible and Empire: Postcolonial Explorations* (Cambridge: Cambridge University Press, 2005), 118.

[61] Notable exceptions are the work of Paul de La Hausse. Paul La Hausse, *Restless Identities: Signatures of Nationalism, Zulu Ethnicity and History in the Lives of Petros Lamula (c. 1881–1948) and Lymon Maling (1889–1936)* (Pietermaritzburg: University of Natal, 2000).

exist, they are usually a mediated product where the missionary functions as a scribe, editor or translator and the convert-informant narrates a personal history.[62]

The last few decades have seen the publication of the voices of African scholars who represent the intellectual descendants of the *amakholwa*, the first groups of Africans to enter the discourse of European-style intellectual training and writing life. It is now from some of them, like South African anthropologist Hlonipha Mokoena, that a recovery of the voices of those first converts is occurring. There are a few Zulu converts, the *amakholwa*—believers, who became a class of intellectuals oddly positioned in the emerging colonial rule, representing the "success of mission acculturation and the failure of imperial liberalism and humanism"[63] at the same time. Besides William Ngidi, another *kholwa*—believer—in Colenso's ministry was Fuze. Magema Fuze's writings provide a rare, but strangely conditioned insight into their negotiation of self, faith, and community. He was brought to Colenso's Ekukhanenyu mission as a child, was educated there, and eventually became a printer for Colenso's Ekukhanyeni mission.[64] He also wrote a Zulu text ambitiously titled *The Black People And Whence They Came,* which was finally translated and published posthumously in 1979.

After Colenso's death, he published a Zulu version of his own account and assessment of Colenso's ministry in the Zulu newspaper *Llanga Lase Natal.* Since there is such a dearth of voices of converts, Fuze's contribution is noteworthy and fortuitous. His writing offers insight into the process of the introduction of literacy into an oral culture and the emergence of local black male intellectuals.[65] Certain accounts of the *kholwa* question the possibility for any independent indigenous cultural expression, while others see them as a class of nascent native nationalists, rendering them either as a marginalized class or a dominant local elite.[66] One of the earliest pieces of Fuze's writing gives us paradoxical hints of both Colenso's high pedagogical aspirations paired with the irony that the schoolboys were asked to ring the bells for segregated services, the first one for "white men," the second for "black men." This made another young black convert wonder how and why blacks were different from whites, despite being taught that they were created by the same God.[67] In a telling and heartrending comment on what the children picked up on race, skin

---

[62] Hlonipha Mokoena, "The Queen's Bishop: A Convert's Memoir of John W. Colenso," *Journal of Religion in Africa* Vol. 38 (2008): 313.

[63] Ibid., 316.

[64] Draper, "Bishop and the Bricoleur," 441–2.

[65] I am here largely following Mokoena's argument in Mokoena, "Queen's Bishop," 314, 316.

[66] Ibid., 317–18.

[67] Ibid., 319.

color and identity, Fuze reports how Sarah Frances Colenso, the Bishop's wife, tricked some of the children into bathing by telling them they would become white if they let themselves be scrubbed in the tub: "The children were very happy when they heard they would be transformed into Englishmen, but they were being tricked, it was to make them enjoy being bathed."[68] This vignette resonates eerily with an illustration in Anne McClintock's *Imperial Leather*, an ad for a soap that depicts a black child being bathed white in a British type bathtub, involving, of course, a spurious, but culturally loaded claim about colonial products, body policing, and conversion coded as racial and socio-economic transformation.[69]

Colenso's interlocutor Magema Fuze saw his relationship to Colenso as foreordained. This raises questions of how aware the child might have been of settlers' encroachment or whether it was indeed a prophetic event. Fuze describes his conversion as not merely a personal "decision" but as a move that required parental consent, thereby complicating the question on what level a conversion—*s'il y en a*—is personal, on what communal.[70] To Fuze's father's surprise, Colenso lets the new student pick his own Zulu baptismal name rather than, as other missionaries have practiced, choosing a name from the New Testament for them. Colenso's practice opens up the possibility of cultural agency even with conversion.[71] Fuze consciously merges his Christian identity with his "quest for Zulu origins," and "the construction of a Zulu historical consciousness."[72]

Some assessments of Fuze's contribution to an *amakholwa* literature, including the editor, A. T. Cope's preface to *The Black People and Whence They Came*, emphasized the limitations of his historical purview as well as his reliance on Colenso's religious and political stances. This stance may underestimate how unusual the existence of a convert's unredacted writings are, especially one writing his own autobiography as well as an account of a missionary's life and work. Written long after the events and rather defensive of his controversial mentor in the thick of ongoing church politics of the Anglican Church in South Africa, his account can be read as an "act of incitement"[73] less interested in factual accuracy than in stimulating and influencing an ongoing controversy. Though Fuze's account of Colenso is quite hagiographic, depicting him as "saintly and Christlike," the attending subtext offers multiple voices, among them critical assessments of colonial church politics, missionary activities, and current events.[74] Having

---

[68] Ibid., 320.
[69] Ann McClintock, *Imperial Leather: Race, Gender and Sexuality in the Colonial Contest* (New York: Routledge, 1995), 213.
[70] Ibid., 321.
[71] Draper, "Bishop and the Bricoleur," 444.
[72] Ibid., 445.
[73] Mokoena, "Queen's Bishop," 314.
[74] Ibid., 314

established Colenso as a benchmark for Christian moral agency, Fuze proceeds to assess the state of mission and region, thereby inserting "himself and his people into the hegemonic historical discourse of white people." Thus, Fuze creates a text that is a unique bricolage, and participates in a protracted discourse around the origin, history, and identity of his own people.[75] Articulating a "particular brand of prophetic nationalism infused by Christian symbolism," Fuze argues that abandoning Zulu custom and adopting Western culture is not desired by God, and will even result in God's abandonment.[76] One form of intercultural mimicry in colonial settings, however, relates to the question of monarchy. Colonial peoples are generally well aware of the "ideological significance of monarchy in British colonial domination" and in some contexts, in a move of intercultural mimicry, formulated their own national monarchical claims, at least symbolically, for the purpose of redefining chiefly authority and to integrate it both into Christian salvation history and as models for preserving justice and order.[77]

Fuze saw Colenso as the "Queen's bishop," that is, authorized no longer by the Archbishop of Canterbury and the Church of England, but by the monarch Victoria herself. Colenso had appealed to the queen for support when relationships with Bishop Gray and the Church of England turned sour and he was, ultimately, declared a heretic.[78] Fuze conferred upon Colenso honorary Zulu identity, which illustrates his status as fully human: "he became black [human] only after he had arrived here in our country, he abandoned whiteness, and became a true human [black]."[79] Colenso then, perhaps "like his Lord," a phrase Fuze likes to use, became incarnate, incarnate as a Zulu, speaking their language, understanding their lives in such a way that Fuze sees him as one of his people. Colenso the boundary breaker is further lifted up by Fuze for not hiding what other Anglican clerics regarded as esoteric knowledge, namely the theological problems with biblical texts and the hermeneutics of suspicion: "Sobantu did not like to withhold anything in his sermons and teaching."[80] The Colenso controversy thus "was as much about theology as it is about the 'democratic' ethos of Colenso's mission, especially where Africans were concerned," as, over time "colonial whites began to despise Colenso and [Fuze] attributed this to the fact that Colenso did not discriminate." Thus, for

[75] Draper, "Bishop and the Bricoleur," 446.
[76] Ibid., 447–8, 451.
[77] The Zulu and the Maori in New Zealand each founded movements for a king or queen with greater reach than precolonial royalty or chiefs. Draper, "Bishop and the Bricoleur," 450 and Michael King, *The Penguin History of New Zealand* (Auckland: Penguin, 2003), 212–13.
[78] Mokoena, "Queen's Bishop," 315.
[79] Ibid., 325–6. Translation by Hlonipha Mokoena, who notes that the term *umuntu* can refer to both black person and human.
[80] Quoted in Mokoena, "Queen's Bishop," 328.

the Africans, Colenso was "'the king of peace,' for the colonists he was the 'king of kaffirs.' "[81]

After Bishop Colenso's excommunication and subsequent loss of income and therefore institutional and economic support for his missionary venture, the Colensos continued to spend great personal energy and much of their economic substance to defend Zulu monarchy, institutions, and individuals. The family often acted as one, believing that the continuation of certain Zulu institutions would allow the Zulu to survive as an integrated ethnic group and lessen the culture-shattering impact of the colonial economic system. Their struggle was, however, with the abuse of imperial power, not with the fact that their culture is in the position of bringing people along to the European way. Their advocacy and agency pushed for an open engagement with local reasoning and theological questions. In this, the Colensos' conviction that Zulus had a natural theology and access to deity impacted their sense of what mission meant, that is, a knowledge of the divine was already present within them, and hence their conversion had a different shape and urgency than was assumed by many other missionaries surrounding Colenso. The dismantling of Zulu social institutions was working to erode the self-sufficiency and socio-spiritual integrity of the Zulu, while exposing them to British learning.

"Then Who Can Be Saved?" Soteriology and Mission

Colenso's theological anthropology and soteriology have come to differ starkly from, say, the "evangelical gaze [that] perceived Africa as a 'desert.' " The "dark continent" was conceived not as an ecological, but as a "moral wasteland:"

Its inhabitants, peoples of the wild, shared its qualities: Unable to master their environment, they lacked culture and history.[82]

Departing from his strict Calvinist beginnings, Colenso, under the influence of his wife Sarah, who introduced him to the British Evangelical Frederick Denison Maurice, adopted a universalist soteriology. This theological position coheres with his belief in living an exemplary life, the progressive effects of literacy and education, together with an understanding that a benevolent imperialist administration provides the best possible way to interact with the local Zulu and other peoples of southern Africa. Such rereadings juxtapose a universalist salvation with the "backward" times of particularity and ethnocentrism,

---

[81] Ibid., 329.
[82] Comaroff and Comaroff, *Ethnography*, 268.

and look toward a time of progress where industrial capitalism contributes in creating an apex of world history.[83]

This grand narrative of liberal optimism both underlies and informs his critique of the injustice of the implementation of colonial rule. His religious universalism goes easily hand in hand with a certain kind of imperial universalism. The Colenso family's struggle is then not so much against imperialism per se, but against its perversion by British landgrabbers and pursuers of racist policies such as Cecil Rhodes and Robert Baden-Powell (the very same known today mostly as the founder of the scouting movement).

The Colenso mission appears to have wrought only very few converts, as traditionally understood, and one cannot but speculate what role this has played in Colenso's seeing the struggle against certain forms of imperialism (rather than the ones they favored) as the main form of their missionary work. Jonathan Draper argues similarly:

> Colenso's theology [. . .] undermined the logic of conventional mission work. If all are already saved whether they accept the Christian gospel or not, then what they stand to benefit from by baptism is enlightenment, knowledge of what they already possess. Colenso's emphasis on the value and importance of natural religion, of the universal operation of conscience, and of the equality of all races and cultures, made for a "cool conversion" [. . .]. There was no need for an absolute break with their former way of life for his converts, no severance of family and kinship ties [. . .] Instead his teaching encouraged the emergence of a Zulu national identity and cultural revival.[84]

Contemporaries will recognize the dilemma of some liberal and progressive Christian circles, where the work for social justice can come close to replacing theological instruction or conversion preaching. Colenso's rejection of the evangelical theology of his contemporaries and their hellfire preaching, of their self-assured proclamation of what he considered an artificially shielded Bible compelled him to hermeneutically crack it open in the vulnerable setting of the missionary context. He believed theology needed to be opened to questions, preached in humility, while claiming neither divine nor missionary omnipotence or omniscience. Colenso's missionary methodology included looking for the "seeds of religious truths" in customs he became familiar with and looking for compatible patterns between Zulu and English Customs.[85]

---

[83] Jeff Guy, *The Heretic: A Study of the Life of John William Colenso, 1814–1883* (Pietermaritzburg: University of Natal Press, 1983), 168, 171–2.

[84] Draper, "Sola Fide," 490.

[85] Ruth Edgecombe, "Bishop Colenso and the Zulu Nation," *Journal of Natal and Zulu History* III (1980): 17.

Colenso, it has been argued, recapitulates Irenaeus' soteriological theory of *recapitulatio*, arguing in his commentary on Romans that Christ's typological repetition of the "First Adam" repudiates and transforms entirely and for the entire human race the sin and separation from God.[86] This leads him to assume the presence of a natural theology in every culture and person as an expression of something of the sacred, if not in its completion. Colenso

> gives maximum weight to Paul's use of the formulation "as in Adam all die, so in Christ we shall all be made alive," to see Christ as the Head of humanity, encapsulating and restoring humanity in his own person on the cross[.][87]

This includes, for Colenso, a sustained argument for purgatory, where condemnation and hope of redemption coexist.[88] This prolepsis also regrounds the sacraments of the church with a purpose as signs of the divine blessing already given, but without "special privileges" for the Christian over the non-Christian.[89] Colenso's insistence that the entire human race is included in God's mercy and salvation "was one of the conclusions that most outraged the Anglo-Catholic orthodoxy" of his day.[90]

His commentary on Romans was not only a formulation of his own soteriology and therefore missiology, but also aimed at his own church at home. Challenging the racial pride of the British, he argued that they have no reason to see themselves as superior. Though his interpretation does not escape conventional forms of anti-judaistic stereotyping, his rereading of Romans also rewrites Jewish-Christian relationships:

> He wishes to show that the English Christian settlers have no grounds of racial pride over against the Zulu, and makes the same point *vis a vis* modern Jews, namely that Christians have no basis for racial pride over against the Jews. On the contrary, their cruelty and bigotry towards the Jews has made it impossible for Jews to believe in the Christian religion.[91]

Colenso resisted the missionary methodologies he found in Natal, which included the promotion of a heightened sense of the urgency of conversion; an emphasis on the fear of hell as a conversionary motif; and the stark Anselmian penal substitution theories of atonement that formed the basis for christology

---

[86] Jonathan A. Draper, "Introduction," in *Commentary on Romans by John William Colenso*, ed. Jonathan A. Draper (Pietermaritzburg: Cluster Publications, 2003), xxx.
[87] Ibid., xxix.
[88] Ibid., xxxi.
[89] Ibid., xxxii.
[90] Ibid., xxxiii.
[91] Draper, "Sola Fide," 479.

presented by most missionaries.[92] Putting the fear of God into the Zulu, so Colenso, forestalls offering a different metaphor for divine-human relationality, that of Father and children, while the less than exemplary lives of missionaries further serve to alienate Africans from pursuing a positive encounter with the gospel.[93] As in other missionary contexts, the stress on individual conversions served to create the sense that conversion meant separation from ancestors and community of ancestry and to alienation from the culture of birth.

This manifests less a postulated dynamic between "individualistic" and "communal" cultures in problematic juxtaposition between "Western" and "Other" cultures, but rather rearticulates a tension familiar within Judaism and Christianity: that between religious identity as part of ancestral inheritance or conscious choice.

Did Colenso eventually go the way of the propagators of the social gospel that pour themselves out in social and political action but let go of any sense of the Divine as beyond the social order? Did this civilizing mission end up promoting a Protestant work ethic that aimed to transform entire economies and social systems, not just persons? One wonders whether such a development, in concert with weakened progressive and liberal theologies of mission deepened an identity crisis and loss of space of Christian theology in a public European context. With such a generous soteriology, what, beyond work for social justice and the expression of local cultural identity, is the vision for mission? A similar problem appears to affect many denominational churches in the United States, as they mark themselves off of the more Augustinian and Calvinist versions of a "massa damnata" soteriology dominant in more conservative Protestant circles. What kind of resistance can such "generous" missiology echo offer in the face of a creeping secularization, propagating an artificial separation between sacred and secular?

Questions of the relationship between sacred and secular were deeply complicated for missionaries. The Comaroffs report a telling anecdote in which early Methodist missionaries among the South African Tswana proposed a missionary strategy that would not impact the tribal social organization, that is, chiefly power. The assurance that missionaries would not intervene in "chiefly matters," that is, the political realm, proves impossible when the missionaries want to baptize newly born children. The socioreligious economy of baptism here disrupts the integrity of other religiocultural ceremonies that inscribe and recreate tribal social relations. The illusion that a separation of religious and political might be possible comes to an end when baptismal rites and tribal rites presided over by the chief—such as male and female circumcision or naming ceremonies—collide. While missionaries often saw "practical advantage in a strong chieftainship" as it "assured a stable polity within

---

[92] Ibid., 475.
[93] Ibid., 476.

which they could toil to build their kingdom of God," their interventions into regional relations as well as communal "religious" rites "could not but erode Tswana sovereignty."[94]

Colenso's less boundaried missiology was more hospitable, at least potentially, to the ways in which religious, cultural, and economic identities overlap. For him, Christians have the "advantage of knowing and experiencing this good news and the responsibility of sharing it with the rest of the human family." At the same time, he emphasizes the continuity rather than disruption of Zulu religiocultural identity and challenges the sense of superiority among colonial settlers. In his commentary on Romans, Colenso identifies his colonial readers with the positionality of the "Jews" of the letter of Romans, and the Zulu with the persons the letter is written to, the Christians in Rome. He argued that Paul's expressed purpose in the letter of Romans was to counter "feelings of racial privilege and pride." This interpretive strategy put him on a collision course with settler audiences and the Church of England.[95]

Jeff Guy argues that a key factor in the great resistance to Bishop Colenso's work in biblical criticism was that he challenged, and in some eyes weakened, the spiritual, cultural, and social power that the clergy class in England and the colony wielded over the minds and lives of church people.

> Is it here that the explanation lies for the extraordinary antagonism with which Colenso's biblical criticism was received. By questioning the authority of the Bible, Colenso was also questioning the authority of all those in mid-Victorian society who held up the Bible when they exercised their dominance over others.[96]

Colenso received support from a number of British intellectuals, among them Tennyson, Dickens, and Darwin.[97] Colenso's theological aim was to teach and preach in such a manner that people could reconcile faith and reason, the creation account, and the emerging theories of humanity's evolutionary origins. He found it crucial to enable people to integrate rather than deny and ignore scientific theories and knowledge. And he valued the capacity of critical thinking in his Zulu interlocutors, integrating a number of hermeneutical strategies across cultural difference: he negotiated between British and Anglican tendencies to reading scripture as an inerrant document, emerging

---

94 Comaroff and Comaroff, *Of Revelation and Revolution*, 258–9.
95 Draper, "Introduction," xxxiii.
96 Guy, *The Heretic*, 184.
97 Only a few hundred kilometers from Colenso's diocese the oldest known remains of hominids were found in the "Cradle of Humankind" near Sterkfontein in Gauteng. See Philip Bonner and Amanda Esterhuysen, ed., Trefor Jenkis, *A Search for Origins: Science, History and South Africa's 'Cradle of Humankind'* (Johannesburg: Wits University Press, 2007).

scientific data and emerging historical critical readings. At the same time, he valued the different cultural perspectives and religious opinions of his Zulu translators and converts. Many resisted his courageous engagement with difficult texts and facts by arguing that his hospitality to critical inquiry and doubt disrupted the spiritual peace of the faithful. His response to a clergyman's complaint that his teachings, among other drove one young man to suicide was simply, "How fearful a responsibility must rest on *you*—you, teachers of religion—who have kept the people so long in darkness, that they cannot bear the light."[98]

Enlightenment and Light Supremacy: The Metaphorical and the Physical

Colenso's missionary theology and anthropology required him to take seriously questions that were also raised by people in the European churches. He strove to articulate a theology and historiography that did not repress but take seriously the questions of those new to the Christian faith as well as the theological and social controversies in European societies.

Colenso named his mission station *Ekukhanyeni*—light or enlightenment. This term echoes both the New Testament's metaphorical engagement with light and enlightenment of the soul and his own leanings to the critical thinking associated with German and British forms of enlightenment consciousness. Colenso frequently employed metaphors of light and enlightenment.[99] Colonial discourse analysis shows unfortunate conceptual links between the ancient metaphor of light for spiritual awakening, Enlightenment thinkers' use of the metaphor for cultural development and a "light supremacy" that can conflate enlightenment with a "white supremacy" based on gradations of skin-color, in which persons become both enlightened and more "white."[100] This dangerous conflation is deeply embedded in modern missionary rhetoric, and heightened by the intellectual expressions of colonial culture. Colenso established a "Boy's Institution at Ekukhanyeni" for the education of the sons of chiefs as future leaders and "regenerators of Natal."[101]

Colenso's attitude toward the images of Shaka and his estimation of the Zulu chiefs that were the inheritors of the myth changed over his time in Natal. During his initial tour of Natal, he calls Shaka a "monster" and an "African

---

[98] Guy, *The Heretic*, 165.
[99] Ibid., 164.
[100] Catherine Keller, *Face of the Deep* (New York/London: Routledge, 2003), 201.
[101] Edgecombe, "Bishop Colenso and the Zulu Nation," 17.

Attila."[102] Magema Fuze writes in "The Black People and Whence They Came From" of a different monstrosity:

> All of you can see for yourselves that there are no large rivers that could be navigated by ships in this country [Eastern South Africa], and frequented by this enormous monster that used to move about and collecting black children, filling its capacious stomach and then making off with them.[103]

Fuze distinguishes between "evil white men" and men like Colenso, his master, and praises Queen Victoria for abolishing the slave trade (of course this is primarily due to the long and labored lobbying of British Evangelicals of the Clapham Sect and William Wilberforce).

Fuze the convert, printer, native informant, functions as a brokering trickster between colonial and native social entities. Zulu scholar Hlonipha Mokoena argues that Fuze's text is "neither a 'history' of the black people nor a recounting of traditional oral narratives" but highlights its unconventionality and the impossibility of categorizing it precisely. She emphasizes Fuze's break with oral traditions and his attempt to create a new kind of literate discursive community among Zulu converts. Thus aiming to fashion a black identity, his efforts integrate African vocabularies with a "discourse of emancipation and modernity" and represent a first attempt at forming a native intelligentsia. Fuze thus represents the first inklings of a *kholwa*—Zulu for (Christian) believer—intellectual scene. The rising elite of *kholwa*—believers or converts to Christianity, who had been educated at mission schools, are seen by many to be the first generation of South African native intellectuals who consciously articulated "an ethnic nationalism that coexisted in ambiguous fashion with the older, broader pan-South African black nationalism and with new forms of class consciousness."[104]

> Some of these dynamics continue to inform and manifest themselves in contemporary power struggles between post-apartheid South African political and ethnic factions and the continuing large gaps between educated, elite black South Africans and poor citizens.[105]

There appear to be as many motives for entering a mission as there are for erecting one. As a representative, perhaps of a number of southern African women, Tsitsi Dangarembga's novel *Nervous Conditions* explores the borderlands

---

[102] John William Colenso, *Ten Weeks in Natal: A Journal of a First Tour of Visitation Among the Colonists and Zulu Kafirs of Natal*, XIII, X.

[103] Fuze, *The Black People*, 7.

[104] Marks, *Ambiguities of Dependence*, 111.

[105] Ibid., 111.

between oppressions encountered by her main character Tambu: between the strict patriarchalism of the Zimbabwean village where her education matters only once her older brother dies, and the mission school that educates in English history, language, and values may see the "transfer to the mission as [their] reincarnation,"[106] while this rebirth embeds another metanarrative of superiority that African women cannot evade, as they are neither not quite not female, nor "not quite 'not' white." As new knowledge and opportunities beckon, alienation from former life threatens. For some, like the main characters's cousin Nyasha, the result is what Frantz Fanon described as the "nervous condition" of the native. This term describes a desperate, self-destructive need to succeed within the terms of the colonial system, adopting an "Englishness [that will] kill them all if they aren't careful,"[107] while being starkly ambivalent about the alienation from friends and family, their envy, and the identity transformation brought on by an "assimilation [. . .] that was intended for the precocious few who might prove a nuisance if left to themselves."[108] The ambivalent social salvation envisioned in this novel occurs in a religious setting, and involves leaving behind the burdens of a pre-scripted life of hard labor and subservience to men and relatives in a Zimbabwean village, so as to enter an equally prescribed, but materially and intellectually attractive life in the mission school. Such a *Bildungsroman* traces the loss of innocence, names the internal ambivalence and self-hatred of the protagonist, sketches a pedagogy of the oppressed, and projects a future nomadic existence shuttling between identities and contexts.

Missionaries contributed quite consciously to this dynamic by creating the infrastructure through which conversion, education, and complex forms of assimilation became one of the routes through which young Zulus could find ways to enter into an ambiguous zone between indigenous and colonial societies to such a degree that neither one became home. Perhaps the mission station generates people who are in some sense "third culture kids," a term often used for the children of missionaries, military, migrant academics, and diplomats. They are hybrids alienated from both societies and at home in neither one of them, destined to a particular sense of homelessness.

Colenso's partial agreement with certain imperial projects does at the same time pit him against others: His conviction that enlightenment, in whatever form, cannot be enforced but that missionaries, settlers, and converts have to lead by example if missionary successes are supposed to be anything more than superficial makes him a persistent critic of the injustices of colonial administration. We see this classic controversy between the manifestations of mission and imperialism in a number of contexts, certainly in our other two

---

[106] Tsitsi Dangarembga, *Nervous Conditions* (Oxfordshire: Ayebia, 1988), 94.
[107] Ibid., 207.
[108] Ibid., 182.

case studies, Aotearoa/New Zealand and Alaska. Many missionaries distanced themselves from the beginning of their work in stark contrast and controversy with the colonial manifestations of "the white man."[109] One might conjecture that the phrase "white *man*" expresses the particularly hypermasculine frontier economy produced by single white men's interactions with land and native societies. The narrative of the corruption of the noble savage—be they Maori, Zulu, or Athabascan—by the injustice and immorality of the white man of the frontier is a staple of missionary rhetoric, and carries a large degree of historical truth in it.

Translating God: What is the Message?

Just as Martin Luther aimed to put the Bible in the hands of the people and break the stranglehold of interpreters authorized by the Roman Catholic Church, Kwame Bediako has argued, the translation of the Bible into African tongues has loosened the grip of missionaries and mission societies on the Bible, relativizing "their proprietory claim on Christianity."[110] When translation occurs, the long conversation between missionaries and presumptive converts becomes differently angled: If the biblical texts are the first thing you see translated into your language, the history of your language is inextricably interwoven with the Bible. This is as true for Germany, one of the key ethnic areas where Martin Luther's translation of the Bible created modern German language, as for Alaska regarding the dying Athabascan language of the Gwich'in, or in New Zealand, where the first printed version of Maori traces a translated sacred text.

Missionary activities are based on an underlying hermeneutical claim: that the densely contextualized Christian tradition a missionary represents is relevant for persons and communities who may not have encountered its particular teachings before. The host context may seem insignificant, but cannot be separated from the message that is being passed on. The "message" content itself is full of contextual assumptions and frameworks—frameworks that are alien to hearer and missionary both. How this? The translation process is always incomplete. Foreign language, concepts, and culture inform in each translation process an entire "politics of translation." As much as translators may strive for

---

[109] The first frontier of colonialism is often predominantly staffed, in the nineteenth century, by (single) white men, and the economic, sexual, and social impact of their presence is often of a particular nature that has often been a major point of critique for missionaries: The gospel is not promoted well by land annexations by the law of the gun, rape, and related disruptions of indigenous families primarily through the use and abuse of women, the introduction of alcohol, prostitution, and firearms.

[110] Quoted in Gerald West, "On the Eve of an African Biblical Studies: Trajectories and Trends," *Journal of Theology for Southern Africa* Vol. 99 (November 1997): 107.

"faithful renderings,"[111] that is indeed what they are: They inscribe the incarnate faith of those who communicate the faith as much as they transmit faith in an incarnate God. Such incarnate faith becomes reincarnated when its flesh moves and relocates.

To speak of God in a different culture renders visible some of the problematic decisions missionaries have to make when choosing a particular term to represent an already translated concept: What are the implications of using a pre-existing term? Will the Jewish and Christian concepts of God be overwhelmed by the traditions local names carry? Should they simply transliterate the Jewish names for God? As the dominance of Latin was more fully dispatched by the Reformation, Protestants proceeded to develop a cottage industry translating the Bible, with varying priorities and time schedules. Colenso's efforts in translation mirrored his theological positions. His translation of the Greek term *pistis* preferred *temba*, a term indicating "confidence, hope, trust," and explicitly rejects the alternative favored by the American Board Mission, *kolwa*, whose root meaning is "to be satisfied, have enough of a thing, to be satisfied with the evidence of a thing."[112] Hence, Colenso inscribed faith as a sense of trust in God over a notion of assent to a creed, closer to the gospel sense of walking by faith and not by sight. Colenso's translation, an expression of his concern to "maximize the nature of justification as objective, universal gift and human response as a simple trusting reliance,"[113] was indeed the linguistically and theologically more correct one but was only later adopted by the Bible society.

Brokering Gospel and Law

The bishop's longtime friend, and adversary later in life, Theophilus Shepstone, Secretary for Native Affairs in Natal, was a ruthless and clever broker between British settlers, Afrikaner colonists, and Zulu tribes. Shepstone manoeuvered the cultural rifts and crossroads with the skill and deviousness of a broker whose principles in translation included adding to a conflict if it was going to benefit cementing his own position as the main power broker and—for a while—the only person knowledgeable in language and culture of both sides to have a monopoly for the negotiation of relations.[114] For a long time, Colenso and Shepstone were close, and found companionship in each other. They shared certain imperialist convictions, as they both "favoured a gradualist approach to the task of education, evangelising and governing

---

[111] Naomi Seidman, *Faithful Renderings: Jewish-Christian Difference and the Politics of Translation* (Chicago, IL: Chicago University Press, 2006).
[112] Draper, "Sola Fide," 483.
[113] Ibid., 483.
[114] Guy, *The View Across the River*, 35, 44–5.

the black population of Natal."[115] Yet, over time Colenso came to realize that Shepstone's segregationist policies and libelous representations of Zulu culture in fact generated tension and violence rather than moving toward peaceful coexistence.[116] Colenso broke with Shepstone in April 1874 when it became clear the Secretary suppressed evidence in a trial crucial to maintain at least a semblance of integrity of Zulu tribal structure in the face of encroaching settler culture. Colenso vowed to bring the truth to light and started to question Shepstone's colonial justifications which he previously received "with implicit trust."[117] Much like his contemporaries, Colenso believed in Britain's messianic mission in the colonies, for the uplift of other nations. For Colenso, this would occur only if Britain's agents in the world lived exemplarily and implemented exemplary laws and lives. The Colensos saw this exemplary living endangered in the province of Natal, and as time progressed, the viability of the mission diminished, with Britain's government and church so closely identified. As a missionary he was concerned that, especially after the Langalibalele trial, British officials and the policies they implemented were becoming fast associated with "duplicity, treachery, and violence."[118] Furthermore, Colenso was bitterly disillusioned when he realized that he and the Zulus were "in the enjoyment of a fool's paradise because we trusted in the word and good faith of an English gentleman," Bartle Frere. Frere, the British High Commissioner in South Africa, had acted as confidence man when rather than restoring land to the Zulus, as promised, he "guaranteed" it to incoming white farmers.[119] Before long, Colenso, after hours of direct interviews with the current Zulu king, found confirmed "entirely my good opinion" of Cetshwayo and his "detestation of the gross calumnies of Sir B. Frere, which have done so much to poison the minds of the English people against the [Zulu] king, and so furnish an excuse for his own policy."[120] Henceforward, the Colensos vehemently opposed and attempted to counteract the "mass of lying abuse,"[121] the inaccuracies, misrepresentations, and subterfuges of colonial officials and settlers against the Zulus, a fight they would eventually lose, their livelihood and lives spent.[122] The Colensos were furious that disingenuous British colonials made

---

[115] Edgecombe, "Bishop Colenso and the Zulu Nation," 16.
[116] Ibid., 21. Edgecombe describes this with a Latin phrase that all but describes politically motivated hate speech and annunciation of total war until destruction, asserting that "Colenso characterised the tenor of Shepstone's language from the time of the Blood River meeting as "Delendus est Cetshwayo."
[117] Ibid., 19.
[118] Ibid., 21.
[119] Ibid., 23.
[120] Colenso as quoted in Edgecombe, "Bishop Colenso and the Zulu Nation," 27.
[121] Ibid., 29.
[122] Ibid., 29. Edgecombe writes: "The Colenso commitment to the perpetuation of the Zulu nation and its ruling family was fully formed in the 1880s, to the extent that Harriette Colenso frequently referred to 'we Usuthu.' This was a logical working out of Colenso's ideas on the need for co-operation between missionaries and governmental structures.

a move sadly common throughout colonial histories: to justify the subjugation of a native people by claiming to protect them.[123]

Brokering Gospel and Gender: Harriette Colenso and the Translation Process

Alice Werner, linguist at the School of African and Oriental Studies in London, and friend of Harriette Colenso, quotes an *izibongo*, a Zulu praise song composed by Mboza Matahiwulana, in Harriette's honor. It describes her as sister and mother of the Zulu, who, when they were defeated, confronted the powerful like a prophet and confronted their injustice.[124] Where no one could help,

---

[. . .] The king had a crucial role to play in shaping this [emerging] society. [. . .] The king, with his hereditary authority and position in Zulu society, could constitute a vital channel for initiating change and he alone could determine the pace and extent of change."

[123] Guy, *The View Across the River*, 68.
[124] The Praises of the Inkosazana.
 uDhlwedhlwe ong' uMandiza ka' Sobantu.
 The sons of our people were scattered and slain on the hillside –
  Their women were borne -
 to the bed of the foeman—our strong men were even as cattle.
  Whom the lion hath torn.-
 We were hunted and slain—we were dead—yes the worms devoured us -
  An end was of strife. -
 When lo'—no man, but a woman, came forth to save us, -
  And brought back our life.
 O tender hands' O heart of a sister' O mother,
  whose child is our race'-
 O sing her praises, Usutu' there is no such another,
  On the whole earth's face.
 Alone she stood before the face of the mighty -
  She said,—Ye do wrong. -
 No weapon had she but the word of her lips to smite them,
  But, lo' she was strong.
 We lay, as men doomed to death, fast bound in a cavern;
  No light was to see,
 Save a hole that a man might span with his thumb and finger.
  No hope.—then came She.-
 And with only her two bare hands, she clave us an opening,
  And bade us go free.
 What shall the children of Tshaka say, when they praise her'
  Whose tongue hath the skill' -
 O the very brave, the wary- who flew on swift wings of pity,
  To save us from ill; -
 Mandiza, Matotoba, thou child of the Just One, -
  who loved us, -
   Our hearts love thee still. -
    Mboza Matahiwulana 1895. This portion of her Isidingo cited according to Alice Werner, "Harriette Colenso," KCM 6563, Papers of Harriette Colenso, Killie Campbell Africana Library (Durban, South Africa, 1932).

the *izibongo* continues, Harriette Colenso saved the people and restored their life by way of her words on their behalf. A bi-cultural broker, her position between cultures, her knowledge of each, paired with a sharp eye and tenacious courage, enabled her to be a negotiator and broker respected by each side in a conflict.

After the death of her father, Alice Werner writes "Dhlwedhlwe, no longer the staff of another, was left in the forefront of the battle, on her own account."[125] Her deep knowledge of Zulu language and culture, her intricate command of historical, legal, and cultural facts, her striving for unbiased, accurate, and fair depiction of any and all persons can still awe her readers today. Rare then, and rare now, such integrity, such lifelong struggle for a cause that ultimately was to fail. Werner notes elsewhere that there were at least three *izibongo* names that described Harriette: *Udhlwedhlwe*—the staff, referring to her work assisting her father, *uMandiza*—the flying one, referring to her journey to St. Helena to visit the exiled chiefs, *uMatotoba*—she "who walks softly," referring to somebody who advances cautiously, one foot after another, and recalls "the caution, wise caution, which marked all her efforts on [the Zulus'] behalf."[126] Harriette's sketchbook of watercolors contains a pictorial portrait of her eulogist Mboza, painted the same year he wrote the praise song, in 1895. He is depicted with gray hair; the painter, Harriette, is about 38 years old: tenderly and colorfully drawn, Harriette's portrait of Mboza feels more intimate and immediate than the hagiographic praise song or the stiffly posed black and white Victorian portraits of her. The water color sketch rather matches the lively, detailed, intelligent, and dedicated voice of her writing.

A woman who never married, Bishop Colenso's daughter Harriette's life was spent as what one might today call an activist for the rights of Zulu over and against the encroaching Boers and British colonists. Unconventional herself, she grew up living in a mission station with her tightly knit family. After the death of her parents and the departure of some of her siblings, Harriette lived for much of her life in "menage a trois" with her favorite sister Agnes and her good friend and supporter Kate Giles.[127]

Harriette Colenso, too, wrote about the colonial authorities' attempt to "suppress polygamy by legislation" and that it was "as foolish a thing as they can do." She suspected that the difference in customs made the (male) colonists "absolutely jealous of the relative freedom from wants and from cares, which makes the native comparatively independent."[128] The relative independence of subsistence cultures from certain forms of property ownership and monetary

---

[125] Werner, "Harriette Colenso," 16.

[126] Alice Werner, "Source Unknown, Page in Unidentified Journal Page, Authored by Alice Werner," Uncatalogued, Killie Campbell, Colenso Papers.

[127] Guy, *The View Across the River*, 30.

[128] Ibid., 42.

exchange systems was broken down bit by bit by legislation such as the hut tax, which levied the hut of each wife, thereby discouraging polygamy and the economic production that went on in those units. Polygamy presents a dilemma not only for missionaries like Colenso, but for those promoting the cause of the flourishing of women's lives, of all stripes.

Ironically, the collusion of Zulu and Victorian patriarchy is one reason Harriette could act as she could, flying as she did under the flag of being her father's "staff," his representative and messenger. That, and the fact that missionary women, due to their association in Victorian thought with representing the moral center of British civilization, were seen as important teachers of the sexual mores, rendered them effective promoters of a heteropatriarchal "missionary position" advocated by the Christian churches.

As an independent minded woman, child to one of the most controversial figures of the colony, she was in a liminal position, a boundary person, translator, negotiator, activist and legal witness, public author, and lecturer on behalf of the Zulu monarchy. Perched in a privileged position of a female broker between two patriarchal societies, Harriette Colenso finds her own voice in interpreting and negotiating the divide. Brenda Nicholls writes:

> For Shepstone it was clear that the power of the Zulu royal house should be regarded as ended. By contrast Harriette Colenso remained loyal to her father's view. This was that the royal house was the integrating principle for the Zulu people and that it was their loyalty to the Zulu royal house that gave the Zulu people a corporate identity. She abhorred the policy of breaking up the Zulu people that had been followed since the end of the Zulu war and sought to achieve not only re-integration of the Zulu people but also reconciliation between the Zulus and the white government of Zululand, then represented by Havelock.[129]

This kind of integrity was, similar to the work of, say, an NGO aid worker today, based on a set of cultural assumptions. The Colensos' assumptions were in some ways entirely in tune with those of their contemporaries; they assumed that an enlightened and enlightening civilizing mission was indeed the task of the British imperial presence in Africa. Where they differed from their contemporaries is the seriousness, integrity, and exemplary nature with which they aimed to embody this mission. Their goal was social transformation of Zulu society into Western style economic structures, "the creation of communities of individualistic, commodity-producing, commodity-consuming families," that thought independently and dared to ask questions of traditional and

---

[129] Brenda Nicholls, "Zululand 1887–1889: The Court of the Special Commissioners for Zululand and the Rule of Law," *Journal of Natal and Zulu History* Volume XV (1994/1995): Accessed Oct 30, 2008.

foreign forms of authority.[130] It is no coincidence that Bishop John William Colenso names the mission station's farm settlement Ekukhanyeni ("into the light").[131] Education, the acquisition of skills in writing, printing, agriculture, and personal hygiene. And lest contemporary readers feel superior to such cultural arrogance: many NGO aid organizations are still striving to provide the same, and development is often not so far from enlightenment.

Harriette Colenso's influence was felt particularly while her contacts to the Zulu ruler were strong and the colonial challenges to the Zulu were ones which she felt she could help with, rather than new problems such as urbanization and industrialization.[132] Highly respected even by those who did not agree with her support of the "Natives," and referred to as *Inksazana*, a woman of authority, by the Zulu, her integrity and character was much admired on both sides.[133] It is important to try as best possible to conceive the political impetus her support of the Zulu monarchy had. In strongly articulated contrast from Theophilus Shepstone, who had maligned the Zulu royal family and gone to pains to color its rule as bloody and tyrannical, Harriette Colenso supported the rule of "military chieftainships" over the "minor hereditary chiefs," arguing that these were a more efficient way for the Zulu to organize themselves in ways that could marshal a certain degree of power, rather than Shepstone's "divide and conquer" strategy.[134] Her counsel revealed a deep trust in peaceful political action and the colonial legal system. She used her influence to deescalate conflicts and urge the surrender of Dinuzulu and other Zulu that were put on trial for the one or other reason by colonial officials.[135] She identified strongly with the Zulu. On occasion she used the appellation "we Zulus" in her letters and supported some of the indigenous church structures that broke away from colonial churches.[136] Harriette was clear that "she was not a native, but natives were very much like the rest of human beings." She insisted that "her opinion was that of an outsider," and consulting her still meant that "the opinion of the people themselves should be obtained."[137] She argued for the preservation

[130] Jeff Guy, "The Colenso Daughters: Three Women Confront Imperialism," *JSOT Supplement Series* 386 (2003): 351 *The Eye of the Storm: Bishop John William Colenso and the Crisis of Biblical Interpretation*, vol. 386, Jonathan A. Draper (London: T&T Clark, 2003), 345-63.

[131] One textbook of the Maori language is entitled *He Whakamarama*, roughly "the making of light"—or enlightenment—though here, the term might appear reversed, as it is learning Maori that gives enlightenment, or initiation into a culture. John Foster, *He Whakamarama: A Full Self-Help Course in Maori* (Auckland: Reed, 1987).

[132] Shula Marks, "Harriette Colenso and the Zulus, 1874–1913," *Journal of African History* Vol. 4, No. 3 (1963): 411.

[133] Even a newspaper critical of her efforts to support Zulu economic and political independence grudgingly grants Harriette Colenso as having been granted "immense and unparalleled influence." Marks, "Harriette Colenso," 405–6.

[134] Ibid., 407.

[135] Ibid., 408.

[136] Ibid., 409.

[137] Harriette Emily Colenso, "Natal Native Affairs Commission," testimony to the Natal Native Affairs Commission (Natal Archives, 1906), 118, 119.

of whatever Zulu law was still in place, rather than assimilating all Zulu custom into the colonial legal system: "Uniformity was not so important as preserving to the natives whatever was good in their own laws."[138] Quoting a Zulu proverb, she argued that for respect to exist at all it must be mutual, and that the trust and respect had been eroded between the colonial government and the chiefs.

Though she received a fair amount of attention among certain members of the London political establishment, those favoring a harsher imperialist line were not above painting her in the "sexist stereotype of an over-zealous, even hysterical, female" whose actions were "reckless" and "irresponsible."[139] Missionaries like her were often seen as "foreign agitators" by colonials, undermining colonial governance. In a revealing public testimony given before the Natal Native Affairs Commission in 1906, Harriette Colenso opens her testimony by calling the hearings "an opportunity for salvation," given to the Natal colony to set things right and bring a measure of justice to the land. That is, her notion of salvation includes a version of interracial justice, as much as that may be possible in colonial setting. Using the soteriological metaphor of sickness and healing, she addresses the members of the commission as doctors, and encourages them to "diagnose the complaints" of the native population appropriately so they can find the causes and "suggest a remedy."[140] Immediately thereafter, she criticizes the invitation of European witnesses as superfluous and repeatedly points to the need to hear native witnesses themselves, rather than rely upon her to speak for them. This question of who gets to speak also involves, of course, herself and her gender. Thus, her brother Francis found it necessary to remark regarding Harriette's activities that:

> It must be remembered, in the first place, that when we are told to listen to "men on the spot," we have in Miss Colenso, not only an exceptionally well-informed woman on the spot, but one who finds no lack of sympathy among her fellow colonists. And many who deprecate some of her public utterances, appreciate the sincerity of her motives, and recognize the importance of her influence on the Natives.[141]

Harriette Colenso argued that the attempt to "abolish hereditary Chieftain-ships" by putting colonially appointed chiefs in their place will not only not work but will further destabilize the situation and "inflame the tribal senti-ments." It would thus have the opposite effect by strengthening attachment to and identification with hereditary chiefs.[142] Furthermore, Colenso and Alice

---

[138] Ibid., 119.

[139] Guy, *The View Across the River*, 341.

[140] Harriette Emily Colenso, "Natal Native Affairs Commission," 115.

[141] Francis Ernest Colenso, "Miss Colenso as an Aid to Justice and Peace in Zululand," 143, C. 1279, Colenso Collection (Natal Archives, 1908), 2–3.

[142] Harriette Emily Colenso, "Natal Native Affairs Commission," 117.

Werner write, the misunderstanding that Zulu chiefs have supreme powers has been a self-fulfilling prophecy, so that "the Supreme Chief, whatever his impossibility in theory, is an accomplished fact. Like Frankenstein's monster, he has no business to be in existence at all; but there he is."[143] It is not hard to imagine such monstrous authorities imagined and created through colonial misunderstandings help create the dictators of postcolonial African governments. The impression of randomness of changes in colonial law created situations in which Zulus "in many cases only became aware of the existence of a law through being fined and flogged for transgressing its provisions."[144] As in the movie *The Gods must Be Crazy*, the Bushman does not become aware that he is "stealing" a goat until he is imprisoned. His hunter-gatherer life informs what constitutes appropriate behavior, namely sharing the goat he killed with the shepherd. Behaviors appropriate to his hunting ways clash with that of the shepherd, a herder, as well as colonial understandings of private property.

Colonial violence, legal injustices, and the abuse of natives do not, so Colenso, give evidence of a "superior race" claiming to guide others:

> I wonder if any of you have been expecting me to arrive at a reference to "the white man's burden"? What I have to say on that point is that it is hypocritical for us to whine over it while it is so largely of our own manufacture, and we blindly refuse to let those bear their share who are perfectly willing to do so, and far better able than we are; and that the burden is manufactured not only by this Ministry or that, but by us all, by the Executive, by the Legislature, by Parliament's masters, the electors; by any of us who can so much as influence a single vote, and do not try to do so.[145]

Colenso and Werner explicitly compare the state of legal mess to ancient Roman imperial circumstances, arguing that

> when we comment on the *Punica fides* of ancient history, or disapprove of the way in which the Romans treated their barbarian subjects and allies, it will be well for us to remember those passages in our own conduct which to later generations may well appear, to say the least of it, equivocal.[146]

---

[143] Harriette Emily Colenso and Alice Werner, "White and Black in Natal," *Contemporary Review* Vol. 61 (January/June 1892): 210.

[144] Ibid., 211.

[145] Harriette Emily Colenso, "The Principles of Native Government in Natal," An Address by Miss Colenso Delivered before the Pietermaritzburg Parliamentary Debating Society, Colenso Collection (Natal Archives, 1908), 15.

[146] Colenso and Werner, "White and Black in Natal," 212.

Whether confusion, colonial misunderstandings, intentional, outright injustice, and notions of racial superiority, the effects compounded into a state where the relationships between the races were severely damaged, even without the constantly progressing annexation of land, livelihood, and the concomitant impact on cultural-spiritual agency. Rhetorical strategies casting colonial subjects as deceitful and unreliable have a long tradition. The term *punica fides* is used to mark the impression that colonized peoples or peoples beyond the borders are notoriously unreliable or deceitful, whether this expression is used or not, and though "there is no evidence of Germania fides, [. . .] authors not writing long after Varus' disastrous defeat [against Arminius] in 9 A.D., describe the Germans as utterly untrustworthy."[147]

A similar dynamic was manifested regarding the exiled Zulu king, who represented "the major obstacle to capitalist expansion," and "capitalist penetration was seen to be dependent on the king's removal."[148] The Zulu royal family had retained a "powerful grip on the popular imagination,"[149] perhaps especially *because* it in fact had very little real material or political power. In terms used to define the function of a sacrament in common Christian parlance, Harriette Colenso describes the imprisonment and exile of members of the Zulu royal family as "the outward and visible sign to the people of their own general disgrace."[150]

> He and his ancestors were believed to ensure the integrity and well-being of the people. At a time of growing exploitation, when subordinate chiefs were increasingly coming to be seen as subservient to white demands, what could be more natural than the people should turn to the king for protection [. . . While] the king "had no power to abuse"; he could continue to express national sentiment, and precisely because of the state's obduracy in failing to recognize him, people could express their resentment against white rule through their allegiance to the Zulu royal family.[151]

Colenso warns her listeners that "there was no greater mistake than to say that the native was a child," but that "in some respects the native was a very old man indeed, and in all that related to the management of men he was a full-grown man." The colonial ideology of evolutionary superiority was rather a self-fulfilling prophecy as it was built upon a disadvantage in "having a different language and a different way of putting things," as well as the

---

[147] Benjamin H. Isaac, *The Invention of Racism in Classical Antiquity* (Princeton, NJ: Princeton University Press, 2004), 331.

[148] Marks, *Ambiguities of Dependence*, 27–8.

[149] Ibid., 108.

[150] Harriette Emily Colenso, "Zululand: Past And Present," *Journal of the Manchester Geographical Society* (1890).

[151] Marks, *Ambiguities of Dependence*, 111.

disruption of native self-governance which, not surprisingly, led to "a state of utter confusion as to what was his [sic] position and what were his rights, and even what tribe he belonged to," while rendering them "out of the habit of handling their own affairs."[152]

Harriette, manifesting her own version of ambivalence between sensations of British cultural superiority and defending the Zulu against British abuses of power and various cultural arrogances, worked against the colonially convenient "stereotype of the beaten down Zulu female." Given her familiarity with Zulu customs, she had an understanding of their lives. At the same time she found common cause with liberal abolitionism and women's suffrage.

Colenso initially pursued an

alliance with imperial authorities to put a Christian king on the Zulu throne and came to be a fierce defender of Zulu independence and legal rights against the colonialists: first Langalibalele, then Cetshwayo, and then, posthumously through his family, Dinizulu.[153]

Harriette's attempt to convey to colonial officials and the British public some of the history and culture of the Zulu was tied up in an inescapably colonialist venture that never seems to have doubted the validity and legality of Queen Victoria's political designs. As British Royalists, the Colenso's also supported a royal Zulu line, despite a lineage that is as imagined a community and as ideologically loaded as Charlemagne's claim over and against the historic lineage of the Merowingian kings he finally usurped.

The Colenso household was a research and writing machine, and Harriette emerged as its star writer, supplementing and elaborating the writing of the bishop, whose main support, or "staff," Dlhwedhlwe in Zulu idiom, she became. After his death, she and her sisters faithfully continued a struggle for justice as they perceived it, for a Zulu monarchy that would unite the people in the face of the fragmenting power of colonial incursion moving toward total "home rule," that is a colonial government solely and supremely run by European settlers.

The Colensos believed that exemplarily lived Christian lives rather than conversionist preaching were preferred missionary tools, a conviction that cohered with other liberal understandings of missionary presence. This conviction is likely one underlying reason why theological reasoning and argumentation is remarkably absent in Harriette Colenso's writings. She saw her mission rather in living an exemplary life promoting truth and justice for Zulus before a decidedly slanted and often unjust colonial law.

---

[152] Harriette Emily Colenso, "Natal Native Affairs Commission," 121, 122.
[153] Draper, "Sola Fide," 490–1.

Alice Werner, a friend and contemporary of Harriette E. Colenso's and the first woman to be called to a professorship at London's School of Oriental and African Studies, writes in her obituary of Harriette:

[s]he was always careful to respect Zulu conventions–which are fairly strict with regard to the several departments of the sexes, though by no means ensuring the subjection of women to the extent frequently supposed—by explaining that, owing to special circumstances, she had been compelled to do a man's work. I used to think that her personal outlook, in this respect, was somewhat Early-Victorian, till one somewhat disconcertingly found her advocating—or at least sympathizing with the advocates of—women's suffrage and welcoming, where justice to Africans is concerned, support from the most diverse quarters.[154]

In the *Women's Penny Paper: The Only Paper Conducted, Written, Printed, and Published by Women*,[155] Harriette Colenso compared the struggle of women with that of the Zulu

who were apparently happy until we took them under "Protection." Perhaps the Zulu are like women, who begin to find out that protection when it does not mean self-protection, is a more than doubtful boon.[156]

Harriette then was part of a diverse stream of Victorian feminism that was supported by many women who had experiences of living in the colonies. In a setting of less oversight and scrutiny, some settler elite women were able to have considerable influence on social interactions in the colonies and often brokered between natives and colonists, as communicators, negotiators, missionaries, and schoolteachers. As agents of literacy, social mores, gender roles, European civilization and material culture, they taught Zulu children in a well-developed, if dampened manifestation of enlightenment thought that had a certain qualified respect for local cultures and a theology that saw a knowledge of the divine represented in them. Deviating from a then dominant Calvinistically tinged Church of England, they embraced, with some liberal features, a theology both evangelical but also sharing similarities with the Wesley's insistence of something like a prevenient grace, something like Aquinas' natural theology. This theology shaped their missionary approach and it separated them theologically and methodologically from other missionaries, bishops, and increasingly the Church

---

[154] Werner, "Harriette Colenso," 11.
[155] David Doughan describes this paper as containing "lively and uncompromising feminism; the most vigorous feminist paper of its time." www.ampltd.co.uk/collections_az/womensj-nc1/description.aspx, accessed 9/27/08.
[156] Quoted in: Guy, *The View Across the River*, 298.

of England. And yet, their battles were also those that were going to change and redefine the Church of England and modern mainline Protestantism: they reflect the divisions between liberals and evangelical, engage questions of how to read scripture in relationship to history and culture, query the relationship between gospel and culture, and how assumptions about that relationship inform missionary theologies and methodologies.

Harriette was not simply proposing the extension of the social sexual code of upper-class Victorians which advocated women's role as a calming influence on home and society. There are of course times when she seems to have seen herself as a calming influence toward peace, fitting with the focus of many upper-class Victorian women in propagating pacifism.[157] Harriette was convinced that if the disgraceful British treatment of the Zulu continued, it would add to "England's disgrace" and "assuredly throw back . . . Christianity and civilization among the native tribes of South Africa for years."[158]

Eventually, the Colensos were unable to prevent the disintegration of the Zulu economy into the colonial order in which it was going to be a subordinated, vulnerable part. Harriette Colenso estimated that she had spent around 3,000 British Pounds in defense of the Zulu. Hence a substantial part of the bishop's material legacy was "spent in pursuit of his moral and political legacy,"[159] a legacy that has yet to be more fully recovered.

The Missionary Position—Women, Marriage, and the Civilizing Mission

Marriage was to be a victory of the mission civilisatrice of the deportment of the well-born among the disorderly fringe of their own class: their womenfolk. The contours of public eminence were that much more sharply drawn by including even women in the charmed circle of upper-class excellence. As a result, the married couple came to appear in public as a miniature of civic order.[160]

One might be forgiven for assuming this description of the transformation of marriage referred to aspects of nineteenth-century sexual morality and the plural frontiers of colonization: internal and external. The context Peter Brown describes is not a Christian Rome, but a pre-Christian transformation of public social mores. The positionality of Roman matrons and the *exemplum* of Roman virtues she was expected to embody and propagate underlie and

---

[157] See, for example, Heloise Brown, *The Truest Form of Patriotism: Pacifist Feminism in Britain, 1870–1902* (Manchester: Manchester University Press, 2003).

[158] Quoted in Guy, *The View Across the River*, 299.

[159] Ibid., 300.

[160] Peter Brown, *Late Antiquity* (Cambridge, MA: Belknap Press of Harvard University Press, 1987), 12.

inform the framework of Christian notions of sexual relationships. Brown introduces his comments with a graphic description of the female Other that needed to be controlled, noting that

> in *Advice on Marriage*, Plutarch had described how the husband should use the skilled personal guidance associated with the philosopher to bring his young wife, still thought of as a kittenish little creature more interested in her partner's sexual vigor than in his philosophical gravity, into line with the public deportment of the upper-class male.[161]

But, as many have pointed out, it would be a mistake to assume the sexual mores of imperial Christianity were simply Christian; rather, they, too, instantiate a fusion of local mores, imperial and political interests, and an imported new take on messianic Judaism, with elements borrowed from the smorgasbord of Graeco-Roman religious and philosophical options.

Christianity is a syncretism not only of religious but socioeconomic practices and ideas. In its imperial incarnations it was redefined as pure and then continued to denounce other forms of syncretism. Local social and sexual mores and the needs that inform their transformations then have some very distinct influence on the sexual mores of Christianity as a religion on the rise during this time. Peter Brown, Elizabeth Clark, Virginia Burrus, and others have shown at length the particular inflections of masculinity, femininity, marriage, virginity, and asceticism that marked the confluence of Roman society and a Christian doctrinal formation increasingly prepped for prime time by the church fathers.

The destruction of indigenous economies such as the Zulu homestead system *(umuzi)* also led to the dissolution of much of the economic and social and gender relations, creating several problems.

> Post-apartheid structural adjustments—with liberalisation of markets, growing privatisation of services, increased urban unemployment and the simultaneous strong promotion of consumer values—have conspired to propel women's engagements in multiple sexual relationships. Through liaisons that imply an exchange of sexual favours for material gain, a woman can acquire goods that symbolise modernity and confer upon her a certain prestige and public image.[162]

---

[161] Ibid., 12. It is only fair to note that often women were many years the junior of their husbands, and while women were considered to reach *sexual* maturity around age 15, men's civic maturity was not complete until quite a bit later. Hence, as in ancient Greece, couples often belonged to what some cultures today would consider different generations, and, as a result, the numbers of widows were quite high, given their husbands were more than 10 years their senior.

[162] Suzanne Leclerc-Madlala, "AIDS in Zulu Idiom: Etiological Configurations of Women, Pollution, and Modernity," in *Zulu Identities: Being Zulu, Past Present*, Benedict Carton, et al. (Scottsdale: University of Kwa-Zulu Natal Press, 2008), 561.

This has led to gender relationships that manifest a number of societal transformations, hence, as "marital rates have plummeted and material transactions—usually gifts from boyfriends to girlfriends" have become common in
heterosexual relationships.[163] In many ways, "with the possibility of marriage
all but disappearing, money and gifts, from food to cell phone 'air time', typi-
cally given by men to women, facilitate intimate relationships." This transactional sexual economy also mirrors the spread of HIV/AIDS along gender and
age divides, as the infection rates of older men follow those of younger single
women with whom they are involved in transactional forms of sex.[164] Hence,
many of the urban migrant labor force of young men are "more likely to be
'providers outside of marriage,' a route to contemporary manhood that pulls
them into the vortex of a lethal pandemic."[165]

During the 2008 U.S. presidential campaign, a video of a Kenyan Assembly
of God minister praying over Sarah Palin, the vice-presidential candidate, was
leaked online to make people aware of what people assumed was her belief in
witchcraft, as the priest prays for her to be protected from witchcraft. The cultural crossroads of a Kenyan Assembly of God pastor invoking African witchcraft practices in the context of rural Alaska, a place often infused with native
spiritual energy, is an interesting thing to consider.

One of the more oblique ways in which women become marginalized is
accusations of witchcraft. Tight socioeconomic circumstances come together
with religious beliefs in which witches are targeted as scapegoats and "public enemy number one, capable of harming or killing others, and need to
be eliminated."[166] Grandmothers and older aunts are often targeted here, as
historically many societies have engaged in "death-hastening" activities when
times run rough and food is low. Identifying certain elders, especially women,
as witches occurs particularly during famines and other events that threaten
communal survival.

Bishop Colenso's approach to dealing with the often problematic (which can
scapegoat, and mark, and disable members of the community accused of it)
presence of witchcraft was to honestly examine his own heritage as well as the
African heritage of witchcraft. Thus he writes:

> How is it possible to teach the Zulus to cast off their superstitious belief in
> witchcraft, if they are required to believe that all the stories of sorcery and

---

[163] Mark Hunter, "IsiZulu-Speaking Men and Changing Households: From Providers Within
Marriage to Providers Outside Marriage," in *Zulu Identities: Being Zulu, Past Present*,
Benedict Carton, et al. (Scottsdale: University of Kwa-Zulu Natal Press, 2008), 566.

[164] Hunter, "IsiZulu-Speaking Men," 570.

[165] Ibid., 571.

[166] Raymond Fisman and Edward Miguel, *Economic Gangsters: Corruption, Violence, and the
Poverty of Nations* (Princeton and Oxford: Princeton University Press, 2008), 140.

demonology which they find in the Bible . . . are infallibly and divinely true . . . I, for one, cannot do this.[167]

That is, Colenso argues that theological honesty requires challenging conceptions of healing and health in the Christian religion in the light of modern medicine and the challenge witchcraft represents both to colonial and indigenous communities. Rather than externalizing the problem by claiming it is something that is only practiced by non-Christians, Colenso sees it as a problem internal to the Christian tradition. He refuses to do the self-splitting move Fanon observes in many colonial relations and refuses to collapse the complexity of his own context in the encounter with another equally complex context, resisting easy oppositions and claims to one-sided superiorities. This admission points to a repressed similarity between the psychophysical energies of African religions and Christian practices and the importance of finding creative approaches to the social and economic dynamics that inform religiously framed accusations.[168] In a certain district in Tanzania, just as poor as others, witch doctors offer a cleansing ritual that promises to rid accused older women from any supposed past "witchcraft 'sins.' "[169] Thus, in the absence of a viable pension system that supports elders, a viable option appears in the form of a religious solution.

Polygamy, Heteronormativity, Homosexuality, and HIV/AIDS: Sexual Politics in Colonial and Post-Apartheid South Africa

Gavin Whitelaw argues that the Central Cattle Pattern—which supports a patriarchal polygynous culture centered on cattle as brideprice—

endured for 1600 years because it represents the mechanism that theoretically gave *all* men access to power. This allowed it to survive even the great

---

[167] Quoted in Draper, "Sola Fide," 473.

[168] The Comaroffs state in Vol. 2 that the Christian pastor or priest's role could not be easily separated from that of the healer or medicine man/shaman. Until today, of course, Christians have engaged in a variety of healing practices, some more seemingly "miraculous" because instantaneous, and others more humble and with a longer time frame. Whether it is Pentecostal healing prayers or the liberative practices of contextual Bible studies that aim to give space to anger, frustration, sense of abandonment and aloneness in the face of HIV/AIDS, it is clear that the relationship between religious claims to power and truth and its psychophysical embodiment are complex. Comaroff, John, and Jean Comaroff. *Of Revelation and Revolution: The Dialectics of Modernity on a South African Frontier, Vol. 2.* (Chicago, IL: Chicago University Press, 1991), 333.

[169] Fisman and Miguel, *Economic Gangsters*, 144.

upheavals of the early stages of colonisation. Indeed, one has to wonder if its persistence in the modern era is not partly a consequence of colonisation and apartheid, of the denial to Africans of an alternative route to power.[170]

The majority of white settlers and colonial officials were deeply offended and strongly opposed what they saw as a form of slavery—of multiple wives held in slavery by their husbands. But the moral grounds that they often claimed for this opposition were not the only ones: Polygamous households also bolstered and sustained self-sufficiency for the Zulu, and many white settlers who could neither compete economically with them nor get Zulu to work for them pushed for the ban on polygamy.

> In the minds of [. . .] prominent colonists, the barbaric slavery of polygamy hindered the establishment of a civilised commercial society in Natal. Well-known settler Thomas Phipson argued that if it were not for the savage state of African society, the white settler "would be able to sell his labour or produce in a fair market" and would be able to afford "the food and clothing appertained to civilised life."[171]

African economic activity was so self-sufficient and self-contained that white settlers could not get traction with Africans either as customers or as laborers: "That colonial power could extract local resources hardly impressed white farmers who irritably complained that the African reserve system bolstered self-sufficiency and encouraged a huge pool of labour to ignore their demands for workers."[172] Ownership of cattle represented, in some instances, "freedom from the labor market," ironically, by turning cattle into cash and escaping from the "cycle of migration and want."[173]

Consumer-relations and capitalist economic relationships have for a long time now worked to override the confines of family, clan, tribe, and nation. "Non-Western" peoples' status is measured in their ability to consume and participate as "good citizens" in a religiopolitical system that has strapped social acceptance to a person or group's consumption potential, either as commodity

---

[170] Gavin Whitelaw, "A Brief Archaelology of Precolonial Farming in KwaZulu-Natal," in *Zulu Identities: Being Zulu, Past and Present*, ed. Benedict Carton, John Laband, and Jabulani Sithole (Scottsville, South Africa: University of KwaZulu-Natal Press, 2008), 57.

[171] Jeremy Martens, "Enlightenment Theories of Civilization and Savagery in British Natal," in *Zulu Identities: Being Zulu, Past and Present*, ed. Benedict Carton, John Laband, and Jabulani Sithole, PL (Scottsville, South Africa: University of KwaZulu-Natal Press, 2008), 129.

[172] Benedict Carton, "Faithful Anthropologists: Christianity, Ethnography and the Making of 'Zulu Religion' in Early Colonial Natal," in *Zulu Identities: Being Zulu, Past and Present*, ed. Benedict Carton, John Laband, and Jabulani Sithole, PL (Scottsville, South Africa: University of KwaZulu-Natal Press, 2008), 153.

[173] Comaroff and Comaroff, *Ethnography*, 148.

or consumer. Christianity, it might appear, has been indelibly fused with not only capitalist over Marxist, but also capitalist over subsistence pastoralist and agriculturalist, as well as subsistence hunters of the climes where agriculture is not feasible. Methodism, having emerged during the industrial revolution and shaped by it, had been successful in Britain in addressing and engaging the growing working class and bolstering its sense of purpose and work ethic. "Drawing on metaphors from the factory and the foundry, it spoke of individual salvation through arduous self-construction."[174] The Christian working class self promoted by it clashed with people initially reluctant to enter industrial capitalism as its workforce, both in post-War Europe[175] and in Africa.

Laziness, long having had a solid career as one of the Catholic mortal sins, sloth, became a secularized symbol opposed to the industriousness of and age drunk on production, and people living in economies that did not comply sufficiently were marked as "lazy Kafir" and similar epithets.[176] One could argue that those who are not willing to work for the kind of prosperity we have seen become commonplace even for common people through industrial capitalism and some of what came after, should not have access to that kind of prosperity. But it also highlights the need for different models of work ethic and different ways of life that legitimately and sustainably combine multiple ways to care for self, family, and community.

Most missionaries participated willingly in much of this, partly because they saw no other way for their charges to survive without being completely disenfranchised, and partly because they sincerely believed this was the best way to go. Many missionaries thus "prepared" the people they were sent to "for wage labor" as they "instilled in them 'wants' that could only be satisfied through entry into the colonial economy." A cynical way of how the Christian gospel itself was spread would seem to find that similar dynamics obtained: many spiritual economies were not perceived to be lacking in ways of regulating and explaining the local social and sacred world.[177] Many missionaries were the salesmen of these goods. But a market had yet to be created for them, and that market creation often seemed to involve a civilizational confinement of Christian faith. It is the rare missionary who could extricate themselves even

---

[174] Ibid., *Ethnography*, 161.

[175] Victoria De Grazia, *Irresistible Empire: America's Advance Through 20th-Century Europe* (Cambridge: Beknap Press, 2005).

[176] Comaroff and Comaroff, *Ethnography*, 161.

[177] Witness the many accounts of first encounters between missionaries and natives that indicate that the concepts of sin, salvation, and damnation were not only unknown, but also unattractive and appeared unnecessary. In the spiritual economy then, they were goods that were neither needed nor desired. The missionaries were the reeducators and salesmen of the goods of salvation. The reader may find this a one-sided cynical reading, but since this reading so often aligns with the accounts we have, theological reimaginings of such exchanges are key to unhitching this overly close link of social and material soteriological discourses.

just partly from these tsunami-like dynamics that they, too, had been indoctrinated with. These issues are a challenge not only for Christian religion but perhaps for simple human pragmatism that pervades many cultures, to adopt the practices that bring advantage to our selves and communities. The tradition of "prosperity theology" is ancient, as ancient as the disciples asking "what will we gain for following you"? Comparative theology is tried and true as a missionary strategy. It should perhaps not further surprise us that such strands in the tradition are a fertile seedbed for certain prosperity theologies of a variety of proveniences, but perhaps particularly the variety currently shilled about America and Africa by the Creflo Dollars of the world.

The Colensos had significant reservations about how much civilizational confinement had to go along with adoption into the Christian faith, and while theirs was a more open version, willing to tolerate not only multiple cultural belongings but also potentially multiple religious belongings, the differentiation between culture and religion remains problematic and only somewhat sustainable in a seemingly secularized environment.

These ideas and assumptions are still very much with us and deeply enshrined in current policies, global and local, as well as in the nonprofit industry. It will require far more beyond-the-box thinking to come up with models that do not simply reiterate hegemonic ideologies. The crisis of neoliberal economics and neo-conservative politics should give cause to reassess what our options are in such encounters and renegotiations. The Comaroffs have held that

> among Southern Bantu-speakers in general, livestock fostered the growth and expression of great discrepancies of wealth. In much the same way as capital, they served both as standards of value and as a means of accumulating and transforming it into other kinds of wealth in the political economy at large.[178]

With the imposition of a more wage-based economy, the province of Kwazulu Natal went from a place that "subsidized the welfare costs of the migrant laborer" to a region where the great majority of inhabitants became dependent on the wages of "migrants and commuters to the 'white economy'" for their economic survival. Eighty percent of the wages earned in the "white economy" went back into it, while emptying the province of men, rendering the capital-deprived Kwazulu of the 1980s a place of women whose men worked in mines, farms, and factories in white South Africa.[179]

The effects of colonial economics on gender relations in South Africa continued to be devastating and form one factor in the spread of HIV/AIDS today, which has its epicenter in Kwa-Zulu Natal.

---

[178] Comaroff and Comaroff, *Ethnography*, 141.
[179] Marks, *Ambiguities of Dependence*, 115.

The Missionary Position and
Colonial Gender Economics

Anglican Churches have been deeply involved in the struggle about variations on the colonial "missionary position," that is, a metaphor for the "well-
documented efforts by missionaries to inscribe European (white) norms on
the sexual practices and beliefs of their converts."[180] Missionaries' bodies
and bodily practices are part of the missionary message; everything about
them speaks, but is read in multiple, at times unpredictable, ways. Offered
by ethnographers, this following assertion may prove a powerful reminder
also for theologians and churches: "human experience everywhere tends stubbornly to reassert the inseparability of physical and social being."[181] From the
above it becomes clear that one of the reasons Colenso pleaded for the acceptance of polygamy had to do with the economic self-sustainability of Zulu
society. Beyond that, there were mixed motives and mixed issues: economic
sustainability, which was, of course, built upon the productivity of the bodies
of Zulu women but allowed resistance.

In the encounter between settlers, missionaries, and natives, two different
kinds of political economy clashed. Patriarchal, both of them, but sufficiently
different in their organization of cattle, agricultural processes, women and
children, designations of acceptable expressions of sexuality, power and religion, they rub against each other and trigger reconsiderations and transformations on both sides. Observing some of the local ways in which people respond
to the HIV/AIDS pandemic, we find familiar images, the wandering womb
and the toothy vagina, ancient mediterranean "bio-moral mode"[182] that linked
women's body features to gendered morals and diseases.

> The theme of "wet" vagina associated with sexually transmitted diseases and
> an ability to cause all manner of "dirt" to stick to its walls, are features in
> both men's and women's discourses of HIV transmission. One young nurs-
> ing student referred to the higher incidence of HIV infection among women
> as being due to the fact that "women are wet down there, therefore when
> they are exposed to infections the germs just stick inside." One young man
> expressed similar anxieties: "Inside a woman it is dark, wet, not nice. AIDS
> can live there, waiting, and you wouldn't know. Even the woman herself
> wouldn't know because it just sticks inside. She really needs a blood test to
> know for sure."[183]

---

[180] Laurel C. Schneider, "Changing the Missionary Position: Facing Up to Racism and
Nationalism," The Castañeda Lecture (Chicago Theological Seminary, 2007), 6.
[181] Comaroff and Comaroff, *Ethnography*, 90.
[182] Leclerc-Madlala, "AIDS in Zulu Idiom," 562.
[183] Ibid., 558.

Both men and women hold views that reflect a symbiotic relationship between women's bodies and disease in general. As a place where disease-causing "dirt" is especially likely to be "hiding," the vagina is widely thought to be an open-ended passage that leads up into the womb. This belief underlies a widespread fear that condoms might "go up" and "get lost." Many women express anxiety that should a condom break or slip off during intercourse, it may "float around inside" and eventually find its way up into the body cavity to cause grave illness.[184]

Labor migrations uproot and deconstruct pre-colonial family structures, and can lead to oversaturation of men within cities and women in rural areas. Thus, "[w]idespread migration impoverished domestic resources, placing increased weight upon matrilateral ties—and on women, who were left to make what they could of the depleted rural economy."[185] Religious responses include a transplanted version of the U.S. Christian Catholic Apostolic Church in Zion. Preceding Pentecostal movements, founded in Chicago in 1896 a lower-class context, "among impoverished urban workers and petty tradesmen" and hence responding among others to industrialized life in growing cities, this church offered a way to come to spiritual terms with what adherents perceived as alienation and "estrangement from the world of the establishment," especially that of capitalist elites and rising bourgeoisies. The disruption of larger social systems and the attempted remaking of Africans into more individually defined subjects whose relationships to family can become supplanted by that to goods and colonial religion are hence mapped on the bodies of men and women. The "sickness" of industrial capitalist production was here, however, "metaphors of affliction would seem to have been depoliticized" and were instead rewritten as a story of spiritual disease in need of divine healing. Instead, "signs of sickness" became a "local dialectic of bodily space and ruptured margins," signifying an "unceasing battle between the healing Spirit and malign forces for the possession of human beings."[186] Zionists used particular rituals to express bio-power they felt they still had access to, despite colonial capitalisms:

Hence, the ambivalent reshaping of African bodies into "the biophysical individualism of the West"[187] represents an "extreme example of the stripping

---

[184] Ibid., 557.

[185] Comaroff and Comaroff, *Ethnography*, 85.

[186] Ibid., 85.

[187] Amartya Sen warns of "civilizational confinement," that is, the sole identification with certain forms of science, governance, religion, or culture with one over another so-called "civilization" (whatever that may be), and hence an artificial simplification of features of societies. Thus he argues that the "Western world has no property right over democratic ideas," and reminds that much unfortunate historiography claimed associates certain cultural practices particularly with "the West" as if ideas such as printing, explosives, mathematics, and so forth were not coproductions rather than an "immaculate Western

of the body's capacity to signify the social," though one might have to qualify this resonant insight in a variety of ways. The Comaroffs indicate as much: "for every visitor who affirmed the emerging stereotype that, like all native Africans, the 'Bechuana' placed communal over personal concerns, collective rights over personal property, ascriptive norms over human achievement and initiative, another spoke of their rampant individualism."[188] Though, in the context of the Comaroff's narrative, the pulsing from hierarchical to autonomous social organization among the Tswana occurs in the context of transformations caused by colonial presences, caution is recommended when vestiges of the device of the noble savage are held up as romantic lenses of internal imperial critique. Different ways of shaping social and individual worlds do not mean the absence of either individual agency or communal cohesion, though it does indeed look quite different in capitalist consumerism than in settings of subsistence economies.

The Zulu notion of land tenure appears similar to the notions of land-use among a variety of native peoples. Thus Harriette Colenso testifies that "the original idea of the native in regard to this matter was that no one could buy or sell land; it all belonged to the people, and the King or Chief, as Trustee, could not really give away the title."[189] Ideally, then, the chief is simply the mouthpiece of the people, rather than the determinant of their action, and the colonial policy of trying to separate natives from their land by empowering certain colonially chosen natives as leaders functioned to divide the native community and to conquer native lands.

Many missionaries in South Africa actively promoted social and economic differentiation, to demonstrate that converts' lives were improving, despite the losses of community and cultural belonging, and promised access to some of the privileges of colonial society.[190] For some missionaries the circumstances created through such economic transformation embodied an independence not even accessible to contemporary Britons, allowing every *kholwa* Zulu farmer to live, in biblical terms, "under his vine and fig tree."[191]

> It was out of the mid-Victorian vision of a "progressive world order," based on the virtues of free labor, secure property rights linked to a free market in land and individual tenure, equality before the law, and some notion of "no taxation without representation" that African Christians in the nineteenth century constructed their world.[192]

conception." Amartya Sen, *Identity and Violence: The Illusion of Destiny* (New York: W. W. Norton, 2006), 56–7.

[188] Comaroff and Comaroff, *Ethnography*, 100.
[189] Harriette Emily Colenso, "Natal Native Affairs Commission," 120.
[190] Marks, *Ambiguities of Dependence*, 46.
[191] Ibid., 46.
[192] Ibid., 48.

This vision was hindered, however, by the ideologies of race and imperialism. While imperialism provided a certain upward mobility, and by the need for an unlimited, unskilled labor force in the factories of industrial capitalism. Thus, there was little room left for an enfranchised black middle class.[193] Through a series of circumstances, over time, the previously flourishing mission stations became "rural slums" as many people evicted settled on *kholwa*-owned land.[194] As we can see from these sobering facts, the economy of a missionary presence is rather complex and far surpasses the initial labors of translation, education, and transformation. The complex reverberations of colonial, missionary, and convert activity continue to shape contemporary African religious and economic life.

Works Cited

Anderson, Benedict. *Imagined Communities: Reflections on the Origin and Spread of Nationalism*. London: Verso, 1983.

Appiah, Kwame Anthony. *Cosmopolitanism: Ethics in a World of Strangers*. New York: W. W. Norton & Company, 2006.

Bonner, Philip, and Amanda Esterhuysen, eds, Trefor Jenkis. *A Search for Origins: Science, History and South Africa's 'Cradle of Humankind'*. Johannesburg: Wits University Press, 2007.

Brown, Heloise. *The Truest Form of Patriotism: Pacifist Feminism in Britain, 1870–1902*. Manchester: Manchester University Press, 2003.

Brown, Peter. *Late Antiquity*. Cambridge, MA: Belknap Press of Harvard University Press, 1987.

Carton, Benedict. "Faithful Anthropologists: Christianity, Ethnography and the Making of 'Zulu Religion' in Early Colonial Natal." In *Zulu Identities: Being Zulu, Past and Present*, edited by Benedict Carton, John Laband, and Jabulani Sithole, PL, 153–67. Scottsville, South Africa: University of KwaZulu-Natal Press, 2008.

Colenso, Francis Ernest. "Miss Colenso as an Aid to Justice and Peace in Zululand." 143, C. 1279. Colenso Collection. Natal Archives, 1908.

Colenso, Harriette Emily. "Natal Native Affairs Commission." Testimony to the Natal Native Affairs Commission. Natal Archives, 1906.

—."The Principles of Native Government in Natal." An Address by Miss Colenso Delivered before the Pietermaritzburg Parliamentary Debating Society. Colenso Collection. Natal Archives, 1908.

—."Zululand: Past And Present." *Journal of the Manchester Geographical Society* (1890).

Colenso, Harriette Emily, and Alice Werner. "White and Black in Natal." *Contemporary Review* Vol. 61 (January/June 1892): 205–13.

Colenso, John William. *A Letter to His Grace the Archbishop of Canterbury Upon the Question of the Proper Treatment of Cases of Polygamy, as Found Already Existing in Converts from Heathenism*. London: Macmillan and Co., 1862.

---

[193] Ibid., 57.
[194] Ibid., 65.

—.*Ten Weeks in Natal: A Journal of a First Tour of Visitation among the Colonists and Zulu Kafirs of Natal.* Cambridge: MacMillan & Co., 1855.

Comaroff, John, and Jean Comaroff. *Ethnography and the Historical Imagination.* Boulder, CO: Westview Press, 1992.

—.*Of Revelation and Revolution: Christianity, Colonialism, and Consciousness in South Africa, Vol. 1.* Chicago, IL: Chicago University Press, 1991.

Dangarembga, Tsitsi. *Nervous Conditions.* Oxfordshire: Ayebia, 1988.

De Grazia, Victoria. *Irresistible Empire: America's Advance Through 20th-Century Europe.* Cambridge, MA: Beknap Press, 2005.

Draper, Jonathan A. "The Bishop and the Bricoleur: Bishop John William Colenso's Commentary on Romans and Magema Kamagwaza Fuze's The Black People and Whence They Came From," eds, Gerald West and Musa Dube, 415–54. Leiden: Brill, 2001.

—."Bishop John William Colenso's Interpretation To The Zulu People Of The *Sola Fide* In Paul's Letter To The Romans." In *SBL 2000 Seminar Papers*, 465–93. Atlanta, GA: SBL, 2000.

—."Introduction" In *Commentary on Romans by John William Colenso*, edited by Jonathan A. Draper, ix–xxxix. Pietermaritzburg: Cluster Publications, 2003.

Edgecombe, Ruth. "Bishop Colenso and the Zulu Nation." *Journal of Natal and Zulu History* III (1980): 15–29.

Fisman, Raymond, and Edward Miguel. *Economic Gangsters: Corruption, Violence, and the Poverty of Nations.* Princeton and Oxford: Princeton University Press, 2008.

Fletcher, Richard. *The Barbarian Conversion: From Paganism to Christianity.* Berkeley, CA: University of California, 1999.

Foster, John. *He Whakamarama: A Full Self-Help Course in Maori.* Auckland: Reed, 1987.

Fuze, Magema Magwa. *The Black People And Whence They Came.* Pietermaritzburg: University of Natal Press, 1979.

Geary, Patrick J. *The Myth of Nations: The Medieval Origins of Europe.* Princeton, NJ: Princeton University Press, 2002.

Guy, Jeff. "The Colenso Daughters: Three Women Confront Imperialism." *JSOT Supplement Series* 386 (2003)*The Eye of the Storm: Bishop John William Colenso and the Crisis of Biblical Interpretation.* Vol. 386, Jonathan A. Draper. 345-363. London: T&T Clark.

—.*The Heretic: A Study of the Life of John William Colenso, 1814–1883.* Pietermaritzburg: University of Natal Press, 1983.

—.*The View Across the River: Harriette Colenso and the Zulu Struggle Against Imperialism.* Charlottesville, VA: University of Virginia Press, 2001.

Hammond-Tooke, W. D. "Cattle Symbolism in Zulu Culture." In *Zulu Identities: Being Zulu, Past and Present,* edited by Benedict Carton, John Laband, and Jabulani Sithole, PL, 62–8. Scottsville, South Africa: University of KwaZulu-Natal Press, 2008.

La Hausse, Paul. *Restless Identities: Signatures of Nationalism, Zulu Ethnicity and History in the Lives of Petros Lamula (c. 1881–1948) and Lymon Maling (1889–1936).* Pietermaritzburg: University of Natal, 2000.

Hunter, Mark. "IsiZulu-Speaking Men and Changing Households: From Providers Within Marriage to Providers Outside Marriage." In *Zulu Identities: Being Zulu, Past Present,* Benedict Carton, et al., 566–72. Scottsdale: University of Kwa-Zulu Natal Press, 2008.

Isaac, Benjamin H. *The Invention of Racism in Classical Antiquity.* Princeton, NJ: Princeton University Press, 2004.

Keller, Catherine. *Face of the Deep.* New York/London: Routledge, 2003.

King, Michael. *The Penguin History of New Zealand.* Auckland: Penguin, 2003.

Leclerc-Madlala, Suzanne. "AIDS in Zulu Idiom: Etiological Configurations of Women, Pollution, and Modernity." In *Zulu Identities: Being Zulu, Past Present,* Benedict Carton, et al.,554–65. Scottsdale: University of Kwa-Zulu Natal Press, 2008.

Lyman, Rebecca. "The Politics of Passing: Justin Martyr's Conversion as a Problem of Hellenization." In *Conversion in Late Antiquity and the Middle Ages: Seeing and Believing,* eds Anthony Grafton and Kenneth Mills, Rochester, NY: University of Rochester Press, 2003.

Marks, Shula. *Ambiguities of Dependence in South Africa: Class, Nationalism, and the State in Twentieth-Century Natal.* Baltimore, MD: Johns Hopkins University Press, 1986.

—."Harriette Colenso and the Zulus, 1874–1913." *Journal of African History* Vol. 4, No. 3 (1963): 403–11.

Martens, Jeremy. "Enlightenment Theories of Civilisation and Savagery in British Natal." In *Zulu Identities: Being Zulu, Past and Present,* edited by Benedict Carton, John Laband, and Jabulani Sithole, PL, 122–32. Scottsville, South Africa: University of KwaZulu-Natal Press, 2008.

Mokoena, Hlonipha. "The Queen's Bishop: A Convert's Memoir of John W. Colenso." *Journal of Religion in Africa* Vol. 38 (2008): 312–42.

Ndlovu, Sifiso. "A Reassessment of Women's Power in the Zulu Kingdom." In *Zulu Identities: Being Zulu, Past and Present,* eds, Benedict Carton, John Laband, and Jabulani Sithole, 111–21. Scottsville, South Africa: University of KwaZulu-Natal Press, 2008.

Nicholls, Brenda. "Zululand 1887–1889: The Court of the Special Commissioners for Zululand and the Rule of Law." *Journal of Natal and Zulu History* Vol. XV (1994/1995): Accessed Oct 30, 2008.

Ntshingila, Futhi. *Shameless.* Scottsville: University of KwaZulu-Natal Press, 2008.

Parker, John, and Richard Rathbone. *African History: A Very Short Introduction.* Oxford: Oxford University Press, 2007.

Schneider, Laurel C. "Changing the Missionary Position: Facing Up to Racism and Nationalism." *The Castañeda Lecture.* Chicago, IL: Theological Seminary, 2007.

Seidman, Naomi. *Faithful Renderings: Jewish-Christian Difference and the Politics of Translation.* Chicago, IL: Chicago University Press, 2006.

Sen, Amartya. *Identity and Violence: The Illusion of Destiny.* New York: W. W. Norton, 2006.

Sugirtharajah, R. S. *The Bible and Empire: Postcolonial Explorations.* Cambridge: Cambridge University Press, 2005.

—.*The Bible and the Third World: Precolonial, Colonial, and Postcolonial Encounters.* Cambridge: Cambridge University Press, 2001.

—.*Postcolonial Criticism and Biblical Interpretation.* Oxford: Oxford University Press, 2002.

Thomas, Linda. "Survival and Resistance In An African Indigenous Church." *Journal of Theology for Southern Africa* No. 98 (July 1997).

Werner, Alice. "Harriette Colenso." KCM 6563. Papers of Harriette Colenso. Killie Campbell Africana Library. Durban, South Africa, 1932.

—."Source Unknown, Page in Unidentified Journal Page, Authored by Alice Werner." Uncatalogued. Killie Campbell, Colenso Papers.

West, Gerald. "On the Eve of an African Biblical Studies: Trajectories and Trends." *Journal of Theology for Southern Africa* Vol. 99 (November 1997): 99–115.

Whitelaw, Gavin. "A Brief Archaelology of Precolonial Farming in KwaZulu-Natal." In *Zulu Identities: Being Zulu, Past and Present*, eds, Benedict Carton, John Laband, and Jabulani Sithole, 47–61. Scottsville, South Africa: University of KwaZulu-Natal Press, 2008.

Chapter 6

Itinerary III:
Regifting the Theological Present: Economies
of Exchange between Maori and Anglicans

The Wealth of Whales: Guides, Hunted,
Beached, Traded, Betrayed

Every few years, a number of whales beach themselves, many in the South Pacific.
A few years ago, a sizable number mysteriously floundered on a remote part of
Aotearoa/New Zealand's North Island.[1] Many died, while some were pushed
back into the sea and survived. The mysterious stranding of whales in what can
seem like suicidal urgings captures people's imagination across cultures, especially in a time when these animals have been decimated and brought near
extinction. Some human cultures have related strongly to whales, the largest
mammals, creatures that sound the depths, breach waves, travel seasonally,
and on occasion strand themselves on shores. Mythical whales feature in narrative and literature: Job's Leviathan, Jonah's whale, Kahu/Paikea's ancestral
guardian in Maori ancestral lore, Melville's Moby Dick. Whales have fueled the
colonial imagination of the South Seas and colonial economics when whale
bodies were hunted to extinction while their blubber fueled the expansive
economy of colonial North America prior to the arrival of electric light and
petroleum energy. Theological and philosophical ruminations on gift economies in the work of Marcel Mauss, Jacques Derrida, and John Milbank intersect with James Cook's journeys on the *Endeavour*, Herman Melville's colonial
male heroes, and the Maori author Witi Ihimaera's 1987 novel and 2002 film
The Whale Rider.

These literary texts broaden the archive on missionary-native and intercultural encounters in the colonial context and offer unexpectedly revealing
glimpses into the notions of gift, exchange, and trade as we navigate ancestral worlds and the ambivalent "gifts" of modern Christendom's imperialism

---

[1] Reuters, "Whale Strandings in New Zealand, Australia," *CNN.Com*, Tuesday, November 30
   2004, www.cnn.com/2004/TECH/science/11/30/australia.whales.reut/.

in the spaces of imagination spanning the North Atlantic and the South Pacific. These narratives are set on the South Pacific shores of the British Empire and tell of contestedly reciprocal encounters between two worlds. In these texts we find negotiations of women and indigenous peoples as two incarnations of otherness to the self of North Atlantic colonial masculinity.[2] I want to examine the ambivalent practice of the gift as a corrective transcultural theological resource, a response to the destructive perversions of hypercapitalist imperialism. This helps challenge notions of unilateral, unreciprocated giving, human and divine, and to probe spaces of responsible reciprocity in recognition of the persistent realities of power scenarios. Such exploration of gift exchange may offer a locus for coming to terms with Christian involvement in modern imperial enterprises, in this case, the colonial churches' complicity with the expansionist "civilizing mission" of the British Empire.

The history and present of British colonialism are inseparable from the present shape of the Anglican Communion.[3] Thinking "beyond colonial Anglicanism"[4] here means expansion of theological sources, archives, and genres, quite distinct from John Milbank's Anglo-Catholic hearkening back to a vision of idealized conformity in matters of faith. Agreeing with Milbank that "we must oppose the sacrifice of individuals to the state, to globalization," I suggest that such opposition must, however, include a critical reading, recognition, repentance of the colonial past and present, and credible moves toward transformed relationships.

Traversing Seas, Weaving Whakapapa

The imported Anglican faith of the British colonists flourished. Christianity is portable. It does not rely on anything being intact. It can be practiced and understood in a city or in the country, under a roof, or out in the open, by any people, anywhere. The faith of the Maori is specific to New Zealand. It can't be packed up and taken anywhere

---

[2]   On these early exploratory travels, women could only go as stowaways. My perspective resembles somewhat an invisible presence with limited access vision, starved for light and air, for freedom of movement and speech. Apparently, large numbers of stowaways regularly were able to get on board such ships, as demonstrated by New Zealand's first shipwreck which uncovered the astonishing number of 46 stowaways, including at least two women. King, *History of New Zealand*, 119.

[3]   Ian T. Douglas, "Authority After Colonialism," *The Witness* 83:3 (March 2000): 10–14 and Ian T. Douglas, "The Exigency of Times and Occasions: Power and Identity in the Anglican Communion Today," in *Beyond Colonial Anglicanism: The Anglican Communion in the Twenty-first Century*, edited by Ian T. Douglas and Kwok Pui-Lan (New York: Church Publishing, 2001), 25–46.

[4]   Ibid.

easily. To resurrect a nature-based spiritual society, you need to protect the sources of awe that inspired spirituality in the first place.[5]

There are a number of common, understandable, but also questionable assumptions in the statement above (in all fairness, made by a non-theologian, but therefore even more forcefully demonstrating certain uninterrogated commonplaces in the public register). While elements of Christian faith and practice certainly seem portable in some forms, there are societies that have not been particularly compatible with certain aspects of its incarnations. India, in particular, is an example. The author of the above repeats the trope of Christianity as a cultureless religion that can be easily assimilated, dualistically juxtaposed with indigenous religions as space-dependent. The more careful reader will remember, however, that Hebrew writings were initially oral, "indigenous," rather place-specific, and only over time, and following exile and diaspora were adapted to different living and settlement patterns. Even a cursory look at Israel/Palestine's ongoing troubles show how attached to place all three Abrahamic religions continue to be, and how some indigenous traditions, including Maori religious culture, have already undergone major transformation through migration. That is, place, migration, and reestablishment in new places have long been part of many religious systems, and it seems imprecise and unhelpful to juxtapose these dynamics based upon persistent but imprecise stereotypes of "migratory" versus "sedentary" systems or to align migratory religious systems with a lack of ecological consciousness.

The adaptation of Christian features shows a relative consistency across cultural, geographic, and temporal variation. Many have become accustomed to condemning one version as "civilizing mission" and celebrating the other as salutary "inculturation." Yet, it is not so much the process of polydox blending that separates the two, but rather the claims attached to them. What once was an indigenization over time has become associated with a universal mode. It is not a helpful response to try to undo previous inculturations of Christian contents, as if that were possible, and pretend the possibility of a "universal" message that can be discerned apart from its cultural incarnations. Nor does it mean inculturating Christian content so profoundly that it becomes completely indistinguishable from historical and geographical adaptations. Rather, it appears that most incarnations of Christian content (whatever that may mean in each occasion) negotiate the cultures of the biblical texts (and not just the gospel!), the cultures of the missionaries, and the cultures of the resident communities, creating a complex set of polydoxies that go beyond

---

[5] James Prosek, "Maori Eels: New Zealand's Maori Defend an Extraordinary Creature—and Themselves," *Orion*, July/August 2010, www.orionmagazine.org/index.php/articles/article/5610/.

just belief systems but involve economic political and social organization. The results are often puzzling, if not vexing, and highly complex to negotiate.

The Maori are often believed to have made the canoe journey to the two South Sea islands they settled around thirteenth century AD.[6] They came traveling across oceans, mapping that terrain well, and then reattached and mapped their understanding of their lifeworld onto a new terrain, its elements, flora and fauna, displaying significant creativity and adaptability. The same adaptive skill can be found in inculturated forms of Maori Christianity, and the prophetic movements beyond the purview of colonial churches. CMS missionaries brought a British-inflected Christianity with Calvinist, evangelical elements, and a particular sense of material and social culture. Maori adopted some of it, adapted other things, and mixed and blended in elements of their own culture, using forms of logic that aimed to make sense of the changes occurring in place and time. That is, adaptation happens, and it continues to generate hybrid forms of cultural negotiation of both indigenous and colonial heritage. Whiti Ihimaera's *The Whale Rider*,[7] in striking difference from the popular movie, features two parallel storylines. One speaks about the fate of whales below the seas, while the other concerns itself with a Maori community on the eastern coast of the North Island of Aotearoa/New Zealand. This narrative is only semi-fictional. There is a historic ancestor, Paikea, on the east coast, who is thought to have come to these shores on the back of a whale. This story of entanglement suggests that the destinies of whales and humans are related, at least since the time they shared fellow migratory travel to those shores. What is more, whales "became known as the helpers of men lost at sea. Whenever asked, the whale would attend the call, as long as the mariner possessed the necessary authority and knew the way of talking to whales."[8] Ihimaera suggests that each group has suffered incursions in their territory, has been hunted down, experienced a decrease in population and lifeforce, and is now struggling to find the internal coherence, vision, and force to survive the destruction of their lifeways.

The ancient whale [. . .] had noticed more cracks in the ocean floor, hairline fractures indicating serious damage below the crust of the earth. Now, some weeks later, the leader was still unsure about the radiation level in the

---

[6] Michael King, *The Penguin History of New Zealand* (Auckland: Penguin, 2003), 48.

[7] The Maori name for the Northern Island is *Te Ika a Maui*, the fishhook of Maui, the trickster god who has pulled up the island from the bottom of the sea, using his grandmother's jaw. Ihimaera has a publicity shot of himself as Maui, who pulls up worlds from the sea, perhaps pointing to his literary work as it participates in recreating what it means to be Maori in a blended cultural environment with new possibilities and new challenges. Timotheos Roussos, "A Man's 'True Face': Concealing/Revealing Masculinities in Novels by Alan Duff and Witi Ihimaera," *Philament* Vol. 5 www.arts.usyd.edu.au/publications/philament/issue5_Critique_Roussos.htm

[8] Witi Ihimaera, *The Whale Rider* (Auckland: Reed, 1987), 43.

sea trench. He was fearful of the contamination seeping from Moruroa. He was afraid of the genetic effects of the undersea radiation on the remaining herd and calves in this place, which had once, ironically, been the womb of the world.[9]

The beached, endangered whale functions as a symbol of the Maori beached on the sands of an unlivable environment, often showing seemingly little or no impulse to retreat into the sea, the only place where survival can be found. The mystery of why whales beach themselves, in what seems a self-destructive suicidal move, is paralleled by the scenario of a Maori community that has lost its center of identity, and its will to get back into its elements for survival and flourishing beyond the confinements of colonialism and its own stifling patterns of patriarchy.

Herman Melville's 1851 *Moby Dick* tells the story of another community's relationship to whales, a radically different one. The book can be read as an economic and spiritual parable that exposes the complexity of exchanges that blur the boundaries between colonizer and colonized, gift economy and consumer capitalism, the quest and pursuit of wealth and power. The initial purpose of the whaler *Pequod*'s trip is to provide a rare and much-demanded source of energy for the U.S. economy, sperm whale oil, which in Melville's time was still a major source of fuel for lamps and candles.[10] Roaming the seas of the world for this precious substance, the cosmopolitan carrier converts the whale and everything on the ship into its monetary value back in port: "Don't ye love sperm? There goes three thousand dollars, men!—a bank! a whole bank! The bank of England."[11] The whale's wondrous body converted into monetary currency dwarfs the worth of a human being, especially that of a slave. Thus, when the black crew member Pip falls overboard and the crew has to let a whale get away in order to pull him back in, overseer Stubb retorts: "We can't afford to lose whales by the likes of you; a whale would sell for thirty times what you would, Pip, in Alabama."[12] Colonizer and colonized are uncomfortably united in situations where race and class dynamics constantly destabilize the common quest for fuel, adventure, and riches. Human solidarity is put in question by such calculations.

There are three colonized subjects among the harpooners of the *Pequod*, representing three areas of the globe colonized by Britain. In this racially and economically tiered ship's economy, these harpooners perform the most physically enormous, most important, and most dangerous job on the whaler. Melville bluntly writes of a Protestant work ethic outsourced: "be it said, that

[9]　Ibid., 59.
[10]　Herman Melville, *Moby Dick* (New York: Signet, 1955), 340.
[11]　Ibid., 340.
[12]　Ibid., 395.

at the present day not one in two of the many thousand men before the mast employed" are born American, but rather that the "American liberally provides the brains, the rest of the world is generously supplying the muscle."[13] The harpooners are Tashtego, a Native American from Martha's Vineyard, Daggoo, from Africa, and Queequeg from "Kokovoko, an island far away to the West and South." Melville further comments: "It is not down in any map; true places never are."[14] And yet, there are clues that might help us find it on a map:

> Having come themselves from a highly maritime culture, even though they had long since ceased to make ocean voyages by canoe, Maori turned out to be excellent crew members on European ships. They began to join ships' companies in the 1790s. [. . .]. By the first decade of the nineteenth century Maori were visiting Sydney regularly, and from the following decade travelling on vessels around the Pacific—Herman Melville's tattooed harpooner Queequeg in *Moby Dick* was in all probability based on a Maori crew member whom the author had met on the whaling ship *Lucy Ann*—and on to North America and England.[15]

In his reading of *Moby Dick*, Graham Ward comments that "Queequeg only has a voice so far as the narrator (and the author) gives it to him."[16] However, in Queequeg's actions, even as seen through Ishmael's eyes, we can glean facets of a complex character pointing beyond the limits of the page. I cannot, nor do I want to try to give voice to Queequeg, beyond attempting a small midrash, but there are a few things that might suggest Queequeg was more than a device used by Melville. We learn from Queequeg's own narrative that he was on board by his own will, stealing on board at night. Having descended from ancestors who were formidable sailors, Queequeg participates in this voyage of discovery and exploitation and participates in the merciless hunt after the white whale. His spear skills translate nicely into harpooning skills, making him thus one of the most important men

---

[13] Ibid., 127. This may indicate a self-consciousness of Americans as inheritors of the British Empire.

[14] Ibid., 70.

[15] King, *History of New Zealand*, 128–9. Many young Maori men were recruited for the whaling fleets, so much so that missionary Johann Wohlers believed that "far too many young Maori men were lost at sea through their passion for boating and whaling." Some Maori were as much exploited in this venture as their European and Euro-American shipmates, while others were able to make a successful career of it. They also brought back knowledge about the Northern societies, and adopted technologies into their own daily lives. Some Maori women participated fully in these exchanges. See Tānia Ka'ai, John C. Moorfield, Michael P. J. Reilly, and Sharon Mosley, *Ki Te Whaiao: An Introduction to Maori Culture and Society* (Auckland: Pearson Education, 2004), 144–5.

[16] Graham Ward, *True Religion* (Malden, MA: Blackwell, 2003), 107.

on board, but also one of the most dangerously employed.[17] His presence on the ship causes deep reactions in Ishmael. His initial fear and repulsion and his ensuing intimate physical and emotional connection to Queequeg profoundly change and challenge Ishmael culturally, erotically, religiously, and economically. For Ishmael it may be what he sees as Queequeg's exotic beingness and masculinity that "allows" the eroticism of the shared cabin's "marriage bed" of the two men to unfurl. Although it is Ishmael who admits that he was "bent upon narrowly observing so curious a creature," though "he treated me with so much civility and consideration, while I was guilty of great rudeness; staring at him from the bed, and watching all his toilette motions," we wonder whose subtly Orientalist reading of the Other fuels this homoerotic encounter.[18]

Despite the power differential of Ishmael's voyeuristic gaze, and the implied ambivalences of noble savagehood, consider the hybridic transformations these visual encounters occasion. Who might be transforming whom, who is "colonizing" whom? The equivocal nature of the gift also can be seen in the "gifts" captain James Cook brought to the Maori of Aotearoa/New Zealand. Cook and his fellow travelers tried to induce Maori interest in the tools and goods they had with them, partly to divert them from possible hostile actions, but partly also, surely, to civilize them by trade. The "civilization" thus acquired, brought with it an ideological opposition between capitalism and communism. Later, the Native Land Act aimed to give settlers easier access to Maori land that was communally owned in order to "break down the beastly communism of the tribe."[19] The forcible transition from communal guardianship and usage rights of *whenua* (land) to capitalist ownership of real estate in Aotearoa/New Zealand was brought about by a particular version of commerce by deception, or what Maori have called land "taken by sale." Thus, one of the main misunderstandings and conflicts between Maori and Pakeha has been that of the nature of the *rangatiratanga*/sovereignty ceded to Queen Victoria with the Treaty of Waitangi. Many Maori voices understand sovereignty as having the "meaning of chieftainship rather than anything to do with the rights of ownership of land. *Rangatiratanga* here, according to one Maori Anglican voice, means "oversight or headship," so there is no contradiction in that "the Maori chiefs ceded sovereignty of their lands to the Queen, and the Maori understanding of *rangatiratanga* as oversight—which had nothing to do with the ownership of land."[20] For many Maori the treaty had legal and spiritual connotations, in

[17] Anne Salmond, *Between Worlds: Early Exchanges Between Maori and Europeans 1773–1815* (Honolulu: University of Hawaii Press, 1997), 320.

[18] Ibid., 45.

[19] M. P. K. Sorrenson, "How To Civilize Savages: Some 'Answers' from Nineteenth-Century New Zealand," *The New Zealand Journal of History* Vol. 9, No. 2 (October 1975): Sorrenson, "How To Civilize Savages," 107.

[20] Te Ahukaramū Charles Royal, ed., *The Woven Universe: Selected Writings of Rev. Māori Marsden* (Masterson, NZ: The Estate of Maori Marsden, 2003), 129.

part because that is the kind of language some Anglican missionaries used to explain the terms and significance of the treaty:

> The role of the English missionary in determining Maori understanding, therefore, was crucial through the way explanations were given. It determined that Ngapuhi, in particular, would understand the treaty as a special kind of covenant with the Queen, a bond with all the spiritual connotations of the biblical covenants; there would be many tribes, including the British, but all would be equal under God.[21]

It can be argued that, "for the majority of chiefs present, the Gospel represented ethical, moral and spiritual wellbeing," which the missionaries verbally associated with the treaty, and the chiefs "understood at that moment in time, first and foremost, the Gospel as a way for a life and a future for their iwi."[22] Today, this means that "the hope of the Anglican Church is for the complete restoration of the Treaty's covenantal value. The Anglican Church in Aotearoa has its history of resistance by Maori who have struggled for justice."[23]

Polydoxy and the Ambivalence of the Gift

The gift can appear as a *pharmakon*, both "the remedy and the poison"[24] for a disease. The gift can enrich and impoverish, poison and heal, the communities it moves between.[25] While "traditional gift exchange is an agent of social cohesion," there are gifts that challenge the "demands of the collective" in such a way that roles become shifted, technologies are introduced, and silences become articulated, while exclusions are challenged.[26] Thus, in many cultures, the gift, like the trickster, can have the function of prodding a society or culture to come to terms with new circumstances. It often introduces technologies and cultural innovations crucial for survival, but with a dangerous side. Gift and *pharmakon* "can never be simply beneficial."

---

[21] Claudia Orange, *The Treaty of Waitangi* (Sydney/London: Allen & Unwin, 1987), 57.

[22] *Iwi* describes a larger tribal group. Moeawa Callaghan, "Look to the Past to See the Future," *First Peoples Theology Journal* Vol. 4, No.1 (June 2006): 106.

[23] Callaghan, "Look to the Past to See the Future," 107.

[24] Note that the German word *Gift* is rendered as poison in English. Jacques Derrida, *Dissemination*, trans. Barbara Johnson (Chicago, IL: University of Chicago Press, 1981), 94. Hence one could say in Germlish *Das Gift vergiftet* (The gift poisons). See John D. Caputo, *The Prayers and Tears of Jacques Derrida: Religion Without Religion* (Bloomington and Indianapolis: Indiana University Press, 1997), 166.

[25] For an exploration of the various ways in which gifts can function, see Derrida's discussion of "Plato's Pharmacy" and especially some of the sections on the *pharmakon* in Derrida, *Dissemination*, 95–155.

[26] Lewis Hyde, *Trickster Makes This World: Mischief, Myth, and Art* (New York: Farrar, Straus and Giroux, 1998), 133.

Certainly this is the case for gift exchanges in encounters occurring within the reach of the British Empire.[27]

The status and economies of the gift in a colonial context are a complicated, nuanced, and notoriously messy affair. However, as the French sociologist and anthropologist Marcel Mauss stressed in his classic 1925 study *The Gift*, Romantic notions of "native" gift economies reflect more the cultural context of the researcher than that of the people observed. He suggested that the European search for a pristine gift economy revealed that "there has never existed, either in the past or in modern primitive societies, anything like a 'natural' economy."[28] The form of Romantic Orientalism critiqued by Mauss mirrors a matching Occidentalism, as James Carrier has observed: the Occidentalism of ascribing "impersonal commodity relations" as essential to the West "makes sense only when it is juxtaposed with its matching orientalism, the society of the gift. Compared to such societies, the West *is* the society of the commodity—these two essentializations defining and justifying each other dialectically."[29] As European ethnographers like Marcel Mauss considered Pacific regions to investigate the gift among indigenous peoples such as Melanesians, Polynesians, and Native Americans of the Pacific Northwest, the economies of both colonized and colonizer were beginning to be profoundly changed by those and other encounters—by beginning to trade with European cultures.[30] Accounting for postmodern as well as postcolonial exchanges must then occur in the context of those trading exchanges, economic, theological, and always inspirited and embodied. As we have seen, in the process of colonization, boundaries were crossed and relationships formed, while economies of goods, faith, and land changed hands. This suggests that essentializing distinctions are representative of only a small amount of the realities. James G. Carrier hence argues that there was and is more variety in both European and indigenous societies, but that few anthropologists had studied the gift in the modern West and others are ignoring "commodity relationships in village societies."[31]

---

[27] Derrida, *Dissemination*, 99.

[28] However, Mauss's own fictions include that he was able to describe "the gift" in a way that has tended to universalize that notion across differences and hence potentially propagate "orthodox" notions about "the gift." Thus, his account has at least two effects: A reality check for Western notions of a "pure gift" and a tendency to claim a total description. Marcel Mauss, *The Gift: Forms and Functions of Exchange in Archaic Societies* (New York/London: W. W. Norton & Company, 1967), 3.

[29] James G. Carrier, "Maussian Occidentalism: Gift and Commodity Systems," in *Occidentalism: Images of the West*, ed. James G. Carrier (Oxford: Clarendon Press, 1995), 94.

[30] Cf. Derrida's *Given Time* and his account of the presence of Tobacco in the European Salon. On the effects of other colonial cargo such as sugar, coffee, and tea for European masculinity, femininity, and respectaiblity cf. also Woodruff D. Smith, *Consumption and the Making of Respectability, 1600–1800* (London and New York: Routledge, 2002), pp. 161–9.

[31] Carrier, "Maussian Occidentalism," 95.

"We Must Give Ourselves to Voyaging:"
Theology, Exploration, and Missionary Travels

Postmodern philosophical and theological discussions of the gift often take place in an ideal theoretical location that urgently needs to be decolonized. Consider, for example, John Milbank's comment that "giving, therefore, is primarily a matter of shared expenditure and celebration. 'Primitive' societies know this, and group themselves around such ecstatic transition, not around accumulated illusions."[32] Milbank's comment on the gift in primitive societies assumes a static "native" whose relationship to the gift appears to be pristine and perpetuates the dualistic distinctions Mauss and Carrier aim to critique and unveil as ideologically convenient fiction. Nevertheless, Milbank proposes "the recovery of mutual giving"[33] through a more fully lived reciprocity among humans. But what would such reciprocity look like in an imperial context where one of the tasks at hand may be to rethink how power, empire, and theology intersect? The absence of an encounter that actually could be described as close to reciprocal (where both sides engage in dialogue and where some mutual recognition and exchange can take place) in Milbank's dismissals of liberation theologians' critiques of capitalism and empire does not seem to keep this promise.[34] Milbank's call to resistance against capitalism and globalization, beyond its caricature as being starkly distinct from "primitive gift" economies, his conflation of liberation thought with liberalism and capitalism, thus remains at odds with his continued investment in a hegemonic sense of "Western" orthodoxy.

By the same token, a call for the "abolition of capitalism and the production of a socialist market,"[35] even if it were a realistic goal, might not be the reciprocal action demanded by the present theological *kairos*. Rather, I suggest that a form of agency readily accessible to Christians who profess faith in a redemptive and liberative relationality between God and creation, in a divine economy that seeks to subvert the oppressive confines of a divinized hypercapitalism may best be found in a variety of subversive strategies, witnessing words and actions. Milbank assumes that ethical exchanges among

---

[32] Milbank, *Being Reconciled*, 181.

[33] Ibid., 155.

[34] My concern in this exploration of colonial give and take is not so much to establish who "really gave" and who "really took," but rather, to trace some of the instability of various degrees of exchange, reciprocal or not, and how they fluctuate across time and place. For Milbank's critique of liberation and political theology, focusing on the way in which these theologies have engaged enlightenment in a "mediating theology" that, so he claims, produces a "futile cycle," see John Milbank, *Theology and Social Theory: Beyond Secular Reason* (Oxford & Cambridge: Blackwell, 1990), 207, 233. Again, I do not so much disagree with some of his criticisms, but with his unhelpful dismissals and apparent inability to appreciate these theologians' contributions.

[35] As paraphrased by Stephen Long in D. Stephen Long, *Divine Economy: Theology and the Market* (New York: Routledge, 2000), 260.

human agents are reciprocal, in critical distance from an ethic of sacrifice that argues that a "true" gift must be without strings attached, and hence also from an im/possible Derridean absolute gift.[36] However, he reserves redemption and forgiveness as a divine "true gift." God remains only a giver and is never a recipient in a gift exchange. Thus, the God-given gift is a "transcendental category"[37] in a way that structures theological discourse about creation, grace, incarnation, atonement, the church, and spirit, all of which have been described as a "gift." This gifting, and the related *methexis* as a "sharing of being and knowledge in the Divine,"[38] appear to flow only in one direction: from God to humans, and from there to other humans, but never toward "him." The intention appears to be to preserve divine sovereignty and power, but from a theology that assumes greater divine permeability and relationality, such contentions continue to de-emphasize humanity's real responsibility and effects on God and the divine economy. The strict assumption of divine unilateral agency articulates a problematic distinction between the need to act reciprocally and responsibly towards other human agents, yet not in relationship with God. In Christian traditions, divine grace is often described as undeserved and unforceable. There are good reasons to assert this, as it counteracts certain problematic tendencies in human relationality to the divine, especially the tendency to bargain, compel, and attempts to force by various means divine support for one's own purposes. But does divine grace, the sense of creation community and the fragile, relational existence of our lives, not oblige responsible reciprocity in some sense? In a context of looming environmental destruction and likely unavoidable severe climate change, is it useful or tenable to promulgate that divine grace does not need a responsible human agent? Does a sense of creation as "gift" in this context not compel a rethinking of what responsible human relationships to the land might look like?

Gift, Land Use, and Sovereignty

The sovereign lack of the need for reciprocity is echoed in representations of British colonial sovereignty.

One of the most famous portraits of Queen Elizabeth I, the Ditchley portrait by Marcus Gheeraerts the Younger, shows her standing astride the globe. Written in Latin on the picture are three fragmentary statements describing

---

[36] This move is critical toward notions of the absolute gift in Jacques Derrida and Jean-Luc Marion. These discussions generally refer to Marcel Mauss's influential study *The Gift*. Marcel Mauss, *The Gift: Forms and Functions of Exchange in Archaic Societies* (New York/London: W.W. Norton & Company, 1967).

[37] Milbank, *Being Reconciled*, ix.

[38] Ibid., ix.

Elizabeth, which stress a particular sort of power. They have been reconstructed and translated as "She gives and does not expect. She can, but does not take revenge. In giving back she increases." Also on the portrait are the remains of a sonnet on the sun, reflecting an established rhetorical tradition of comparison of the monarch's power with that of the sun, as the inexhaustible source of all that is good.[39]

There are certain obvious echoes between theological and imperial language: the image of sun, who gives light but does not receive anything back, God, the ungiven giver, and the sovereign who "gives and does not expect." These echoes resound troubling resonances in how such discourse represents and reflects the sovereign divine/imperial power's relations (the rare woman at the helm of a growing empire) projecting stereotypically princely male power over "Woman, Native, Other."[40]

This theological image of grace as a gift all too closely parallels imperial propaganda. The God image reiterated by Milbank builds upon a long, but increasingly problematic tradition of casting God as a propertied male owner and humanity as an impoverished, lacking, feminized recipient. We are in our nothingness before "him,"[41] and yet the metaphor is unstable, and nothingness is gendered, a kind of "feminine lack" in giving.[42] Milbank reiterates classic tropes of divine economy such as the commerce of the *conubium*, whereby a "genuinely erotic body" is "restored" to humanity "in Christ, who offers it to his bride, the Church." This image of redemption perpetuates a problematic gendering of the human-divine relationship where a masculinized, propertied divine bridegroom seeks to marry a feminized, unworthy whore-bride, giving "her" a new body.[43] God occupies here the position of the traditional husband, king (and in more contemporary terms), CEO in a structure that equates God with the Good, Abundance, Wealth, and juxtaposes it with Evil, Lack, and Poverty.[44] This mode of power does not request permission, cannot

---

[39] Murray, *Indian Giving*, 55.

[40] Trinh Minh-Ha, *Woman, Native, Other* (Bloomington: Indiana University Press, 1989).

[41] Note Milbank's insistent use of the male pronoun for God. Milbank, *Being Reconciled*, 46 et passim.

[42] I have explored the feminization of giving in strands of traditional interpretations of women in the gospels and their excessive giving (which has also been read as foreshadowing Jesus' abundant giving of his life) in more detail in Grau, *Of Divine Economy*, 99–107.

[43] John Milbank, "The Midwinter Sacrifice," *The Blackwell Companion to Postmodern Theology*, Graham Ward, ed. (Oxford: Blackwell, 2001), 128.

[44] This gendered economy appears to be of one piece with Milbank's affirmation of the unilateral gifting of a *creatio ex nihilo*. See Milbank, *Being Reconciled*, 2, 4. For a critical investigation in the power and theodynamics of the *creatio ex nihilo* see Catherine Keller, *Face of the Deep: A Theology of Becoming* (New York: Routledge, 2003). I am not here claiming that poverty is not often a form of evil and degradation; however, it therefore seems even more important to question the elevation of riches to the level of the divine and the problematic identification of the human condition as poverty.

be responded to, and is seemingly irresponsible to the masses of feudal serfs, peasants, and workers.

To retain this colonial image of God in a time when the promotion of irresponsible agency in politics, law, and finance continues to be iterated in seemingly ever greater fashion and with increasingly disastrous results appears unhelpful, if not complicit. While Milbank might argue that positioning God as "ungiven giver" guarantees "his" sovereignty, might the image not flip and to drain the divine giver, emptying out the generosity? And what if God's grace is emptied out without reciprocity, invoking the stereotype of the self-emptying and ever-giving woman? Can such talk of abundance without responsibility to the giver in fact serve to surbordinate the exploitation of God as well as the indigenous inhabitants of lands colonized, who are put in the role of abundant givers, needing no response to their "gift," of hospitality, of land? Is there a possibility that, not unlike the colonial dynamic of extracting more gifts from colonial cultures than are willingly given, and refusing to reciprocate gifts, God's unilateral "givingness" is assumed, while abused by the human assumption (and, in the case of prosperity theologies, the insistence) that the purpose of God's giving and promise is to fulfill human needs and desires, or the colonizer's desires? Similarly, the "native" in colonial discourse is often imagined as passive recipient of colonial culture and religion, while many indigenous peoples who can carry in their traditions strong positive values associated with giving, are asked to keep on giving land, resources, and culture. Their often Romanticized generosity continues to be abused in the process of colonization. Hence, as we have seen in the actual ambivalences of the gift, the giver is not (always) the only person with power in a relationship. Might God's generosity, as imagined by much of Christian theology, be as problematic as the colonial view of the "Woman, Native, Other," either as idealized giver or as passive recipient of civilization and religion? Woman, native, other (according to Barth, God is "the wholly Other") alike would thus be open to exploitation in colonial theological accounts. The complex situations we find ourselves in, where certain forms of technologically enhanced human agency have radical consequences for life on the planet, need a more complex account, and finegrained analysis of the reciprocal relations between God and humanity, between colonizer and colonized, one that does not serve to reinforce a dynamics of exploitation. Giving and taking in colonial relations are indeed full of ambivalence:

> The instability of colonial give and take is exemplified in accounts of "Indian giving" as leaving the status of the colonists undecided as taker, traders, or thieves, as a counterpoint to Europeans' long-standing presentation of themselves as bringers of gifts, specifically, the gifts of civilization and Christianity. [. . .] These were gifts so huge that they dwarfed any negative aspects that might come along with them and justified taking the bounty

of the New World. So powerful and persistent has been the idea of Western civilization as the source of all that is important and valuable that recent emphasis on what "we" owe to Indians culturally as well as materially is felt to be claiming something new and controversial.[45]

Stephen Greenblatt's lucid investigation of the theological underpinnings of such gift rhetoric suggests that giving and taking can be mobilized in multiple ways, and by different actors.

Under these ambivalent conditions, colonial encounters have caused culture clashes that find indigenous peoples struggling to find constructive ways to survive and thrive under colonial hegemony. Colonial encounters confronted the people of the land with severe challenges to their values, economies, and way of life before the term "postmodern" ever crossed the North Atlantic. Hence, according to Michel-Rolph Trouillot,

> if the collapse of metanarratives alone characterized the postmodern condi-
> tion, then some of those populations outside of the North Atlantic that have
> been busily deconstructing theirs for centuries, or that have gone through
> mega-collapses of their own, have long been "postmodern," and there is
> nothing new under the sun. [. . . But] even if we concede, for the sake
> of argument, that metanarratives once were a prerequisite of humankind
> and are now collapsing everywhere at equal rates (two major assumptions
> indeed), we cannot infer identical reactive strategies to this collapse.[46]

While most elite Maori were still in charge of resources and offered needed protection to traders and whalers, they also had some control over trades and exchanges. Note that Queequeg, for example, engages in his own informal economy. He is trying to find buyers for his *moko mai*, his preserved head, but, as the landlord in Ishmael's Nantucket inn notes, the market is saturated: "I told him he couldn't sell it here, the market's overstocked."[47] Melville's Queequeg understands monetary exchange well enough, and knows how to profit from it. Melville's "noble savage" does not match Romantic projections of pure indigenous identity or innocence. Rather, exchange goes both ways,

---

[45] David Murray, *Indian Giving: Economies of Power in Indian-White Exchanges* (Amherst: University of Massachusetts Press, 2000), 18.

[46] Trouillot, *Global Transformations*, 11. Trouillot's phrasing about a "collapse" of metanarratives may be so strong as to seem untenable. The questioning of metanarratives seems a more appropriate term, given that the discourse and practices of empire and capitalism are alive and well in the world today.

[47] Melville, *Moby Dick*, 36. Many items were traded between the residents of Aotearoa and European and American visitors and traders, too many to lay out in detail here. Some of them were: flax, muskets, heads, agriculture, livestock, sexual partners, language, writing, spiritual knowledge, the gospel, marine skills (harpooning), tattoos, and various other items of "curiosity."

people trade with each other, certainly in often unequal ways, but each side has its own interests and desires of what it wants out of the exchange.

Misfits in Mission: Missionaries, Converts, Prophets

In encounters in mission, power flows in multiple directions, depending on place and time, and often involves greater complexity than missionaries and anthropologists may consider. Concerning missionary encounters in Aotearoa/ New Zealand, historians have proposed multiple scenarios. Harrison Wright proposed a three-tiered structure with stages of initial shock, cultural assertion, followed by increased confusion and cultural breakdown.[48] One of Wright's main claims is that in a pre-colonial missionary setting, where the indigenous framework was strong and coherent, things and events occurred that the indigenous culture's own terms could neither explain or control. That is, the turning point in mission is not the strength of the Christian framework, but the loss of the integrity of the Maori framework. Thus, it is the encounter with new technologies, diseases, and social forces upsetting socioreligious explanatory systems that precedes, and leads to, religious diffusion, and under certain circumstances to what the various missionary communities frame as, each in their own terms, conversions.[49] Different criteria are being used to assess practices of conversion: baptism, church attendance, cultural association, consent to doctrinal orthodoxy, adoption of dress, demeanor, economic agency, technology, literacy, and so forth.[50] Some Christian communities, for a variety of reasons including both theological preference and clerical availability, have taken different approaches to who is baptized, catechized, and so forth.

Owens emphasizes the resilience, diversity, and agency of Maori responses to Christianity.[51] Judith Binney postulates a similar succession of phases in the history of early missions in Aotearoa/New Zealand, where an initial phase of little to no impact was followed by a somewhat "sudden breakthrough" at which time both conversions to "orthodox" Christianity occur and rival alternative movements form that merge Christian models and previously existing Maori frameworks. This period was followed by a phase during which the power of the Christian God was widely considered to be significant in comparison with

[48] J. M. R. Owens, "Christianity and the Maoris to 1840," *The New Zealand Journal of History* Vol.2, No. 1 (April 1968): 19.

[49] Ibid., 21.

[50] Conversion harbors its own ambivalence hovering somewhere between "superficial conformity" and an, often problematic and ill-defined, ideal of "complete transformation" that may include some forms of social transformation, though the definition of what constitutes an appropriate transformation and who defines it will remain elusive. Owens, "Christianity and the Maoris to 1840," 23.

[51] Ibid., 39–40.

traditional notions of the divine.[52] In the North Island setting, the missions had a rough start in large part because missionaries were entirely dependent on tribal patrons for food, protection, and space for agency. For a chief, a missionary meant access to the trade goods that would be coming in and through such a person.[53] In this pre-settler context, missionaries did not have much independence, and hence little effect, but once they "showed [economic] independence their words began to take effect." Perhaps this ought to be understood as the equivalent of these missionaries acquiring a sense of *mana* of power and charisma in Maori terms. In many other ways, Binney argues, missionaries were able to gain entrance for their ideas through folding it in with skills or items more desirable to Maori. Hence, there was mutual angling for one's own objectives on both sides obtained, thereby creating a strange kind of reciprocity, arguably, at this point, to some degree "mutually beneficial". Maori received access to goods and technologies, the missionaries made inroads both in "civilizing" and in spreading various forms of the gospel.[54]

How could or should the manifold interpretation and expression not only of the New Testament but also the adoption and elaboration of Old Testament cultures, social, and religiously expressive patterns be monitored and engaged in? Protestant missionaries' reference to the "book" meant that "Maori Christians also soon learned that an appeal to 'The Book'" in the context of interpretations and arguments was a crucial location of power.[55] Hence, a missionary wife recalled a Maori preacher challenging the local elders about divine creative power: "You tell us Mawi [i.e. Maui] made the world, but where is your proof? Where is Mawi's sacred book?"[56] The adoption of the discourse of "proof," referring to the superiority of printed writing as "literally" true, over orally passed on myth and the kind of truth it may speak, is striking. The mode of transmission, its seeming tangibility, appears at least here to override the solidity of the oral tradition. Allan Davidson summarizes the controversy about why Christianity began to take hold among Maori, saying that "what is clear is that Maori during the 1830s were attracted by both the medium and the message. The medium of literacy had a powerful force throughout primal societies, notably in Polynesia."[57]

Meanwhile, the class relations the Europeans knew at home were rebuilt into hierarchical race relations in numerous missionary contexts. Missionaries often created households separate and boundaried from indigenous peoples,

---

[52] Judith Binney, "Christianity and the Maoris to 1840: A Comment," *The New Zealand Journal of History* Vol.3, No. 1 (April 1969): 144.

[53] Ibid., 144–6.

[54] Ibid., 152.

[55] Owens, "Christianity and the Maoris to 1840," 37.

[56] Ibid., 37.

[57] Allan Davidson, "The Interaction of Missionary and Colonial Society in Nineteenth-Century New Zealand," *Studies in World Christianity* Vol. 2, No. 2 (1996): 148.

thereby replicating and foreshadowing future colonial racial relations and discrimination.[58] The rhetoric they employed with regard to Maori replicates middle class ressentiments towards the "undeserving poor in England, resisting the sermons that would transform them into godly mechanics."[59] Indeed, the first emissaries of the CMS were artisan missionaries, showing the civilizing priorities of this particular phase and practice of mission.[60] But these boundaries were often fragile, and some crossed them. Both societies were highly stratified. Social mobility was accessible in different ways, and at times negotiated between systems.

As the influence of colonial and settler cultures increased, resistance to Christian worship waned, for a variety of reasons. While initially seeking patronage from Maori tribal elites, in this phase, preaching to slaves and the sick became a priority for some missionaries. Their words fell on presumably more fertile soil with those isolated and in socially lower position, while providing a link to other tribal communities, as slaves were generally composed of members of other tribes.[61] Over time, missionaries noted that the rapid conversion of southern Maori was due to the presence of Maori preachers, resulting in the conversion of people "who never saw a European."[62] The same pattern can be seen in other contexts.

Due to the prevalent Calvinist inflection in the theology of the often deeply conservative evangelical CMS missionaries of the time, strongly Calvinist elements were seeded into the emerging Maori Christianity,[63] which then developed in different ways than some of the European churches' theologies, some of which, over time, moved away from more Calvinist emphases toward more Wesleyan, Roman, or Arminian inflections. Some missionary theological tropes focused on biblical and figural elements thought to be of particular attraction to these communities. Thus, they juxtaposed the tribal narratives of the Hebrew scriptures with the figure of the Prince of Peace—a common supersessionist logic that here is employed in a culture war as some British colonial presences were interested in pacifying Maori—contrasting christologies of Christ the peacemaker with images "Jehovah, the God of Vengeance."[64]

---

[58] Examples from a variety of contexts abound. Owens, "Christianity and the Maoris to 1840," 36.

[59] Ibid., 37–8.

[60] Davidson, "Interaction," 147.

[61] Binney, "Christianity and the Maoris to 1840: A Comment," 156.

[62] Ibid., 163.

[63] Ibid., 164.

[64] Binney does not mention the supersessionist framework of the missionary message of the Prince of Peace, though it is hardly a stretch considering the habitual supersessionism of Christian theologies. Binney, "Christianity and the Maoris to 1840: A Comment," 164. Perhaps the questions of the "Maori Jews" also have to do with a rejection of the Prince of Peace and the retention of *utu* warfare? See Huie-Jolly Mary, "Maori 'Jews' and a Resistant Reading of John 5.10–47," in *Postcolonial Biblical Reader* (Oxford: Blackwell, 2006), 224–37.

Here, as elsewhere, theological prejudices, conventions, and stereotypes mix in ways that preserve problematic interpretive structures and make them newly fertile for a different social context, in which their potential was, at least potentially, liberative.

> The Bible had a profound effect on Maori. They learnt the Bible off by heart, they wove its message into their own beliefs in ways that did not always easily cohere with the missionaries' teaching. Maori were not passive recipients of the missionaries' message.[65]

Thus, the acceptance, response to, and adaptation of Christian ideas and cultural practices occur, as ever, in a densely complex context that cannot be grasped by looking at theology, economy, sociology, or anthropology, or indigenous, biblical and colonial narrativity separately. An interdisciplinary approach promises to be more realistic. Indigenous evangelists, often without the knowledge of the missionaries, went ahead and passed on pieces of Christian practice, ritual, and narrative. Thus, Henry Williams, as a first European entering a certain village found himself surprised by the fact that the entire village knew to sing and speak the correct reponses for the evening prayer he recited. Hence, a Maori-inflected Christianity began to emerge by 1840.[66]

But for some Maori the powerful new narratives found in this book were not assimilable without certain adjustments that were often communally specific. Missionary presence, especially when deeply suspicious of Maori religioculture, did not necessarily offer enough bridges of meaning-making. In an explosion of creative adaptation, Maori made powerful connections between ancestral and biblical traditions, religion and politics, protest and accommodation.[67] Bronwyn Elsmore has mapped some of the varieties in which Maori adapted and blended biblical and Maori narrativity until it addressed the concerns of their own communities. One of the main hermeneutical effects of missionary presence was the opening up of different social and self-fashioning options along with multiple theological-political narratives.[68] This had, as does all cultural adaptation, predictably, mixed results, both then and now, no matter which criteria one applies.

Another classic missionary pattern repeats Daniel of Winchester's interpretive historiographic move articulated in a letter to Boniface, encouraging the comparison of previous states of people according to the pattern "your present is our past, and our present is your future," while highlighting the welfare that could be obtained by conversion to Christianity. In a variation on the theme,

---

[65] Davidson, "Interaction," 148.
[66] Ibid., 149.
[67] Ka'ai, Moorfield, Reilly, and Mosley, *Ki Te Whaiao*, 171.
[68] Binney, "Christianity and the Maoris to 1840: A Comment," 157.

CMS missionary Henry Williams opines that "once we were as you are, clad as you are, living in houses similar to yours, but you see now we possess all things."[69] Likewise, Samuel Marsden preached

> God's omnipotence by stressing his practical powers, for God, he said, unlike the tapu system, *could* heal wounds, restore health, and prevent death. The teachings of the missionaries were based on a fundamental error: the confusion of technological superiority with moral superiority.[70]

Seen from another angle, the seemingly bridgeable difference is still quite problematic. In the oral tradition of the Maori Anglican priest Maori Marsden, Henry Williams is reported to have rejected a fighting chief and *tohunga* (expert practitioner, priest, healer) of Nga Puhi, Hone Ngapua's offer to enter the "Mihinare Priesthood" (the Anglican CMS-mediated priesthood), as a man "whose hands were polluted with the blood of his fellowmen and his teeth polluted with human flesh." Hone Ngapuha is said to have replied that "if your God won't have me, then I'll return to my own."[71] Conflicting notions of *tapu*, sacred, pollution, and purity collide here, as Williams rejects the legacy of cannibalism among warring Maori tribes as potentially irredeemable. The economies of *tapu* and *noa* (that which is filled with sacred energy, and that which has been rendered neutral or safe for life) structured Maori lives, but were often seen by missionaries such as Thomas Kendall as hindering the acceptance of a new form of religious economy.

> Tapu, the sustaining religious force which bound together the whole fabric of social organization, and which was most concerned with the natural resources needed by the society, the most highly valued cultural objects, and man himself, was directly challenged as the main obstacle to the civilization and improvement of the heathen.[72]

This often meant that one religious system was lifted above another by way of false parallels, and claiming sacred authority by denying previous sacred authority. Thus, for Marsden and Kendall, tragically, "the preaching of Christianity meant the preaching against tapu observances, mourning customs, and so on. Jehovah would not be 'angry' at transgressions against the Maori social system

---

[69] Ibid., 152.

[70] Judith Binney, *The Legacy of Guilt: A Life of Thomas Kendall* (Wellington: Bridget Williams Books, 1968), 84.

[71] Te Ahukaramū Charles Royal, "Editor's Introduction," in *The Woven Universe: Selected Writings of Rev. Māori Marsden*, Woven Universe (Masterson, NZ: The Estate of Maori Marsden, 2003), xxxi.

[72] Binney, *Legacy of Guilt*, 82.

but only at those against the European social absolutes."[73] The *moko,* a form of writing employing facial and corporeal tattoo, was replaced by literacy of the Bible. In the late nineteenth century, facial tattoos became a forbidden art and were strongly discouraged.[74] Some, but not all, missionaries agreed with this supersessionist rather than synthetic approach to mission.

Several of the Church Missionary Society (CMS) missionaries in Aotearoa possessed a "high view of revelation" which led to an emphasis on textual trans-lation, reproduction, and theological argumentation based on scripture and textuality.[75] Their understanding of sin was Augustinian and featured a well-developed sense of the tragic fallenness of humans. This was complemented by a sense of the cross as propitiation offered for human sins and by which humans became justified. Salvation was not earned by good deeds, but rather those deeds demonstrated the reality of faith. They read biblical texts primar-ily as guides to holy life, rather than historical and intellectual exegesis.[76]

CMS missioniaries were often working class and experienced resistance to their class as well as their "enthusiasm." The CMS was an evangelical mission-ary society that recruited from a particular segment of society both in Britain and abroad, influenced by Wesley's and Whitefield's revivals, filled with a sense of evangelical fervor and missionary impetus toward "non-English" souls.[77] Evangelical faith emphasized the heart, experience, and a seriousness of com-mitment that often, as in William Wilberforce's case, took public and political commitment to move the faithful person outside of the sphere of the home.[78]

Curiously, some of the first CMS missionaries were German, as English missionaries had been impossible to recruit and the society hired some "good German Lutherans in place of their more desirable English cousins."[79] Here national boundaries could be overridden in a pinch, whereas class bounda-ries proved less penetrable. Most missionaries came from lower middle classes, aiming to be upwardly mobile from their background as artisans, journeymen, and clerks.[80] A few single women, a group that made major contributions to "missionary advance" across the globe, also made it to New Zealand in the early years. They came, over time, to outnumber the men.[81] Yet, eventually, due to the dearth of qualified ordained clergy in the CMS, in part due to

---

[73] Ibid., 84.
[74] Terence Barrow, *An Illustrated Guide to Maori Art* (Auckland: Reed, 1984), 21.
[75] Robert Glen, "Those Odious Evangelicals: Origins and Background of the CMS Missionaries in New Zealand," in *Mission and Moko: Aspects of the Work of the Church Missionary Society in New Zealand, 1814–1882,* ed. Robert Glen (Christchurch: Latimer Fellowship of New Zealand, 1992), 19–20.
[76] Ibid., 20–1.
[77] Ibid., 14.
[78] Ibid., 17.
[79] Ibid., 28.
[80] Ibid., 33. Quoting Andrew Walls.
[81] Ibid., 35–6.

Bishop Selwyn's resistance to ordaining Maori clergy, Maori lay leaders kept missions going.[82] Many CMS missionaries went from being misfits at home to being "normalized" as representatives of their context of origin's religious landscape. This brought many problems with it. It meant that when some missionaries acted in less than honorable ways, the reputation of the entire group, and at times of the church, and Christianity at large, could be impacted. Many missionaries had mixed motives as they convinced Maori tribal leaders to sign a treaty ceding sovereignty to the Crown, while retaining an ambiguously defined sense of ownership and use rights.

> This highly political action by the Protestant missionaries was in response to what they perceived as the detrimental impact of European settlement in New Zealand and the arrival of the first group under William Wakefield's scheme of planned migration. The missionaries were wanting to defend their own interests and in benevolent and paternalistic ways try and protect Maori against the rough edges of a European invasion.[83]

The great respect Maori leaders had for the missionaries was all but lost when even the Queen's Governor accused missionary Henry Williams of unfairly acquiring large tribal lands, and he was dismissed. Other missionaries tried to stem the rampant and deceitful acquisition of land by an influx of settlers, but without success. The following wars were disastrous for the missionary churches, as missionaries were often trying to minister both to Maori and settlers at the same time, and often betrayed Maori.[84] The epitome of Maori rejection of missionary Christianity came with the killing of the German CMS missionary Carl Völkner, who appeared to some Maori to be a government informant, and was thus seen as disloyal to the Maori he was serving in Opotiki. In this situation of betrayal by missionaries, Maori devised new prophetic movements that featured narrative variations on biblical narratives that were sympathetic to Maori causes of independence.[85] The Parihaka movement used civil disobedience and passive resistance, while others were along a spectrum from militantly anti-settler to envisioning an eventual future of peaceful cohabitation. The theological adaptations often took the form of associating the missionaries with the New Testament and Christ, and the Maori with Jews, since Maori often turned to the Hebrew scriptures to find support. Thus, CMS missionary James Stark wrote insightfully:

> It is not to be wondered at, that when they broke away from their European guides and tried to conceive of God for themselves, that the result of their

---

[82] Ibid., 37.
[83] Davidson, "Interaction," 149.
[84] Ibid., 150.
[85] Ibid., 151.

independent study of Holy Writ was to convince them, that Jehovah was the God of the sons of Shem, the family to which they believed themselves to belong, and the Lord Jesus the God of the sons of Japhet, the family to which the English belong.[86]

Yet, Maori religious movements represent a rejection of the particularities of missionary Christianity, rather than Christianity. The failure to allow Maori into ordained church leadership increased the motivation for some Maori to create their own structures, theologies, and movements.[87] Elsewhere, one of the most memorable and oft referenced ways in which some missionaries could contribute services that worked well with pacifist readings of the Christian gospel is their work as peacemakers between the tribes,[88] an activity that was seen to echo the Sermon on the Mount's injunction, "blessed are the peacemakers."[89]

Most cross-cultural encounters occur between individuals who occupy rather atypical locations in either society, that is, those who are often not the most typical representatives of that context. This recognition adds to the insight that generalization from the location of certain particular encounters can dangerously normalize and reduce entire cultures, societies, and churches on either side to a caricature, giving only a shadow image of the diversity that exists in each society and each church.

What follows is a cursory account of an example of one such very particular encounter and theological adaptation. In contrast to the setting in Natal, there had not been a Shaka-like figure in Aotearoa/New Zealand that had first subjugated, and then subsumed and included, other tribal communities as Zulu, a colonially expanded identity to generate cohesion. Thus many different communities, in different forms of relationship with colonial forces, missionaries, and settlers, responded differently.

Te Whiti, a charismatic leader who founded the millennial Parihaka community, proclaimed himself as "Jehovah's mouthpiece" or "small Christ," and claimed powers over the ordering of the earth. Despite arrests, the leaders rebuilt the community with all the trappings of "Maori Christian modernity" as a center of peaceful resistance.[90] Many of these charismatic movements had to do with land issues, reclaiming ancestral land, healing diseases that became prevalent with the settlers, and providing a sense of constructive transition into a changing environment. Some responses involved military action against

---

[86] Ibid., 152, quoting James Stark.
[87] Ibid., 155.
[88] Owens, "Christianity and the Maoris to 1840," 20.
[89] Though Owens claims there is evidence the claim that weariness of warfare made some Maori tribes more susceptible to Christianity may be questionable. Owens, "Christianity and the Maoris to 1840," 29. See also Binney, "Christianity and the Maoris to 1840: A Comment," 148.
[90] Ka'ai, Moorfield, Reilly, and Mosley, *Ki Te Whaiao*, 175.

colonial forces, while other Maori interaction with the missionaries led them to reject killing, and to imagine a peaceful movement that would lead, with great ascetic sacrifices, to the yet unfinished construction of a new temple that would signify the future peaceful cohabitation of Maori and Pakeha in Aotearoa.

Many of these responses are particular to a community, as is Witi Ihimaera's story of *The Whale Rider*, which talks about a very particular historical ancestor and weaves a prophetic history around them, reconstructing a narrative of retraditioning, survival, and identity formation that blends cultural elements, theological concepts, and religious figures. As such, it is "a movement which has been set up by Maori people precisely for the purpose of making a foreign system acceptable."[91] As with many of such movements, our circumambulation meets the *unheimlich* territory of stumbling over randomly preserved fragments, as "the details of the doctrinal dimension of the Kohiti faith can no longer be fully recovered," while the author hopes that "enough has been pieced together" to give a good sense of this movement.[92]

The Te Kohititanga Marama response to the gospel is one of many prophetic movements that combined features of Maori on the east coast and CMS-mediated Christian religiocultural systems and attempted to bring them into some coherence for the community adjusting to the transformations. The Maori *atua*, the sense of life forces at work in the universe, the God of the Old Testament and the figure of Christ, Pentecost, and the Second Coming were reinterpreted. The movement Te Hahi o te Kohititanga Marama (The Church/Religion of the New Moon), developed in a particular region of the east coast of the North Island, in the region of Wairoa. Under the leadership of a local visionary Matenga Tamati, the movement envisioned a new lunar cycle as signifying a new world of changed relationships with divine and human forces.

The presence, first of whalers, and later of missionaries in the region of the Wairoa district, in Northern Hawke's Bay eventually led to the first instruction in the gospel by former captives of the Ngapuhi raiders who had been freed by the missionaries and taught the elements of Christian faith by them. Hence, the first gospel instruction in the region occurred through local teachers, rather than missionaries themselves.[93] This was not necessarily seen as an advantage by every chief, and so some of the missionaries, here James Hamlin, received complaints that the Maori teachers had "acted most inconsistently in their manner of addressing men of rank; which seemed to have prejudiced the minds of many not a little against the truth."[94]

---

[91] Peter Nabokov, *Where The Lighting Strikes: The Lives of American Indian Sacred Places* (New York: Penguin, 2006), 15.

[92] Bronwyn Elsmore, *Te Kohititanga Marama: New Moon, New World* (Auckland, NZL: Reed, 1998), 10.

[93] Ibid., 20.

[94] Ibid., 21, quoting James Hamlin.

Another relatively common reaction in the early missionary period consisted of groups who had given up or rejected Christian faith by professing
themselves as "Jews," which signifies an identification with how "the Jews" in
New Testament texts were portrayed, namely as skeptical of Jesus' teaching,
rather than a conversion to Judaism. Three specific reasons given for this particular rejection were the "lack of effectiveness of the new religion," not only
in terms of economic advantage but also in terms of what benefits the people,
the fact that Maori rather than being protected died from new, unknown diseases that perhaps the new deity smote them with, and that the mission was too
slow to provide a teacher.[95] The pockets of "Jews" also seem to have to do with
the bad example or behavior of Christian converts or other social problems
that Christians were seen to have introduced.[96] When a woman healer named
Tangaroa found a way to integrate the two systems, the missionary Hamlin
showed great antipathy and a refusal to even engage her, most likely out of a
great resistance to perceived "syncretism" and the fear of pollution. Yet, the
large following she attracted showed the "great need of the people for both
healing, and a system which bridged the great gap between the cultures of the
Maori and the Pakeha."[97]

The "truth" these groups were seeking did not fit easily into either one or
other culture's structures, rituals, and care of the soul. Rather, as so often,
"political trauma correlates with theological innovation"[98] and moves toward
an explanatory system that makes spiritual and historical sense of what is happening to the people. Once the Old Testament had been translated into Maori
and enough instruction in it had occurred, many Maori found a ready model
for their situation and many of the prophetic movements "displayed a strong
element of identification of the Maori with the Hebrews—both racially, as
some of the early missionaries believed and had told the people, and in their
situation."[99]

It is likely that Matenga Tamati co-signed the letter opposing the Maori
King movement, professing his loyalty to Queen Victoria.[100] He sensed that
he was called to fulfill the work begun by the prophet and leader Te Kooti,
and to build a temple for the Lord.[101] Missionary William Williams rejected
such movements and saw them in strong antithesis to his work. But a "growing
spiritual need" that remained unaddressed led the Maori to look for their own

[95] Ibid., 22. See also Huie-Jolly Mary, "Maori 'Jews' and a Resistant Reading of John 5.10–47."
[96] Ibid., 23.
[97] Ibid., 27.
[98] Laurel C. Schneider, *Beyond Monotheism: A Theology of Multiplicity* (London: Routledge, 2008), 40.
[99] Elsmore, *Kohititanga Marama*, 28 Again, we see evidence of the missionary belief that Maori represented the lost tribes of the people of ancient Israel.
[100] Ibid., 36.
[101] Ibid., 37.

religious narratives. Matenga saw the details for the construction of the temple revealed in a manner that reminds of the manner in which the God of the
Hebrew scriptures mediated instructions for tabernacle or tent of meeting in
the wilderness. The temple was to be built of 12 logs or pillars for the 12 tribes
of Israel, but without walls or roof; they were to function simply as a marker of
sacred space, inside which an Ark of the Covenant was to be placed.

Upon completion of the tabernacle, Matenga believed God would speak
to the people from the temple.[102] Matenga and some of his followers in the
community went to the bush, to fell the trees for the pillars. They prepared
themselves through ascetic abstentions from smoking, drinking, spitting, and
inappropriate utterances. Had the men had enough faith, Matenga promised
the logs would move themselves. But infractions happened, and the moving
of the trunks proved to be an immense task, and thus a great test of faith.[103]
After a torrential flood, the logs were finally swept out to the sea, and eleven of
them beached themselves where Matenga predicted. The leading log, Hohepa
(Joseph), playing on the brother who had gone before his brothers into Egypt,
where they could survive, traveled further. A cart was chartered to reunite him
with his brothers.[104] Since their arrival on the beach, the pillars have been
regarded to be full of *tapu*, sacred power that can hurt those who approach it
unwisely.[105] As in the time of Salomon, the present generation would not see
the completion of the temple, but in the meantime, the Kohiti followers should
gather at the time of the new moon to pray and ask for guidance[106] for when
the inauguration of a new age of Maori and Pakeha living together in peace
was to come. This faith was peaceful, it saw forward to an age of harmony and
unity between Maori and Pakeha, and the new moon was symbolic of this new
world to come.[107]

This vision of harmony, so Bronwyn Elsmore ventures, was however limited
to a particular time and place. Though begun by a charismatic leader and in
some ways continuing the Ringatu movement, Kohititanga appears to have
been a transitional movement to help people adjust spiritually to a changing
universe and economy. Te Matenga did not institute a succession, hierarchy, or
institution. In fact, it seems as if he was convinced that it would have been up
to God to move further actions. A celebration of the new moon was a retrieval
of Maori tradition and parallel to Hebrew scriptures, but Elsmore assumes the
primary issue is that of "abiding by scriptural command rather than adopting
the customs of Jewish religion."[108]

---

[102] Ibid., 38.
[103] Ibid.,39.
[104] Ibid., 60–1.
[105] Ibid., 43.
[106] Ibid., 45.
[107] Ibid., 46–7.
[108] Ibid., 71.

The rationale for choosing these passages specifically, as determining practice, however, may no longer be retrievable. Elsmore gives hints: certain retraditioning aspects are primary, water and moon feature prominently, neither Maori nor Christian forms of priesthood or leadership are included (though this is certainly an exception from other charismatic Maori leaders). There appears to be a de-emphasis of Christian motifs and institutions, which may have been more associated with the colonial powers.[109]

This interpretation of the Hebrew scriptures integrates features that were suggested by the missionaries themselves, using the trope of the lost tribes as well as the felt similarity between both tribal societies.[110] Many Maori have a strongly developed sense of the importance of their ancestry—*whakapapa*—and the option of seeing themselves as descendants of the Israelites and the prophets presented itself quite naturally. Reading themselves into this narrative allowed them to both adapt to the empire of Pharaoh and attempt an exodus from the increasing problems of settler society and missionary distance. This cultural bricolage allowed them to articulate a theology of divine action on their behalf, and hope for sustenance, survival and thriving. It addressed the "general feeling among Maori that the new religion of Christianity failed in its appreciation of the holistic nature of the universe—God was removed from the creation," and allowed people to reimagine a time when "the atua were with the people and the two had an active and continuing relationship." The Kohiti faith showed God as concerned specifically with the local people, "his people, to the point of intervening on their behalf"[111] and showing them signs pointing toward accompaniment for the times of spiritual transition.

The 12 logs continue to lie on shore, as if waiting for the time to come. They are at times reshuffled by the meanderings of waves, tides, and storms. On the same beach, and offshore, the search for oil that fuels the oil-intensive economies of present capitalism presses upon the community who sees its spiritual resources strained by the temptation for oil money.

Commercializing Conversion

Commerce was seen, by some of the British, as a means of "civilizing" the Maori, and indeed some Maori appear to have been quick studies (Queequeg perhaps one of them) in bartering and trading, so much so that some British observers noted with regret that a form of consumerism became apparent. Samuel Marsden, the founder of the Anglican mission in Aotearoa/New Zealand, participated in trade "for his personal profit," believing that distribution of

[109] Ibid., 74.
[110] Ibid., 52.
[111] Ibid., 82.

tools and goods would lead to an inevitable "very rapid progress in the attainment of the necessary comforts of civil life."[112] The hope was that commerce would turn the Maori away from the pursuit of intertribal warfare and would advance "their civilization."[113] Others seem to have been saddened by what they felt was a corruption of the Maori into consumers, as they became "irrevocably enslaved by wants which were unfelt by their ancestors."[114] Here, as so often, the gospel traveled in close companionship with European modes of capitalism and commerce, and some of the empire's agents, such as Marsden, saw in "agriculture and trade the first steps in civilization, and in turn, the adoption of Christianity." Other local missionaries reversed the order and proceeded to focus on the propagation of the gospel first.[115] The theological conversion strategies outlined by Judith Binney matched quite closely those promulgated in the ninth century by Daniel of Winchester: The missionaries argued that Christian society was a result of God's favor and that with it came material prosperity.[116] But this change of strategy did little to challenge the naive assumption by the British that they would be able to control how their goods—and their religion—would be received, interpreted, and adapted by these tribal societies. In fact, the transmission of Christian theological traits proved far from under the control of the missionaries, of Western theological or cultural orthodoxies. The Evangelicals' millennialist eschatologies, for example, morphed into Maori prophetic movements resistant to British settlement and expansion while adapting "the gospel" to the purpose of survival

---

[112] As quoted in Sorrenson, "How To Civilize Savages," 99.

[113] J. S. Polack quoted in Ibid., 100.

[114] Ibid., 100.

[115] Ibid., 99–101.

[116] Binney, "Christianity and the Maoris to 1840: A Comment," 152. CMS missionaries further emphasized, true to Puritan form, a strong Augustinian notion of sin. (Robert Glen, "Those Odious Evangelicals: The Origins and Background of CMS Missionaries in New Zealand," in *Mission and Moko: The Church Missionary Society in New Zealand, 1814–182*, ed. Robert Glen [Christchurch: Latimer Fellowship of New Zealand, 1992], 20.) Thus having talked up human depravity, which was not a concept familiar or obvious to Maori, they attempted to convey the notion of redemption via the cross. While the missionaries found the *tapu* restrictions of Maori society a great hindrance to conversion, they ironically claimed sickness is a result of sin (which one could in some sense compare to the breaking of a *tapu* restriction). Maori fear of imported diseases came in handy in stressing that the British had better medicine (ironically not a better form of faith healing) and was problematically merged with a "European religion of rewards (and punishments)" (Binney, "Christianity and the Maoris," 153–4). Ironically, the missionaries' efforts were hampered by their own emphasis on keeping themselves separate from the Maori, as well as on isolating converts from the villages, and often proved the wrong strategy for propagating the gospel. Owens argues that the missionaries transferred British class divisions onto interracial relationships, treating Maori as lower-class people with whom they would not intermarry or socialize. Not surprisingly, then, native catechists were far more effective, being able to express the gospel as they understood it in Maori terms (John Morley R. Owens, "Christianity and the Maoris to 1840," *The New Zealand Journal of History* Vol. 2, No.1 [April 1968]: 29 and Binney, "Christianity and the Maoris," 163).

and resistance:[117] "Maori did not so much convert to Christianity as *convert Christianity*, like so much else that Pakeha"—people of non-Maori descent— "had brought, to their own purposes."[118] The gift of religion was here received in a manner, in many ways as much if not more, on the terms of the recipients than on those of the givers. The gift, once again, reveals its ambivalence as the poison. The dosage, administration, and particular context in which it functions can contribute more to the articulation of a component of cultural transmission than attempts to control the outcomes.

Gift, Obligation, Reciprocity

But a theology of land that does justice to the Maori affinity with their whenua and Pakeha conquest and occupation is impossible. The Biblical images of the people of Israel entering the promised land and conquering it at the expense of others, the Jubilee with its redistribution of land and Jesus pointing his followers away from the things of this earth to the kingdom of heaven present seemingly irreconcilable models.[119]

Little about the care of the land is as simple as it may seem. A sense of connection with land and the care for it can be found across ethnic difference. And at times even people of the land do not make decisions that benefit both in the long term. Settler populations engage in practices that destroy and ways of safeguarding land, often in conflict and competition with those of previous inhabitants. The many ways of living on the land recall the complex and conflicting notions of relationship to the land that are part of the biblical tradition: itinerancy, settlement, being a foreigner, moving into a land that was previously settled and being first guest, usage rights versus property ownership, struggles for dominance and imperial invasion. All these experiences and the attending conflicts around them reflect experiences that continue in our time. What would it mean to reimagine postcolonial land relationships? We need more complex instruments to measure and ways to engage than the dualistic stereotypes that so often have marked past relationships. In a postcolonial, transcultural world, there is a need for thinking multiple modes of reciprocity between humans in terms of time, degree, location, and differences in power, culture, and knowledge. At the same time, there is a profound need to rethink and reenact the divine-human-world relationship. A variety of exchanges partake in the formation of the hybrid identities of transcultures. To address these issues, it is important to recognize and deconstruct the hierarchical gender dynamic that often overlaps with the structural economy of colonizer-colonized.

[117] Bronwyn Elsmore, *Mana from Heaven: A Century of Maori Prophets in New Zealand* (Auckland: Reed, 1989).
[118] King, *History of New Zealand*, 144. Italics mine.
[119] Davidson, "Interaction," 163.

Consider the rhetoric of British colonial propagandist and Anglican cleric Samuel Purchas who argued that the "Virgin Portion" of North America had been divinely allocated to his countrymen, "God in wisdom having enriched the savage countries, that those riches be attractive for Christian suitors."[120] In colonial travel and propaganda literature, the trope that "the American continent was a richly endowed virgin bride awaiting a husband enjoyed considerable usage" in early colonial times.[121] Other instances equally revealed the dangerous side of imagining the gift as gendered exchange. Cook's journal often notes that a canoe with "people" came by his ship. This may indicate the presence of women in Maori war canoes. However, Maori women, in these encounters narrated by Cook and company, are even more silenced, perhaps doubly so, by the hypermasculine world of a floating homosocial imperial naval society that often overlaid its particular sexist assumptions and needs on native communities. Some Maori women, particularly if unmarried or commoners, became sexual partners of the erotically starved male ship population and often the first recipients of sexually transmitted disease viruses introduced by sailors. At times, sex was traded, by the women and the sailors. Sometimes male heads of families and chiefs sent women to shops once it became clear that goods could be traded for intercourse.[122] Yet, whether the women "were involved in fleeting or sustained relationships, they were critical in mediating cross-cultural difference and forging a new and common set of understandings."[123] Soon they would also be mothers, and hence the main producers of intercultural genetic exchanges, harnessed in the cause of assimilation through the "amalgamation of races" policy as pursued by the British during some phases of the colonization of New Zealand.[124]

Early accounts of travels to North America were "characterized by promises of abundance, even excess,"[125] though the early settlers were heavily dependent on credit from home. Furthermore, the "New World" was considered to be possessed of "an abundance that was permanent and natural and therefore needed none of the hierarchies and hoardings that followed from a scarcity economics."[126] The lust for gold soon did away with such Romantic ideas.

---

[120] James, *British Empire*, 12.

[121] Ibid., 12. On Columbus's use of the same trope see also Catherine Keller, *Apocalypse Now And Then: A Feminist Guide to the End of the World* (Boston: Beacon, 1996), 154–6.

[122] Ka'ai, Moorfield, Reilly, and Mosley, *Ki Te Whaiao*, 145.

[123] Ibid., 146.

[124] Sorrenson, "How To Civilize Savages," 103. This policy remains unsuccessful in many ways in part because many indigenous peoples, among them Maori, resist the Western notion of identification of blood/race/ethnicity with cultural, communal belonging. Hence, in contemporary Aotearoa New Zealand, while there is a great degree of intermarriage, there is increased resistance to assimilation when it means the erasure of Maori culture, and great resistance to identifying as Maori as having to do with the amount of person's blood content. http://maaori.com/whakapapa/fullblood.htm

[125] Murray, *Indian Giving*, 49.

[126] Ibid., 51.

Assumptions of divine and natural abundance merged with other constructions to form the dissonant, mixed messages of colonial imagery: "What we
have is a persistent presentation of Europeans as the givers, and a stress on the
power of giving, *alongside* the counteridea of the New World as a bountiful,
fecund place from which to take."[127]

This resonance of the double givingness, parallels and redoubles theological troping, and hides the violence of colonial exploitation (rather than trade)
behind decidedly ambivalent notions of double abundance. It serves as an
apology for empire as royal and divine sovereignty are merged together to subordinate land and inhabitants, while claiming a superabundance of giving and
of resources that are inexhaustible. In colonial exchanges, power moves unsta-
bly across boundaries. It fluctuates between giver and receiver, and the trope
of the gift can function in several ways in colonial propaganda, missionary
theological narrative, and native response. Colonial explorers often remarked
upon the abundant nature of resources they encountered on their travels.
Hence, James Cook, who served, in many ways, as a bioprospector for the merchants of empire, drew tidy and accurate maps to many "treasure islands" later
visited by seal-hunting and whale-hunting ships (such as the *Essex*, the factual
antecedent of the fictional *Pequod*) and finally by European settlers in South
Pacific Islands.[128] It took only 40 years of exploiting the "abundance of the
New Zealand fur seal" reported by Cook for that population to crash, and the
whaling industry in pursuit of whale oil as fuel for industry and lamps peaked
not long after.[129]

Today, Cook's journals are used by Maori as a source for lands and resources
claims staked in the Waitangi tribunal.[130] In reclaiming some of the land and
resources disenfranchised during the process of colonization, Maori have
taken advantage of Cook's detailed prospecting:

"We've survived colonial oppression by being proactive," Tracey [Tangihere]
said, "and by adapting Western skills to our own ends." To illustrate this,
she showed me a three-hundred-page "working paper" for a land claim one
local tribe had filed with the government. To prove such claims, tribes had
to demonstrate a long-term pattern of use and settlement. "Cook's one of
our best sources," Tracey said. With a surveyor's eye, Cook had carefully

---

[127] Ibid., 60. My italics.
[128] Cf. Londa Schiebinger, *Plants and Empire: Colonial Bioprospecting in the Atlantic World*
(Cambridge, MA: Harvard University Press, 2004).
[129] The depletion of fur seals was intimately connected with a new addiction the British had
picked up during their imperial adventures: Sealskins functioned as payment for tea from
China. King, *History of New Zealand*, 118, 121.
[130] "The Tribunal is a permanent commission of inquiry charged with making recommen-
dations on claims brought by Maori relating to actions or omissions of the Crown, which
breach the promises made in the Treaty of Waitangi." See www.waitangi-tribunal.govt.nz/
about/waitangitribunal/.

delineated the boundaries of villages, the location of shell mounds, the use of fishing nets. At one point, the *Endeavour*'s men saw fishing canoes more than twelve miles offshore—evidence the Maori now use to determine the extent of their traditional fishing ground. [. . .] "It's come full circle, eh?" Tracey said. "Cook led to the destruction of our world, and now we're using him to put it back together again. "[131]

This is not a simple act of resistance by a colonized culture against the culture of the colonizer. It is a sophisticated transcultural act, using the tools of the master as unexpected product of the "gift of civilization."[132] This is made possible by the inherent ambivalence of such cultural practices and technology. One way to begin to appreciate more fully the agency and contribution of colonized peoples is to recognize transcultural creativity through resistant adaptations.[133]

This agency can be caught between giving in to the pressure for assimilation and the attempt to go entirely native—whatever that may mean—and most likely ends up with a more or less well-conceived and functional melange. Many of these adaptive processes are still being formed, and have to contend with the great damage that has been done to land rights, mindset, and morale of indigenous peoples. Yet, it is key to move beyond the liberal "bleeding heart" depiction of natives only as victims of merchants and missionaries. Transcultural boundary infractions, intercontinental trade, and cultural exchange have been commonplace throughout history in most societies. Cultural purity and

---

[131] Horvitz, *Blue Latitudes*, 130. This should not give the impression, however, that resources in pre-European settlement Aotearoa/New Zealand were uncontested. Much of inter-tribal warfare concerned contested resources.

[132] In contemporary Aotearoa/New Zealand, Maori continue to struggle to deal with the gifts/poisons received from British and now American civilizations. In the wake of the North Atlantic merchants and missionaries came the social scientists. Maori were somewhat of a favorite with anthropologists, since at one time race and diffusionist theories harbored by European scientists ranked the South Polynesian Maori above Africans and Australian "sons of Ham," and they were at times identified as the "lost tribes of Israel." "Indeed the Maori had the good fortune to be ranked higher than most other 'savages.' Exponents of the Great Chain of Being invariably put the Maori somewhat above the unfortunate Hottentots or the Australian Aborigines who were usually placed in the last links in the chain between man and the apes. [Similarly,] the Maori, with their sedentary agriculture and skilled arts, were usually placed on the border between savagery and barbarism and assumed to be capable, with proper guidance, of graduating to civilization." See Sorrenson, "How To Civilize Savages," 97, 98. James Cook considered them a "warlike people" (Horvitz, *Blue Latitudes*, 117) and noted their sedentary agricultural economy, something that indicated a level of "culture" to imperialist Englishmen. It seemed, however, that for the most part, the Maori remained a very ambivalent encounter for European visitors to Aotearoa, because they defied the labels of both "barbaric" peoples and "noble savage."

[133] Assimilation here appears as the pressure to conform to a hegemonic culture, something that was asked of Jews in Germany. The psychological costs of assimilation are, however, immense.

stability is generally an untenable fiction. Societies can enhance and revive through intercultural exchange. Whether such an exchange is reviving or can become genocidal has much to do with the conditions under which it occurs and the power relations that shape the conditions under which intercultural exchange occurs. There can be places of creative hybridity, places on the "edge of chaos,"[134] where divine *dynamis* offers a space for healing transformation to all involved. Such salutary processes do not come easy or fast, and need to be based on changing power relations.

In the transcultural networks that can foster such exchanges, the lines may run less and less along ethnic, gender, and even class boundaries and are increasingly being redrawn around issues such as justice, peace, ecological sustainability, and the desire to form societies built on more equitable exchanges between indigenous peoples and settler populations. Transcultural encounter, under less hegemonic terms, if indeed possible, must move to mutual understanding that goes far deeper than exotic observations about the other that in the end are self-mirroring and shore up an oppositional identity formation or serve as narcissistic self-enhancement.[135] That such self-mirroring inflects a great deal of research about other peoples has ceased to be a secret. One might say that, in a reflection of what Westerners know as the Heisenberg principle, the observer not only changes what they observe but brings themselves into the process, and the narration of the process of observation, which is perhaps better named an exchange, an economy of knowledge exchange, however it may be constructed.

In his investigation of European/North American discourses around native practices of potlatch, Christopher Bracken contends that the Canadian legislation to forbid the potlatch and the controversy around it implied that "when Canada finally delivered itself to its western border, it found Europe already embodied in a group of cultures that white Canadians wished to define themselves against. Europe was already there among the very First Nations that European Canada, Europe-in-Canada, considered absolutely different from itself."[136] Bracken argues that the notion that there had once been societies that practiced a "true gift" was a quite recent invention: "for Mauss the distinction between a gift, conceived as an event that brings nothing back to the giver, and an exchange, understood as a reciprocal circulation of goods and services between two or more parties," is a "fairly recent" development, "peculiar to Western European societies." Referencing among other, Aotearoa/New Zealand, anthropologist Marcel

---

[134] For a theological exploration of chaos theory and the dynamics of systems oscillating between versions of chaos and order, see Keller, *Face of the Deep*.

[135] Something I am aware this essay could be seen to be involved in.

[136] Christopher Bracken, *The Potlatch Papers* (Chicago: University of Chicago Press, 1997), 2. Hence, it is no surprise that, as Bracken further contends, Mauss's investigations were conditioned not so much by his Romanticism about "primitive peoples," but by his culture's (ibid. 155).

Mauss ponders the real and imagined differences between the economies of indigenous and capitalist cultures, aiming to lay to rest the romanticized sense of the indigenous gift, as free and capitalist economies as notoriously drenched in obligation. Instead, he argues, there is no such thing as a free gift, and obligations and limitations are always part of exchanges, whether in "civilized" or "primitive" settings. Hence, he critiques one of the basic hermeneutic moves of early anthropologists and ethnographers, namely that the indigenous social system represented an unchanged, archaic, primitive system of social arrangements that was interesting perhaps primarily as the (imagined) "antecedent" of the cultures which Europe sees itself as representing, depending on one's position, an apex of civilization or a perversion of social accountability. This means a particular historiography, imprinted in the European mind among others by Hegel, and his comments on the history of cultures is subtly but profoundly challenged in this moment.[137] While such projection may well be part of the structure of life as many people know it, and can likely not be avoided, a greater awareness of and accountability for the internal needs for such projection are crucial for projections to transcend into actual encounters with an other. It will take some work then to move beyond rejection formation and to get a more realistic sense of what the differences and similarities between cultures, persons, and modes of being might consist in.

Similar things can be said about the practice of theology. A person's biography—including one's gender, cultural, language, and class background—will inform his or her theological framework. That fact, in itself, does not immediately carry value. Rather, it depends on how such contextualization is embodied in relation, and becomes an enacted hermeneutic of text and world. A person or group's history and vulnerability influence profoundly the way they see and experience not only other people, but notions of the Divine, God, or the Sacred. A healthier sense of self and group will enable a healthier encounter with the Divine and a more centered articulation and promulgation of that relationship. To put it plainly, the more twisted the self in community, the more twisted the theology and relationship to the Divine. And the more important are healing measures both on the personal, communal, and theological level, and the shape of encounter with the Divine. One oft-stated difference between Western modern capitalist cultures and indigenous cultures is that in many indigenous cultures, generous giving (which of course is predicated on the acquisition of enough resources to be generous) enhances status as "the giver gains rank."[138]

Giving is then the marker of social status, whereas within capitalist cultures, taking and owning have been the dominant indicators of social status.[139] Such

---

[137] Frederick Weiss, ed., *Hegel: The Essential Writings* (New York: Harper & Row, 1974), 310.

[138] Carl Olson, "Excess, Time, and the Pure Gift: Postmodern Transformations of Marcel Mauss," *Method & Theory in the Study of Religion* 14 (2002): 357.

[139] As evidenced by many detailed accounts of extreme capitalism such as Juliet B. Schor, *The Overspent American: Upscaling, Downshifting, and the New Consumer* (New York: Basic Books,

gaps in social priorities can serve to culturally disadvantage one group: If one were to remain true to the cultural priority of social recognition through generous giving, one's own exploitation may be facilitated, as the cultural priority of societal recognition through personal acquisition might create a dynamic that moves most goods to their side. Such dynamics generate a culture shock on steroids, where survival may necessitate the abandonment or creative adaptation of one's own cultural values. But rather than mark these cultural differences so starkly dualistic, to break through the ease of projection and move toward more understanding and creative relation building, it is crucial to try as best as possible to get a sense of difference in degree, rather than in kind. That is, to look for where each culture deals with a particular issue in similar ways, but with different emphases, and different priorities and strategies. Rather than simple "opposites" then, cultural differences can be perceived as "sameness but different" and "different, but the same."

From some standpoints, many Maori have a particularly developed sense of reciprocity and obligation in economies of exchange. Anne Salmond notes that "it has often been remarked by European scholars that there is no precise word for 'gratitude' in Maori. This is probably because words are an inadequate return for kindness, or help in time of need."[140] Yet the absence of a particular concept does not mean it is not embedded elsewhere, if implicitly. And Mauss observes about the *hau*,[141] the "spirit of a thing given," that *taonga* ("treasures")[142] have a form of *mana* (which Mauss defines as "magical, religious and spiritual power," that can destroy a recipient if "the law, or rather

---

1998), Dell deChant, *The Sacred Santa: Religious Dimensions of Consumer Culture* (Cleveland, OH: Pilgrim Press, 2002); Thomas Frank, *One Market Under God* (New York: Anchor Books, 2000). This does not exclude the existence of strong expectations of charitable giving or of "giving back" to one's alma mater. However, these, too, are not simply "gifts" but expectations of reciprocity.

[140] Thus Anne Salmond begins her acknowledgements in Anne Salmond, *Two Worlds: First Meetings Between Maori and Europeans 1642–1772* (Honolulu: University of Hawaii Press, 1991), 9.

[141] The missionary and ethnographer William Williams gives several meanings, among them "wind, air," "property, spoils," and "return gift" in Herbert William Williams, *Dictionary of the Maori Language* (Wellington: Legislation Direct, 2003, 7th ed. revised and augmented), 38–9.

[142] While Mauss concentrates on *taonga* relations between people, the term includes the "treasure" of the land that Maori are set over as guardians (see King, *History of New Zealand*, 160, and Hirini Moko Mead, *Tikanga Maori: Living by Maori Values* [Wellington: Huia, 2003], 186–7. Land was regarded as the ultimate gift and could be something given in return for help in armed conflicts or to entice a future husband to live with the bride's family). Hence, Maori *taonga* are mentioned in the Treaty of Waitangi, often considered the "founding document" of New Zealand. (On the history and terms of the treaty, see Claudia Orange, *The Treaty of Waitangi* [Wellington: Allen and Unwin, 1987].) The treaty, a highly contested document due to its problematic genesis and differing versions in two languages, guarantees unequivocally that Maori will enjoy full power over their *taonga*. This includes *whenua*, land, though later the treaty was soon used in ways that justified the phrase that land was "taken by sale," confiscated, or otherwise alienated.

the obligation, about making a return gift is not observed."[143] Thus, as Mauss sees it, "[t]he *taonga* and all strictly personal possessions have a *hau*, a spiritual power. You give me *taonga*, I give it to another, the latter gives me *taonga* back, since he is forced to do so by the *hau* of my gift; and I am obliged to give this one to you since I must return to you what is in fact the product of the *hau* of your *taonga*."[144] Likewise, "[the] obligation attached to a gift itself is not inert. Even when abandoned by the giver, it still forms a part of him [sic]."[145] Hence, even though giving may convey high status, it is part of a cycle of reciprocity that is quite tightly knitted, perhaps more tightly than a setting in which a gift without reciprocity continues to be imagined and idealized. In such a cultural setting it is also possible to imagine that one can take without abandon, without consideration of "externalities" such as people and the cycles of the elements. It would seem to be intimately connected to the idea that the giving of the creator carries no obligation for response. While it is impossible to give as we have received, we can engage in a responsible stewardship of what is in our sphere of action. Jacques Derrida, pondering of gift, exchange, and economy—writes the following, inhabiting fellow French Jew Marcel Mauss' influential book *The Gift*:

> Now this equivalence of giving-taking is precisely stated in the form of a "beautiful Maori proverb" that, once again as epiloguing epigraph, comes to close the "Moral Conclusions":
> "Ko Maru kai atu
> Ko Maru kai mai
> Ka ngohe ngohe"
> "Give as much as you take, all shall be very well."[146]

This old Maori proverb reoccurs as a form of Kaupapa Maori, as a principle of sustainable management, in contemporary resource management of fisheries and land, and as a principle involved in negotiating claims to the Treaty Of Waitangi.[147] Yet, as all principles, how it becomes applied shows how difficult such negotiations are when applied in actual situations of exchange when multiple agents and multiple interests are negotiated. Does becoming assimilated to some of the more impactful forms of less reciprocal and not globally sustainable economic and social interaction then also mean to stop being so "naive" (as defined in Western culture) as to "always give," foolishly expecting

---

[143] Mauss, *The Gift*, 8–9.
[144] Ibid., 9.
[145] Ibid., 9.
[146] Jacques Derrida, *Given Time: I. Counterfeit Money*, trans. Peggy Kamuf (Chicago, IL: University of Chicago Press, 1992), 67.
[147] www.csiwisepractices.org/?read=62andwww.waitangi-tribunal.govt.nz/reports/viewchapter.asp?reportID=7df6e15e-2c4d-4dd0–9e60–50a88ffb48a9&chapter=7.

reciprocity in giving? Does becoming assimilated, becoming a capitalist, then also mean prioritizing taking and abandoning giving? Is putting one's own tribe's interests above else, even above sustainable use of land, any different than the principles of the externalizing dynamics of neoliberal economics, just on a different scale? This notion of the gift without any concomitant reciprocal obligation also bolsters the theological notion of God as boundless giver and could influence assumptions that such a gift does not oblige responsible reciprocity in their relations with God and world. One anti-imperialist argument raised both by peoples within and without North Atlantic colonizing cultures has been that "it is a problem of whites, and therefore of the entire earth, that they always take and never give."[148]

A tempting juxtaposition via a pop cultural reflection comes to mind. The scene is from *The Life of Brian*, a happily anachronistic British satire of the human condition as it manifests itself in the life of a man who could have been Christ. In particular, the film flays common patterns of cultural and religious madness and inconsistency. In one scene, representatives of various Palestinian resistance groups—congregated in a Roman colosseum to plot an uprising—are pondering the question "what have the Romans ever done for us?" and in spite of themselves list aqueducts, sanitation, irrigation, roads, public baths, games, wine, and so on. The movie's self-ironic impetus hits a nerve also because British culture has internalized a highly Romanized culture as apex of its notion of civilization, blending languages, practices, governmental systems, and teaching Latin in schools as a cultured language. This highly ambivalent perception of having unwillingly, yet quite profoundly, been transformed by contact with a colonizer whose presence is also profoundly disruptive is very real for a great many populations of the earth. It constitutes an initially forced hybridity that can no longer be excised, and has become part of one's identity, acknowledged or not. This hybridity makes it an even more difficult venture to posit a distinct mode of being that resists colonial excess, rather than simplistically rejecting any kind of foreign influence or culture. When one of Witi Ihimaera's characters wonders whether adaptation to new technologies and mindsets will allow Māori to still be Māori,[149] he is asking a crucial question: what makes or breaks identity, personal, tribal, cultural, national? Identities both of colonizer and colonized can become more permeable in these encounters on the boundary. This increased permeability triggers a multiplicity of responses. Increased mobility also means increased instability. Instability can be perceived as chance and as threat.

---

[148] Heiner Uber, "Die Aktivistin: Amerikas Farmer Wollen Wieder auf Büffeljagd Gehen—the Indianerin Winona LaDuke Will es Verhindern," *Die Zeit* Nr. 2 (7 January 1999): 54. Translation mine.

[149] "Will we have prepared the people to cope with the new challenges and the new technology? And will they still be Maori?" Ihimaera, *The Whale Rider*, 71.

Lakota activist, and U.S. Green Party member, Winona LaDuke argues that some of the more ambivalent "gifts" of Euro-American culture (technology, literacy, culture, monetary capitalism), however, can and should be used, for the survival of her people.[150] But the gifts that Western cultures claim to have brought also have poisonous uses. The gift, Jacques Derrida has often pointed out, is somewhere between cure and poison, and many of its effects have to do with the dosage applied. The Greek term *doron* is related to *dosis*, and the word "gift" in German means poison. Some cultures affected by colonialism have sustained more toxic buildups than others. Resistant agency occurs in adapting the gifts/poisons of the colonizer to survival.[151] Thus, giving and taking yet again emerges as far more complex than essentialist imperialist or anti-imperialist rhetoric can capture. Resistant agency of a more questionable kind is also expressed in the sometimes highly contentious nature of intertribal competition and a culture of complaint that continues the problem of paternalism by continuing to feed it.

It seems far too simplistic to assert, as those Mauss addresses in *The Gift*, that "primitive" cultures are based on gift giving, and "civilized" cultures are based on property capitalism in some simple way. Rather, we might get a step closer if we look at how the various cultures involved in an economic exchange understand and conceptualize giving and taking, property, use rights, and exchange, and how the two systems interact and overlap, interact, and adapt to each other.

Regifting the Theological Present: Justice, Grace, and Reciprocity

Let us consider Milbank's suggestion that the only thing required of humans in response to forgiveness is acceptance and penance: "Christ's atonement is without measure and without price, and the only penance demanded of us in return" is the "non-price of acceptance."[152] Milbank here seems to cryptically both concede and deny reciprocity, exemplifying the paradoxical non/reciprocity of his approach. His claim that forgiveness is either an "aneconomic economy of pardon" (without strings attached) or does not exist forces a false alternative. Milbank, who seeks to "outwit nihilism" through the proclamation of a radical orthodoxy, appears to find support for his project in those

---

[150] Uber, "Die Aktivistin," 54.

[151] This adaptation would be distinct from the policy of the "amalgamation of the races" pursued by the British settlers, the goal of which would have been assimilation rather than creative, flexible adaptation and a truly bi-cultural society—something that is still a hope rather than a reality in Aotearoa/New Zealand.

[152] Milbank, *Being Reconciled*, 47.

"radical pietists" who realized that "to be human means to reckon with an immense depth behind things."[153] The only possibility for escaping "nihilism," Milbank sees, is to "trust the depth, and appearance as the gift of depth, and history as the restoration of the loss of this depth in Christ."[154] What then, would it mean to "trust the depth," as Milbank suggests? Investigating the deep means paying a depth charge, resisting the simple answers, and examining received orthodoxies. Catherine Keller's theological analysis of depth in the first verses of Genesis and their afterlives, biblically and otherwise, suggests that "the deep" emerges as neither simply trustworthy nor scarily abysmal, but as a site of complexity, of "chaosmos," that we may need to face in order live honestly and faithfully within the fullness of the created world.[155]

Similarly, the gift of "the Christian tradition" is only simplistically seen as either trustworthy or untrustworthy. If we want to carve out possibilities of living faithfully with this gift, then it is crucial to acknowledge it in its complexity, and wrestle with it in its depth. Such regifting resists a neat conflation with creedal orthodoxy. The unified one-voicedness hides a multiplicity of local options. The imperial monologue often resists absorbing more deeply the issues of gender, class, race, ethnicity, and the need to decolonize creedal formulations formulated under the eyes of the newly Christian empire, and under imperial duress. All these factors need to be taken into consideration in a theology that wants to decolonize Christian faith and tradition to allow for a more equitable economic and social world. It is important to pursue this without either discarding or uncritically affirming dogmatic decisions made on the basis of some very particular contingencies that are not necessarily the final enunciation of a cultural interaction between Jewish, Christian and Hellenistic, Platonic ideas.

Some argue that among many Pakeha, a pretense continues to be upheld, in universalist language, that "we are all the same," echoing Busby's pronouncement after the signing of the Treaty of Waitangi by a delegation of Māori leaders that "we are now one people." The position that there should be "no special treatment" for Maori has meant that all citizens were to be assimilated in the Pakeha way of doing things, and cease to be "different." As Trinh Minh-ha has accurately analyzed: "Gone out of date, then revitalized, the mission of civilizing the savage mutates into the imperative of 'making equal.'" Again, the colonizers speak: "*They* decide who is 'racism-free or anti-colonial' and

---

[153] John Milbank, "Knowledge: The Theological Critique of Philosophy in Hamann and Jacobi," in *Radical Orthodoxy: A New Theology*, John Milbank, Catherine Pickstock, and Graham Ward, eds (London: Routledge, 1999), 32.

[154] Ibid., 32.

[155] Keller borrows this term from Joyce's *Finnegan's Wake* and suggests that the deep hosts a matrix of possibilities. Catherine Keller, *Face of the Deep: A Theology of Becoming* (New York: Routledge, 2003), 12.

they seriously think they can go on formulating criteria for us, telling us where and how to detect what they seem to know better than us: racism and colonialism. Natives must be taught in order to be anticolonialist and de-Westernized; they are, indeed, in this world of inequity, the handicapped who cannot represent themselves and have to either be represented or learn to represent themselves."[156] Beyond Milbank's claims that modernity can be reduced to "nihilism" and "secularism," some of the subplots of modernity—Reformation, colonialism, Enlightenment—likewise witnessed explosions of new forms of religiosity (such as Romanticism, Pietism, awakenings, missionary cultures, and so on).

It is crucial to recognize the ambivalence resident in the Christian tradition, as in any other tradition—that we are barred any access to a "pure," uncontaminated past, to radical roots that would represent an "originary" sense of Christianity. Rather, the "roots" and hence the radicality of Christian traditions may function more like a rhizome, the root network of plants such as potatoes and mushrooms, which are multiple and remain invisible to the eye, though the way this structure fuses "connection and heterogeneity" is crucial for the formation and survival of the plant system.[157]

Forgiveness may be unachievable in human understanding, as Milbank claims, even when "inaugurated" by the "divine humanity"[158] of Christ, but acts of restorative justice can at least begin to cease some of the abuse, whether physical, structural, or epistemological, even as imperialism's effects continue. For colonized peoples (and colonizers, as well), an easy time warp skipping modernity would instantiate a form of dangerous amnesia on the part of the colonizer and make a mockery of the lives of those under the influence of imperialism. Restorative justice in theological discourse, then, must strive to come to terms with colonial theologies of give and take. Since there is no pure

---

[156] See Trinh Minh-Ha, *Woman, Native, Other*, 59 (Bloomington, IN: Indiana University Press, 1989). The danger and constant temptation is to repeat the scripts of the North Atlantic "geography of imagination" and to use differences as devices in rhetoric to reinscribe "the West" as the "better savage" ("better," or "more authentic" than the actual native person, a dynamic based on a strong binary division between self and Other/Native). Trouillot recommends: "The 'us and all of them' binary, implicit in the symbolic order that creates the West, is an ideological construct and the many forms of Third-World-ism that reverse its terms are its mirror images. There is no Other, but multitudes of others who are all others for different reasons, in spite of totalizing narratives, including that of capital." Michel Trouillot, *Global Transformations*, 27 (New York: Palgrave Macmillan, 2003). Theologians in transcultures would do well to defer the rhetoric of otherness in a way that is neither assimilationist nor nationalist, but that writes and preaches new possibilities for intertextuality and the adaptation (as distinct from the assimilation) of ancient tribal narratives and contemporary transcultures.

[157] The writers discuss the rhizome in the introduction. Gilles Deleuze and Felix Guattari, *A Thousand Plateaus: Capitalism and Schizophrenia*, Brian Massumi, trans. and foreword (Minneapolis: University of Minnesota Press, 1987), 7.

[158] Milbank, *Being Reconciled*, 61.

space in Christianity (or any other culture for that matter) that allows a retreat before a certain time of "spoilage." The task at hand might be to come to terms, not only with the hybridities that have existed in all cultures, but with those new ones generated by new phases of imperialism and colonialism: how to find a sense of culture and identity that is neither impermeable nor completely assimilated, how to trade in economies that allow most people to satisfy their basic needs and be able to live in relative comfort while restoring much of the integrity of colonized lands.

How to construct Christian theologies, which neither simply repeat the cultural expressions of the missionaries, nor search for some pure lost expression of indigenous religion, seems to be one of the challenges of the future. Such theologies need to see beyond an "either/or"[159] approach to theological loci, periods, and discourses and instead come to theological terms with the ambivalent exchanges inherent in colonial trades, theological and economic. Accounting for our complex history allows for the repentance of the Christian complicity with exploitation and empire and searches for ways to embody restorative justice and less antagonistic, more cooperative and conciliatory relationships among humans. The question is, how do we find clear-sighted, hopeful, and creative responses to the divine spirit calling us beyond guilt-ridden despair and disengagement or forgetful denial and resentment toward new iterations of divine economies? To accept the "gift of depth" would then mean to bring into our presen/ce/ts the extensive ties that have been formed between cultures since modern anthropologists (and colonists and missionaries before them) set out to describe "gifts" among "natives." We might then have to learn to live in the presence of unstable economies of giving. We ignore their ambivalent locations at the peril of being unable to discern God's agency in a way that may help heal the abuses of imperial theologies and economies of exchange.

> Human understanding (as opposed to human control) requires reciprocal exchange, for all its hazards—your wisdom for mine (wanaanga atu, wanaanga mai), as we cross our thoughts together (whakawhitiwhiti whakaaro). In New Zealand, at least, a collaboration between Maori and Western knowledges seems possible. It may lead, eventually, to studies of cross-cultural encounters that do justice to the ancestors on both sides, and the potent, perilous pae—the edge between them.[160]

---

[159] John Milbank, "Knowledge: The Theological Critique of Philosophy in Hamann and Jacobi," in *Radical Orthodoxy: A New Theology*, John Milbank, Catherine Pickstock, and Graham Ward, eds (London: Routledge, 1999), 32.

[160] Anne Salmond, *Between Worlds: Early Exchanges Between Maori and Europeans 1773–1815* (Honolulu: University of Hawai'i Press, 1997), 513.

Works Cited

Barrow, Terence. *An Illustrated Guide to Maori Art*. Auckland: Reed, 1984.

Binney, Judith. "Christianity and the Maoris to 1840: A Comment." *The New Zealand Journal of History* Vol.3, No. 1 (April 1969): 143–65.

—.*The Legacy of Guilt: A Life of Thomas Kendall*. Wellington: Bridget Williams Books, 1968.

Bracken, Christopher. *The Potlatch Papers*. Chicago, IL: University of Chicago Press, 1997.

Callaghan, Moeawa. "Look to the Past to See the Future." *First Peoples Theology Journal*, June 2006, 104–9.

Davidson, Allan. "The Interaction of Missionary and Colonial Society in Nineteenth Century New Zealand." *Studies in World Christianity* Vol. 2, No. 2 (1996): 145–66.

Derrida, Jacques. *Given Time: I. Counterfeit Money*. Trans. Peggy Kamuf. Chicago, IL: University of Chicago Press, 1992.

Douglas, Ian T., and Kwok Pui-Lan. *Beyond Colonial Anglicanism: The Anglican Communion in the Twenty-first Century*. New York: Church Publishing, 2001.

Elsmore, Bronwyn. *Te Kohititanga Marama: New Moon, New World*. Auckland, NZL: Reed, 1998.

Glen, Robert. "Those Odious Evangelicals: Origins and Background of the CMS Missionaries in New Zealand." In *Mission and Moko: Aspects of the Work of the Church Missionary Society in New Zealand, 1814–1882*, Robert Glen, ed., 14–37. Christchurch: Latimer Fellowship of New Zealand, 1992.

Huie-Jolly Mary. "Maori 'Jews' and a Resistant Reading of John 5.10–47." In *Postcolonial Biblical Reader*, 224–37. Oxford: Blackwell, 2006.

Ihimaera, Witi. *The Whale Rider*. Auckland: Reed, 1987.

Ka'ai, Tānia, John C. Moorfield, Michael P. J. Reilly, and Sharon Mosley. *Ki Te Whaiao: An Introduction to Maori Culture and Society*. Auckland: Pearson Education, 2004.

King, Michael. *The Penguin History of New Zealand*. Auckland: Penguin, 2003.

Nabokov, Peter. *Where The Lighting Strikes: The Lives of American Indian Sacred Places*. New York: Penguin, 2006.

Orange, Claudia. *The Treaty of Waitangi*. Sydney/London: Allen & Unwin, 1987.

Owens, J. M. R. "Christianity and the Maoris to 1840." *The New Zealand Journal of History* Vol.2, No. 1 (April 1968): 18–40.

Prosek, James. "Maori Eels: New Zealand's Maori Defend an Extraordinary Creature—and Themselves." *Orion*, July/August 2010. www.orionmagazine. org/index.php/articles/article/5610/.

Roussos, Timotheos. "A Man's 'True Face': Concealing/Revealing Masculinities in Novels by Alan Duff and Witi Ihimaera." *Philament* Vol. 5. http://sydney.edu.au/arts/publications/philament/issue5_Critique_Roussos.htm

Royal, Te Ahukaramū Charles, ed. *The Woven Universe: Selected Writings of Rev. Māori Marsden*. Masterson, NZ: The Estate of Maori Marsden, 2003.

—."Editor's Introduction." In *The Woven Universe: Selected Writings of Rev. Māori Marsden*, Woven Universe. Masterson, NZ: The Estate of Maori Marsden, 2003.

Salmond, Anne. *Between Worlds: Early Exchanges Between Maori and Europeans 1773–1815*. Honolulu: University of Hawaii Press, 1997.

Schneider, Laurel C. *Beyond Monotheism: A Theology of Multiplicity*. London: Routledge, 2008.

Weiss, Frederick, ed. *Hegel: The Essential Writings*. New York: Harper & Row, 1974.

Chapter 7

In Transit

This chapter offers some examples for negotiating the space of mutual mission, of indigenous adaptations of Christian faith and practice for survival and flourishing. They move beyond purity, while struggling for authenticity and the integration of various cultural knowledges to creative, adaptive retraditioning.

Recovering Identities: Struggling for Authenticity

Fanon recognizes the crucial importance, for subordinated peoples, of asserting their indigenous cultural traditions and retrieving their repressed histories. But he is far too aware of the dangers of the fixity and fetishism of identities within the calcification of colonial cultures to recommend that "roots" be struck in the celebratory romance of the past or by homogenizing the history of the present.[1]

Cultural expressions of living in right relationship with God are highly disputed. The particular arrangements and compromises that were negotiated between the cultures of the gospel and local religiocultures inform what each community sees as conforming to divine intent, what they consider to be in need of urgent change, and where they discern personal and social salvation. Some of this salvation may come in the form of estrangement for many of us, of acquiring a greater sense of the relocation of the home and the world—the unhomeliness—that is the condition of extraterritorial and cross-cultural initiations.[2] This unhomeliness has not always been redemptive. Some of it has been imposed, some of it has been manifest as deep displacement of self, community, and land. There are great differences in how this displacement is experienced, and whatever new relations are formed in the aftermath of colonialism have to face the loss, the depth of anger, and despair still experienced. The gap of experience, the pace of movement, and

[1]   Homi Bhabha, *The Location of Culture* (London/New York: Routledge, 1994), 9.
[2]   Ibid., 9.

the need for healthy, mutual engagement are crucial elements. There are tensions between the need to transcend abusive relationality and the combating of intercultural transference of past and present colonial relations. A helpful theological metaphor for such healing, but not consuming relationships is Mayra Rivera's notion of the "touch of transcendence"[3] as mutual touch rather than encompassing grasp or complete detachment. Since the influence of colonial religions transcends the mere visible attendance of church services and explicit, official theological expressions, it is necessary also to look at how some of the unintended, and at times undesirable, effects of contact with colonial cultures interact.

The following creative adaptations may offer the potential to make connections with indigenous Christian expressions outside the colonial churches found in many different contexts, ranging from local prophetic movements to separate faith bodies.

Land and People: "The Sacred Place Where All Life Begins"[4]

The Caribou are God's way of giving us life. They are too sacred for self-interest. Politics is not in our (traditional) system. When the caribou migrate they use the energy of this planet. Now the energy is all screwed up. It is a matter of spirituality and the global environment. You can't rely on money out there, these are the cycles of nature. Without the cycle of life, without ANWR, the cycle of life is over, all for money.[5]

Alaska Natives were the first human inhabitants of the Americas. Some have distinct cultural ties with indigenous Siberians, having come across via Siberia and the Bering Strait from Eurasia.[6] Many of them have subsisted on coastal whaling and fishing, others are caribou, river and fish people. Athabascans, one of five distinct Alaska Native tribal groups, call themselves Dene, "the people," and are kin to Athabascans in Canada and the Navajo in the southwest of the United States, with whom they share linguistic and cultural features.[7] The modern history of Alaska is marked by periods of intensive resource

---

[3] Mayra Rivera, *The Touch of Transcendence: A Postcolonial Theology of God* (Louisville, KY: Westminster John Knox, 2007).

[4] In the Gwichin' dialect, "Gwats'an Gwandaii Goodlit", cf. http://gwichinsteeringcommittee.org/

[5] Gwich'in Native quoted in Standlea, *Oil, Globalization*, 113.

[6] See for example Walter R. Borneman, *Alaska: Saga of a Bold Land* (New York: Harper Collins, 2003), 18, Jared Diamond, *Guns, Germs, and Steel: The Fates of Human Societies* (New York: W. W. Norton & Company, 1997), 44–5, and Spencer Wells, *The Journey of Man: A Genetic Odyssey* (Journey of Man: Random House, 2002), 139–44.

[7] Karl W. Luckert, *The Navajo Hunter Tradition* (Tucson, AZ: University of Arizona Press, 1975), 9.

exploitation: first colonized in modernity by Russians, who traveled there for beaver skins, then sold to the United States, and mining when gold in the Yukon became a major attraction. The most recent resource exploitation concerns fossil fuels at Prudhoe Bay and the "opening up of ANWR". For decades environmentalists and the Gwich'in have fought the opening of the Arctic National Wildlife Refuge (ANWR) for petroleum exploitation.

The ancient calving grounds of the Porcupine Caribou herd of northeastern Alaska and northwestern Canada are known by several names, depending on who names them and what context and place they speak from. *Ivvavik* is an Inuvialut Gwich'in term for a "place for giving birth," and one might say that the story of this place is a real-time and real-space parable of the earth as an "ecosystem that does not know political boundaries,"[8] a nexus that reveals truths about our pasts, presents, and futures that are worth considering.

The Eskimos undeniably got a good deal in the Native Claims Settlement Act, but it was good only insofar as they agreed to change their way—to cherish money, and to adopt the concept (for centuries unknown to them) of private property. [. . .] The forest Eskimos' relationship with whites has made them dependent on goods that need to be paid for: nylon, netting, boat materials, rifles, ammunition, motors, gasoline.[9]

The particular form of "landgrab" that took place in Alaska was distinct from the expropriation processes witnessed in the "lower 48." In its own time the *Alaska Native Claims Settlement Act* (ANCSA) was hailed as the most liberal settlement ever achieved with Native Americans, granting large amounts of money and land to a new entity: native for-profit corporations.[10] Under the pressure of corporate presences desiring access to native lands, this treacherous settlement converted "native claims" to almost all land in Alaska into shares distributed among tribes for a limited time (i.e. shares of ownership in the corporations will not be passed down to descendants.) Thus, many tribes have been reorganized into for-profit corporations. Effectively, then many tribal entities are now structured as businesses, and in many cases tribal decision-making is as profit-driven as that of any other business corporation.

The direct impact of drilling for oil, oil production, and transportation (which are often conveniently left out of the calculation) are only a small fraction of what threatens earth habitat: the longer-range impact of global

---

[8] Borneman, *Alaska*, 534.

[9] John McPhee, *Coming Into the Country* (New York: Farrar, Straus, and Giroux, 1976), 34, 37.

[10] See an account of the history of ANCSA in John Strohmeyer, *Extreme Conditions: Big Oil and the Transformation of Alaska* (Anchorage, AK: Cascade Press, 1997); and a survey of native communities after ANCSA in Thomas R. Berger, *Village Journey: The Report of the Alaska Native Review Commission* (New York: Hill and Wang, 1985).

warming is also disproportionately affecting the Arctic, and Alaska, rendering this context an important location for people all over the world to watch and learn from. Indigenous peoples, or better, people of the land, and the land they want to continue to belong to, continue to be the miner's canary, of what happens when we disrupt our vital ties to the land to replace them with other forms of dependency and addictions. Modern myths of "independence" may in the end have served to enslave us even more thoroughly and far more tragically to machines, substances, and mindsets. The people of the land are, of course, not immune to the addictions imported by industrialized capitalist systems. This is the case for peoples of the Arctic around the world as the Arctic "has been transformed into the planet's chemical trash can, the final destination for toxic waste that originates thousands of miles away. Atmospheric and oceanic currents conspire to send industrial chemicals, pesticides, and power-plant emissions on a journey to the Far North."[11]

During a legislative hearing, former Alaska Senator Frank Murkowski infamously lifted up a white placard, arguing that the Arctic Refuge was nothing but this, most of the year: white, empty, nothing, useless. A tabula rasa, a *terra nullius*,[12] unused, and hence not to be preserved, waiting to be made "useful." Maps reveal the politics and ideology of the mapmaker. Other maps diverge. This place is far from useless in the mind map of the people of that land. Birthing place of the caribous, nesting place of many bird species that travel endless miles south and north during its winter, lichen that sustain the caribou. What happens if we lay these maps on top of each other rather than conveniently erase its details?

The debates on whether the Arctic Refuge—or really any place—is "pristine" shows a problematic use of the term, as well as a tendency to either/or logic that fails to correspond to meaningful senses of reality: If a place is not "pristine" then why resist fully exploiting and accessing it? If the native peoples are not fully "authentic" and "pristine" in their own lifestyles, why should one stop disrupting ecosystems and cultures? The linguistic power politics of purity often emerge around notions of "pristine" and "authentic." Pro-drilling discourse tactics can dispute the worthiness of protection by resorting to devaluing land and people as "empty, and people as inauthentic because they have adopted some modern ways of life, or have become dependent on the Alaska Permanent Fund, a dividend paid to Alaska residents due to oil money sloshing through the Alaska government. Pristine, no, but these silent pollutants highlight even more how much is at stake! Debates about purities of culture,

---

[11] Marla Cone, "Dozens of Words for Snow, None For Pollution," *Ode* Volume 3, Issue 9, (November 2005): 47.

[12] See also Whitney Bauman's essay on "Creatio ex Nihilo, Terra Nullius, and the Erasure of Presence" in eds., Laurel Kearns and Catherine Keller, *Ecospirit: Religions and Philosophies for the Earth* (New York: Fordham University Press, 2007) 353–72.

nature, and so forth, deftly cover up key issues at stake for the Gwich'in, as for many in more densely human population centers: How ought we to live within the place and time we find ourselves? How ought we to "use its resources rightly"[13] —neither destroy nor completely withdraw ourselves from them? And what do animals and people need to survive and thrive? Trying to find answers to these questions is where the debate becomes complicated and embattled. And it reveals many favorite myths, half-truths, lies, and assumptions, as well as great wisdom and reliable truths. To sift through them may not promise easy or final answers, but the debate itself reveals much that shows where the questions themselves may not yet be probing deep enough.

> The Arctic Refuge "war" takes on real and symbolic value of historic and global significance and needs to be understood in context of global (spatial) and historical (temporal) scales for its value as a precursor of events to come.[14]

Though David Standlea may here have overstated the global visibility and importance of the resource war around the Alaskan Arctic, it is certainly a "uniquely American environmental battle" and has, for many U.S. Americans, perhaps embodied the most visible and persistently recurring case of ideological clashes around environmental issues in decades, perhaps in the history of the United States.

The issues concerning the Arctic span a great distance. Oil, a local resource, is desired and embattled in contexts far beyond Alaska. Fossil fuel use has caused climate change, that is experienced disproportionately in Arctic regions, where its effects have been reported by indigenous Alaskans for decades. Each place on this planet is vitally connected to the Arctic which generates and sustains present climatic patterns and ocean currents. Continued dependency on oil not only endangers the local patterns of survivance and subsistence of the Gwich'in, in the larger scheme of things, but each ecosystem that is connected to the Arctic is at stake as well. Hence these two questions are related: What is at stake for the Gwich'in Athabascans in particular? What is at stake for those of us living in other places of the world?

The battle around the Arctic Refuge has become an endless struggle that reveals a number of issues crucial not only in the immediate context of Alaska. It takes place within a nation-state with aspirations to imperial unilateralism based on a capitalist system, whose "superior economic and military power" is fueled by the extraction of carbon-based fuels from increasingly endangered

---

[13] Form IV of the Prayers of the People, Holy Eucharist Rite II, *Book of Common Prayer* of the Episcopal Church USA, 388. New York: Church Publishing, 1979.

[14] Standlea, *Oil, Globalization*, 11.

locations.[15] Alaska's particular location and history make it an unusually clear example of a colony governed so as to facilitate land grab, then annexed into statehood to facilitate resource extraction, indigenous genocide, and more recently environmental cultural imperialism.[16] Global climate change has continued to threaten the resolve to keep the area protected, as it might become more accessible due to retreating ice. Meanwhile, the trans-Alaska pipeline is becoming more endangered as permafrost retreats and makes the foundation for the pipeline more fragile. The horrific spill from Deepwater Horizon in 2010 has brought the dangers of offshore oil exploration closer to home to many more, but the addiction to oil sits deep, and with it come many layers of denial. We only rarely realize how place matters in our lives. As Anne Daniell writes in her theology of place:

> If one of the reasons for engaging in theology is to better discern, appreciate, and learn ways of caring for that which is sacred in our lives, then places, as relational nexuses of which humans are a constitutive part, are an essential subject for theology.[17]

Hence, observing how some of the controversies around this particular place are framed, and which important themes and issues need to be included in mapping the struggle can inspire us to read, write, listen, pray, teach, and act more sustainably in the future. The fight of the Gwich'in to prevent oil drilling in a fragile environment shares several similarities with other struggles around land, ecosystems, and indigenous rights elsewhere in the world.[18] The Gwich'in are fighting for the land as for their lives, their culture, and its survival. The sacred, sacramental body of the caribou, for the Gwich'in, a major source of their life substance and energy, is endangered. Evon Peter, former chief of the Arctic Village Gwich'in, states:

---

[15] What is worse, for some Anglican Christians in former colonies, the confirmation of an openly gay and partnered bishop has seemed like another unilateralism on the part of the American Episcopal Church, rather than a concession to local theology and pastoral concerns.

[16] There are those who argue that this "war" is simply a skirmish to distract "liberals" from paying attention to what U.S. neoconservatives and oil industry lobbyists really want—tax breaks, energy subsidies, and anti-federal legislation—should that be the case, we have good cause to broaden the scope of our vision even more widely. Standlea lists Ralph Nader as one of those who have argued that "ANWR was a smokescreen and a brilliant strategy" to get to domestic oil and tax breaks. Nevertheless, especially given the need to see through a variety of smokescreens and greenwashing manoeuvers, the need to develop a wide-angle perspective on current and future resource wars becomes a great caveat. Standlea, *Oil, Globalization,* 68, 101.

[17] Anne M Daniell, "Incarnating Theology in an Estuary-Carnival Place: New Orleans in the Pontchartrain Basin," Ph.D. diss. (Madison, NJ: Drew University, 2005), 12.

[18] This is also suggested in Standlea's focused study on the Arctic Refuge: David M. Standlea, *Oil, Globalization, and the War for the Arctic Refuge* (Albany, NY: SUNY Press, 2006), 11.

The animals, the rivers—we're essentially a voice for things that cannot talk. We don't see ourselves as separate from those things. If the rivers and animals are poisoned, the poisons will work their way into us, too.[19]

Some have argued that the Christian identity of the Nets'aii Gwich'in of Arctic Village "represents communal *resistance* to colonial domination, as well as the ability to blend past and present traditions." When asked what could be done to support the Gwich'in in their struggle against drilling for oil and the protection of the Porcupine Caribou herd that is their lifeblood, the answer the Gwich'in gave was: Help us to restore our church.[20] Steven Dinero, a professor of human geography, who assisted the Gwich'in in rebuilding the historical Episcopal chapel in Arctic Village, states that "the degree to which Native Americans have embraced Christianity should not be constructed as acceptance of assimilation or willingness to participate in their own cultural destruction."[21] Beyond the distinctions of academia and faith commitments, people have come to understand that for the Gwich'in, the restoration of a church building that symbolizes part of their history, identity, and work of their ancestors, seemingly a submission to colonial influence, embodies in fact a part of their ability to maintain a core strength in their resistance to the stampedes of the footsoldiers of profit.

The story of Athabascan Episcopalians represents a fortuitous case of a more gentle inculturation, largely due to the particular charisma of the people involved. One resident of Arctic Village reports: "We were the last ones to be contacted by the so-called Columbus discovery [. . .] The Russians came from north, and the French from the south," but the remote Gwich'in semi-nomadic villages were encountered by Europeans only quite recently.[22] The Rev. Robert MacDonald began his missionary work in Alaska in 1862 and stayed there for 40 years. He studied the Gwich'in language, created an orthography using the Bible and the Book of Common Prayer, and thanks to him records of the language in its mid-nineteenth century form survive. He translated many hymns into Tadukh, the name he gave the language.[23] Using the vernacular to frame the message of the gospel greatly aided its adaptation by the Gwich'in. Sarah James, for example,

> still believes in the old ways, she says, carrying those fish in through the
> back door [. . .] and giving nearly ceaseless thanks to the land—but "now

---

[19] Evon Peter is a former chief of the Neetsaii Gwich'in from Arctic Village in northeastern Alaska and currently chairperson of Native Movement (nativemovement.org). Quoted on www.oilonice.org/toolkit/html/community.html

[20] Personal conversation with Bishop Mark MacDonald.

[21] Dinero, "The Lord Will Provide," 4.

[22] Rick Bass, *Caribou Rising: Defending the Porcupine Herd, Gwich'in Culture, and the Arctic National Wildlife Refuge* (San Francisco: Sierra Club Books, 2004), 60.

[23] Dinero, "The Lord Will Provide," 7.

I believe in the Episcopal church. Now I believe in Jesus. It teaches us good things we already practiced," she says, speaking of Christianity.[24]

The Rev. Albert Tritt, the first Nets'ai Gwich'in Episcopal priest and a resident of Arctic Village, was an indigenous evangelist who was very effective due to his knowledge of Athabascan culture and language. The chapel he built from 1910 to 1917 plays a central role in the village until today.[25] The former Bishop of Alaska, the Right Rev. Mark MacDonald has put himself in the midst of controversy between Euro-Episcopalians (some pro-, some anti- drilling) and tribal groups that either oppose or support drilling. It is largely through his initiative that the Episcopal Church in Alaska and later also the national body of the church has supported the Gwich'in in their struggles. In 2005, the Episcopal Church co-sponsored and cowrote a document on the issues at stake in the decision to drill or not to drill.[26] The church's standpoint meaningfully connects human rights issues with environmental issues, a helpful advancement over some environmental organizations' tendency to strive to preserve places without people.[27]

The poisoning of land and people will eventually affect all of us, even those who currently have a cocoon of privilege yet wrapped around them. Whether or not there will be drilling in the Arctic Refuge, the ecosystems of the Arctic have already been compromised significantly. There is no return to Eden, but there are possibilities for preserving broken and compromised landscapes and for working toward healing them and us together. The Arctic is a "wounded sacred" that recognizes its sustaining and healing capacity along with its compromised and endangered integrity as "degraded but still glorious, wounded but still alive."[28] Moving away from the romanticizing rhetoric of purity in much of the anti-drilling language, we need to understand that the "wounded sacred" is as much worth our love, care, and action as the fantasy of pristine lands, "untouched by human hand." Recognizing a place and a people (including ourselves!) as wounded and sacred does not give us permission to continue bringing about its degradation. In fact, the "wounded sacred" calls us even more to change our ways, so the entire ecosystem, humans included, can survive and flourish. The wounded sacred are also the

---

[24] Bass, *Caribou Rising*, 72.

[25] Dinero, "The Lord Will Provide," 12–13.

[26] Much of the content of this document is based on the UN Charter of Human Rights. Gwich'in Steering Committee, The Episcopal Church, and Richard J. Wilson, "A Moral Choice For the United States: The Human Rights Implications for the Gwich'in of Drilling in the Arctic National Wildlife Refuge" (2005), http://gwichinsteeringcommittee.org/GSChumanrightsreport.pdf.

[27] On this issue see also Aaron Sachs, *Eco-Justice: Linking Human Rights and the Environment*, Worldwatch Paper (Washington, DC: Worldwatch Institute, 1995).

[28] Wallace, *Finding God in the Singing River*, 145.

last small indigenous peoples holding out. One Sunday in Arctic Village, Rick Bass hears priest Trimble Gilbert preach:

> "We are the last people," he tells his congregation [. . .] "I hope you under-stand that. All the people with money are against us but we don't want to lose our culture.

> "Because we don't have money, they think we are a poor people." He speaks of the meek inheriting the Kingdom of God. "When the time comes, maybe we're goin' to be the ones who go first," he says, into that kingdom. "For sure, we try to save the earth."[29]

The real wealth here is not in money, but in the land, which will guarantee future survival for many generations ahead. Maintaining the integrity of the land, not temporally limited financial interests in what is extracted from it, is key for the Gwich'in. The wealth of the coastal plain, as Alaska's Serengeti, is not in the least diminished by the fact that it is populated by caribou only for a short time during the summer months, during the calving season, as some pro-drilling Alaska politicians have argued. The worth of the land cannot be measured by how "effectively" it is "used" by animals, humans, or others. Fallow time and winter time are the sabbaths of nature and the ancestors of all our cultures honored those. We fail to disrespect them today at the peril that the land will neither carry us, our descendants, nor its other inhabitants anymore. If this huge landscape is there for animals "only," then so be it. Barry Lopez suggests that

> the advantages of these dismal regions [. . .] are several. The number of predators is low, wolves having dropped away from the herds at more suit-able locations for denning to the south. Food plants are plentiful. And these grounds either offer better protection from spring snowstorms or experi-ence fewer storms overall than adjacent regions.[30]

Sacramental Time and Place

There's a prophecy, it's called voice from the north, there's gonna come a time when a voice from north is gonna rise. When that voice from the north rises, it signifies a time for human kind to change their ways. (Faith Gemmill, Gwich'in Steering Committee)[31]

---

[29] Bass, *Caribou Rising*, 60.
[30] Barry Lopez, *Arctic Dreams* (New York: Vintage Books, 1986), 169.
[31] As quoted on the site of Southwest Research and Information Center "Voices from the Earth," www.sric.org/voices/2005/v6n1/caribou.html

The time has come, the *kairos* is here. The Arctic places of the world, the regions of glaciers, permafrost, snow, wind, and ice, are changing. The people of those lands have said so for decades, before Western scientists were able and willing to acknowledge the reality of global warming. A large factor in climate change is a widespread, systemic dependency on carbon-based fuels to power infrastructure, industries, and homes across the world. Fossil fuels have been the main power source to fuel commerce at home and abroad. This energy does not come without severe costs for the places it is extracted from, transported to, refined at, and finally consumed. What are the implications for people of faith across the world? What visions of a different life do we need to empower changed action? How might a theology of Arctic place inform and affect theologies of place and action in contexts across the world?

The hotly embattled Arctic National Wildlife Refuge (ANWR) is a roadless, remote region in the "bush" of Alaska. The Arctic Refuge is located several hundred miles north of the city of Fairbanks. Some have argued that "the 1.5 million-acre coastal plain of the Arctic Refuge is the most fought-over chunk of wilderness in the world."[32] One main source of the opposition to drilling in the Arctic Refuge comes from indigenous Athabascans, the Gwich'in nation, in particular, who fear that fossil fuel exploitation will significantly impact the life and migratory patterns of the Porcupine Caribou herd, which is the foundation of their life and culture. They have been in contact with Anglican and Episcopal missionaries and priests since the 1860s and continue to affirm that affiliation as part of their tribal identity until today.[33] In 1988, the Gwich'in Steering Committee was formed to address the increasing threat to the coastal plain, the calving grounds of the caribou.

Under the leadership of the Right Rev. Mark MacDonald, Bishop of the Episcopal Diocese of Alaska, the Episcopal Church has supported its Gwich'in members in their fight for survival and subsistence at local, regional, and subsequently national levels. Indigenous peoples have responded to biblical messages as mediated by missionaries in a myriad of ways.

A theology of place takes form as a theopolitics[34] striving beyond imperial conditions. It knows its biblical traditions of prophecy, protest, and life of witness, listens to voices that represent the needs of land and people, witnesses to the unsustainability of ideologies, technologies, and lifestyles, and encourages needed changes of heart and hand. During travels within the Diocese of

---

[32] Ken Madsen, *Under The Arctic Sun: Gwich'in, Caribou & the Arctic National Wildlife Refuge* (Englewood, CO: Westcliffe Publishers, 2002), 174.

[33] See Steven C. Dinero, "'The Lord Will Provide': The History and Role of Episcopalian Christianity in Nets'aii Gwich'in Social Development—Arctic Village, Alaska," *Indigenous Nations Studies Journal* Vol. 4, No. 1. (Spring 2003): 7.

[34] As used by Catherine Keller in reference to theological interpretations of political actions in Catherine Keller, *God and Power: Counter-Apocalyptic Journeys* (Minneapolis, MN: Fortress, 2005), 55 et passim.

Alaska, and to native communities such as Arctic Village, I have been struck by how land, faith, economic, social, and ecological concerns are interwoven for Alaska Natives and other indigenous peoples, and how distinct, though not unrelated, their concerns are from their siblings in faith in other rural, but also in suburban and urban contexts. The challenges faced by the Athabascan Episcopalians that I encountered in Anchorage, Fairbanks, Minto, and Arctic Village manifest as "transdisciplinary," that is, there is not "one" problem that could be easily isolated and delegated to either scientists, social workers, environmentalists, or ministers and theologians. Rather, even upon casual observation a nexus of issues becomes visible for responses that necessitate a wide-ranging vision: the colonial heritage of missionary theologies and church bodies, the task of contemporary theological work in facing this heritage, the issues of economy and ecology as they intersect with culture-cide and ecocide, the survival of indigenous Episcopal Christians in a capitalist global culture that continues to mark native lands as "corporate sacrifice zones"[35] from where to exploit the fuel for globalization, the intransigence of fossil fuel dependency across cultures and societies, the lack of commitment to develop the viable alternatives, and find visionary ways for people to meaningfully combine a variety of ways of existing within a place.

When the problems we are confronted with are multi-compounded, our constructive proposals for theology, for faithful and determined action ought to be transdisciplinary as well. Such a nexus of issues might be mapped helpfully as the rhizome described by Deleuze and Guattari. Hence, the approach I am employing here is better conceived as a map fostering "connections between fields," removing the blockages and entering into the rootweb, through "multiple entryways."[36] A theopolitics then must look closely at the nexus of issues at hand, as best they can be discerned, indicate how theological questions and concerns are interwoven with the very fabric of this weave of life, and develop a vision for faith, thought, and practice.[37] It offers a rendering of what is spiritually, economically, and ecologically at stake in this particular place, outlines some key components of a theology of Arctic place, and shows how the ongoing controversy about the Arctic Refuge exposes the spiritual crisis of sustainable human life on this planet.

---

[35] Mark I Wallace, *Finding God in the Singing River: Christianity, Spirit, Nature* (Minneapolis, MN: Fortress, 2005), 57.

[36] Gilles Deleuze and Felix Guattari, *A Thousand Plateaus: Capitalism and Schizophrenia*, Brian Massumi, trans. and foreword (Minneapolis: University of Minnesota Press, 1987), 12.

[37] If we fail to look at problems like this by eliminating the false separations between economy, ecology, indigenous sovereignty and sustainability, colonial expansion of church and capitalism, we fail to grasp to address them adequately and fully, and we will fall short in crafting hopeful alternatives. I use the work of economists, ecologists, energy specialists, historians, and journalists who have all written extensively on the issues of oil, ecology, indigenous peoples, and Arctic Place.

Witnessing to Devastation as Transformative Mission: Contextual Bible Study in South Africa

Healing held a pivotal place in [Africans'] conceptions of power; apart from all else, it was the site, par excellence, of mediation between the human and the divine.[38]

Then and now, the question of medicine, healing, and power, is tightly intersected not only with the narratives of African religiosity but also with the biblical narratives that continue to shape European and African approaches to sickness and disease.[39] The intercultural confusion around the question of how healing and medicine were related to sacred power has many facets and a *Wirkungsgeschichte* as forked as the delta of the Nile.[40] These questions also concern the tangible effects of salvation, and the mediation of human and divine elements as understood through its psychosomatic effects. The ways in which healing, technology, medicine, salvation, and redemption are narrated and embodied in and between cultures speak of a signifying body that is expected to display, in some ways, evidence of salvation, physical or at least spiritual. This relationship between health, sickness, death, and healing is negotiated in complex ways among poor and rich people, between traditional healing and modern medicine. One of the sites of such negotiation is the work of the Ujamaa Centre at the University of Kwa-Zulu Natal in Pietermaritzburg.

The "open bible"[41] as a pervasive cultural presence can be employed to foster open conversations, voicing grief and lament, and to uncover oppression. An example of the combination of academic biblical studies and education for liberation can be found in the University of Kwa-Zulu Natal Ujamaa Centre's Contextual Bible Studies. Working with concepts like gender violence, suffering, HIV/AIDS, economic issues, the contextual Bible studies as offered by the Ujamaa Centre for Community Development at the University of KwaZulu-Natal in Pietermartizburg, South Africa, arose out of simple coincidence. In the aftermath of a massacre, staff from the School of Theology participated in interviewing some of the survivors and witnesses and recording their stories.

---

[38] John Comaroff and Jean Comaroff, *Of Revelation and Revolution: The Dialectics of Modernity on a South African Frontier,* Vol. 2 (Chicago, IL: Chicago University Press, 1997), 333.

[39] Theologians have thematized disability, stigma, and the construction of community, identity, and sacred power in relationship to able-bodiedness. See Nancy Eiesland, *The Disabled God: Toward a Liberatory Theology of Disability* (Nashville, TN: Abingdon Press, 1994) and Sharon Betcher, *Spirit and the Politics of Disablement* (Minneapolis, MN: Fortress, 2007).

[40] See for example Margaret Midgley, *Science as Salvation: A Modern Myth and Its Meaning* (New York: Routledge, 1992), Donna J. Haraway, *Modest_Witness@Second_Millennium. FemaleMan©_Meets_OncoMouse™* (New York/London: Routledge, 1997), 4.

[41] In contrast to the "closed bible" as cultural object of numinous power that is symbolic and powerful, but remains unread. See Gerald West, "Mapping African Biblical Interpretation: A Tentative Sketch," in: *The Bible in Africa: Transaction, Trajectories, and Trends,* 28–53 (Leiden: Brill, 2000), 48.

When asked about their own profession and told of their work with the Bible, they were invited to return because, the people said, the people said that they could not hear God's voice anymore. The creators of the biblical studies projects, among them Gerald West, talk openly about employing biblical texts in particular ways; far from value-free, these are texts chosen because they will free communities to talk about and name traumatizing dynamics within their communities as well as structural problems.

One Bible study, focused on the rape of Tamar (2 Samuel 13:1–22), thematizes rape, male exploitation, and complicity in silence and denial. Although the biblical narratives are "texts of terror," it is exactly that quality that allows women to articulate their own terror, to find their voices in response, naming and implicating those responsible and complicit in the biblical texts, as well as in their own context.

> Women felt that the story of Tamar was empowering because it was a story in the Bible and therefore could be used in the church and community to break the silence surrounding rape and abuse.[42]

The selected Bible passage, and the very carefully chosen questions, allow participants to explore violence and trauma via the authoritative text of the Bible. The fact that these stories are found in the Bible gives many of the participants a sense of authority to speak about difficult subjects in a space that legitimates their speaking. The polygynous past and its postcolonial reverberations are thus explicitly addressed, and voiced, reading the biblical text through a liberation hermeneutics. Thus, the liberative qualities of the biblical text, apart from its often problematic institutional representation and repressive use in various churches, can be unleashed. Texts of terror allow the naming of the terror, and proceed toward lament, and healing of soul, if not body. Often, community members feel especially empowered by unfamiliar texts outside of lectionary or common liturgical usage, such as the Tamar story, Job 3, and others.[43] In circumstances where the Bible is present as a cultural object, but distant in terms of its relation to life's circumstances, it was opened and given to the people, rather than authority figures. It spoke to them in ways that affirmed, not condemned them: "what had brought judgment, stigma and discrimination now brought healing, hope, and life."[44]

---

[42] Gerald West and Phumzile Zondi-Mabizela, "The Bible Story That Became A Campaign: The Tamar Campaign In South Africa (and Beyond)," *Ministerial Formation* Vol. 103 (July 2004): 5.

[43] Gerald West and Bongi Zengele, "The Medicine of God's Word: What People Living with HIV and AIDS Want (and Get) from the Bible," *Journal of Theology for Southern Africa* Vol. 125 (July 2006): 55.

[44] Ibid., 57, 58.

The Bible studies start with "community questions," which first manifest the "public transcript" and continue with "critical consciousness questions" that elicit some of the hidden transcripts resident within the community. Then, from there, beyond literary questions, the process moves to sociohistorical questions. The Bible study, though constructed consciously by biblical scholars to allow for a liberative discussion of difficult topics, gives ample space for regular people to engage with the biblical texts before leading to the concerns that biblical scholars would have to offer to the conversation.

> Equally importantly, by waiting for the questions to arise from the participants, we can be sure that we are answering questions of interest to them rather than questions of interest to us biblical scholars (on which the industry of biblical scholarship is based).[45]

The last question opens a space for immediate reaction: "What will you do now in response to this Bible Study?" Particularly powerful in this model of biblical reading is the cooperation of "ordinary" and "scholarly" interpreters working together. The Bible studies move between community consciousness and critical consciousness, combining critical and community consciousness. Each Bible study begins and ends with community consciousness.

By doing Bible studies focused on a generative concern from the context, and engaging in continued reflection and action about where the community wants and needs to go next, the Ujamaa Centre has produced a number of different Bible studies. Sharpened by trial and error, they enable a transformative practice that can raise consciousness; in a Freirian sense it is education for emancipation. CBS employs the "See-Judge-Act method."[46] As reality shifts, the see-judge-act hermeneutical feedback loop shifts.

By 1997, the HIV/AIDS pandemic was reaching catastrophic levels in South Africa. Ujamaa felt a need to get involved with the issue of HIV/AIDS, but felt it was important to receive a "call" from the community. It came in the form of an invitation from Edendale Drop-In-Centre in Pietermaritzburg. Black women were the first to come in and named the group *Siyaphila*, Zulu for "We are well" or "We are alive."[47] The name itself expresses resistance to a society that treated them as unwell, if not already dead. The group founded itself and now is a movement with local full and part-time staff. For most people, free clinics are the first stop if one is unwell; if you're middle class you go to your doctor. The clinics are not a formal health care system, but will treat everybody for free. They are also a place for people to talk and pray. The Pietermaritzburg clinic has become somewhat of a model for other places in

---

[45] West and Zondi-Mabizela, "Tamar Campaign," 8.
[46] West and Zengele, "The Medicine of God's Word," 55.
[47] Ibid., 52.

South Africa. Contextual Bible Study (CBS) functions as part of a whole, as a form of therapy that can help build resilience. CBS provides a theology—assuring the solidarity of Jesus to those suffering from HIV/AIDS.

Gerald West tells of somebody sick with AIDS asking, "Why should I not kill myself?" and responding to them that Job asks for God to take or erase his life, but never talks about taking his own life (Job 3). Rather, Job continues to feel what he is feeling and is given the space to articulate his anger over and over again. God is angry at the friends, not at Job. God can bear the anger of a suffering person. The text provides a vocabulary to express repressed "negative" emotions, which are not easily expressed directly to God in a context of evangelical piety. The text allows venting of anger against God without feeling guilty or judged. It ends with exhaling and breathing, so that the lamentations become liturgical expression.

Siyaphila is firmly in the control of women. Many patriarchal patterns continue to be deeply ingrained in the culture, including anticolonial conspiracy theories of AIDS itself being a Western conspiracy. HIV/AIDS provides an X-ray of South African society,[48] of its precolonial patriarchal polygynous society, its colonial and apartheid economic exploitations, and post-Apartheid afterlives. Like an X-ray, the hidden dynamics in Mark 3, Jesus brings the sick person to the center of the community where the Torah is. Too often, people talk about the sick as if they do not exist, and cannot speak for themselves. The people at the Ujamaa Centre became increasingly frustrated and angry when they saw that the churches were rejecting sick people. Like Jesus, they felt anger at the judgmental attitudes of the religious authorities towards the plight of the poor. In the text in Mark, Jesus and the disciples are in the boat, with Jesus asleep, and a storm comes up. The storm is raging, but Jesus remains asleep, unaware of the threat and the anxiety. Sometimes, the people felt, God is with you, but as if asleep.[49] Colonial texts and biblical studies are engaged as co-learners, learning and teaching from below.

How might these examples inform a changing sense of mission and soteriology? Given the multiplicity of metaphors that have traditionally been employed to try to circumscribe or circumambulate redemption, the impossibly complex processes and events imagined and associated with mission and conversion, how might we conceptualize salvation, within a panoply of immensely and often uncomfortably diverse inculturations and localizations of "the gospel"? Is one of the preconditions of "redemption"—observing it through the lens of this fundamentally economic concept—about being called to be free to be

---

[48] Cf. Jon Sobrino's suggestion that a catastrophe serves as an X-ray of a society, revealing its real nodes and links of power rather than being, as routinely is suggested, a form of divine punishment. Jon Sobrino, *Where is God? Earthquake, Terrorism, Barbarity, and Hope* (Maryknoll, NY: Orbis, 2004), 3.

[49] West 2003, emerging from Bible study on the Solidarity of Jesus: Mark 3.

who we are, without repression of our religiocultural identities, without the repression of elements of resident and Christian cultural patterns that keep us from being so, while keeping open the possibility for mutual transformation?

Works Cited

Betcher, Sharon. *Spirit and the Politics of Disablement*. Minneapolis, MN: Fortress, 2007.

Bhabha, Homi. *The Location of Culture*. London/New York: Routledge, 1994.

Comaroff, John. and Jean Comaroff. *Of Revelation and Revolution: The Dialectics of Modernity on a South African Frontier, Vol. 2*. Chicago, IL: Chicago University Press, 1997.

Eiesland, Nancy. *The Disabled God: Toward a Liberatory Theology of Disability*. Nashville, TN: Abingdon Press, 1994.

Haraway, Donna J. *Modest_Witness@Second_Millennium.FemaleMan©_Meets_OncoMouse™*. New York/London: Routledge, 1997.

Kearns, Laurel, and Catherine Keller. *Ecospirit: Religions and Philosophies for the Earth*. New York: Fordham University Press, 2007.

Lopez, Barry. *Arctic Dreams*. New York: Vintage Books, 1986.

Midgley, Margaret. *Science as Salvation: A Modern Myth and Its Meaning*. New York: Routledge, 1992.

Rivera, Mayra. *The Touch of Transcendence: A Postcolonial Theology of God*. Louisville, KY: Westminster John Knox, 2007.

Sobrino, Jon. *Where is God? Earthquake, Terrorism, Barbarity, and Hope*. Maryknoll, NY: Orbis, 2004.

West, Gerald. and Bongi Zengele. "The Medicine of God's Word: What People Living with HIV and AIDS Want (and Get) from the Bible." *Journal of Theology for Southern Africa* Vol. 125 (July 2006): 51–63.

West, Gerald, and Phumzile Zondi-Mabizela. "The Bible Story That Became A Campaign: The Tamar Campaign In South Africa (and Beyond)." *Ministerial Formation* Vol. 103 (July 2004): 4–12.

Chapter 8

Holding Patterns

Fractal Iterations

When life is in transit, in a holding pattern, things are changing within and around. Such complexity is best approached with a flexible, but resolute epistemology. Holding patterns then means to hold patterns we think we may have recognized in an open palm, lightly and not in a stranglehold, are crucial in such situations. Remaining open to the touch of transcendence in immanence in each moment precludes holding too tightly what cannot be held other than in a wide space. The purpose of naming a number of patterns here is not to claim a grasp on the situations or occurrences described, not to provide answers, but rather to sketch certain cross-cultural, cross-temporal, and cross-geographic similarities in difference. Not unlike what we find in chaos theory, where fractals are repeated at different scales and with different repetition rates, a number of patterns can be recognized. As in chaos theory, what we find often hovers between solidly defined forms of chaos and order, teetering on the edge of chaos, as repetition in difference.[1] In these unruly patterns, we might discern certain rhythms, certainly not harmonies, that allow moving with and around the iterating flow and friction of patterns, rather than simply being subsumed into them, or fighting a losing battle against them. Perhaps there even beckons an epiphany or two.

Cultures are enriched, destabilized, and transformed through a variety of intercultural dynamics that have different effects and are experienced in different ways. As go-betweens, missionaries, travelers, and traders bring to consciousness questions about the generative forces of life and community. Trade in materials, goods, technologies of self and community engages spirit and matter, the many layers of life and often generates tensions between desires to access material goods and negotiating it with the spiritual goods of the "good news." The losses incurred within these exchanges can be unfathomable. They extend to life, livelihood, land, and identity. The colonial impact, as a mate-

---

[1]   Catherine Keller, *Face of the Deep* (New York/London: Routledge, 2003), 168–9.

rial and a spiritual regime, often disrupts the local logic in profound ways, denigrating, disregarding, and supplanting previous lifeways.

There is no one way in which such dynamics occur. At times this theological logic is enforced and part of the civilizing mission. At other times, local populations use pieces of this logic in creative adaptations that do not simply repeat the intent to civilize but actively engage features that strengthen survival and flourishing. Sometimes the logic of the oppressor is mimicked; in more rare cases, the gospel is understood as a force that opposes colonial dynamics and economic regimes. Most forms of this negotiation constitute blends between assimilation and subversion, constantly being recalibrated for different spaces and times.

Itinerant Idiosyncracies

It has been said that "the past is another country where things are done differently [and in which even] the best interpreters still remain biased strangers."[2] If the past is a different country, the past *in* a different country is doubly so. Many encounter past and present differences as upsetting and explosive, as dangerous memory, as much as the comfort and sustenance of ancestral knowledge. Indeed, actual engagement with a different culture can resemble playing the game "Minesweeper" on a computer. In most instances of playing the game, it is a matter of time *when* the "bomb" goes off, rather than *whether* it will explode. When we step on sacred ground, insult a person, take liberties that offend, refuse to pitch in, or do too much, talk too much or too little, are too careless, barge into events or spaces not open to us, think we should have access everywhere, think people should trust us right off the bat, while we ourselves may reserve not to trust them, and so forth, we are stepping on hidden landmines. Some hosts will just smile and we may never know we offended, but others will be happy to let us know.

During my stay at *Te Rau Kahikatea*, the Māori *tikanga* at St. John's Seminary in Auckland, I involuntarily infringed upon Māori *tapus*. I did not realize this had happened until I was called to task for it. I felt stuck between the tension of the duties of a guest not to offend and the impossibility of knowing how to avoid offense in the absence of the information I needed to avoid doing so. This, too, appears as a common issue in intercultural relations: the reality of offense, often unconsciously due to adhering to one's own culture's assumptions, is close to unavoidable and will be bound to happen, especially if there is a cultural taboo or unwillingness to orient newcomers explicitly to a code of

---

2   The quote slightly modifies the opening line of English novelist L. P. Hartley's novel *The Go-Between*, which is: The past is another country: they do things differently there. As quoted in John Comaroff and Jean Comaroff, *Ethnography and the Historical Imagination* (Boulder, CO: Westview Press, 1992), 14.

encounter. At best, one can liken it to learning a complex circle dance. First we may observe, sway with the music, get a feel for the movement, then imitate the movements, then join into the dance, needing to pay attention to our own movements and those of the other persons, in a way that preserves both their space and ours. There is never a guarantee against bumping into each other or stepping on each other's toes, breaking each other's stride. Despite the dangers of encounter and the seeming ease disengagement may tempt us with, we are daily knit into a tight, often scripted dance of global relations, and dance we must, with as much skill and care as we can muster.

Given human contextuality, it is impossible to report about other people's practice without "reading from this place," namely our own. Different interpreters display different levels of bias, reading skills, and abilities to conceptualize and represent other cultural practices. Things get lost in representation and translation and the danger of overlaying the terms of one's own cultural context on others is a constant threat to intercultural communication and negotiation.

When encountering difference, most people will try to frame and fit what they perceive into their known and existing frameworks. Whether missionaries are trying to conceptualize ethnic groups new to them in biblical terms in Christian historiography as the "lost tribes," or whether—as Navajo, upon encountering horses and sheep imported by settlers, adjust their creation stories to mark them as created by the Holy People of the Four Corners of Navajoland—claims about including and integrating what previously was not known in one's own logic of existence are made. Even as the power differential allows some of these integrative accounts to achieve dominance, and marks others as curiosities, similar epistemological dynamics seem to persist. In other words, the adaptation of other cultural knowledge, information, or materials is not only a colonial practice, but a hermeneutic practice of adaptive integration of knowledge resulting in culturally hybrid narrativity, engaging with the strangeness of the past and present and making it more familiar.

The question of knowledge generation, acquisition, and claims for primary validity has great importance in missionary encounters, both for indigenous and missionary interlocutors. What is the proper form of education, who oversees it, what community holds and informs this education, what are the goals, what should be learned, by which means and through what systems of generating, ordering, and disseminating knowledge? The question of knowledge, with knowing one's identity and belonging (as a Christian, as a Jew, as Maori, or Zulu, for example), also informs thinking about salvation, especially when salvation is linked by missionaries to conscious conversion and most likely some form of cognition, adopted narrativity, self and communal identity. Within the variety of polydox senses of postcolonial mission it may be important to rethink conversion as a process of conscious, embodied reasoning, feeling, and acting. It is crucial to ponder the relational axes of conversion with thinking, practice, and ritual, its processual quality, and its continued possibility for accommodating multiple religious belongings, including the relationship between ritual action and internal affirmation of contents of faith or cultural knowledge.

Forgotten Crossroads

It is easy to underestimate the degree to which trade, exchange, and religious practice interpenetrated each other over the course of history. Some of these connections are simply no longer known historically, others are being unearthed anew. Few are aware, for example, that a Buddha statue found its way to Denmark in the so-called dark ages,[3] highlighting our forgetfulness of intercontinental travel and the resulting self-centered assumptions in claiming that only now, after "modernity" we live in a "global" age. While it is likely that few ancient persons other than local elites had access to precious goods and cultural knowledge from afar, such trade connections stretch back far longer than we commonly imagine. People traveled and migrated widely across the Pacific and across the Atlantic Oceans tens of thousands of years before modernity. Transfer of technology and trade were common in many societies. Over time, the roles of colonizer and colonized often changed.

The forgetfulness of ancient crossroads can contribute to the generation of self-serving historiographies that highlight in particular one's own cultural contributions, and, perhaps quite naturally, see one's own culture at the center of the world, as the benchmark of comparison, and as having invented things that were in fact gifts or adaptations from other cultures. This dynamic can bolster binary thinking, where one's own culture constitutes one extreme and either one's own past or the past or present of other presumably distinct groups are cast as the opposite extreme.

Negotiating Similarity and Difference

The comparison of different human experiences is as common as it is problematic, especially at the intersection of culture and religion. When expected patterns are not found or recognized, the seeming absence of a practice, concept or structure can lead to erroneous claims about their absence or meaning. Colonial travel literature can claim that a certain group of indigenous peoples seemingly has "no religion," but quite likely such statements remark on the absence of something that corresponds to Christianity in particular, especially before the term religion was employed to religious practices other

---

[3]   Peter S. Wells, *Barbarians to Angels: The Dark Ages Reconsidered* (New York: W. W. Norton & Company, 2008), 126, 144.

than the direct successor to Roman "religio." Hence, this contextual claim may be more usefully transcribed as "these people do not practice Christianity in ways we recognize."

Missionaries in particular can tend toward "false parallels"[4] such as attempting to link the doctrine of atonement for sin and notions of payment, reparation, to the Maori practice of *utu*, thereby providing "easy illusions" of similarity that become hardened and resistant to revision past the first impressions upon which they were founded. The overdetermination by patterns from one's home culture and familiar theological concepts can affect the representation of ideas of others in such a way that they become deeply obscured.[5] Ethnographers and missionaries can, as in the case of Io in Maori creation narratives, and also potentially in the case of the postulation of a Zulu "supreme deity," plant quasi-equivalents of Christian concepts in the host culture. At times it becomes impossible to try to untangle what became entangled. It occurs with some degree of frequency that persons arguing for the indigeneity of a particular notion or theological concept include the "planted" elements in their articulation of indigeneity. At times, persons may assume access to "pure" indigenous practices long after contact, despite the attendant inability to determine with any degree of security what may constitute precolonial practice. This can be a function of a politics of recognition, with the impetus to be recognized as legitimate in the eyes of the colonial Christian representation. More resistant to fashioning oneself in the panopticon of the "colonial Christian observer," it becomes a consciously and admittedly constructive adaptation between cultures, admitting the developmental shifts in theological expression, both within traditional Christianity and its successive iterations. Such processes are reminiscent of the production of *logos* theology in early Christianity and its creative adaptation from Stoic sources and Philo of Alexandria. One might then ask why it should matter whether Io was adopted later into Maori cosmology, if it seemed to fit well enough and filled a gap in explanation, as did logos theology. Is the fact that it was, possibly inadvertently, "planted'" sufficient grounds to dismiss it as problematic, because it does not fit a sense of historic originality? Ironically, then, claims for originality represent a function of historicism rather than respecting the subversive potential of adaptation. Such creative friction in adaptation is less concerned about originality than engaging in bricolage, using the means at hand, no matter what their provenance. Even if the first articulation of a creative adaptation was a strategy of legitimation within a changing cultural scheme, and thus potentially polemic and apologetic, other versions of these shifts articulate the

---

[4]   Judith Binney, *The Legacy of Guilt: A Life of Thomas Kendall* (Wellington: Bridget Williams Books, 1968), 83, 128.

[5]   Ibid., 128.

constant changes and developments of theological expressions and its creative, integrative shape.

Certainly, the kinds of claims attached to such adaptation vary, and at times
reconstruct cultural authenticity, as for example the integration of sheep and
horses into Navajo creation narratives and claiming indigenous authenticity
for Athabascan fiddling. This technique may not be unlike ancient storytellers integrating elements of the book of Genesis to resonate with the themes of
creation stories of Babylon. Storytellers and theologians improvise upon their
themes engaging questions of sacred ethnogenesis: the narratives show concern with what constitutes the group, what allows life to flourish, what phases of
transition and learning have been passed through. They recount the deeds of
ancestors, how they inform the present, and the ambivalent acts that occur on
the way of a community's travels to finding, losing, and keeping their place of
life and way of life. We hear about arrangements made with difficult neighbors,
wars being fought, the management of gender relations, and how divine agency
moves people through space and is involved in negotiating space. Sometimes
divinity features as central to space negotiations, sometimes marginal to the
narrative. Sometimes ideologies are hard to distinguish from what might be
dedication. Many biblical narratives articulate the tension between the tribal
focus of the divine-human relationship and care for creation beyond one
region. In indigenizing biblical narrativity, people often reinscribe the narrative upon their local landscape, overlaying geography with additional meaning.
This allows a people to move with meaning through sacred itineraries.

Similar patterns might be discerned in the phenomenon of cargo cults,
which integrate information from Christian theological narratives with the
hitherto unknown material goods and technologies brought by missionaries
and traders in the terms of local culture. Cargo cults appear to be especially
prominent where Christian faith and practice is introduced along with a great
deal of "cargo" that constitutes new materials, material practices, or technology. Thus, cargo is not understood as "secular" but as spiritually imbued materials that affect the lifeworld spiritually and materially. Cargo cults strive to
make sense of their religiocultural power, their material and spiritual effects
on daily acts and relationships between colonizer and colonized. They engage
the question of what the commitment of the divine to the local people may be,
and why it is that other peoples have so apparently been blessed with "cargo."
The "theodicy" question here becomes the question of why it is that the divine,
or the ancestors, have withheld or given goods to some, but not others. That
is, these could be seen as questions concerning "divine economy," or salvation
history (and indeed perhaps be informed by missionaries or other colonial
presences) within a sacred cosmos, and the distribution of blessings and things
within it. Cargo cults might then offer a sacred narrative that explains the
world as it is now, why distributions of power are as they are, or what has to
occur to set these injustices right.

Some of the more solid difficulties in missionary encounters have been the negotiation of resident polytheisitic and animistic senses of the world with a colonially formed and expressed monotheism. There are instances of polytheistic imperial ideologies such as Babylon, Egypt, Greece, and Rome, where the integration of local deities into a polytheistic pantheon was a way to organize and solidify a growing empire on the level of sacro-political governance,[6] indicating that empire and polytheism are not necessarily exclusive to each other. Christian imperialism, on the other hand, has sought to combine religious and political "monotheism," and generally advocated a replacement over an additive approach to deities. Biblical texts are marked by the strife between local polytheisms and a tribal deity writ large and eventually transformed into an imperial monolatry.

Many of the dynamics of encounter, observed in these pages, could be characterized as a blend between partial adaptation and partial rejection: rejecting the colonial church, but claiming Christianity for oneself and one's community. This is echoed in many postcolonial church settings. Indigenizing movements make space and create religious movements that combine elements from each religioculture to form something that can bridge the gap for the community it serves, at times only for a certain segment and a certain time period. Moses and Abraham have been key figures around whom communities have articulated heritage, identity, and power. Thus, inherited interpretations of a text are both honored, repeated, dislodged, and reclaimed by readers, who both assimilate and resist their antecedents.

Christian faith arrives embodied in a variety of accommodations, political, linguistic, cultural, and economic, translated into new technologies of writing, narrating, and forming subjects. Within Near Eastern and Mediterranean cultures the main deities are male. When polytheisms feature female and male deities, many of them arranged in complementary couples, reduce all powers into one deity, that deity is most often male, and the more the feminine images of the divine are either erased, subsumed, or subordinated, the more starkly male the monotheistic deity becomes, and the greater the loss of feminine religio-cultural imagery.[7] When female ancestors and female deities are repressed, so are the women in society as roles of honor and pride are lost. Imperial monotheism appears to have had this effect both in converting pagans in Northern Europe and in modern colonial missionary encounters.

The global resurgence of indigenous and pagan spiritualities may also have to do with the return of the repressed feminine divine that could not

---

[6] Jan Assmann, *Of God and Gods: Egypt, Israel, and the Rise of Monotheism* (Madison, WI: University of Wisconsin Press, 2008).

[7] Gro Steinsland, "Fra Yggdrasils Ask Til Korsets Tre—Tanker Om Trosskiftet," in *Fra Hedendom Til Kristendom: Perspektiver På Religionsskiftet i Norge*, ed. Magnus Rindal (Oslo: Ad Notam Gyldendal, 1996), 24.

be accommodated in classical theisms focused on an all-male trinity.[8] Some inhabitants of post-Christian societies may have repressed this loss of identity, having internalized the missionary logic that in conversion theirs was only gain and not loss. But as so often happens, the repressed returns, perhaps also through a fascination with "exotic" indigenous peoples, their histories, languages, and stories. May the longing for a "noble savage" also provide a mirror on European pre-Christian pasts, manifesting a longing filling its emptiness with cultural contraband? With colonial prosthesis?

We are left to wonder what may have been different if the forms of Christianity adopted and within the range of possible polydoxy, had been more open to sacred sites, and if their elemental fullness in water, earth, air and fire, and had been more open to women's embodied and ancestral sacrality, and a sense of immanent divine? What might it mean to encourage, within the established church bodies, to integrate, and retradition lost and dismissed locations and the traditions attached to them? What might it mean to not just allow but further the "resacralization of place"[9] in both locations that have to be involved in decolonization: colonized and colonizers alike? Is the strong increase of pilgrimages one—circumambulating—way of retracing the steps of the ancestors, a way that is perhaps not focused so much on iterating contents of the faith apart from the world of senses, of travel, of numinous space, encountering in landscape and fellow travelers also the divine in grace-filled entangled reciprocity? Such pilgrimages will not be cushy package deals, keeping us close to the known tourist traps, but include some uneven terrain, lost turns, and plenty of questionable characters. The sacred is never safe. For every Egeria and Helena there are a gaggle of the pilgrims of the Canterbury Tales, rude, self-interested, lusty, conceited, greedy, fallible, exposing the foibles, hypocrisies, and prides of their guilds, status, and societies. They, too, make up the panoply of polydox expressions of Christian religiocultures.

Multiple religious belongings constitute a significant reality also among church members who find the sacred in many places: in Buddhist meditation, in yoga classes, in Rumi's poetry.[10] This marks another realm of the polydox, a more generous sense of orthodoxy, less obsessed with tight boundary controls and policing perceptions of divine power. A more capacious sense of the Christian divine may both de-exoticize other religious options and re-exoticize Christianity's own wild spaces. Stretching beyond the atrophies of Roman traditionalisms and Protestant dogmatisms, themselves localized but often encrusted options we may yet see a shift in retraditioning, resacralizing

[8]   See, for example, Jone Salomonsen, *Enchanted Feminism: The Reclaiming Witches of San Francisco* (New York: Routledge, 2002).

[9]   Lisbeth Mikaelsson, "Locality and Myth: The Resacralization of Selja and the Cult of St. Sunniva," *Numen* Vol. 52 (2005): 191.

[10] See Catherine Cornille, *Many Mansions: Multiple Religious Belonging and Christian Identity* (Maryknoll, NY: Orbis, 2002).

and readapting Christian faith and practice in both the North and the South, gaining rather than losing integrity. Between the stale localizations of the past and the pressure to assimilate into more easily consumable religious options, where might the difficult ways of resolute creative adaptation lie? What friction is productive, what merely destructive?

Claiming Ancestry, Translating Power

The tenuous relationship of Christians to Jews and Judaism has informed, in multiple ways, their encounter with actual Jews as well as peoples "new" to them. Jews continued to be highly prized converts living among Christians, and the patterns of relationality with them inform colonial missionary relations. Many missionaries perceived a special affinity between tribal peoples and the Israelites of the Hebrew scriptures, and saw commonalities in their "primitive qualities." This comparison can be leveraged in a variety of ways, depending on what the assessment of the Israelites is in the theological shape of the missionary's framework and its reception within the indigenous framework. Some Maori prophetic movements made a point to counter and reject the claims of the missionaries through their reading of the gospel of John and associating themselves with "the Jews" that reject Jesus' claim to cultural authority. They saw themselves as the people of the land, resisting the claims of a European Christ, parallel to the ways in which some Jews resisted Jesus' messianic claim, perhaps as a claim foreign to their cultural self-understanding.[11]

When one translates, especially in a language that does not have a long tradition of interaction with one's resident language and the biblical languages, unforeseen associations render polysemy profoundly dynamic and unpredictable, with sometimes comical, but often serious consequences. Missionaries may find that candidates for translation of theological terms will present them with wanted and unwanted resonances that continue to have hermeneutic trickster effects. The history of a term is carried forward into translation, where its repressed meanings can reassert themselves beyond conscious control.

The transition from oral to textual cultural expressions of narrativity brings with it a number of epistemological and hermeneutical issues, involving questions of anamnesis and the processes involved in it. Walter Ong argues that oral cultures have to be more "literalist" in order to maintain coherence of a canon of narrativity, potentially limiting quite strictly the

---

[11]   See R. S. Sugirtharajah, *The Bible and the Third World: Precolonial, Colonial, and Postcolonial Encounters* (Cambridge: Cambridge University Press, 2001), 128.

variations among different storytellers.[12] Indeed, there is evidence that certain forms of oral knowledge and content are deeply difficult to transform, and can, in certain settings, be more resistant to transformation than even a written text. Or, the two modes of "writing" and remembering are combined in a way that heightens the effect by generating a strangely static moment: Thus, missionaries in Aotearoa/New Zealand reported that certain Maori took a certain set of biblical injunctions rather literally, at least in the eyes of the missionaries, while completely ignoring others. Certainly, the same could be said about colonial interpreters and their selective hermeneutics. Some Zulu pointed out that humans were encouraged to wear animal skins and considered their British interlocutors disobedient to this commandment, while the hide-wearing Zulu found easy resonance with their own practices. On the other hand, not eating shellfish would have been inconceivable for Maori and against their own cultural practice. There can be cohesion between taking practices and beliefs compatible with the receiving culture particularly seriously, while overlooking and resisting others, and certainly, this dynamic between recognition and blind spots is not exclusive to any particular culture.[13]

Neutralitas Non Valet In Regno Dei—There is No Neutrality in the Reign of God

Colonial societies for a number of reasons did not provide a very encouraging environment for the development of missionary Christianity among indigenous peoples.[14]

Missionary encounters have often been situated in sociopolitically complex sites. All sides have to negotiate claims to validity across the religiocultural spectrum: thereby, these encounters get invariably caught up in political and economic power struggles that heighten when settler populations arrive or compete with indigenous residents that were the first ones to enter into the "long conversation" between missionaries and local people.

---

[12] Walter Ong, *Orality and Literacy: The Technologizing of the Word* (New York: Routldedge, 1982), 41–2.

[13] Postcolonial biblical scholar R. S. Sugirtharajah offers helpful tags for commonly employed hermeneutical methods within colonial contexts, including examples that show how common and consistent some of them are. Dissident and resistant readings, nativist (some of the indigenous prophetic movements and indigenous churches), liberationist and postcolonial approaches. Sugirtharajah, *The Bible and the Third World*, Chapters 6 through 8.

[14] Allan Davidson, "The Interaction of Missionary and Colonial Society in Nineteenth Century New Zealand," *Studies in World Christianity* Vol. 2, No. 2 (1996): 155.

The relations sought out by missionaries in their attempts to make contact with potential converts varied. Persons of a certain social status often were preferred sites of connection. It was often assumed that going to "the leader" of a community would result in a kind of "trickle down effect," and at least a nominal communal conversion. At times the conversion of persons tied into a strong communal network could only be significantly affected by directly challenging the local power structure and its cohesion; at others, missionaries were dependent on the support of local leaders. Community leaders did eventually have to be engaged, in some way, as some of the claims made by missionaries touched upon the logic and practices that held the community together. At other times, when a community was intact and seemed impenetrable to missionaries, they focused on persons that had been marginalized for the one or other reason within those communities. In Central and Northern Europe, Christian missionaries aimed to convert chiefs, royalty, and nobles, who found through Christianity access to literacy and education. Some of the same strategy is later exported with colonial missions, and, as some missionary historians have pointed out, evokes comparison of the involved intercultural dynamics in the various contexts.

Missionaries often had to negotiate sites of economic survival for themselves, within dynamics of local tribal authorities. Questions of loyalty are raised almost immediately, sites of friction appear in the fragile places of boundary renegotiation. Missionaries and local interlocutors in their relating may stress and fray other relations and loyalties. Missionaries inadequately educated and insufficiently supported by their sending agencies must find other ways to sustain themselves, but may lose social standing and social capital (e.g., *mana*) in the process, which impacts their effectiveness as missionaries.

Kendall's greed and insensitivity, his theological crisis and isolation compromised his ability to engage in a mutual mission. Colenso's advocacy for the Zulu, though in a paternalistic key, and his attempt to use new theological resources to address the theological problems resulting from encounters that took Zulu cultural experiences seriously, led to his condemnation as a heretic.

How does the desired access to goods and technologies, to "cargo," structure the exchanges between divine and material goods? What constitutes the "economic" friction of power-laden exchanges between those engaged in negotiating such sites? The negotiation of the other's culture occurs necessarily with a limited understanding thereof, couched in a number of layers that impact the encounter: social status, colonial status, gender/sexuality, ethnic and cultural expressions, marital status, education, ability to function interculturally, personal characteristics, theological and conceptual understandings as communally enforced and personally represented, and abilities to transmit them in effective ways.

The Psychopathologies of Post/Colonial Intercultural Encounter and "The Healing of Nations"

Local interlocutors renegotiate their religiocultural identity between local and imported knowledges. Depending on their social location in the local society, loss of cultural connection threatens, or beckons with the promise of increased belonging, personal and social fulfilment in a new religious community. Sometimes orphans, women, or lower caste individuals find themselves able to access more expansive spaces, while at the same time risking the loss of cultural heritage and the fraying of social relationships. The presences of settler and military colonial presences heightens the friction and may add the threat of the crushing of body and spirit, the dismantling of indigenous self-sustainability and independence from colonial law, the imposition of new forms of labor and its division, the depropriation of communally inhabited and managed land toward the English common law's notion of private property of land, resources, and goods. The destruction and deconstruction of the particular link between place, community, and religious inhabitation of these spaces by a community leads to a variety of intersecting postcolonial conditions that can generate serious psychosocial dysfunctions, as well as opportunities for the painful, struggling regeneration of personal and communal identity. The efficiency of healing practices in local and missionary culture can have a striking effect on conversions, whether or not the efficiency of healing practices is due to faith healing or to medicinal techniques.

Colonial trauma in soul and society does not always easily accommodate calm complexity as injured selves and communities may tend toward more polarized political positions that do not hold up on closer examination. Yet, there appear many incentives to maintain them, some political, some opportunist, some emotionally abusive, continuing to embody a profoundly tragic "master-slave" relationship. Sometimes such reconstruction is able to constructively integrate a blend of religiocultural and socioeconomic practices, but certainly with varying results: some liberating, some extending the ability of disproportionate use of power and exploitation, sometimes informing and equipping resistance against corporate interests, as in the case of Gwich'in resistance against oil exploration in Alaska, in the contextual Bible studies in Kwa-Zulu Natal, and in liberative Christian and non-Christian movements elsewhere, in the creative adaptive processes of indigenous theories like *kaupapa maori*. Other persons within the same populations have been too profoundly wounded by the incarnations of colonial churches to be able to find a healing relationship to them and instead attempt to formulate more nativist or purist identities.

The negotiation of a new identity, a converted self, often produces "nervous conditions." Indeed, one may say that such differential power relationships across religiocultures occasion an entire set of psychopathologies of

colonial/postcolonial friction. Those psychopathologies are of course relational, as Frantz Fanon articulated many decades ago. They involve splitting
of self and some degree of reaction formation and a distortion of the self in
relation to others. To move missionary encounters towards mutual lure and
persuasion may include embodying an erotic power of mission that does not
abuse the power of social status by molesting its subject through a missionary
im/position, but rather gestures towards a radiant, yet apophatic, unknow-
ing "touch of transcendence." Rather than enact coercive threats of colonial
seduction, we are on a mission to find possible spaces of mutual liberation,
recognition, and peacemaking within the many vexing complications and
barriers to such encounter.

   bell hooks has powerfully articulated one way to overcome the straitjacket of
victim identity, while holding accountable those who enable it partly through
white guilt and narcissist self-aggrandizement.[15] What she writes about the
intersection of white-black and male-female oppressive dynamics in the United
States can, mutatis mutandis, identify a particular pathological—soulsuffer-
ing—pattern elsewhere. After identifying the victim identity and its attendant
problems of deferring agency on those that have oppressed one, she argues
for the need to claim agency and not look to others for salvation. In a transformative reiteration of the co-dependency inherent in what Hegel articulated
so persuasively as the master-slave dynamic, she argues that oppressor and
oppressed's identities are mutually constructed, and to break through to transformation must occur on both sides. For many who find themselves located in
the spaces of colonial power, whether inherited or enacted, their work will be
in transforming fragile selves from the temptations of narcissistic self-identifi-
cation by claiming superiority, from "saving" victims of colonization, to opening themselves up to the challenges to perceived ego power necessary for a
genuinely mutual relationship.[16]

Missionary Positions: Sexual Perversions and
Erotic Power

Much of the psychopathology of colonial relations is negotiated through sexual encounters. The history of the symbolic native female body and what was
projected and ejaculated toward it, fills many volumes. One of the mysteries of
intercultural encounter involved profound misreadings, misunderstandings,
and misappropriations of particularly female bodies and sexuality. Zulu and
Maori notions of young femininity were widely different. While an unmarried

---

[15]   bell hooks, *Killing Rage: Ending Racism* (New York: Henry Holt Co., 1995).
[16]   Ibid., 51–61.

Maori woman was free to chose multiple sexual partners and became monogamous after commitment to one man, the virginity of young Zulu women was tied into the cattle exchange and hence of great value to tribal and familial relations. Overall, the familial structures were often radically different between the cultures that engaged in these encounters, involving many intimate dynamics.

Depending on the context, patriarchal structures of colonial hierarchy, and those of traditional local masculinity can be symbiotic, heighten misogyny, and displace more equitable gender relations. The impact of transnational feminism is highly complex and not easily tracked or described. Dismissals of all feminist logic and practice as colonialist are unhelpful, and often used not only to resist "metropolitan feminists" but increasingly by Nativist misogynist rhetoric employed to shut up and shut down local women who seek to raise issues of women's health, violence against women, and other issues critical to women, especially if they claim to be informed by feminism, which was, at least initially framed locally in "Western" contexts.

Power to Convert and Converting Power

Claims to greater power have served as a key strategy for how missionary discourse negotiates divinity. "Strength tests" as proof of greater efficiency of the Divine seem closely related to the issue of conversion. Missionaries have to make a case that the new divine power regime is preferable over the previous one, or at least is worth integrating into the existing sacral power hierarchies. Thus, the discourse over who is "the strongest God"[17] can be articulated explicitly, or be tied to questions that are about the power to heal and sustain body and mind, in finding the most effective option that will amend and help the ailments persons and communities are struggling with. In the presence of colonial forces that involve military, technological, agricultural, or educational aspects in particular, the connections between civilizational aspects and religious claims will inform meaning-making and evaluation of religious options.

At least since the emperor Constantine, political agents who seek to guarantee and enhance their own socioreligious power may seek to ally or align themselves with a religious option in ascendancy or dominant in a society. From Clovis to Charlemagne to Olav Tryggvason and onward, rulers negotiated, quite naturally, sacropolitical power. Claims to political power were always already also claims to a particular relationship with the spiritual power of the universe. Only within a secularist framework would these links be thought to be remarkable or "abnormal" (whatever that would mean) or seem to need to

---

[17] Heretaunga Pat Baker, *The Strongest God* (Blenheim, NZL: Cape Catley Ltd, 1990).

be critiqued. The links between spiritual and political power are not exclusive to imperial religions, and they do not necessarily involve some form of claim that the ruler represents divine power, but rather may suggest that the ruler is the principal intermediary to the divine.

When this claim to power is linked to claims of patriarchal masculinity or military prowess, the "weak" and hence potentially "effeminate" Christ of the cross can be reinterpreted as a masculine presence. We see this in a text such as the *Heliand*, where a redemptive masculinity in indigenous terms is conferred upon the defeated Saxons. Christ is represented within the terms of the masculine warrior culture, the cross as a heroic sacrifice for war comrades. The "Saxon savior" raises, pars pro toto, the question of the limits of indigenizing the gospel, what forms of indigenizing are appropriate in time and context, and the need to continue revising such indigenizations when they become themselves problematic because they are open to problematic hierarchical relations.[18]

Healing movements or prophets who feature claims to spiritual and physical healing can be prominent among the responses to colonial presences—which can often feature new ailments such as influenza, and particularly also colonial Christianity. The particular combination of ritual, spiritual, and cultural health care offered by an indigenous healer with a profound understanding of the setting was often misunderstood by missionaries: as competition at best, and as detrimental at worst. The claims to healing powers negotiated between local healers, missionaries working in concert with Western medicine as well as Christian faith healing constitute a complex, contested field of negotiation and are potentially contiguous within industrialized societies with the contestations around the "placebo effect" and the power of faith and prayer in the healing process.

A great need for healing in intercultural communication obtains between the understanding of "private property" and "usage right of land". Many indigenous communities understand the negotiation of land *use* as something that is given temporarily to a group, family, for a certain time and purpose. Colonizing societies often have an understanding of Lockean private property, enshrined in English common law. This crucial difference in the understanding of central terms of economic transactions, of property, land and lease continues to underlie a great many of postcolonial socioeconomic struggles. Without reconceiving issues of land use and property in mutual mission, theological utterances about justice, gospel, and love mean little. If we can convert heart and economy toward changing relationships to land and people, the Spirit may be able to find us again in new ways.

---

[18] See Anthony W. Bartlett, *Cross Purposes: The Violent Grammar of Christian Atonement* (Harrisburg: Trinity Press International, 2001).

Per/Versions of the Good Message

The relationship between gospel and culture is notoriously complicated. That is, if there is such a thing as "the gospel." *S'il y en a*, as the ghost of Jacques Derrida might whisper. Is the gospel what the missionaries say it is or what local interpreters glean? If missionaries and local interpreters both are recipients of the gospel, meaning may be found in the interactive space of their encounter. The message transmitted and received becomes embodied in religiocultural formations. The phrase "the gospel," a present absence, accounts for the many ways in which the "closed Bible"—the Bible as an artifact and material object—is negotiated at the same time as the "open Bible"—the Bible that is read—and the education and literary technologies needed to move from the closed Bible to the open Bible. There are many other ways in which Christian messages have been delivered. Definitions of mission, or for what constitutes mission, vary over time and context. There are forms of Christian faith that do not consider mission central to their life. Mission within expanding empires looks different than territorially stable societies. While Christian practice may always have included some degree of change in cultural practice, many of the modern missions have been overshadowed by material exchanges and colonial property patterns to the detriment of local bodies and lands. Like any other form of discourse, theology represents an economy of power and is expressed through certain forms of power, including multiple forms of self-fashioning technology. Multiple incentives must be negotiated in any conversion process. Some conversions are partial, and remain so. Some have to do with geopolitical concerns, with the stabilization of power, and solidifying group cohesion. In other settings, group pressures and loyalty to religious conformity no longer obtain in ways they used to, thus removing some of the incentives to participate in religious group activities. Others include the integration of previous practices and concepts into the transformed relationship to the divine. Mission can include the continuation of a narrative tradition and attempts to name and rename a narrative of connection to the divine in the incarnate body of person and community.

Transforming relationships need a recognition and awareness of all forms of baggage, theological, intercultural, personal. Recognition of the reality of baggage enables moving beyond it to more genuine encounters "in the desert" where we both leave behind and become more aware of what perturbs us inside (and often comes from outside, from our relationships and experiences). The central question for me here has been: What is the future of Christian expressions in the present context? These expressions relate to other forms of religiosity, including Judaism and Islam, indigenous shamanism, revivals of paganism, and seemingly ad hoc forms of spirituality. They involve people coming to terms with the ambivalence of their own and foreign traditions,

negotiating the terms of blended commitments, religiously, ethnically, culturally. It is in this mix that we discern the Divine, and specifically, Christian
notions of the Divine.

The understanding of God's power in relation to humanity informs missionary encounters. The transcendence of God can be described in terms
of "colonial omnipotent power" or as immanent transcendence that infuses,
rather than invades, gently touches rather than tortures or rapes, that refuses
to claim or inhabit such power over others, since they are not the most persuasive and compelling kinds of power, but rather distorted attempts to it. For
Whitehead, God's greatest power is in worship, in doxology, which polydoxy
aims to make room for. Such worship is more praiseworthy under the conditions of persuasive rather than coercive power. Some of us, or our ancestors,
did not have much of a choice. But we can opt for the friction of polydox
mutual mission.

The distortions of self and other that occur in the space of encounter carry
the potential of tragic relationality as well as the potential for liberation, but
only if continuously negotiated toward mutual mission. What we can say for
sure is that abusive power relationships do not promote any gospel worth promoting, that coercion to conversion does not constitute a sense of mission
informed by the generosity of many encounters we have witnesses of in gospel
texts. Rejection and misunderstanding, too, are part of these transactions in
the zones of religiocultural encounter, as numerous gospel stories inform us
as well. Sand shaken off sandals, curses spoken, threaten already at the earliest circumambulations of Judaean zones of interaction. But rather than hide
this evidence of the volatility of missionary encounters, perhaps, we must, like
polydoxy, simply embrace the multiple, despite its dangers. If we want to continue engaging in mission, the fullness of these passionate encounters with the
divine, with the human, with the earthly—able to engender both great attraction and great suffering—then we must indeed embrace the unresolvably dangerous memory of these encounters, and how they might inform our own.

Being open to perceiving the many connections and exchanges between
cultures that defy simplistic dualisms, seeing them as in flux and mutually
transforming toward greater justice, is a feature of a polydox sense of mutual
mission. While some forms of missionary theological thinking and teaching
continue to discourage independent thinking, and can continue to prefer
rote repetition and reproduction of traditional theologies weighted toward
those produced in the missionary cultures—understandably producing a certain level of frustration in some students—the proposed approach to mutually transformative mission questions any emphasis on Christian belonging
as uniformly orthodox that is both unenforceable, and inhospitable to multiple religiocultural belongings. In some cases, colonial epistemologies and
theologies can become internalized and affirmed as legitimate orthodoxy, in
a form of internalized colonial episteme. When this episteme is challenged by

changed situations in the cultures that initially helped induct this knowledge, it may cause theological whiplash, as the status of colonially implanted orthodoxies has become so reified as to seem unchangeable and delegitimizing of the power projected onto the cultures from which missionaries once came. In an exercise of metonymy, the missionary comes to stand for an entire culture, and when that culture itself proves to be more complex than its partial representative, the entire representational chain can be perceived as threatened. Applying a postcolonial hermeneutics to such intercultural frustrations can help to come to terms with the complexity of each religiocultural expression and the continued process of reinterpreting the good news in each place and time. While the application of postcolonial concepts like ambivalence, mimicry, and hybridity may disturb in its embrace of inconclusion, or raise the specters of relativism, the intended effect is a resistance to epistemologically and practically unhelpful essentialisms. At the same time, polydox missiology is committed to reading, understanding, and responding complex processes of transformation, accepting the need for continued watchful discernment.

If there is no neutrality, then perhaps we may choose between two gospel sayings that have long marked some of the flux of the polydox space of the *basileia tou theou*: Rather than "who is not with me is against me" (Matthew 12:30), we will here stand with the paradox juxtaposition of it, equally gospel: "Who is not against us is for us" (Mark 9:40). Thus, a polydox sense of mutual mission would be robustly planted in one tradition, secure in a flexible identity that can engage hospitably with Christian and other religious difference by neither romanticizing nor simply rejecting its multiple incarnations. This polydox sense does not forestall strong critiques of the abuse of religious and cultural power both within and without one's own tradition/s, but rather provides a more flexible epistemology, methodology, and hermeneutics for identifying objectionable theological speech and ethical practice.

Rather than suspecting a threatening "relativism" in the admission that theology arises from context, such weighty gravitas follows as a consequence of taking the incarnation of the Logos seriously. The rest is in the details: How our context figures into our encounters with the divine, and how we speak about it and express it—that is, do theology, is a matter of negotiation. Context represents a powerful datum, and certainly suggests powerful priorities, vocabularies, epistemologies, and conceptual frameworks. How a person or community chooses to live out of it and into it, adjacent to it, or in resistance to it, is a matter of continual unfolding. Such unfolding engages in what Catherine Keller identifies as one of the great struggles of contemporary Christianity in the United States—and perhaps elsewhere in the Northern hemisphere: Many find themselves caught between the extremes of strong truth claims and the dangers of relativism, between "the absolute and the dissolute."[19] Keller

[19]   Catherine Keller, *On the Mystery: Discerning God in Process* (Minneapolis: Fortress, 2008), 2.

proposes a third way where "all human truth-claims are relative to context and perspective. But why would it follow that truth, or value, is *nothing but* that perspective?"[20] Though we may "relinquish certainty," we need to be able to speak and act with *"confidence."*[21]

Works Cited

Assmann, Jan. *Of God and Gods: Egypt, Israel, and the Rise of Monotheism.* Madison, WI: University of Wisconsin Press, 2008.

Baker, Heretaunga Pat. *The Strongest God.* Blenheim, NZL: Cape Catley Ltd, 1990.

Bartlett, Anthony W. *Cross Purposes: The Violent Grammar of Christian Atonement.* Harrisburg: Trinity Press International, 2001.

Binney, Judith. *The Legacy of Guilt: A Life of Thomas Kendall.* Wellington: Bridget Williams Books, 1968.

Comaroff, John, and Jean Comaroff. *Ethnography and the Historical Imagination.* Boulder, CO: Westview Press, 1992.

Cornille, Catherine. *Many Mansions: Multiple Religious Belonging and Christian Identity.* Maryknoll, NY: Orbis, 2002.

Davidson, Allan. "The Interaction of Missionary and Colonial Society in Nineteenth Century New Zealand." *Studies in World Christianity* Vol. 2, No. 2 (1996): 145–66.

hooks, bell. *Killing Rage: Ending Racism.* New York: Henry Holt Co., 1995.

Keller, Catherine. *Face of the Deep.* New York/London: Routledge, 2003.

—.*On The Mystery: Discerning God in Process.* Minneapolis, MN: Fortress, 2008.

Mikaelsson, Lisbeth. "Locality and Myth: The Resacralization of Selja and the Cult of St. Sunniva." *Numen* Vol. 52 (2005): 191-225.

Salomonsen, Jone. *Enchanted Feminism: The Reclaiming Witches of San Francisco.* New York: Routledge, 2002.

Steinsland, Gro. "Fra Yggdrasils Ask Til Korsets Tre—Tanker Om Trosskiftet." In *Fra Hedendom Til Kristendom: Perspektiver På Religionsskiftet i Norge,* ed. Magnus Rindal, 20–30. Oslo: Ad Notam Gyldendal, 1996.

Sugirtharajah, R. S. *The Bible and the Third World: Pre-colonial, Colonial, and Postcolonial Encounters.* Cambridge: Cambridge University Press, 2001.

Wells, Peter S. *Barbarians to Angels: The Dark Ages Reconsidered.* New York: W. W. Norton & Company, 2008.

[20]   Ibid., 4.
[21]   Ibid., 8.

Chapter 9

Aporias: No Way Out

What should theologians writing on mission in the post-colony consider as they write constructive, subversive approaches to mission today? Informed and sobered by the tragic encounters of past and present, they must aim to wrestle a reluctant blessing from them. They are called to sharply observe the rapidly changing landscape of mission and theology and propose where next steps may need to lead.

What has compelled human beings, then and now, to enter into the sign and symbol system as well as the material and ritual practices of the Christian faith? What role did the imperial embedding of Christian faith and practice play in the missionary ventures launched to Christianize Europe and Europe's own Anglo-Protestant missions in the Southern hemisphere? What changes to socioreligious, ethnocultural practices have occurred, and what is lost and gained? What were and are the contributions made by peoples that encounter Christian faith and practice? What other ways of expressing the gospel are being engendered? Which losses and which gains do we need to remember and allow to inform us as we move forward? Which hermeneutical and methodological assumptions about Christian faith and practice limit and circumscribe how we perceive conversion and the gospel? How do the religiocultural identities of persons in community become impacted and transformed?

I have approached these questions through concentric circumambulations, employing select case studies from across time and space. They were chosen for their accessibility (to me), the amount and quality of usable material available in the archive of mission history, contextual responses to Christian texts and practices, and the revelatory and instructive potential of the missionary encounters in these archives.

What I have found on these itineraries reveals the gospel as a form of trickster knowledge that, in the words of a well-worn truism, can comfort the afflicted and afflict the comfortable, in ways that give profound contour and depth to this overused phrase. The use of a polydox methodology has the potential to show the multi-layered thinking and action patterns, the many motivations, juxtapositions, and pitfalls that accompany such encounters.

We have seen the complex set of circumstances, spiritual and material realities, that compound the encounter with Christian faith and practice. Having discerned the dense relation between sacred and profane spheres, and the impossibility to effectively separate them, we can see that conversion is negotiated within and across the totality of religiocultural relations, including economic, political and socio-sexual aspects. The observed patterns inform the theological construction of doctrinal themes and topics in conversation with the knowledges of the many cultures that have shaped and been shaped by a great variety of Christian text, words, thoughts. We may have discovered that what we thought of as isolated rivers are connected through a delta, their waters blending.

In the transformation of religiocultural identity and the presencing of Christian contents in cultures in particular, certain forms of violence and abuse of power do occur. The heritage of these forms of violence is a toxic residue that continues to maim and repress possibilities of flourishing. These losses are real and need to be acknowledged and mourned. Lament and remembrance can help to move from victimhood to survival, and if the process is mutual, empowering, and power imbalances can be named and renegotiated, some measure of reconciliation and modes of just reciprocity can be moved toward. Where we thought we were safeguarding ourselves from abuse, instrumentalization, self-sabotage, or self-interest, we may recognize how easily we slip into it in intercultural encounters.

The parabolic itineraries of Chapters 4–7, entered through my own nodes of intersection with the complex of Western Christianities, give cause for lament, display reciprocal exchange and transformation, and offer signs of cautious, modest glimpses of hope. They have shown multiple layers of meaning, power, and adaptive negotiation that obtain in colonially negotiated mission. They warn of the ambivalence of collapsing gospel and culture and simply juxtaposing them with each other. They warn of abuses of power, lack of vision and education, of damaging senses of self and other, us and them, that impact theology and conceptions of God. We see damage being done when this embodied set of relations to the divine becomes static or offers too little cohesion, rather than being well constructed and flexibly resolute. In these tales of caution, there are lessons for what lies on the road not taken.

We know the sacred, God, the gospel, through our cultural projections and conceptions, and this knowledge is embodied through language and practice. In this sense, then, mission has always been "civilized" and "civilizing," if by that we mean it tends to shape subjects, communities, and ideas of divine and sacred. The question is not whether or not this occurs but how! Does the gospel function to compel us to become more disciplined members of our own societies and cultures, or subvert the very terms of these cultures? This basic dilemma, already expressed in the tensions between biblical prophets blessing the mighty or pointing out their abuses, the gospel that divides families or enforces conformity with the household, is still with us. None of these questions are new, though we must ask them anew in changing scenarios and spacetime.

Ancient hermeneutical patterns for relating to religious and cultural otherness have had a great and lasting influence on how missionaries, anthropologists, historians, and philosophers have engaged cultural and historical difference. By taking a closer look at early medieval missionary encounters, we have learned that Boniface's ambivalent position toward local tribes and regal authority both empowered and compromised his mission, of the gospel moving northward through a manifold of processes, prominent among them geopolitical considerations, shaping an *Adelskirche* intent on unifying realms and sustaining sacropolitical power. The layering of promises for dynastic and cultural power obtained with conversion was interlaced with religious conviction, association with Roman civilization and order, and geopolitical designs. In Scandinavia, we have considered the rediscoveries of Inuit identity in Lutheran Greenland and a rediscovery of pilgrimage and Saint Sunniva in Protestant Norway.

We have seen that the terms of the Christianization of Europe were as multiply motivated as the conversions to Christianity within the scope of British missions to New Zealand and Natal in the nineteenth century: desires for access to expansive power, agency in spiritual life worlds, reorienting person and community in shifting cultural worlds, the desire for access to education, material and spiritual technologies, the shifting relations to land and property, to law and civilizing practices all form part of multilayered shifts in allegiance and identity formation.

The echoes of these past missions and conversion reverberate into our own time, informing and impacting what we fear, dread, and desire in terms of mission. Mission may be imagined as a *pharmakon*, a remedy that can both heal and maim, depending on dosage, context, and interactions with other practices.

The inflexible prioritizing of the missionary's cultural interests often rendered the missionary churches' credibility vulnerable. When missionaries and missionary societies betrayed the interests of those they had brought the gospel to by promoting, complying, or assisting with colonial depropriation of natives, converts turned away from missionary churches, and founded their own, or created new religious movements in a "syncretistic" fashion. When missionaries did take the side of natives, like the Colenso family in Natal, or some missionaries in Aotearoa/New Zealand, they could risk disciplining and expulsion from their sending bodies, defunding, and profound marginalization from settler communities who wanted spiritual support for settling and recreating churches of the homeland in a colonial setting. Some of these divisions of interest, of asking churches for support for communities of opposing concerns have persisted into post-settler government societies and their fraught relationships with indigenous communities.

The polydox theology of mission, proposed within the preceding pages, then has aimed to construct a method capable of perceiving and describing a complex range of theological conceptions, interests, motivations, and dynamics that obtain in missionary encounters. Gospel and culture, sacred and secular, do not function as opposites, or even complements. Indeed, the copula *and* points toward an additive approach, imagines gospel *as* culture and secular *as* sacred. The cultures of the gospel are sets of practices and beliefs that function as negotiation grounds for differently embodied *doxa*. Sitting in the presence of the ancient possibilities of paradox, polydox approaches to mission, conversion, and faithful practice, we may discern polydox mission as enunciating polymorphic gospels, in many guises.[1] Likewise, each cultural setting retells, reimagines, and produces faithful renderings.

The polydox hospitality/hostility to the *angelus*, the messenger of mission, and to the paradoxical gospels that can spiral out of control, necessitates several movements of therapeutic theology: recognizing loss—recognizing complex interaction—recognizing creative adaptation—and movement toward relocating theologies while practicing reconciliation in reciprocity. We have attempted to trace here some of the contributions of gospel adaptations from South Africa, Aotearoa/New Zealand and Alaska, that move within sacrally arced spaces within and beyond colonialism. Polydox gospels manifest in ever-changing ways, moving not simply outside of orthodoxy, but manifesting multiple orthodox spaces within the wide stream of Christian traditions. Important questions that will need to be asked regarding the terms of any inculturation of Christian faith and practice: Who are the agents of inculturation? Who is left out, invisible, underrepresented? Who dominates, takes up more energy and time? What kinds of stereotypes and assumptions block the gentle spirit of careful transmutation and adaptation?

Just because some amorphous "community" informs the process of inculturation does not mean it is by definition more "just" or equitable. Who is this community, and what are their motivations and goals? It is as important to avoid the romanticism of the noble savage as to avoid idealizing postcolonial hybridity when it comes to resemble an easily assimilable commodity of late neo-imperial consumer capitalism. The many hybrid incarnations of mission and polydox gospels have produced hybrid Christian identities that encompass many levels of internal tension. They are one of the results of colonial missions

---

[1] During the canonization of the biblical texts, the veritable multiplicity of early written gospel narratives was reduced not to one, but limited to a four-foldness that were considered to be within the realm of sound doctrine, yet preserving a certain level of polydoxy, variations within the canon. Considerations on what other gospels posterity may have benefitted from cannot be entertained here. Suffice it to say that there is much that can be learned from the discovery of others, such as the Gospel of Thomas, the Acts of Paul and Thecla, and some Gnostic texts, none of which are, however, without their own set of problems.

as much as European Christian identities were informed by the lingering influence of Christian Rome. The mimetic processes of colonial Christian logic in its ancient and contemporary versions retain their problematic nature, but they are not helpfully countered by idealizing authenticity, indigeneity, and locality or regarding as forever tainted the translation of an imagined essential Christian faith and practice into those of another culture.

Tracing the contours of this interpretive, translating hermeneutic process of the multiply motivated messengers of mission, is a crucial practice for identifying patterns we may want to affirm from those we need to resist and discourage. This discernment is a communal process, but it is not fail-safe, and will be both blessed and cursed, bounded and gifted by contextualities. It traverses toxic territories, must make room for lament, the remembering of loss and take courageous steps of restitution, before it can move to inklings of reconciliatory action and transformative relation across colonial divides. Only then do we have cause for cautious hope in the hard, slow work of salvific subversion as grace-filled, entangled reciprocity with the Divine in earth, cultures, others, selves.

In the End, Aporias: No Way . . . ?

What does this all mean for living in contemporary societies where religious/secular relations are being reshuffled? What conclusions can be drawn? In this mottled context what does mission mean? Or, *via negativa*, what does it *not* mean? Affirming a polydox sense of mission avoids talk of an essence or core of the gospel or of mission, it resists aggressive absolutisms and defeatist dissolutions. It resists the progressive tendency of being "ashamed of the gospel of Jesus Christ" in reaction-formation to conservative imperial missions, resists paralyzing and narcissistic forms of white guilt, moving instead toward a modestly witnessing confessional reciprocity. It resists the reduction of mission to development work and affirms the careful, holistic embodiment of polydox Christianities that can also affirm the truths and gifts of other religions. It resists Nativist reductions of Christianity to colonial domination and mind control and the seduction of declarations of "authentic," "indigenous" practices as if these were somehow now beyond critique, as well as claims to the superiority of "new indigenous Christianities" as morally and spiritually superior to those of a "decadent West" and the imported culture wars that inform such unhelpful juxtapositions.

Via Positiva: Some of the most compelling recent articulations of mission are summarized by the five marks of mission: (1) to proclaim the Good News of the kingdom of God, (2) to teach, baptize, and nurture new believers, (3) to respond to human need by loving service, (4) to seek to transform unjust structures of society, and (5) to strive to safeguard the integrity of creation and sustain and renew the life of the earth.[2] Polydox mission moves toward a reciprocal resolute articulation and practice of Christian faith. It involves creative friction and adaptation rather than assimilation or simple rejection. Within these zones of encounter and friction, it discerns multiple productive modes of encountering gospel and carefully discerns attendant gifts and dangers. Cultural hybridity and mimicry are embedded in multifaceted encounters. Polydox Christianities emerge at the complex, constantly negotiated intersection of the cultures of the gospel and the good news found in a variety of cultural practices. Polydox Christianities are found when there is creative interaction between multiple hermeneutic styles and methods, openness to creative transformation, and critical challenges to both local and gospel cultures, when they interpret each other, and identify and critique tendencies to violent domination in each setting.

At the conclusion of these itineraries is not a goal or resting place, but depending on where you, dear reader, depart from this text, you may find further crossroads open up, pointing towards further *aporias*. Lacking a precise map, route, or clearly marked signposts, we are better off knowing the baggage we carry with us, along with a diagnostic instrumentarium with potential for pattern recognition, assessing the terrain of encounter we engage, feeling the history of its wounds and blessings, as we learn from it for future encounters. When encountering cultural, religious, and power differences with painful histories, you might want to consider (1) the history of the community and the encounters with past and present others that shape it; (2) how these encounters were informed by certain persons, circumstances, groups, and events; (3) the profound ambivalence in many of our encounters with the Sacred and with each other; (4) what we can learn from history and mission studies for constructive theology.

As we end, we will also find that we have asked ourselves: what makes for sacred commerce? The sacred conversions of meaning and matter, how do they become truly blessing rather than curse? The questions, rather than the answers, are the gifts needed to expand the horizon of encounters in mission. Herein just a few of them were able to be raised.

---

[2] Andrew Walls and Cathy Ross, eds *Mission in the 21st Century: Exploring the Five Marks of Global Mission* (Maryknoll, NY: Orbis, 2008), xiv.

Index